PROGRESS IN COMPUTER RESEARCH
VOLUME I

PROGRESS IN COMPUTER RESEARCH
VOLUME I

FRANK COLUMBUS
EDITOR

Nova Science Publishers, Inc.
Huntington, New York

Senior Editors: Susan Boriotti and Donna Dennis
Coordinating Editor: Tatiana Shohov
Office Manager: Annette Hellinger
Graphics: Wanda Serrano
Book Production: Matthew Kozlowski, Jonathan Rose and Jennifer Vogt
Circulation: Cathy DeGregory, Ave Maria Gonzalez, Ron Hedges and Andre Tillman

Library of Congress Cataloging-in-Publication Data
Available Upon Request

ISBN 1-59033-010-2.

227 Main Street, Suite 100
Huntington, New York 11743
Tele. 631-424-6682 Fax 631-425-5933
E Mail: Novascience@earthlink.net

Printed in the United States of America

CONTENTS

PREFACE

This series presents the leading-edge research in the field of computer research, technology and applications. Each contribution has been carefully selected for inclusion based on the significance of the research to the field. The coherence of each book rests in its fit within the larger framework of the series and its goals.

ASYNCHRONY IN PARALLEL COMPUTING: FROM DATAFLOW TO MULTITHREADING*

JURIJ ŠILC†, BORUT ROBIČ‡, AND THEO UNGERER§

Abstract. The paper presents an overview of the parallel computing models, architectures, and research projects that are based on asynchronous instruction scheduling. It starts with pure dataflow computing models and presents an historical development of several ideas (i.e. single-token-per-arc dataflow, tagged-token dataflow, explicit token store, threaded dataflow, large-grain dataflow, RISC dataflow, cycle-by-cycle interleaved multithreading, block interleaved multithreading, simultaneous multithreading) that resulted in modern multithreaded superscalar processors. The paper shows that unification of von Neumann and dataflow models is possible and preferred to treating them as two unrelated, orthogonal computing paradigms. Today's dataflow research incorporates more explicit notions of state into the architecture, and von Neumann models using many dataflow techniques to improve the latency hiding aspects of modern multithreaded systems.

Key words. parallel computer architectures, data-driven computing, multithread computing, static dataflow, tagged-token dataflow, threaded dataflow, cycle-by-cycle interleaving, block interleaving, multithreaded superscalar

AMS subject classifications. 68-02, 68M05, 68Q10

1. Introduction. There are many problems that require enormous computational capacity to solve, and therefore present opportunities for high-performance (parallel) computing. There are also a number of well-known hardware organization techniques for exploiting parallelism. In this paper we give an overview of the computers where parallelism is achieved by executing multiple asynchronous threads of instructions concurrently.

For sequential computers the principal execution model is the well known *von Neumann model* which consists of a sequential process running in a linear address space. The amount of concurrency available is relatively small [229]. Computers having more than one processor may be categorized in two types, SIMD or MIMD [83], and allow several *multiprocessor von Neumann* program execution models, such as *shared memory* (with actions coordinated by synchronization operations, e.g. P and V semaphore commands [76]), or *distributed memory* (with actions coordinated by message passing facilities [119, 136], e.g. explicit operating system calls). A MIMD computer in principle will have a different program running on every processor. This makes for an extremely complex programming environment. A frequent program execution model for MIMD computers is the *single-program multiple data* (SPMD) model [63] where the same program is run on all processors, but the execution may follow different paths through the program according to the processor's identity.

In multiprocessor systems, two main issues must be addressed: *memory latency*, which is the time that elapses between issuing a memory request and receiving the corresponding response, and *synchronization*, which is the need to enforce the ordering of instruction

*This work was partially supported by the Ministry of Science and Technology of the Republic of Slovenia under grants J2-7648 and J2-8697.

†Computer Systems Department, Jožef Stefan Institute, Jamova cesta 39, SI-1000 Ljubljana, Slovenia (Jurij.Silc@ijs.si).

‡Faculty of Computer and Information Science, University of Ljubljana, Tržaška cesta 25, SI-1000 Ljubljana, Slovenia, and Computer Systems Department, Jožef Stefan Institute, Jamova cesta 39, SI-1000 Ljubljana, Slovenia (Borut.Robic@fri.uni-lj.si).

§Department of Computer Design and Fault Tolerance, University of Karlsruhe, P.O.Box 6980, D-76128 Karlsruhe, Germany (Ungerer@ira.uka.de).

executions according to their data dependencies. The two issues cannot be properly resolved in a von Neumann context since connecting von Neumann processors into a very high speed general purpose computer also brings bottleneck problems [20].

As an alternative, the dataflow model was introduced as the radically new model capable of properly satisfying the two needs [8, 17, 67, 89]. Dataflow models use dataflow program graphs to represent the flow of data and control. Synchronization is achieved by a requirement that two or more specified events occur before an instruction is eligible for execution [192]. For example, in the *graph/heap model* [66] an instruction is enabled by the presence of simple tokens (i.e., data packets) on the arcs of copies of the dataflow graph, whereas the *unraveling interpreter model* (U-interpreter) [19] enables instructions by matching tags that identify the graph instance to which a token belongs. In [159] a detailed implementation of an unraveling dataflow interpreter of the Irvine Dataflow (Id) programming language is proposed. Dataflow models have also guided the design of several multithreaded computers [71].

Unfortunately, direct implementation of computers based on a pure dataflow model has been found to be an arduous task. For this reason, the impact of the convergence of the dataflow and control-flow was investigated [16, 126, 128, 142, 170]. In particular, *Nikhil* and *Arvind* posed the following question: *"What can a von Neumann processor borrow from dataflow to become more suitable for a multiprocessor?"* and offered the answer in terms of the P-RISC (Parallel RISC) programming model [165]. The model is based on a simple, RISC-like instruction set extended with three instructions that give a von Neumann processor a fine-grained dataflow capability [16]. It uses explicit *fork* and *join* commands. Based on P-RISC programming model a multithreaded Id programming language is implemented [163, 164]. Another model designed to support nested functional languages using sequential threads of instructions is the Multilisp model [115, 116, 117, 147]. Multilisp is an extension of the Lisp dialect Scheme with additional operators and semantics to deal with parallel execution. The principal language extension provided by Multilisp is $future(x)$. Upon executing $future(x)$, an immediate *undetermined* value is returned. The computation of x occurs in parallel and the result replaces *undetermined* when complete. Of course, any use of the result would block the parent process until the computation is finished.

The incorporation of conventional control-flow thread execution into the dataflow approach resulted in the *multithreaded* computer architecture which is one of the most promising and exciting avenues for the exploitation of parallelism [10, 43, 88, 129, 152, 160].

2. The day before yesterday: Pure dataflow. The fundamental principles of dataflow were developed by *Jack Dennis* [66] in the early 1970s. The dataflow model [8, 69, 94, 192] avoids the two features of von Neumann model, the program counter and the global updatable store, which become bottlenecks in exploiting parallelism [27]. The computational rule, also known as the *firing rule* of the dataflow model, specifies the condition for the execution of an instruction. The basic instruction firing rule, common to all dataflow systems is as follows: *An instruction is said to be executable when all the input operands that are necessary for its execution are available to it.* The instruction for which this condition is satisfied is said to be *fired*. The effect of firing an instruction is the consumption of its input values and generation of output values. Due to the above rule the model is *asynchronous*. It is also *self-scheduling* since instruction sequencing is constrained only by data dependencies. Thus, the flow of control is the same as the flow of data among various instructions. As a result, a dataflow program can be represented as a directed *graph* consisting of named *nodes*, which represent instructions, and *arcs*, which represent data dependencies among instructions [65, 139] (Fig.2.1 a,b). Data values propagate along the arcs in the form of data packets, called *tokens*. The two important characteristics of the dataflow graphs are *functionality* and *composability*. Functionality means that evaluation of a graph is equivalent to evaluation of a mathematical function on the same input values. Composability means that graphs can be combined to form new graphs.

In a dataflow architecture the program execution is in terms of receiving, processing and sending out tokens containing some data and a tag. Dependencies between data are translated into tag matching and transformation, while processing occurs when a set of matched tokens arrives at the execution unit. The instruction which has to be fetched from the instruction store (according to the tag information) contains information about what to do with the data and how to transform the tags. The matching and execution unit are connected by an asynchronous pipeline, with queues added to smooth out load variations [137]. Some form of associate memory is required to support token matching. It can be a real memory with associative access, a simulated memory based on hashing, or a direct matched memory. Each solution has its proponent but none is absolutely suitable.

Due to its elegance and simplicity, the pure dataflow model has been the subject of many research efforts. Since the early 1970s, a number of dataflow computer prototypes have been built and evaluated, and different designs and compiling techniques have been simulated [17, 67, 89, 152, 169, 186, 197, 206, 209, 217, 220]. Clearly, an architecture supporting the execution of dataflow graphs should support the flow of data. Depending on the way of handling the data, several types of dataflow architectures emerged in the past [15]: *single-token-per-arc dataflow* [73], *tagged-token dataflow* [23, 230], and *explicit token store* [172]. We describe them in the following subsections.

2.1. Single-token-per-arc dataflow. The *single-token-per-arc* (or *static*) architecture was first proposed by *Dennis* [73] (Fig.2.1 c). At the machine level, a dataflow graph is represented as a collection of *activity templates*, each containing the *operation code* of the represented instruction, *operand slots* for holding operand values, and *destination address fields*, referring to the operand slots in subsequent activity templates that need to receive the result value. The static dataflow approach allows *at most one token* to reside on any one arc. This is accomplished by extending the basic firing rule as follows [68]: *A node is enabled as soon as tokens are present on its input arcs* and *there is no token on any of its output arcs*. To implement the restriction of at most one token per arc, *acknowledge signals*, traveling along additional arcs from consuming to producing nodes, are used as additional tokens. Thus, the firing rule can be changed to its original form.

The major advantage of the single-token-per-arc dataflow model is its simplified mechanism for detecting enabled nodes. Unfortunately, this model of dataflow has a number of serious drawbacks [15]. Since consecutive iterations of a loop can only partially overlap in time, only a pipelining effect can be achieved and thus a limited amount of parallelism can be exploited. Another undesirable effect is that token traffic is doubled. There is also a lack of support for programming constructs essential to any modern programming language. Despite these shortcomings, several machines were constructed and the most important are listed below. They made a tremendous impact on the field of computer architecture by introducing radically new ways of thinking about massively parallel computers. They also served as a basis for subsequent dataflow computers.

MIT Static Dataflow Architecture: This machine was designed at the Massachusetts Institute of Technology (MIT) (Cambridge, Ma, USA) [67, 68, 70, 73] as a direct implementation of a single-token-per-arc dataflow model. It consisted of five major subsystems:

a memory section, a processing section, an arbitration network, a control network, and a distribution network. All communication between subsystems was by asynchronous packet transmission over the channels. A prototype was built consisting of eight processing elements (emulated by microprogrammable microprocessors) and an equidistant packet routing network using 2 × 2 routing elements; it was used primarily as an engineering model [72].

LAU System: Researchers at the CERT (Toulouse, France) carried out the first research effort to go through the entire process of graph, language, and machine design. Their system, called LAU [50, 51, 176, 212], was built in 1979. "Language à assignation unique" (LAU) is a French acronym for single-assignment computation. The LAU system used static graphs and had its own dataflow language based on single-assignment.

TI's Distributed Data Processor: The Distributed Data Processor (DDP) [52, 53] was a system designed by Texas Instruments (USA) aimed to investigate the potential of dataflow as the basis of a high-performance computer. The DDP was not commercially exploited, but a follow-on design with Ada as the programming language [103] had application in military systems.

DDM1 Utah Data Driven Machine: DDM1 [64] was a computing element of a recursively structured dataflow architecture designed at the University of Utah (Salt Lake City, Ut, USA) and was completed at Burroughs Interactive Research Center (La Jolla, Ca, USA). The machine organization was based on the concept of recursion. It was tree structured, with each computing element connected to a superior element (above) and up to eight inferior elements (below). Each processing element consisted of an agenda queue, which contained firable instructions, an atomic memory (providing the program memory), and an atomic processor.

NEC Image Pipelined Processor: NEC Electronics (Japan) has developed the first dataflow VLSI microprocessor chip μPD7281 [48, 134, 135, 214, 215]. Its architecture was a pipeline with several blocks, or working areas, organized in a loop. A link table and function table stored object code, while the data memory was used for temporary storage of the tokens to be matched. The address generator and flow controller matched two tokens, which were temporarily stored in the queue before they were processed by the processing unit.

Hughes Dataflow Multiprocessor: The Hughes Dataflow Multiprocessor (HDFM) project began in 1981 at Hughes Aircraft Co. (USA), prompted by the need for high performance, reliable, and easily programmable processors for embedded systems. The HDFM [42, 90, 226, 227] consisted of many, relatively simple, identical processing elements connected by a global packet-switching network. The interconnection (3-D bussed cube) network was integrated with the processing element for ease of expansion and minimization of VLSI chip types. The communications network was designed to be reliable, with automatic retry on garble messages, distributed bus arbitration, alternate path packet routing, and failed processing element translation table to allow rapid switch-in and use of spare processing elements. The communication network was able to physically accommodate up to an 8 × 8 × 8 configuration or 512 processing elements. Candidates proposed for the HDFM network were evaluated in [82]: a 3-D bussed cube network, a multi-stage network, a hypercube network, a mesh network, and a ring network. The processor engine was a three-stage pipelined processor with three operations overlapped: instruction fetch and dataflow firing rule check, instruction execution, and result and destination address combining to form a packet.

2.2. Tagged-token dataflow. The performance of a dataflow machine significantly increases when loop iterations and subprogram invocations can proceed in parallel. To achieve this, each iteration or subprogram invocation should be able to execute as a separate instance of a reentrant subgraph. However, this replication is only conceptual. In the implementation, only one copy of any dataflow graph is actually kept in memory. Each token includes a *tag*, consisting of the address of the instruction for which the particular data value is destined, and other information defining the computational context in which that value is used. This context is called the values *color*. Each arc can be viewed as a bag that may contain *an arbitrary* number of tokens with different tags. Now, the firing rule is: *A node is enabled as soon as tokens with identical tags are present at each of its input arcs.* Dataflow architectures that use this method are referred to as *tagged-token* (or *dynamic*) dataflow architectures (Fig.2.1 d). The model was proposed by *Watson* and *Gurd* at the University of Manchester (England) [230], and by *Arvind* and *Nikhil* at MIT [23].

The major advantage of the tagged-token dataflow model is the higher performance it obtains by allowing multiple tokens on an arc. One of the main problems of tagged-token dataflow model was the efficient implementation of the unit that collects tokens with matching colors. For reasons of performance, an associative memory would be ideal. Unfortunately, it would not be cost-effective since the amount of memory needed to store tokens waiting for a match tends to be very large. Therefore, all existing machines use some form of hashing techniques which are typically not fast enough compared with associative memory. In what follows, we list the most important tagged-token dataflow projects.

Manchester Dataflow Computer: The researchers at the University of Manchester focused on the construction of a prototype dataflow computer [28, 29, 38, 44, 45, 93, 108, 109, 110, 111, 112, 113, 130, 185, 219, 230, 231]. The graph structure in this machine was static with token labels to keep different procedure calls separate. The machine was first implemented as a simulation program in 1977/78, and as the hardware prototype in 1981. It consisted of a single processing element and a single structure storage module connected together via a simple 2×2 switch. The processing element had pipelined internal structure [60], with tokens passing through a queue module, a matching unit [61] and an instruction fetch unit before being processed by one of 20 function units in a parallel array that provided the computational power. The function units were microcoded, and different instructions took quite different times to execute. To overcome the restriction in the Manchester machine that only two successor instructions could be specified in one instruction, the TUPlicate operator (iterative instruction) was introduced [36, 37]. Using TUPlicate operator reduced the size of code and led to a significant reduction in execution time especially for large programs. The Extended Manchester Dataflow Computer (EXMAN) from Indian Institute of Science (Bangalore, India) [175] incorporated three major extensions to the basic machine: a multiple matching units scheme, an efficient implementation of the array data structure, and a facility to concurrently execute reentrant routines. To allow all storage functions to be performed concurrently also a prototype parallel structure store was developed [140].

MIT Tagged-Token Dataflow Machine: This project originated at the University of California at Irvine (Ca, USA) and continued at MIT. The Irvine dataflow machine [21, 99, 100] implemented a version of the U-interpreter [98] and array handling mechanisms to support *I-structure* concepts [20, 23, 24, 158]. An I-structure may be viewed as a repository for data values obeying the single-assignment principle. That is, each element of the I-structure may be written only once but it may be read any number of times. The machine was proposed to consist of multiple clusters interconnected by a token ring. Each cluster (four processing elements [22]) shared a local memory through a local bus and a memory controller. The MIT machine [17, 91] was a modified Irvine machine, but still based on the Id language. Instead of using a token ring, an N $\times$ N packet switch network for interprocessor communications was used.

SIGMA-1: The SIGMA-1 [122, 123, 194, 233] system is a supercomputer for large-scale numerical computation and has been operational since early 1988 at the Electrotechnical Laboratory (Tsukuba, Japan). It consists of 128 processing elements and 128 structure elements interconnected by 32 local networks (10 $\times$ 10 crossbar packet switches) and one global two-stage Omega network. Sixteen maintenance processors are also connected with the structure elements and with a host computer for I/O operations, system monitoring, performance measurements, and maintenance operations [121].

PATTSY Processor Array Tagged-Token System: PATTSY [161] was an experimental system that had been developed at the University of Queensland (Brisbane, Australia), which supported the dynamic model of dataflow execution. PATTSY had a host computer that provided the user-interface to the machine and accepted user programs which it converted into dataflow graph. These graphs were mapped onto the processing elements (PEs), but the actual scheduling of operation was carried out at runtime. An 18 processor prototype of the machine was operational. It used an IBM-PC as the host and the PEs were built from Intel 8085 based single board microcomputers.

NTT's Dataflow Processor Array System: The dataflow processors array system [213] from Nippon Telephone and Telegraph (Japan) was a dynamic tagged-token design intended for large scientific calculation. A hardware experimental system Eddy [13], consisting of 4 $\times$ 4 processing elements, was built and used to test some applications.

Q-p One-Chip Data-Driven Processor: The Q-p [25, 145, 167] is specifically designed to be a one-chip functional element which is easily programmable to form various dedicated processing functions. Particular design considerations were taken to achieve high flow-rate data-streams processing capabilities. In the Q-p, a novel bi-directional elastic pipeline processing concept was introduced to implement token matching. The Q-p was developed jointly by Osaka University, Sharp, Matsushita Electric Ind., Sanyo Electric, and Mitsubishi Electric (Japan).

DDDP Distributed Data Driven Processor: The DDDP [141] from OKI Electric Ind. (Japan) had a centralized tag manager and performed token matching using a hardware hashing mechanism similar to that of the Manchester Dataflow Computer. A prototype consisting of four processing elements and one structure store connected by a ring bus achieved 0.7 MIPS.

SDFA Stateless Data-Flow Architecture: SDFA was designed at the University of Manchester and inspired by the Manchester Dataflow Computer. As its name implies, the SDFA system [205, 206] had no notion of states. There were no structure stores, and only extract-wait functionality was provided in the matching stores. All the instructions in the instruction-set were simple and based on RISC principles. There were no iterative or vector style instructions producing more than two tokens per execution.

CSIRAC II: The origins of the CSIRAC II dataflow computer date from 1978 [79]. It was built at the Swinburne Institute of Technology (Hawthorn, Australia). The architecture is unusual in that the temporal order of tokens with the same color on the same graph arc is maintained [77, 78].

PIM-D Parallel Inference Machine: The PIM-D was proposed to be one of the candidates for a parallel inference machine in the Fifth Generation Computer System and was a joint venture of ICOT and OKI Electric Ind. (Japan) [131, 132, 133]. This machine was constructed from multiple processing elements and multiple structure memories interconnected by a hierarchical network and exploited three types of parallelism: OR parallelism, AND parallelism, and parallelism in unification.

2.3. Explicit token store. One of the main problems of tagged-token dataflow architectures is the implementation of an efficient token matching. To eliminate the need for associative memory searches, the concept of an *explicitly address token store* has been proposed [172]. The basic idea is to allocate a separate memory frame for every active loop iteration and subprogram invocation. Each frame slot is used to hold an operand for a particular activity. Since access to frame slots is through offsets relative to a frame pointer, no associative search is necessary (Fig.2.1 e). To make this concept practical, the number of concurrently active loop iterations must be controlled. Hence, the constraint condition of *k-bounded loops* was proposed in [18, 54], allowing the number of concurrently active loop iterations to be bounded by a constant.

The explicit token address store principle was developed in the Monsoon project, but is applied in most dataflow architectures developed more recently (see Subsection 3.2. below), i.e. as so-called direct matching in the EM-4 and Epsilon-2.

Monsoon: The Monsoon dataflow multiprocessor was built jointly by MIT and Motorola (USA) [56, 173, 193, 218]. Monsoon dataflow processor nodes are coupled by a packet-communication network with each other and with I-structure storage units. The main objective of the Monsoon dataflow processor architecture was to alleviate the waiting/matching problem by explicitly using address token store. This is achieved by a dataflow processor using an eight-stage pipeline. The first pipeline stage is the instruction fetch stage which is arranged prior to the token matching, in contrast to dynamic dataflow processors with associative matching units. The new arrangement is necessary, since the operand fields in an instruction denote the offset in the memory frame that itself is addressed by the tag of a token. The explicit token address is computed by the composition of frame address and operand offset. This is done in the second stage, which is the first of three pipeline stages that perform the token matching. In the third stage a presence bit store access is performed to find out if the first token of a dyadic operation has already arrived. If that is not the case, the presence bit is set and the current token is stored of the frame slot in the frame store in the fourth stage. Otherwise the presence bit is reset and the operand retrieved from the frame store in the fourth pipeline stage. The next three stages are execution stages in the course of which the next tag is also computed concurrently. The eighth stage forms one or two new tokens that are sent to the network, stored in a user token queue, a system token queue, or directly recirculated to the instruction fetch stage of the pipeline (see next section). Several small Monsoon systems have been built and installed at universities and research institutes.

3. Yesterday: Combining control-flow and dataflow. Pure dataflow computers based on the single-token-per-arc or tagged-token dataflow model usually perform quite poorly with sequential code. This is due to the fact that an instruction of the same thread can only be issued to the dataflow pipeline after the completion of its predecessor instruction. In the case of an 8-stage dataflow pipeline, an instruction of the same thread can be issued at most every eight cycles. If the load is low, for instance for a single sequential thread, the utilization of the dataflow processor drops to one eighth of its maximum performance. A further drawback is the overhead associated with token matching. Before a dyadic instruction is issued to the execution stage, two result tokens are necessary. The first token is stored in the waiting-matching store, thereby introducing a bubble in the execution stage(s) of the dataflow processor pipeline. Only when the second token arrives is

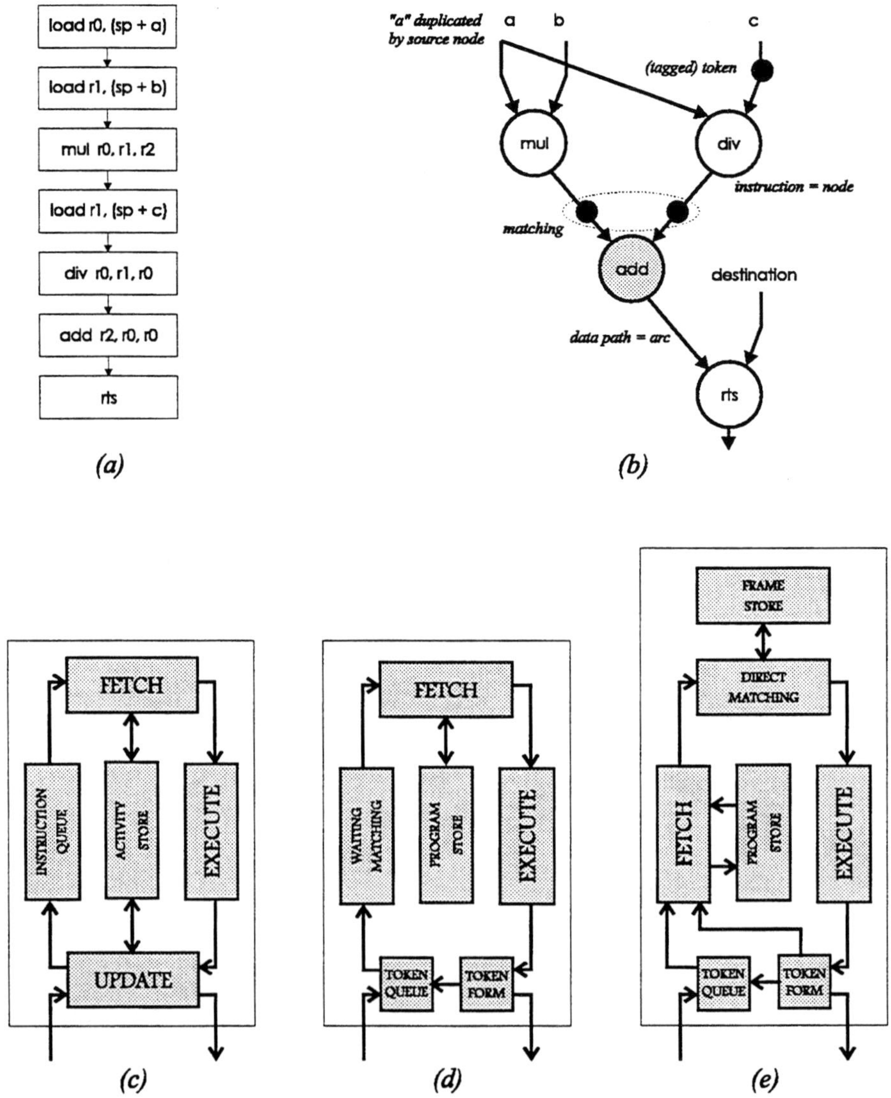

Fig. 2.1 – Computing $a \cdot b + \frac{a}{c}$ with: (a) control flow; (b) dataflow. Pure dataflow basic execution pipeline: (c) single-token-per-arc dataflow; (d) tagged-token dataflow; (e) explicit token store dataflow.

the instruction issued. For example, the pipeline bubbles sum up to 28.75 % executing a Traveling Salesman program on the Monsoon machine [173].

Since a context switch occurs in fine-grain dataflow after each instruction execution, no use of registers is possible. Use of registers could optimize the access time to data values, avoid pipeline bubbles caused by dyadic instructions, and reduce the total number of tokens during program execution.

One solution of these problems is combining the dataflow and control-flow mechanisms. The symbiosis between dataflow and von Neumann architectures is represented by a number of research projects developing von Neumann/dataflow hybrids [41, 128]. The spectrum of such hybrids is very broad, ranging from simple extensions of a von Neumann processor with a few additional instructions to specialized dataflow systems attempting to reduce overhead by increasing the execution grain size and employing various scheduling, allocation, and resource management techniques developed for von Neumann computers. These developments illustrate that dataflow and von Neumann computers do not necessarily represent two entirely disjoint worlds but rather are the two extreme ends of a spectrum of possible computer systems (Fig.3.1 a,b,c).

After *early hybrid dataflow* attempts, several techniques for combining control-flow and dataflow have emerged: *threaded dataflow* [174], *large-grain dataflow* [128], *RISC dataflow* [165], and *dataflow with complex machine operations* [81]. We describe them in the next five subsections (for a comparison of the techniques see [31]).

3.1. Early hybrid dataflow. The first attempts towards hybrid dataflow computing were made already in the early 1980s in quite diverse directions. Some of them are listed below.

JUMBO Newcastle Data-Control Flow Computer: The JUMBO [221] was built at the University of Newcastle upon Tyne (England) to study the integration of dataflow and control-flow computation. It has a packet communication organization with token matching. There are three principal units (matching unit, memory unit, processing unit) interconnected into ring by FIFO buffers.

MADAME Macro Dataflow Machine: The MADAME architecture from Jožef Stefan Institute (Ljubljana, Slovenia) was suitable for execution of acyclic dataflow (sub)graphs and supported synchronous dataflow computing [198, 199, 200, 201]. The advantage of such computing over pure dataflow is that more efficient runtime code can be generated because instructions can be scheduled at compile-time rather than at runtime.

PDF Piecewise Dataflow Architecture: The PDF architecture addressed Lawrence Livermore National Laboratory's (Livermore, Ca, USA) needs for supercomputing power. This architecture [178, 179] blended the strengths found in SIMD, MIMD, and dataflow architectures. The PDF contained a SIMD processing unit and a scalar processing unit that managed a group of processors (MIMD). Programs that ran on the PDF were broken into basic blocks and scheduled for execution using dataflow techniques. Two levels of scheduling divided responsibility between the software and hardware. The time-consuming analysis of when blocks can overlap was done in the compile-time, before program executions began. Individual instruction scheduling was done in hardware.

MUSE Multiple Stream Evaluator: The MUSE machine [40] from University of Nottingham (England) was a structured architecture supporting both serial and parallel processing which allowed the abstract structure of a program to be mapped onto the machine in a logical way. The MUSE machine had many features of dataflow architecture but in its detailed operation it steered a middle course between a pure dataflow machine, a tree machine, and the graph reduction approach.

RAMPS Real Time Acquisition and Multiprocessing System: RAMPS [30] was a parallel processing system developed at EIP Inc. (USA) for high performance data acquisition and processing applications. RAMPS used dataflow at a macro level while tasks were executed using a sequential model of computation.

DTN Dataflow Computer: The DTN Dataflow Computer [228] (developed by the Dutch company Dataflow Technology Nederland) is a high-performance workstation well suited for applications containing relatively small computing-intensive parts with enough parallelism to execute efficiently on the dataflow engine. The DTN Dataflow Computer contains a standard general purpose host, a graphical subsystem (four microprogrammable systolic arrays), and a dataflow engine. The dataflow engine consists of eight identical modules connected by a token routing network. Each module contains four NEC Image Pipelined Processors, interface chip, and image memory.

ETCA Functional Dataflow Architecture: A functional dataflow architecture has been developed at ETCA (Arcueil, France) and is dedicated to real-time processing [191]. Two types of data-driven processing elements, dedicated respectively to low and mid-level processing are integrated in a regular 3-D array. Its design relies on close integration of dataflow principles and functional programming. For the execution of low-level functions, a custom dataflow processor with six bi-directional I/O ports was developed [177].

3.2. Threaded dataflow. In a dataflow program each subgraph that exhibits a low degree of parallelism can be identified within a dataflow graph and transformed into a sequential thread. By the term *threaded dataflow* we understand a technique where the dataflow principle is modified so that instructions of a sequential instruction stream can be processed in succeeding machine cycles. A thread of instructions is issued consecutively by the matching unit without matching further tokens except for the first instruction of the thread. Threaded dataflow covers the repeat-on-input technique in the Epsilon-1 and Epsilon-2 processors, the strongly connected arc model of EM-4, and the direct recycling of tokens in Monsoon. Data passed between instructions from the same thread is stored in registers instead of writing them back to memory. These registers may be referenced by any succeeding instruction in the thread. Thereby single-thread performance is improved. The total number of tokens needed to schedule the instructions of a program is reduced thus saving hardware resources. Pipeline bubbles are avoided for dyadic instructions within a thread. Two threaded dataflow execution techniques can be distinguished: the *direct token recycling*, and *consecutive execution* of the instructions of a single thread. The first technique, used by the Monsoon dataflow computer, allows a particular thread to occupy only a single slot in the 8-stage pipeline, which implies that at least 8 threads must be active for a full pipeline utilization to be achieved. This cycle-by-cycle instruction interleaving of threads is used in a similar fashion by some multithreaded von Neumann computers (Section 4.). To optimize single-thread performance the Epsilon-processors and the EM-4 execute instructions from a thread consecutively. The circular pipeline of fine-grain dataflow is retained. However, the matching unit has to be enhanced with a mechanism that, after firing the first instruction of a thread, delays the matching of further tokens in favor of issuing all instructions of the thread consecutively. By this mechanism cycling of tokens through the pipeline for the activation of the next instruction is suppressed. The three highly influential projects are given below.

Monsoon: The Monsoon dataflow processor can be viewed as a cycle-by-cycle interleaving multithreaded computer [174] due to its ability of direct token recycling. By use of this technique a successor token is directly fed back in the eight-stage Monsoon pipeline bypassing the token store. Another instruction of the same thread is executed every eighth processor cycle. Monsoon allows the use of registers (eight register sets are provided) to store intermediate results within a thread, thereby leaving the pure dataflow execution model.

Epsilon-2: Epsilon-2 machine [101, 102] developed at Sandia National Laboratories (Livermore, Ca, USA), supports a fully dynamic memory model, allowing single cycle context switches and dynamic parallelization. The system is built around a module consisting of a processor and structure unit, connected via a 4×4 crossbar to each other, an I/O port, and the global interconnect. The structure unit is used for storing data structures such as arrays, lists, and I-structures. The Epsilon-2 processor retains the high performance features of the Epsilon-1 prototype, including direct matching, pipelined processing, and a local feedback path. The ability to execute sequential code as a grain provides RISC-like execution efficiency.

EM-4 and EM-X: In the EM-4 project [35, 143, 182, 183, 184, 187, 188, 189, 190, 207] at Electrotechnical Laboratory (Tsukuba, Japan), the essential elements of a dynamic dataflow architecture using frame storage for local variables are incorporated into a single chip processor. In this design a *strongly connected* subgraph of a function body is implemented as a thread that uses registers for intermediate results. The EM-4 was designed for 1024 nodes. Since May 1990 the EM-4 prototype with 80 nodes (EMC-R gate-array processor) is operational. In 1993 the EM-X [144] (upgrade of EM-4) was designed to support latency reduction by fusing the communication pipeline with the execution pipeline, latency hiding via multithreading, and runtime latency minimization for remote memory access.

3.3. Large-grain dataflow. This technique, also referred to as *coarse-grain dataflow*, advocates activating macro dataflow actors by the dataflow principle while executing the represented sequences of instructions by the von Neumann principle [34, 62, 81, 128]. Large-grain dataflow machines typically decouple the matching stage (sometimes called signal stage, synchronization stage, etc.) from the execution stage by use of FIFO-buffers. Pipeline bubbles are avoided by the decoupling. Off-the-shelf microprocessors can be used for the execution stage. Most of the more recent dataflow architectures fall in this category and are listed below. Note, that they are often called *multithreaded machines* by their authors.

TAM Threaded Abstract Machine: The TAM [55, 57] from the University of California (Berkeley, Ca, USA) is an execution model for fine-grain interleaving of multiple threads, that is supported by an appropriate compiler strategy and program representation instead of elaborate hardware. TAM's key features are placing all synchronization, scheduling, and storage management under explicit compiler control.

**T:* The *T (pronounced "start" [166]) is a direct descendant of dataflow architectures, especially of the Monsoon, and unifies them with von Neumann architectures. *T has a scalable computer architecture designed to support a broad variety of parallel programming styles including those which use multithreading based on non-blocking threads. A *T node consists of the data processor (executing threads), the remote-memory request coprocessor (for incoming remote load/store requests), and the synchronization coprocessor (for handling returning load responses and join operations), which all share local memory. This hardware is coupled with a high performance network having a fat-tree topology with high cross-section bandwidth. A modified version of the *T [166] was implemented in cooperation by MIT and Motorola, based on a 88110 superscalar microprocessor (called 88110MP [32, 33]). Despite its name the StarT-ng [14, 47] bears no resemblance to its predecessor *T and to dataflow machines. It defines a rather conventional multiprocessor with PowerPC 620 processors augmented with special hardware for message-passing and shared memory access.

ADARC Associative Dataflow Architecture: In the Associative Dataflow Architecture ADARC [210, 211, 234] the processing units are connected via an associative communication network. The processors are equipped with private memories that contain instruction sequences generated at compile-time. The retrieval of executable instructions is replaced by the retrieval of input operands for the current instructions from the network. The structure of the network enables full parallel access to all previously generated results by all processors. A processor executes its current instruction (or instruction sequence) as soon as all requested input operands have been received [210]. In [234] it is shown that that ADARC is well-suited to implement neural network models. ADARC was developed at J.W.Goethe University (Frankfurt, Germany).

Pebbles: The Pebbles architecture [181] from Colorado State University (Fort Collins, Co, USA) is a large-grain dataflow architecture with a decoupling of the synchronization unit and the execution unit within the processing elements. The processing elements are coupled via a high-speed network. The local memory of each node consists of an instruction memory which is read by the execution unit and a data memory (or frame store) which is accessed by the synchronization unit. A ready queue contains the continuations representing those threads that are ready to execute. The frame store is designed as a storage hierarchy where a frame cache holds the frames of threads that will be executed soon. The execution unit is a 4-way superscalar microprocessor.

From Argument Fetch Dataflow Processor to MTA and EARTH: The EARTH (Efficient Architecture of Running Threads) [156], developed at McGill University and Concordia University (Montréal, Canada), is based on the MTA (Multithreaded Architecture) [87, 127] and dates back to the Argument Fetch Dataflow Processor. An MTA node consists of an execution unit that may be an off-the-shelf RISC microprocessor and a synchronization unit to support dataflow-like thread synchronization. The synchronization unit determines which threads are ready to be executed. Execution unit and synchronization unit share the processor local memory which is cached. Accessing data in a remote processor requires explicit request and send messages. The synchronization unit and execution unit communicate via FIFO queues: a ready queue containing ready thread identifiers links the synchronization unit with the execution unit, and an event queue holding local and remote synchronization signals connects the execution unit with the synchronization unit, but also receives signals from the network. A register use cache keeps track of which register set is assigned to which function activation [127]. MTA or EARTH rely on non-blocking threads. The EARTH architecture [162] is implemented on top of the experimental (but rather conventional) MANNA multiprocessor [92].

3.4. RISC dataflow. Another stimulus for dataflow/von Neumann hybrids was the development of *RISC dataflow* architectures, notably P-RISC [165], which allow the execution of existing software written for conventional processors. Using such a machine as a bridge between existing systems and new dataflow supercomputers made the transition from imperative von Neumann languages to dataflow languages easier for the programmer.

P-RISC Parallel RISC: The basic philosophy underlying the development of the P-RISC architecture [165] can be characterized as follows: use a RISC-like instruction set, change the architecture to support multithreaded computation, add fork and join instructions to manage multiple threads, implement all global storage as I-structure storage, and implement the load/store instructions to execute in split-phase mode (Fig.3.1 d,e). The architecture based on the above principles was developed at MIT. It consists of a collection of PEs and Heap Memory Elements, interconnected through a packed-switching communication network.

3.5. Use of complex machine operations. Another technique to reduce the instruction level synchronization overhead is the use of complex machine instructions, for instance vector instructions. These instructions can be implemented by pipeline techniques as in vector computers. Structured data is referenced in block rather than element-wise, and can be supplied in a burst mode. This deviates from the I-structure scheme where each data element within a complex data structure is fetched individually from a structure store. A further advantage of complex machine operations is the ability to exploit parallelism at the subinstruction level. Therefore the machine has to partition the complex machine operation into suboperations that can be executed in parallel. The use of a complex machine operation may spare several nested loops. The use of a FIFO-buffer allows the machine to decouple the firing stage and the execution stage to bridge the different execution times within a mixed stream of simple and complex instructions issued to the execution stage. As a major difference to conventional dataflow architectures tokens do not carry data (except for the values "true" or "false"). Data is only moved and transformed within the execution stage. This technique is used in the Decoupled Graph/Computation Architecture, the Stollmann Dataflow Machine, and the ASTOR architecture. These architectures combine complex machine instructions with large-grain dataflow, described above. The structure-flow technique proposed for the SIGMA-1 enhances an otherwise fine-grain dataflow computer by structure load and structure store instructions, that move for instance whole vectors from or to the structure store. The arithmetic operations are executed by the cyclic pipeline within a single PE. A more detailed description is given below.

Decoupled Graph/Computation Architecture: In this architecture, developed at the University of Southern California (Los Angeles, Ca, USA), the token matching and token formatting and routing are reduced to a single graph operation called *determine executability* [81]. The decoupled graph/computation model separates the graph portion of the program from the computational portion. The two basic units of the decoupled model (*computational* unit and *graph* unit) operate in an asynchronous manner. The graph unit is responsible for determining executability by updating the dataflow graph, while the computation unit performs all the computational operations (fetch and execute).

Stollman Data Flow Machine: The Stollman dataflow machine [96, 97] from Stollman GmbH (Hamburg, Germany) is a coarse-grain dataflow architecture directed towards database applications. The dataflow mechanism is emulated on a shared-memory multiprocessor. The query tree of a relational query language (such as the database query language SQL) is viewed as dataflow graph. Complex database query instructions are implemented as coarse-grain dataflow instruction and (micro-)coded as a traditional sequential program running on the emulator hardware.

ASTOR Augsburg Structure-Oriented Architecture: The ASTOR architecture [224, 225, 235, 236] from University of Augsburg (Germany) can be viewed as a dataflow architecture that utilizes task level parallelism by the architectural structure of a distributed memory multiprocessor, instruction level parallelism by a token-passing computation scheme, and subinstruction level parallelism by SIMD evaluation of complex machine instructions. Sequential threads of data instructions are compiled to dataflow macro actors and executed consecutively using registers. A dependency construct describes the partial order in the execution of instructions. It can be visualized by a dependency graph. The nodes in a dependency graph represent control constructs or data instructions; the directed arcs denote control dependencies between the nodes. Tokens are propagated along the arcs of the dependency graph. To distinguish different activations of a dependency graph, a tag is assigned to each token. The firing rule of dynamic dataflow is applied: a node is enabled as soon as tokens with identical tags are present on all its input arcs. However, in the ASTOR architecture tokens do not carry data.

4. Today: Multithreading. In a *single-threaded* architecture the computation moves forward one step at a time through a sequence of states, each step corresponding to the

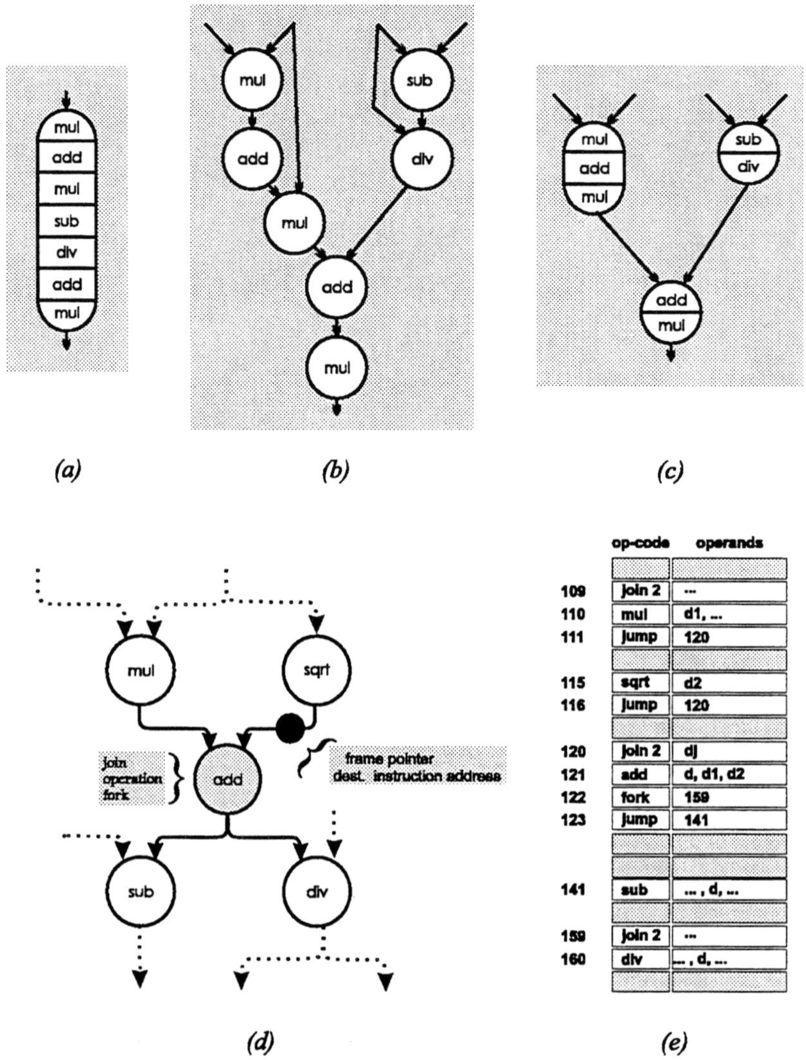

Fig. 3.1 – Spectrum of scheduling models: (a) fully ordered (control flow); (b) partially ordered (dataflow); (c) partially ordered graph and fully ordered grains (e.g. Epsilon-2 hybrid). "RISCifying" dataflow (P-RISC dataflow/von Neumann hybrid): (d) conceptual; (e) encoding of graph.

execution of one enabled instruction. The state of a single-threaded machine consists of the *memory state* (program memory, data memory, stack) and the *processor state* which consists of *activity specifier* (program counter, stack pointer) and *register context* (a set of register contents). The activity specifier and the register context make up what is also called the *context* of a thread. Today most architectures are single-threaded architectures.

According to [71], a *multithreaded* architecture differs from the single-threaded architecture in that there may be several enabled instructions from different threads which all are candidates for execution (Fig.4.1). Similar to the single-threaded machine, the state of the multithreaded machine consists of the memory state and the processor state; the later, however, consists of a *collection* of activity specifiers and a *collection* of register contexts. A thread is a sequentially ordered block of instructions with a grain-size greater than one (to distinguish multithreaded architectures from fine-grained dataflow architectures).

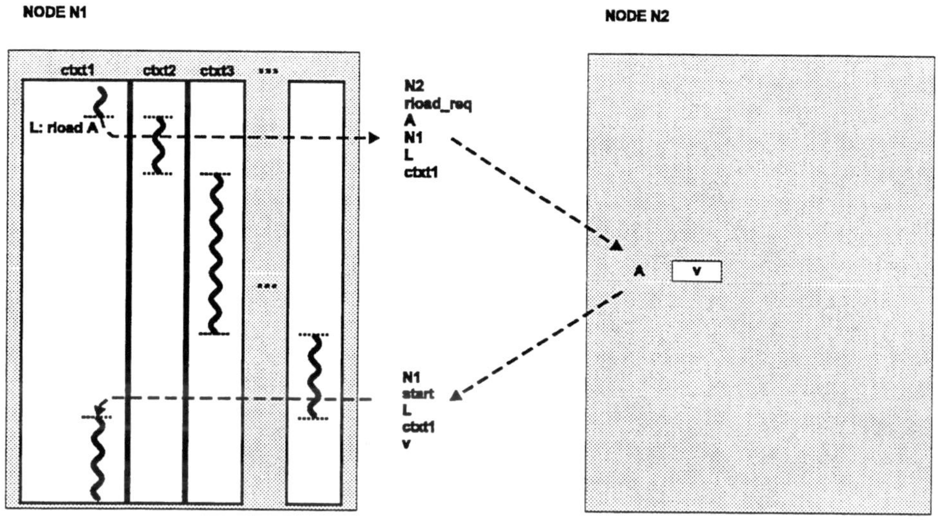

Fig. 4.1 – Multithreading: when a thread issues a remote-load request, the processor starts executing another thread.

Another notion is the distinction between *blocking* and *non-blocking* threads. A *non-blocking thread* is formed such that its evaluation proceeds without blocking the processor pipeline (for instance by remote memory accesses, cache misses or synchronization waits). Evaluation of a non-blocking thread starts as soon as all input operands are available, which is usually detected by some kind of dataflow principle. Thread switching is controlled by the compiler harnessing the idea of rescheduling rather than blocking when waiting for data. Access to remote data is organized split-level by one thread sending the access request to memory and another thread activating when its data is available. Thus a program is compiled into many very small threads activating each other when data become available. The same hardware mechanisms may also be used to synchronize interprocess communications to awaiting threads, thereby alleviating operating systems overhead [160]. In contrast, a *blocking thread* might be blocked during execution caused by remote memory accesses, cache misses or synchronization needs. The waiting time, during which the pipeline is blocked, is lost when using a von Neumann processor, but can be bridged by a fast thread switch in a multithreaded processor. The thread is resumed when the reason for blocking is removed. Use of non-blocking threads typically leads to many small threads that are appropriate for execution by a hybrid dataflow computer or by a multithreaded architecture that is closely related to hybrid dataflow. Blocking threads may be normal threads or whole processes of a multithreaded UNIX-based operating system.

Notice, that we exclude in this section architectures that are designed for the execution of non-blocking threads. Although these architectures often are called *multithreaded*, we categorized them as threaded dataflow (Subsection 3.2.) or large-grain dataflow (Subsection 3.3.) since a dataflow principle is applied to start execution of non-blocking threads. Thus, multithreaded architectures (in the more narrow sense applied here) stem from the modification of RISC or even of superscalar RISC processors. They are able to bridge waiting times that arise in the execution of blocking threads by fast thread switching. This ability is in contrast to RISC processors or today's superscalar processors, that use busy waiting or a time-consuming, operating system based thread switch. One characteristic for such multithreaded architectures is the use of multiple register sets and a mechanism that dynamically triggers the thread switch. Thread switch overhead must be very low, from zero to only a few cycles.

Current microprocessors utilize instruction-level parallelism by a deep processor pipeline and by the superscalar instruction issue technique. A superscalar processor is able to dispatch multiple instructions each clock cycle from a conventional linear instruction stream [74]. DEC Alpha 21164, IBM & Motorola PowerPC 604 and 620, MIPS R10000, Sun UltraSparc and HP PA-8000 issue up to four instructions per cycle from a single thread. VLSI-technology will allow future generations of microprocessors to exploit instruction-level parallelism up to 8 instructions per cycle, or more.

However, the instruction-level parallelism found in a conventional instruction stream is limited. Recent studies showed the limits of processor utilization even of today's superscalar microprocessors. Using the SPEC92 benchmark suite, the PowerPC 620 showed an execution of 0.96 to 1.77 instructions per cycle [75], and even an 8-issue Alpha processor will fail to sustain 1.5 instructions per cycle [223].

The solution is the additional utilization of more coarse-grained parallelism. The main approaches are the *multiprocessor chip* and the *multithreaded processor*. The multiprocessor chip integrates two or more complete processors on a single chip. Therefore every unit of a processor is duplicated and used independently of its copies on the chip. In contrast, the multithreaded processor stores multiple contexts in different register sets on the chip. The functional units are multiplexed between the threads that are loaded in the register sets. Depending on the specific multithreaded processor design, only a single instruction pipeline is used, or a single dispatch unit issues instructions from different instruction buffers simultaneously. Because of the multiple register sets, context switching is very fast. Multithreaded processors tolerate memory latencies by overlapping the long-latency operations of one thread with the execution of other threads - in contrast to the multiprocessor chip approach. While the multiprocessor chip is easier to implement, use of multithreading in addition to a wide issue bandwidth is a promising approach.

Research on multithreaded architectures has been motivated by two concerns: tolerating latency and bridging of synchronization waits by rapid context switches. Three different approaches of multithreaded architectures are distinguished: *cycle-by-cycle interleaving* [118, 174, 203, 216], *block interleaving* [2, 3, 107], and *simultaneous multithreading* [222, 223].

4.1. Cycle-by-cycle interleaving. In the *cycle-by-cycle* interleaving model the processor switches to a different thread after each instruction. In principle, an instruction of the same thread is fed in the pipeline after the completion of the execution of the previous instruction. There must be at least as many register sets (loaded threads) available on the processor as the number of pipeline stages. Since cycle-by-cycle interleaving eliminates control and data dependencies between instructions in the pipeline, pipeline conflicts cannot arise and the processor pipeline can be easily built without the necessity of complex forwarding paths. This leads to a very simple and therefore potentially very fast pipeline - no hardware interlocking is necessary. The latency is tolerated by not scheduling a thread until its reference to a remote memory has completed. This model requires a large number of threads and complex hardware to support them. Interleaving the instructions from many threads also limits the processing power accessible to a single thread, thereby degrading the single-thread performance. The use of the dependence look-ahead technique in HEP, Horizon and Tera gives some help. Some machines that use cycle-by-cycle interleaving are given below.

HEP Heterogeneous Element Processor: The HEP system was a MIMD shared-memory multiprocessor system developed by Denelcor Inc. (Denver, Co, USA) between 1978 and 1985 [138, 146, 202, 203, 204], and was a pioneering example of a multithreaded machine. Spatial switching occurred between two queues of processes, one of these controlled program memory, register memory, and the functional memory while the other controlled data memory. The main processor pipeline had eight stages, matching the number of processor cycles necessary to fetch a data item from memory in register. Consequently eight threads were in execution concurrently within a single HEP processor. In contrast to all other cycle-by-cycle interleaving processor, all threads within a HEP processor shared the same register set. Multiple processors and data memories were interconnected via a pipelined switch and any register memory or data memory location could be used to synchronize two processes on a producer-consumer basis by a full/empty bit synchronization on a data memory word.

MASA Multilisp Architecture for Symbolic Applications: The MASA was a multithreaded processor architecture for parallel symbolic computation with various features intended for effective Multilisp program execution [86, 118]. MASA featured a tagged architecture, multiple contexts, fast trap handling, and a synchronization bit in every memory word. Its principal novelty was the use of multiple contexts both to support interleaved execution from separate instruction streams and to speed up procedure calls and trap handling (in the same manner as register windows).

Horizon: This (paper) architecture was based on the HEP but extended to a massively parallel MIMD computer. The machine was designed for up to 256 processing elements and up to 512 memory modules in a $16 \times 16 \times 6$ node internal network. Like HEP it employed a global address space, and memory-based synchronization through the use of full/empty bits at each location [95, 149, 216]. Each processor supported 128 independent instruction streams by 128 register sets with context switches occurring at every clock cycle.

Tera MTA Multi-Threaded Architecture: The Tera MTA [9, 11, 12] is based on the Horizon architecture and currently under construction by Tera Computer Company (Seattle, Wa, USA) (after many delays introduction to market is scheduled for Spring 1997). The machine is a vast multiprocessor with multithreaded processor nodes arranged in 3D mesh of pipelined packet-switch nodes. In the case of the maximum configuration of 4096 nodes, arranged in a $16 \times 16 \times 16$ mesh, there are up to 256 processors, 512 memory units, 256 I/O cache units, 256 I/O processors, and 2816 switching nodes. Each processor is 64-bit custom chip with up to 128 simultaneous threads in execution. It alternates between ready threads, using a deep pipeline. Inter-instruction dependencies are explicitly encoded by the compiler. Each thread has a complete set of registers. Memory units have 4-bit tags on each word, or full/empty and trap bits [12]. The Tera MTA exploits parallelism at all levels, from fine-grained instruction-level parallelism within a single processor to parallel programming across processors, to multiprogramming among several applications simultaneously. Consequently, processor scheduling occurs at many levels, and managing these levels poses unique and challenging scheduling concerns [11].

SB-PRAM and HPP: The SB-PRAM [1, 26] or HPP (High Performance PRAM) [84, 85] is a MIMD parallel computer with shared address space and uniform memory access time due to its motivation: building a multiprocessor that is as close as possible to the theoretical machine model CRCW-PRAM. Processor and memory modules are connected by a butterfly network. Network latency is hidden by pipelining several so-called virtual processors on one physical processor node in cycle-by-cycle interleaving mode. A first prototype (SB-PRAM) [26] is running with four processors, a second prototype (HPP) is under construction. In the SB-PRAM 32 virtual processors are scheduled round-robin for every instruction [84]. The project is running at the University of Saarland (Saarbrücken, Germany).

4.2. Block interleaving. The block-interleaving approach, exemplified by the MIT Sparcle processor, executes a single thread until it reaches a long-latency operation, such as a remote cache miss or a failed synchronization, at which point it switches to another context. The Rhamma processor switches contexts whenever a load, store or synchronization operation is discovered.

In the *block* interleaving model a thread is executed for many cycles before context switching. Context switches are used only to hide long memory latencies since small pipeline delays are hidden by proper ordering of instructions performed by the optimizing compiler. Since multithreading is not used to hide pipeline delays, fewer total threads are needed and a single thread can execute at full speed until the next context switch. This may also simplify the hardware. There are three variations of this model. The *switch-on-load* version switches only on instructions that load data from shared memory while storing data in shared memory does not cause context switching (since local memory loads and other instructions all complete quickly and can be scheduled by the compiler). However, context switches sometimes occur sooner than needed: If a compiler ordered instructions so that a load from shared memory was issued several cycles before the value was used, the context switch should not have to occur until the actual use of the value. This strategy is implemented in the *switch-on-use* model [155]. Here, a *valid bit* is added to each register. The bit is cleared when the loading from shared memory to the corresponding register is issued and set when the result returns from the network. A thread context switches if it needs a value from a register whose valid bit is still cleared. A benefit of this model is that several load instructions can be grouped together thus prefetching several operands of an instruction. Instead of using valid bits, an explicit context switch instruction can be added between the group of loads and their subsequent uses. This model, which is called *explicit-switch* [57, 166], is simpler to implement and requires only one additional instruction.

The multithreading with caching approach adds *caches* to the block interleaving model. Only those loads that miss in the cache have long latencies and cause context switches. By filtering out many of the remote references, caching reduces the number of threads. In [39], it is shown that for most applications just two or three threads per processor is sufficient. There are three variations of the cache-extended block interleaving model. The *switch-on-miss* model [5] context switches if load from shared memory instructions misses in the cache. Such a context switch is not detected immediately, however, so a number of subsequent instructions have already entered the CPU pipeline and thus wasted CPU time. The *switch-on-use-miss* model [107] context switches when an instruction tries to use the (still missing) value from a shared load that missed in the cache. The *conditional-switch* model provides the benefits of grouping (of the explicit-switch model) and caching. In this model, the explicit switch instruction is ignored if all load instructions (in the preceding group) hit the cache; otherwise, the context switch is performed. In what follows, we describe five representatives of the block interleaving model of multithreading.

CHoPP Columbia Homogeneous Parallel Processor: The CHoPP [155] was a shared memory MIMD with up to 16 powerful computing nodes. High sequential performance is due to issuing multiple instructions on each clock cycle, zero-delay branch instructions, and fast execution of individual instructions. Each node can support up to 64 threads.

Sparcle Processor in Alewife System: The MIT Alewife multiprocessor [3, 4, 5, 6, 7, 148] is based on the multithreaded Sparcle processor. The Sparcle processor is derived from a Sparc RISC processor. The eight overlapping register windows of a Sparc processor are organized in four independent non-overlapping thread contexts, each using two windows (one as register set, the other as a context for trap and message handlers). Thread switching is triggered by external hardware when a remote memory access is detected. Emptying the pipeline from instructions of the thread that caused the context switch and organizational software overhead sum up to a context switching penalty of 14 processor cycles. The Alewife multiprocessor has been operational since May 1994 [4]. It uses a low-dimensional direct interconnection network. Despite its distributed-memory architecture, Alewife allows efficient shared-memory programming through a multilayered approach to locality management. Communication latency and network bandwidth requirements are reduced by a directory-based cache-coherence scheme referred to as LimitLESS directories. Latencies still occur although communication locality is enhanced by runtime and compile-time partitioning and placement of data and processes.

MSparc: An approach similar to the Sparcle processor is taken at the University of Oldenburg (Germany) with the MSparc processor [157, 180]. MSparc supports up to four contexts on chip and is compatible to standard Sparc processors. Switching is supported by hardware and can be achieved within one processor cycle. The multithreading policy is block interleaving with the switch-on-cache-miss policy as in the Sparcle processor.

J-Machine: The MIT Jellybean Machine [59, 168] is so called because it is to be built entirely of a large number of "jellybean" components. The initial version uses an $8 \times 8 \times 16$ cube network, with possibilities of expanding to 64K nodes. The "jellybeans" are message driven processor (MDP) chips, each of which has a 36-bit processor, a 4K word memory, and a router with communication ports for 6 directions. External memory of up to 1 M words can be added per processor. The MDP creates a task for each arriving message. In the prototype, each MDP chip has 4 external memory chips that provide 256K memory words. However, access is through a 12-bit data bus, and with an error correcting cycle, the access time is four memory cycles per word. Each communication port has a 9-bit data channel. The routers provide support for automatic routing from source to destination. The latency of a transfer is 2 microseconds across the prototype machine, assuming no blocking. When a message arrives, a task is created automatically to handle it in 1 microsecond. Thus, it is possible to implement a shared memory model using message passing, in which a message provides a fetch address and an automatic task sends a reply with the desired data.

Rhamma: The multithreaded Rhamma processor [104, 105] from the University of Karlsruhe (Germany) uses a fast context switch to bridge latencies caused by memory accesses or by synchronization operations. Load/store, synchronization and execution operations of different threads are executed simultaneously by specialized functional units within the processor. The units are coupled by FIFO buffers and access different register sets. Each unit stops the execution of a thread when it recognizes an instruction intended for another unit. To perform a context switch the unit passes the thread tag to the FIFO buffer of the unit that is appropriate for the execution of the instruction. Then the unit resumes processing with another thread of its own FIFO buffer. The Rhamma processor is most similar to the Sparcle. However, the execution unit of the Rhamma processor switches the context whenever it comes across a load, store or synchronization instruction, and the load/store unit switches whenever it meets an execution or synchronization instruction (switch-on-load policy). In contrast to Sparcle, the context switch is in an early stage of the pipeline, thus decreasing context switching time. On the other hand, the overall performance of the Rhamma processor suffers from the higher rate of context switches unless the context switch time is very small. Software simulations showed the need for extremely fast context switching. Therefore a VHDL representation of Rhamma with optimizations towards fast context switching was developed, simulated and synthesized. Specific implementation techniques reduce switching costs to zero or at most one processor cycle. These techniques use a context switch buffer which is a table containing the addresses of instructions that already yielded a context switch.

4.3. Simultaneous multithreading or multithreaded superscalar. The *simultaneous multithreading* or *multithreaded superscalar* approach [153, 195, 196, 222, 223] combines a wide issue superscalar instruction dispatch with the multiple context approach by providing several register sets on the multiprocessor and issuing instructions from several instruction queues simultaneously. Therefore, the issue slots of a wide issue processor can be filled by operations of several threads. Latencies occurring in the execution of single threads are bridged by issuing operations of the remaining threads loaded on the processor. In principle, the full issue bandwidth can be utilized. Project dependent details are briefly discussed below.

Media Research Laboratory Processor: The multithreaded processor of the Media Research Laboratory of Matsushita Electric Ind. (Japan) [124, 125] is the first approach to simultaneous multithreading. Instructions of different threads are issued simultaneously to multiple functional units. Simulation results on a parallel ray-tracing application showed that using 8 threads a speed-up of 3.22 in case of one load/store unit and of 5.79 in case of two load/store units can be achieved over a conventional RISC processor. However, caches or TLBs are not simulated, nor is a branch prediction mechanism.

Simultaneous Multithreading: The *simultaneous multithreading* approach from the University of Washington (Seattle, Wa, USA) [80] surveys enhancements of the Alpha 21164 processor [223] and of a hypothetical out-of-order issue superscalar microprocessor that resembles R10000 and PA-8000 [222]. Simulations were conducted to evaluate processor configurations of an up to 8-threaded and 8-issue superscalar. This maximum configuration showed a throughput of 6.64 instructions per cycle due to multithreading using the SPEC92 benchmark suite and assuming a processor with 32 functional units (among them multiple load/store units) [223]. The second approach [222] evaluated more realistic processor configurations and reached a throughput of 5.4 instructions per cycle for the 8-threaded and 8-issue superscalar case. Implementation issues and solutions to register file access and instruction scheduling were also presented.

Multithreaded Superscalar (Sigmund & Ungerer): While the simultaneous multithreading approach [223] surveys enhancements of the Alpha 21164 processor, the *multithreaded superscalar* processor approach from the University of Karlsruhe [195, 196] is based on a simplified PowerPC 604 processor. Both approaches, however, are similar in their instruction issuing policy. The multithreaded superscalar processor implements the six-stage instruction pipeline of the PowerPC 604 processor (fetch, decode, dispatch, execute, complete, and write-back) [208] and extends it to employ multithreading. The processor uses various kinds of modern microarchitecture techniques as e.g. separate code and data caches, branch target address cache, static branch prediction, in-order dispatch, independent execution units with reservation stations, rename registers, out-of-order execution, and in-order completion. However the instruction set is simplified (using an extended DLX [120] instruction set instead). A software simulation evaluated various configurations of the multithreaded superscalar processor. While the single-threaded 8-issue superscalar processor only reached a throughput of about 1.14 instructions per cycle, the 8-threaded 8-issue superscalar processor executed 4.19 instructions per cycle (the load/store frequency in the work load sets the theoretical maximum to 5 instructions per cycle). Increasing the superscalar issue bandwidth from 4 to 8 yields only a marginal gain in instruction throughput - a result that is nearly independent of the number of threads in the multithreaded processor. A multiprocessor chip approach with 8 single-threaded scalar processors reaches 6.07 instructions per cycle. Using the same number of threads, the multiprocessor chip reaches a higher throughput than the multithreaded superscalar approach. However, if the chip costs are taken into consideration, a 4-threaded 4-issue superscalar processor outperforms a multiprocessor chip built from single-threaded processors by a factor of 1.8 in performance/cost relation [195].

Multithreaded Superscalar (Bagherzadeh et al.): This *multithreaded superscalar* processor approach [106, 154] combines out-of-order execution within an instruction stream with the simultaneous execution of instructions of different instruction streams. A particular superscalar processor called Superscalar Digital Signal Processor (SDSP) is enhanced to run multiple threads. The enhancements are directed by the aim of minimal modification to the superscalar base processor. Therefore most resources on the chip are shared by the threads, as for instance the register file, reorder buffer, instruction window, store buffer, and renaming hardware. Based on simulations a performance gain of 20 - 55 % due to multithreading was achieved across a range of benchmarks. The project runs at the University of California at Irvine.

5. Coming: Micro dataflow and nanothreading. The latest generation of microprocessors - as exemplified by the Intel PentiumPro [49], MIPS R10000 [232], and HP PA-8000 [150] - displays an out-of-order dynamic execution that is referred to as *local dataflow* or *micro dataflow* by microprocessor researchers.

In the first paper on the PentiumPro, the instruction pipeline is described as [49]: *"The flow of the Intel Architecture instructions is predicted and these instructions are decoded into micro-operations (micro-ops), or series of micro-ops, and these micro-ops are register-renamed, placed into an out-of-order speculative pool of pending operations, executed in dataflow order (when operands are ready), and retired to permanent machine state in source program order."* After register renaming the instructions (or micro-ops) are placed in an instruction window of pending instructions and in a reorder buffer that saves the program order and execution states of the instructions (instruction window and reorder buffer may coincide). State-of-the art microprocessors typically provide 32 (R10000), 40 (PentiumPro) or 56 (PA-8000) instruction slots in the instruction window or reorder buffer. Instructions are ready to be executed as soon as all operands are available. A 4-issue superscalar processor dispatches up to 4 instructions per cycle to the execution units provided that resouce conflicts do not occur. Dispatch and execution determine the out-of-order section of a microprocessor. After execution instructions are retired in program order.

Comparing dataflow computers with such superscalar microprocessors shows several similarities and differences which are briefly discussed below.

While a single thread of control in modern microprocessors often does not incorporate enough fine-grained parallelism to feed the multiple functional units of todays microprocessors, dataflow resolves any threads of control into separate instructions that are ready to execute as soon as all required operands are available. Thus, the fine-grained parallelism potentially utilized by a dataflow computer is far larger than the parallelism available for microprocessors.

Data and control dependencies potentially cause pipeline hazards in microprocesssors that are handled by complex forwarding logic. Due to the continuous context switches in fine-grain dataflow computers and in cycle-by-cycle interleaving machines, pipeline hazards are avoided with the disadvantage of a poor single thread performance.

Antidependencies and output dependencies are removed by register renaming that maps the architectural registers to the physical registers of the microprocessor. Thereby the microprocessor internally generates an instruction stream that satisfies the single assignment rule of dataflow. Modern microprocessors remove antidependencies and output dependencies on-the-fly and avoid the high memory requirements, the often awkward solutions for data structure storage and manipulation, and for loop control caused by the single assignment rule in dataflow computers.

The main difference between the dependence graphs of dataflow and the code sequence in an instruction window of a microprocessors is branch prediction and speculatively execution. The accuracy of the branch prediction is surprisingly high - more than 95 % are reported for single SPEC benchmark programs [46]. However, rerolling execution in case of a wrongly predicted path, is costly in processor cycles especially in deeply pipelined microprocessors. The idea of branch prediction and speculative execution has never been evaluated in the dataflow environment.

Due to the single thread of control, a high degree of data and instruction locality is present in the machine code of a microprocessor. The locality allows to employ a storage hierarchy that stores the instructions and data potentially executed in the next cycles close to the executing processor. Due to the lack of locality in a dataflow graph, a storage hierarchy is difficult to apply in dataflow computers.

The matching of executable instructions in the instruction window of microprocessors is restricted to a part of the instruction sequence. Because of the serial program order, the instructions in this window are likely to be executable soon. Therefore the matching hardware can be restricted to a small number of instruction slots. In dataflow computers the number of tokens waiting for a match can be very high. A large waiting-matching store is required. Due to the lack of locality the likelyhood of the arrival of a matching token is difficult to estimate so caching of tokens to be matched soon is difficult in dataflow.

An unsolved problem in todays microprocessors is the memory latency caused by cache misses. As reported for the SGI Origin 2000 distributed shared memory system [151] these latencies are 11 processor cycles for a primary-level cache miss, 60 cycles for a secondary-level cache miss, and can be up to 180 cycles for a remote memory access. In number of missed instruction slots the latencies should be multiplied by the degree of superscalar. Only a small part of the memory latency can be removed or hidden in modern microprocessors even when techniques like out-of-order execution, write buffer, cache preload hardware, lockup free caches, and a pipelined system bus are employed. So microprocessors often idle and are unable to exploit the high degree of internal parallelism provided by a wide superscalar approach. The rapid context switching of dataflow and multithreaded architectures shows a superior way out. Idling is avoided by switching execution to another context.

An 8-issue (or even higher) superscalar dispatch will be possible in the next generation of microprocessors. Finding enough fine-grain parallelism to fully exploit the processor will be the main problem. One solution is to *enlarge the instruction window* to several hundred instruction slots with hopefully more simultaneously executable instructions present. There are two draw-backs to this approach. First, regarding that all instructions stem from a single instruction stream and that on average every seventh instruction is a branch instruction, most of the instructions in the window will be speculatively assigned with a very deep speculation level (todays depth normally is four at maximum). Thereby most of the instruction execution will be speculative. The principal problem here arises from the single instruction stream that feeds the instruction window. Second, if the instruction window is enlarged, the updating of the instruction states in the slots and matching of executable instructions lead to more complex hardware logic in the dispatch stage of the pipeline thus limiting the cycle rate increase which is essential for next generations of microprocessors. Solutions are the *decoupling of the instruction window* with respect to different instruction classes as in the PA-8000, the *partitioning of the dispatch stage* into several pipeline stages, and *alternative instruction window organizations*. One alternative instruction window organization is the multiple FIFO-based organization in the dependence-based microprocessor [171]. Only the instructions at the heads of a number of FIFO buffers can be dispatched to the execution units in the next cycle. The total parallelism in the instruction window is restricted in favour of a less costly dispatch that does not slow down processor cycle rate. Thereby the potential fine-grained parallelism is limited - a technique somewhat similar to the threaded dataflow approaches described above. It might be interesting to look, with respect to alternative instruction window organizations, at dataflow matching store implementations and dataflow solutions like threaded dataflow as exemplified by the repeat-on-input technique in the Epsilon-2 and strongly-connected arcs model of EM-4, or the associative switching network in the ADARC, etc. For example, the repeat-on-input strategy dispatches very small compiler-generated code sequences serially (in an otherwise fine-grained dataflow computer). Transfered to the local dataflow in an instruction window, a dispatch string might be used where a serie of data dependent instructions are generated by a compiler and dispatched serially after the dispatch of the leading instruction. However, the high number of speculative instructions in the instruction window remains.

Another new idea is the *nanothreading* technique of DanSoft (Košice, Slovak Republic) [114]. Nanothreading dismisses full multithreading for a nanothread that executes in the same register set as the main thread. The DanSoft nanothread requires only a 9 bit program counter, some simple control logic, and it resides in the same page as the main thread. The nanothread might be used to fill the instruction dispatch slots of a wide superscalar approach (like in simultaneous multithreading) without the need for several register sets.

But the main problem of todays superscalar microprocessor may not be found in the instruction window organization. It is the necessity of instruction completion/retirement due to the serial semantic of the instruction stream. For example, if a load instruction causes a secondary-level cache miss, the whole reorder buffer may soon be clogged by succeeding instructions (succeeding in sequential program order) that are already executed. Because of the sequential program order that should be restored by the completion stage, these instructions cannot be retired and removed from the reorder buffer even if the instructions are independent of the load instruction that caused the cache miss. The completion may be the main obstacle for further performance increase in microprocessors.

In principle, an algorithm defines a partial ordering of instructions due to control and true data dependences. The total ordering in an instruction stream for todays microprocessors stems from von Neumann languages. Why should

- a programmer design a partially ordered algorithm, and
- code the algorithm in total ordering because of the use of a sequential von Neumann language,
- the compiler regenerate the partial order in a dependence graph, and
- generate a reordered "optimized" sequential machine code,
- the microprocessor dynamically regenerate the partial order in its out-of-order sec-

tion, execute due to a *micro dataflow* principle,
- and then reestablish the unnatural serial program order in the completion stage?

Ideally, an algorithm should be coded in an appropriate higher-order language (e.g. dataflow-like languages might be appropriate). Next, the compiler should generate machine code that still reflects the parallelism and not an unnecessary serialization. Here, a dataflow graph viewed as machine language might show the right direction. A parallelizing compiler may generate this kind of machine code even from a program written in a sequential von Neumann language. The compiler could use compiler optimization and coding to simplify the dynamic analysis and dispatch out of the instruction window. The processor dismisses the serial reordering in the completion stage in favour of an only partial reordering. The completion unit retires instructions not in a single serial order but in two or more series (as in the simultaneous multithreaded processors). Clogging of the reorder buffer is avoided since clogging of a thread does not restrict retirement of instructions of another thread.

6. Conclusion. Conceptually, the research in parallel computing shows a clear unification of two paradigms, i.e. von Neumann and dataflow computing. One of the key realizations made by the dataflow community is that pure dataflow and pure control-flow are not orthogonal to each other but are at two ends of a "continuum." Hence, the trend in dataflow research was to incorporate explicit notions of state into architecture. As a result, many of the pure dataflow ideas were replaced by abstractions that are more conventional. At the same time, von Neumann computing incorporated many of the dataflow techniques. Based on these and other merging ideas the multithreaded model of computing emerged within the "continuum" with several theoretically and commercially fruitful advantages.

Historically, commercial parallel machines have demonstrated innovative organizational structures, often tied to a particular programming model, as architects sought to obtain the ultimate in performance out of any given technology. The period up to 1985 is dominated by advancements in *bit-level parallelism* (8-bit microprocessors was replaced by 16-bit, 32-bit etc.). Doubling the width of the datapath reduces the number of cycles required to perform an operation. The period from the mid-80s to mid-90s is dominated by advancements in the *instruction-level parallelism*, where the basic steps in instruction processing could be performed in a single cycle, most of the time. The RISC approach was straightforward to pipeline the stages of instruction processing so that an instruction is executed almost every cycle, on average. In order to utilize the parallelism in the hardware, it became necessary to issue multiple instructions in each cycle, called *superscalar* execution, as well as pipelining the processing of each instruction. Although superscalar execution will continue to be very important, barring some unforeseen breakthrough in instruction level parallelism, the leap to the *thread-level parallelism* is increasingly compelling as chips increase in capacity. Introducing thread-level parallelism on a single processor reduces the cost of the transition from one processor to multiple processors, thus making small scale SMPs more attractive on a broad scale. In additions, it establishes an architectural direction that may yield much grater latency tolerance in the long term. To conclude, there are strong indications that multithreading will be utilized in a future processor generations to hide the latency of local memory access [58].

Acknowledgements. The authors are grateful to referees of this paper for their meticulous review and many helpful comments.

REFERENCES

[1] F. Abolhassan, R. Drefenstedt, J. Keller, W.J. Paul, and D. Scheerer, *On the physical design of PRAMs*, Computer Journal, 36 (1993), pp. 756–762.

[2] A. Agarwal, *Performance tradeoffs in multithreaded processors*, IEEE Trans. Parallel and Distr. Syst., 3 (1992), pp. 525–539.

[3] A. Agarwal, J. Babb, D. Chaiken, G. D'Souza, K. Johnson, D. Kranz, J. Kubiatowicz, B.-H. Lim, G. Maa, and K. Mackenzie, *Sparcle: A multithreaded VLSI processor for parallel computing*, Lect. Notes Comput. Sc., 748, Springer-Verlag, Berlin, 1993, pp. 395.

[4] A. Agarwal, R. Bianchini, D. Chaiken, K.L. Johnson, D. Kranz, J. Kubiatowicz, B.-H. Lim, K. Mackenzie, and D. Yeung, *The MIT Alewife machine: Architecture and performance*, in Proc. 22nd ISCA, June 1995, pp. 2–13.

[5] A. Agarwal, G. D'Souza, K. Johnson, D. Kranz, J. Kubiatowicz, K. Kurihara, B.-H. Lim, G. Maa, D. Nussbaum, M. Parkin, and D. Yeung, *The MIT Alewife machine: A large-scale distributed-memory multiprocessor*, in Proc. Workshop on Scalable Shared Memory Multiprocessors, 1991.

[6] A. Agarwal, J. Kubiatowicz, D. Kranz, B.-H. Lim, D. Yeung, G. D'Souza, and M. Parkin, *Sparcle: An evolutionary processor design for large-scale multiprocessors*, IEEE Micro, 13 (June 1993), pp. 48–61.

[7] A. Agarwal, B.-H. Lim, D. Kranz, and J. Kubiatowicz, *April: A processor architecture for multiprocessing*, in Proc. 17th ISCA, June 1990, pp. 104–114.

[8] T. Agerwala and Arvind, *Data flow systems*, IEEE Computer, 15 (Feb. 1982), pp. 10–13.

[9] G. Alverson, R. Alverson, D. Callahan, B. Koblenz, A. Porterfield, and B. Smith, *Exploiting heterogeneous parallelism on a multithreaded multiprocessor*, in Proc. 1992 Intl. Conf. Supercomputing, 1992, pp. 188–197.

[10] ———, *Integrated support for heterogeneous parallelism*, Multithreaded Computer Architecture: A Summary of the State of the Art, (R.A. Iannucci, G.R. Gao, R. Halstead, and B. Smith, eds.), Kluwer Academic, Boston, MA, 1994.

[11] G. Alverson, S. Kahan, R. Korry, and C. McCann, *Scheduling on the Tera MTA*, Lect. Notes Comput. Sc., 949, Springer-Verlag, Berlin, 1995, pp. 19.

[12] R. Alverson, D. Callahan, D. Cummings, B. Koblenz, A. Porterfield, and B. Smith, *The Tera computer system*, in Proc. 1990 Intl. Conf. Supercomputing, June 1990, pp. 1–6.

[13] M. Amamiya, N. Takahashi, T. Naruse, and M. Yoshida, *A dataflow processor array system for solving partial differential equations*, in Proc. Intl. Symp. Applied Math. and Infor. Sci., March 1982.

[14] B.S. Ang, Arvind, and D. Chiou, *StarT the next generation: Integrating global caches and dataflow architecture*, Advanced Topics in Dataflow Computing and Multithreading, (G.R. Gao, L. Bic, and J.-L. Gaudiot, eds.), IEEE Computer Society Press, Los Alamitos, CA, 1995, pp. 19–54.

[15] Arvind, L. Bic, and T. Ungerer, *Evolution of dataflow computers*, Advanced Topics in Data-Flow Computing, (J.-L. Gaudiot and L. Bic, eds.), Prentice Hall, Englewood Cliffs, NJ, 1991, pp. 3–33.

[16] Arvind and S.A. Brobst, *The evolution of dataflow architectures from static dataflow to P-RISC*, Intl. J. High Speed Computing, 5 (1993), pp. 125–153.

[17] Arvind and D.E. Culler, *Dataflow architectures*, Ann. Review in Comput. Sci., 1 (1986), pp. 225–253.

[18] ———, *Managing resources in a parallel machine*, Fifth Generation Computer Architectures, (J.V. Woods, ed.), North-Holland, Amsterdam, 1986, pp. 103–121.

[19] Arvind, K.P. Gostelow, and W. Plouffe, *An asynchronous programming language and computing machine*, Tech. Report 114a, Univ. California at Irvine, Dept. Information and Comput. Sci., Dec. 1978.

[20] Arvind and R.A. Iannucci, *A critique of multiprocessing von Neumann style*, in Proc. 10th ISCA, June 1983, pp. 426–436.

[21] Arvind and V. Kathail, *A multiple processor dataflow machine that supports generalized procedures*, in Proc. 8th ISCA, May 1981, pp. 291–302.

[22] Arvind, V. Kathail, and K. Pingali, *A processing element for a large multiprocessor dataflow machine*, in Proc. Intl. Conf. Circ. Comput., Oct. 1980.

[23] Arvind and R.S. Nikhil, *Executing a program on the MIT tagged-token dataflow architecture*, Lect. Notes Comput. Sc., 259, Springer-Verlag, Berlin, 1987, pp. 1–29.

[24] ———, *Executing a program on the MIT tagged-token dataflow architecture*, IEEE Trans. Computers, C-39 (1990), pp. 300–318.

[25] K. Asada, H. Terada, S. Matsumoto, S. Miyata, H. Asano, H. Miura, M. Shimizu, S. Komori,

T. FUKUHARA, AND K. SHIMA, *Hardware structure of a one-chip data-driven processor: Q-p*, in Proc. 1987 ICPP, Aug. 1987, pp. 327–329.

[26] P. BACH, M. BRAUN, A. FORMELLA, J. FRIEDRICH, T. GRÜN, AND C. LINCHTENAU, *Building the 4 processor SB-PRAM prototype*, in Proc. 30th Hawaii Intl. Conf. Syst. Sci., Jan. 1997, vol.5, pp. 14–23.

[27] J. BACKUS, *Can programming be librated form the von Neumann style? A functional style and its algebra of programs*, Comm. ACM, 21 (1978), pp. 613–641.

[28] P.M.C.C. BARAHONA AND J.R. GURD, *Simulated performance of the Manchester multi-ring dataflow machine*, in Proc. 2nd ICPC, Sep. 1985, pp. 419–424.

[29] ———, *Processor allocation in a multi-ring dataflow machine*, J. Parall. Distr. Comput., 3 (1986), pp. 67–85.

[30] S. BARKHORDARIAN, *RAMPS: A realtime structured small-scale data flow system for parallel processing*, in Proc. 1987 ICPP, Aug. 1987, pp. 610–613.

[31] M. BECK, T. UNGERER, AND E. ZEHENDER, *Classification and performance evaluation of hybrid dataflow techniques with respect to matrix multiplication*, in Proc. GI/ITG Workshop PARS'93, April 1993, pp. 118–126.

[32] M.J. BECKERLE, *An overview of the START (*T) computer system*, Tech. Report MCRC-TR-28, Motorola Technical Report, July 1992.

[33] ———, *Overview of the START (*T) multithreaded computer*, in Proc. COMPCON'93, 1993, pp. 148–156.

[34] L. BIC, *A process-oriented model for efficient execution of dataflow programs*, J. Parall. Distr. Comput., 8 (1990), pp. 42–51.

[35] L. BIC AND M. AL-MOUHAMED, *The EM-4 under implicit parallelism*, in Proc. 1993 Intl. Conf. Supercomputing, July 1993, pp. 21–26.

[36] A.P.W. BÖHM, J.R. GURD, AND Y.M. TEO, *The effect of iterative instructions in dataflow computers*, in Proc. 1989 ICPP, Aug. 1989, pp. 201–208.

[37] A.P.W. BÖHM AND J. SARGEANT, *Code optimization for tagged-token dataflow machine*, IEEE Trans. Computers, C-38 (1989), pp. 4–14.

[38] A.P.W. BÖHM AND Y.M. TEO, *Resource management in a multi-ring dataflow machine*, in Proc. CONPAR88, Sep. 1988, pp. B 191–200.

[39] R.F. BOOTHE, *Evaluation of multithreading and caching in large shared memory parallel computers*, Tech. Report UCB/CSD-93-766, Univ. California Berkeley, Comput. Sci. Division, July 1993.

[40] D.F. BRAILSFORD AND R.J. DUCKWORTH, *The MUSE machine – an architecture for structured data flow computation*, New Generation Computing, 3 (1985), pp. 181–195.

[41] R. BUEHRER AND K. EKANADHAM, *Incorporating data flow ideas into von Neumann processors for parallel processing*, IEEE Trans. Computers, C-36 (1987), pp. 1515–1522.

[42] M.L. CAMPBELL, *Static allocation for a dataflow multiprocessor*, in Proc. 1985 ICPP, Aug. 1985, pp. 511–517.

[43] W.W. CARLSON AND J.A.B. FORTES, *On the performance of combined data flow and control flow systems: Experiments using two iterative algorithms*, J. Parall. Distr. Comput., 5 (1988), pp. 359–382.

[44] A.J. CATTO AND J.R. GURD, *Resource management in dataflow*, in Proc. Conf. Functional Programming Lang. Comput. Arch., Oct. 1981, pp. 77–84.

[45] A.J. CATTO, J.R. GURD, AND C.C. KIRKHAM, *Non-deterministic dataflow programming*, in Proc. 6th ACM European Conf. Comput. Arch., April 1981, pp. 435–444.

[46] P.Y. CHANG, E. HAO, T.Y. YEH, AND Y. PATT, *Branch classification: a new mechanism for improving branch predictor performance*, in Proc. 27th ACM/IEEE Intl. Symp. Microarchitecture, Nov. 1994, pp 22–31.

[47] D. CHIOU, B.S. ANG, R. GREINER, ARVIND, J.C HOE, M.J. BECKERLE, J.E. HICKS, AND A. BOUGHTON, *StarT-NG: Delivering seamless parallel computing*, Lect. Notes Comput. Sc., 966, Springer-Verlag, Berlin, 1995, pp. 101–116.

[48] Y.M. CHONG, *Data flow chip optimizes image processing*, Comput. Design (Oct. 1984), pp. 97–103.

[49] R.P. COLWELL AND R.L. STECK, *A 0.6 μm BiCMOS processor with dynamic execution*, in Proc. Intl. Solid State Circuits Conf., Feb. 1995.

[50] D. COMTE AND N. HIFDI, *LAU multiprocessor: Microfunctional description and technologic choice*, in Proc. 1st Eur. Conf. Parallel and Distr. Proc., Feb. 1979, pp. 8–15.

[51] D. COMTE, N. HIFDI, AND J.C. SYRE, *The data driven LAU multiprocessor system: Results and perspectives*, in Proc. World Comput. Congress IFIP'80, Oct. 1980, pp. 175–180.

[52] M. CORNISH, *The TI dataflow architecture: The power of concurrency for avionics*, in Proc. 3rd Conf. Digital Avionics Syst., Nov. 1979, pp. 19–25.

[53] M. Cornish, D.W. Hogan, and J.C. Jensen, *The Texas Instruments distributed data processor*, in Proc. Lousiana Comput. Exposition, March 1979, pp. 189–193.

[54] D.E. Culler, *Managing parallelism and resources in scientific dataflow programs*, Ph.D. thesis, MIT, Cambridge, MA, June 1989.

[55] D.E. Culler, S. Goldstein, K.E. Schauser, and T. von Eicken, *TAM - A compiler controlled threaded abstract machine*, J. Parall. Distr. Comput., 18 (1993), pp. 347–370.

[56] D.E. Culler and G.M. Papadopoulos, *The explicit token store*, J. Parall. Distr. Comput., 10 (1990), pp. 289–308.

[57] D.E. Culler, A. Sah, K.E. Schauser, T. von Eicken, and J. Wawrzynek, *Fine-grain parallelism with minimal hardware support: A compiler-controlled Threaded Abstract Machine*, in Proc. 4th Intl. Conf. Arch. Support for Programming Lang. Operating Systems, April 1991, pp. 164–175.

[58] D.E. Culler, J.P. Singh, and A. Gupta, *Parallel Computer Architecture - A Hardware/Software Approach*, Morgan Kaufmann Publishers, 1998 (to appear).

[59] W.J. Dally, J. Fiske, J. Keen, R. Lethin, M. Noakes, P. Nuth, R. Davison, and G. Fyler, *The message-driven processor: A multicomputer processing node with efficient mechanisms*, IEEE Micro, 12 (April 1992), pp. 23–39.

[60] J.D.G. Da Silva and J.V. Woods, *Design of a processing subsystem forthe Manchester data flow computer*, in Proc. IEE, 128 (1981), pp. 218–224.

[61] ———, *A pseudoassociative matching storage using hardware hashing*, in Proc. IEE, 130 (1984), pp. 19–25.

[62] K. Dai and W.K. Giloi, *A basic architecture supporting LGDF computation*, in Proc. 1990 Intl. Conf. Supercomputing, 1990, pp. 23–33.

[63] F. Darema, D.A. George, V.A. Norton, and G.F. Pfister, *A single-program-multiple-data computational model for EPEX/FORTRAN*, Parallel Comput., 7 (1988), pp. 11–24.

[64] A.L. Davis, *The architecture and system method of DDM1: A recursively structured data driven machine*, in Proc. 5th ISCA, April 1978, pp. 210–215.

[65] A.L. Davis and R.M. Keller, *Data flow program graphs*, IEEE Computer, 15 (Feb. 1982), pp. 26–41.

[66] J.B. Dennis, *First version of a data-flow procedure language*, Lect. Notes Comput. Sc., 19, Springer-Verlag, Berlin, 1974, pp. 362–376.

[67] ———, *The variaties of data flow computers*, in Proc. 1st Intl. Conf. Distr. Comput. Syst., Oct. 1979, pp. 430–439.

[68] ———, *Data flow supercomputers*, IEEE Computer, 13 (Nov. 1980), pp. 48–56.

[69] ———, *Dataflow computation: A case study*, Computer Architecture - Concepts and Systems, (V.M. Milutinović, ed.), North-Holland, New York, NY, 1988, pp. 354–404.

[70] J.B. Dennis, G.A. Boughton, and C.K.C. Leung, *Building blocks for data flow prototypes*, in Proc. 7th ISCA, May 1980, pp. 1–8.

[71] J.B. Dennis and G.R. Gao, *Multithreaded architectures: Principles, projects, and issues*, Multithreaded Computer Architecture: A Summary of the State of the Art, (R.A. Iannucci, G.R. Gao, R. Halstead, and B. Smith, eds.), Kluwer Academic, Boston, MA, 1994, pp. 1–74.

[72] J.B. Dennis, W.Y.P. Lim, and W.B. Ackerman, *The MIT data flow engineering model*, in Proc. 9th World Comput. Congress IFIP'83, Sep. 1983, pp. 553–560.

[73] J.B. Dennis and D.P. Misunas, *A preliminary architecture for a basic data-flow processor*, in Proc. 2nd ISCA, Jan. 1975, pp. 126–132.

[74] K. Dieffendorf and M. Allen, *Organization of the Motorola 88110 superscalar RISC microprocessor*, IEEE Micro, 12 (April 1992), pp. 40–63.

[75] T.A. Diep, C. Nelson, and J.P. Shen, *Performance evaluation of the PowerPC 620 microprocessor*, in Proc. 22nd ISCA, June 1995, pp. 163–174.

[76] E.W. Dijkstra, *Co-operating sequential processes*, Programming Languages: NATO Advanced Study Institute, (F. Genuys, ed.), Academic Press, London, 1968, pp. 43–112.

[77] G.K. Egan, *The CSIRAC II dataflow computer: Token and node definitions*, Tech. Report 31-009, School of Electrical Engineering, Swinburne Institute of Technology, 1990.

[78] G.K. Egan, N.J. Webb, and A.P.W. Böhm, *Some architectural features of the CSIRAC II data-flow computer*, Advanced Topics in Data-Flow Computing, (J.-L. Gaudiot and L. Bic, eds.), Prentice Hall, Englewood Cliffs, NJ, 1991, pp. 3–33.

[79] G.K. Egan and S. Wathanasin, *Data-driven computation: Its suitability in control systems*, in Proc. Science Research Council's Workshop on Distr. Comput., July 1978.

[80] S.J. Eggers, J.S. Emer, H.M. Levy, J.L. Lo, R.L. Stamm, and D.M. Tullsen, *Simultaneous multithreading: A platform for next-generation processors*, IEEE Micro, 17 (Oct. 1997).

[81] P. Evripidou and J.-L. Gaudiot, *The USC decoupled multilevel data-flow execution model*, Advanced Topics in Data-Flow Computing, (J.-L. Gaudiot and L. Bic, eds.), Prentice Hall, Engle-

wood Cliffs, NJ, 1991, pp. 347–379.

[82] M.R. Exum and J.-L. Gaudiot, *Network design and allocation consideration in the Hughes data-flow machine*, Parallel Comput., 13 (1990), pp. 17–34.

[83] M. Flynn, *Some computer organizations and their effectiveness*, IEEE Trans. Computers, C-21 (1972), pp. 948–960.

[84] A. Formella, J. Keller, and T. Walle, *HPP: A high performance PRAM*, Lect. Notes Comp. Sc., 1123, Springer-Verlag, Berlin, 1996, pp. 425–434.

[85] ———, *HPP: A high performance PRAM*, Tech. Report H 124, 02/96, University of Saarbruecken, 1996.

[86] T. Fujita, *A multithreaded processor architecture for parallel symbolic computation*, Tech. Report MIT/LCS/TM-338, CS Lab., MIT, Cambridge, MA, 1987.

[87] G.R. Gao, *An efficient hybrid dataflow architecture model*, J. Parall. Distr. Comput., 19 (1993), pp. 293–306.

[88] G.R. Gao, J.-L. Gaudiot, and L. Bic, *Dataflow and multithreaded architectures: Guest editor's introduction*, J. Parall. Distr. Comput., 18 (1993), pp. 271–272.

[89] J.-L. Gaudiot and L. Bic, *Advanced Topics in Data-Flow Computing*, Prentice Hall, Englewood Cliffs, NJ, 1991.

[90] J.-L. Gaudiot, R.W. Vedder, G.K. Tucker, D. Finn, and M.L. Campbell, *A distributed VLSI architecture for efficient signal and data processing*, IEEE Trans. Computers, C-34 (1985), pp. 1072–1087.

[91] D. Ghosal and L.N. Bhuyan, *Performance analysis of the MIT tagged token dataflow architecture*, in Proc. 1987 ICPP, Aug. 1987, pp. 680–683.

[92] W.K. Giloi, U. Brüning, and W. Schröder-Preikschat, *MANNA: Prototype of a distributed memory architecture with maximized sustained performance*, in Proc. 5th Euromicro Workshop on Prallel and Distributed Processing, Jan. 1996.

[93] J.R.W. Glauert, J.R. Gurd, and C.C. Kirkham, *Evolution of dataflow architecture*, in Proc. IFIP WG 10.3 Workshop on Hardware Supported Implementation on Concurrent Lang. in Distr. Systems, March 1984, pp. 1–18.

[94] J.R.W. Glauert, J.R. Gurd, C.C. Kirkham, and I. Watson, *The dataflow approach*, Distributed Computing, (F.B. Chambers, D.A. Duce, and G.P. Jones, eds.), Academic Press, London, 1984, pp. 1–53.

[95] R.R. Glenn and D.V. Pryor, *Instrumentation for a massively parallel MIMD application*, in Proc. Intl. Conf. Measurement and Modeling of Comput. Syst., May 1991, pp. 208–209.

[96] E. Glück-Hiltrop, *The Stollman dataflow machine*, in Proc. CONPAR88, Sep. 1988.

[97] E. Glück-Hiltrop, M. Ramlow, and U. Schürfeld, *The Stollman dataflow machine*, Lect. Notes Comput. Sc., 365, Springer-Verlag, Berlin, 1989, pp. 433–457.

[98] K.P. Gostelow and Arvind, *The U-interpreter*, IEEE Computer, 15 (Feb. 1982), pp. 42–49.

[99] K.P. Gostelow and R.E. Thomas, *A view of dataflow*, in Proc. National Comput. Conf., June 1979, pp. 629–636.

[100] ———, *Performance of a simulated dataflow computer*, IEEE Trans. Computers, C-29 (1980), pp. 905–919.

[101] V.G. Grafe and J.E. Hoch, *The Epsilon-2 multiprocessor system*, J. Parall. Distr. Comput., 10 (1990), pp. 309–318.

[102] V.G. Grafe, J.E. Hoch, G.S. Davidson, V.P. Holmes, D.M. Davenport, and K.M. Steele, *The Epsilon project*, Advanced Topics in Data-Flow Computing, (J.-L. Gaudiot and L. Bic, eds.), Prentice Hall, Englewood Cliffs, NJ, 1991, pp. 175–205.

[103] J.D. Grimm, J.A. Eggert, and G.W. Karcher, *Distributed signal processing using data flow techniques*, in Proc. 17th Hawaii Intl. Conf. Syst. Sci., Jan. 1984, pp. 29–38.

[104] W. Gruenewald and T. Ungerer, *Towards extremely fast context switching in a block-multithreaded processor*, in Proc. 22nd Euromicro Conf., Sep. 1996, pp. 592–599.

[105] ———, *A multithreaded processor designed for distributed shared memory systems*, in Proc. Intl. Conf. Advances in Parallel and Distr. Comput., March 1997.

[106] M. Gulati and N. Bagherzadeh, *Performance study of a multithreaded superscalar microprocessor*, in Proc. 2nd Intl. Symp. High-Performance Comput. Arch., Feb. 1996, pp. 291–301.

[107] A. Gupta, J. Hennessy, K. Gharachorloo, T. Mowry, and W.-D. Weber, *Comparative evaluation of latency reducing and tolerating techniques*, in Proc. 18th ISCA, May 1991, pp. 254–263.

[108] J.R. Gurd, *The Manchester dataflow machine*, Future Generations Computer Systems, 1 (1985), pp. 201–212.

[109] J.R. Gurd, C.C. Kirkham, and I. Watson, *The Manchester prototype dataflow computer*, Comm. ACM, 28 (1985), no. 1, pp. 34–52.

[110] J.R. Gurd and I. Watson, *A multilayered data flow computer architecture*, in Proc. 1977 ICPP, Aug. 1977, pp. 94.

[111] ———, *Data driven system for high speed computing, Part I: Structuring software for parallel execution*, Computer Design, 19 (1980), pp. 91–96.

[112] ———, *Data driven system for high speed computing, Part II: Hardware design*, Computer Design, 19 (1980), pp. 97–106.

[113] ———, *Preliminary evaluation of a prototype dataflow computer*, in Proc. 9th World Comput. Congress IFIP'83, Sep. 1983, pp. 545–551.

[114] L. Gwennap, *DanSoft develops VLIW design*, Microprocessor Report, 11 (Feb. 17, 1997), pp. 18-22.

[115] R.H. Halstead, Jr., *Implementation of Multilisp: Lisp on a multiprocessor*, in Proc. ACM Symp. Lisp and Functional Programming, Aug. 1984, pp. 9–17.

[116] ———, *Multilisp: A language for concurrent symbolic computation*, ACM Trans. Programming Lang. Syst., 7 (1985), pp. 501–538.

[117] ———, *Parallel computing using Multilisp*, Parallel Computation and Computers for Artificial Intelligence, (J.S. Kowalik, ed.), Kluwer Academic, Boston, MA, 1988, pp. 21–49.

[118] R.H. Halstead, Jr. and T. Fujita, *MASA: A multithreaded processor architecture for parallel symbolic computing*, in Proc. 15th ISCA, May 1988, pp. 443–451.

[119] R. Hempel, A.J.G. Hey, O. McBryan, and D.W. Walker, *Message passing interfaces (special issue)*, Parallel Comput., 20 (1994), pp. 417–673.

[120] J. L. Hennessy and D. A. Patterson, *Computer Architecture: A Quantitative Approach*, Morgan Kaufmann Publishers, San Francisco, CA, 1996.

[121] K. Hiraki, K. Nishida, S. Sekiguchi, and T. Shimada, *Maintenance architecture and LSI implementation of a dataflow computer with a large number of processors*, in Proc. 1986 ICPP, Aug. 1986, pp. 584–591.

[122] K. Hiraki, S. Sekiguchi, and T. Shimada, *Status report of SIGMA-1: A dataflow supercomputer*, Advanced Topics in Data-Flow Computing, (J.-L. Gaudiot and L. Bic, eds.), Prentice Hall, Englewood Cliffs, NJ, 1991, pp. 207–223.

[123] K. Hiraki, T. Shimada, and K. Nishida, *A hardware design of the SIGMA-1, a data flow computer for scientific computations*, in Proc. 1984 ICPP, Aug. 1984, pp. 524–531.

[124] H. Hirata, K. Kimura, S. Nagamine, Y. Mochizuki, A. Nishimura, Y. Nakase, and T. Nishizawa, *An elementary processor architecture with simultaneous instruction issuing from multiple threads*, in Proc. 19th ISCA, May 1992, pp. 136–145.

[125] H. Hirata, Y. Mochizuki, A. Nishimura, Y. Nakase, and T. Nishizawa, *A multithreaded processor architecture with simultaneous instruction issuing*, Supercomputer, 49 (1992), pp. 23–39.

[126] J.L.A. Hughes, *Implementing control-flow structures in dataflow programs*, in Proc. COMPCON Spring 82, Feb. 1982, pp. 87–90.

[127] H.H.J. Hum, K.B. Theobald, and G.R. Gao, *Building multithreaded architectures with off-the-shelf microprocessor*, in Proc. IPPS 94, April 1994, pp. 288–294.

[128] R.A. Iannucci, *Toward a dataflow/von Neumann hybrid architecture*, in Proc. 15th ISCA, May 1988, pp. 131–140.

[129] R.A. Iannucci, G.R. Gao, R. Halstead, and B. Smith, *Multithreaded Computer Architecture: A Summary of the State of the Art*, Kluwer Academic, Boston, MA, 1994.

[130] Y. Inagami and J.F. Foley, *The specification of a new Manchester dataflow machine*, in Proc. 1989 Intl. Conf. Supercomputing, June 1989, pp. 371–380.

[131] N. Ito, M. Kishi, E. Kuno, and K. Rokusawa, *The data-flow based parallel inference machine to support two basic languages in KL1*, in Proc. IFIP TC-10 Working Conf. Fifth Generation Comput. Arch., July 1985, pp. 123–145.

[132] N. Ito and K. Musada, *Parallel inference machine based on the data flow model*, in Proc. Intl. Workshop High Level Comput. Arch., May 1984.

[133] N. Ito, M. Sato, E. Kuno, and K. Rokusawa, *The architecture and preliminary evaluation results of the experimental parallel inference machine PIM-D*, in Proc. 13th ISCA, June 1986, pp. 149–156.

[134] M. Iwashita and T. Temma, *Experiments on a data flow machine*, in Proc. IFIP Conf., 1987, pp. 235–245.

[135] T. Jeffery, *The μPD7281 processor*, Byte (Nov. 1985), pp. 237–246.

[136] I. Jerebic, B. Slivnik, and R. Trobec, *Library for programming on tourus-connected multiprocessors*, in Proc. PACTA'92, Sep. 1992, pp. 386–395.

[137] C. Jesshope, *Scalable parallel computers*, EURO-PAR Conf. (Stockholm, Sweden), Aug. 1995, Tutorial.

[138] H.F. Jordan, *Performance measurements on HEP: A pipelined MIMD computer*, in Proc. 10th

ISCA, June 1983, pp. 207–212.
[139] K.M. KAVI, B.P. BUCKLES, AND U.N. BHAT, *A formal definition of data flow graph model*, IEEE Trans. Computers, C-35 (1986), pp. 940–948.
[140] K. KAWAKAMI AND J.R. GURD, *A scalable dataflow structure store*, in Proc. 13th ISCA, June 1986, pp. 243–250.
[141] M. KISHI, H. YASUHARA, AND Y. KAWAMURA, *DDDP: A distributed data driven processor*, in Proc. 10th ISCA, June 1983, pp. 236–242.
[142] D. KLAPPHOLZ, Y. LIAO, D. J. WANG, AND A. OMONDI, *Toward a hybrid data-flow/control-flow MIMD architecture*, in Proc. 5th Intl. Conf. Distr. Comput. Syst., May 1985, pp. 10–15.
[143] Y. KODAMA, Y. KOUMURA, M. SATO, H. SAKANE, S. SAKAI, AND Y. YAMAGUCHI, *EMC-Y: Parallel processing element optimizing communication and computation*, in Proc. 1993 Intl. Conf. Supercomputing, July 1993, pp. 167–174.
[144] Y. KODAMA, H. SAKANE, M. SATO, H. YAMANA, S. SAKAI, AND Y. YAMAGUCHI, *The EMC-X parallel computer: Architecture and basic performance*, in Proc. 22nd ISCA, June 1995, pp. 14–23.
[145] S. KOMORI, K. SHIMA, S. MIYATA, AND H. TERADA, *Parallel processing with large grain data flow techniques*, IEEE Micro, 9 (June 1989), pp. 45–59.
[146] J.S. KOWALIK, *Parallel MIMD Computation: The HEP Supercomputer and Its Applications*, MIT Press, 1985.
[147] D.A. KRANZ, R.H. HALSTEAD, AND E. MOHR, *Mul-T: A high-performance parallel Lisp*, ACM SIGPLAN Notices, 24 (1989), no. 7, pp. 81–90.
[148] J. KUBIATOWICZ AND A. AGARWAL, *Anatomy of a message in the Alewife multiprocessor*, in Proc. 1993 Intl. Conf. Supercomputing, July 1993, pp. 195–206.
[149] J.T. KUEHN AND B.J. SMITH, *The Horizon supercomputing system: architecture and software*, in Proc. Supercomputing '88, Nov. 1988, pp. 28–34.
[150] A. KUMAR, *The HP PA-8000 RISC CPU*, IEEE Micro, 17 (March/April 1997), pp. 27–32.
[151] J. LAUDON AND D. LENOSKI, *The SGI Origin: A ccNUMA highly scalable server*, in Proc. 24th ISCA, June 1997, pp. 241-251.
[152] B. LEE AND A.R. HURSON, *Dataflow architectures and multithreading*, IEEE Computer, 27 (Aug. 1994), pp. 27–39.
[153] J.L. LO, S.J. EGGERS, J.S. EMER, H.M. LEVY, R.L. STAMM, AND D.M. TULLSEN, *Converting thread-level parallelism to instruction-level parallelism via simultaneous multithreading*, ACM Trans. Comput. Systems, 15 (1997).
[154] M. LOIKKANEN AND N. BAGHERZADEH, *A fine-grain multithreading superscalar architecture*, in Proc. PACT'96, Oct. 1996, pp. 163–168.
[155] T.E. MANKOVIC, V. POPESCU, AND H. SULLIVAN, *CHoPP priciples of operations*, in Proc. 2nd Intl. Supercomputer Conf., May 1987, pp. 2–10.
[156] O.C. MAQUELIN, H.H.J. HUM, AND G.R. GAO, *Costs and benefits of multithreading with off-the-shelf processors*, Lect. Notes Comp. Sc., 966, Springer-Verlag, Berlin, 1995, pp. 117–128.
[157] A. MIKSCHL AND W. DAMM, *Msparc: A multithreaded Sparc*, Lect. Notes Comp. Sc., 1123, Springer-Verlag, Berlin, 1996, pp. 461–469.
[158] J. MILEWSKI, *Data driven control in I-structures*, in Proc. 2nd Intl. Conf. Parallel Computing, Sep. 1985, pp. 377–382.
[159] J. MILEWSKI AND I. MORI, *Efficient loop handling in a stream-oriented unraveling dataflow interpreter*, Comput. Artif. Intell., 9 (1990), pp. 545–570.
[160] S.W. MOORE, *Multithreaded Processor Design*, Kluwer Academic, Boston, MA, 1996.
[161] V.L. NARASIMHAN AND T. DOWNS, *Operating system features of a dynamic dataflow array processing system (PATTSY)*, in Proc. 3rd Annual Parallel Processing Symp., March 1989, pp. 722–740.
[162] S.S. NEMAWARKAR AND G.R. GAO, *Measurement and modeling of EARTH-MANNA multithreaded architecture*, in Proc. 4th Intl. Workshop MASCOTS'96, Feb. 1996, pp. 109–114.
[163] R.S. NIKHIL, *The parallel programming language Id and its compilation for parallel machines*, Intl. J. High Speed Computing, 5 (1993), pp. 171–223.
[164] ———, *A multithreaded implementation of Id using P-RISC graphs*, Lect. Notes Comput. Sc., 768, Springer-Verlag, Berlin, 1994, pp. 390–405.
[165] R.S. NIKHIL AND ARVIND, *Can dataflow subsume von Neumann computing?*, in Proc. 16th ISCA, May 1989, pp. 262–272.
[166] R.S. NIKHIL, G.M. PAPADOPOULOS, AND ARVIND, **T: A multithreaded massively parallel architecture*, in Proc. 19th ISCA, May 1992, pp. 156–167.
[167] H. NISHIKAWA, H. TERADA, K. KOMATSU, S. YOSHIDA, T. OKAMOTO, Y. TSUJI, S. TAKAMURA, T. TOKURA, Y. NISHIKAWA, S. HARA, AND M. MEICHI, *Architecture of a one-chip data-driven processor: Q-p*, in Proc. 1987 ICPP, Aug. 1987, pp. 319–326.

[168] M.D. Noakes, D.A. Wallach, and W.J. Dally, *The J-Machine multicomputer: An architectural evaluation*, in Proc. 20th ISCA, May 1993, pp. 224–236.

[169] M. Ojsteršek, V. Žumer, and P. Kokol, *Data flow computer models*, in Proc. CompEuro '87, May 1987, pp. 884–885.

[170] A. Omondi and D. Klappholz, *Combining control driven and data driven computation for high processing rate*, in Proc. Intl. Computing Symp., March 1985.

[171] S. Palacharla, N.P. Jouppi, and J.E. Smith, *Complexity-effective superscalar processors*, in Proc. 24th ISCA, June 1997, pp. 206-218.

[172] G.M. Papadopoulos, *Implementation of a general-purpose dataflow multiprocessor*, Tech. Report TR-432, MIT Laboratory for Computer Science, Cambridge, Ma., Aug. 1988.

[173] G.M. Papadopoulos and D.E. Culler, *Monsoon: An explicit token-store architecture*, in Proc. 17th ISCA, June 1990, pp. 82–91.

[174] G.M. Papadopoulos and K.R. Traub, *Multithreading: A revisionist view of dataflow architectures*, in Proc. 18th ISCA, May 1991, pp. 342–351.

[175] L.M. Patnaik, R. Govindarajan, and N.S. Ramadoss, *Design and performance evaluation of EXMAN: EXtended MANchester data flow computer*, IEEE Trans. Computers, C-35 (1986), pp. 229–244.

[176] A. Plas, D. Comte, O. Gelly, and J. C. Syre, *LAU system architecture: A parallel data driven processor based on single assignment*, in Proc. 1976 ICPP, Aug. 1976, pp. 293–302.

[177] G.M. Quénot and B. Zavidovique, *A data-flow processor for real-time low-level image processing*, in Proc. IEEE Custom Integrated Circuits Conf., May 1991, pp. 1241–1244.

[178] J.E. Requa, *The piecewise data flow architecture control flow and register management*, in Proc. 10th ISCA, June 1983, pp. 84–89.

[179] J.E. Requa and J.R. McGraw, *The piecewise data flow architecture: Architectural concept*, IEEE Trans. Computers, C-32 (1983), pp. 425–438.

[180] J. Risau, A. Mikschl, and W. Damm, *A RISC approach to weak cache coherence*, Lect. Notes Comp. Sc., 1123, Springer-Verlag, Berlin, 1996, pp. 453–456.

[181] L. Roh and W.A. Najjar, *Design of a storage hierarchy in multithreaded architectures*, in Proc. 28th MICRO, 1995, pp. 271–278.

[182] S. Sakai, *Synchronization and pipeline design for a multithreaded massively parallel computer*, Advanced Topics in Dataflow Computing and Multithreading, (G.R. Gao, L. Bic, and J.-L. Gaudiot, eds.), IEEE Computer Society Press, Los Alamitos, CA, 1995, pp. 55–74.

[183] S. Sakai, K. Okamoto, H. Matsuoka, H. Hirono, Y. Kodama, and M. Sato, *Super-threading: Architectural and software mechanisms for optimizing parallel computation*, in Proc. 1993 Intl. Conf. Supercomputing, July 1993, pp. 251–260.

[184] S. Sakai, Y. Yamaguchi, K. Hiraki, Y. Kodama, and T. Yuba, *An architecture of a dataflow single chip processor*, in Proc. 16th ISCA, May 1989, pp. 46–53.

[185] J. Sargeant and C.C. Kirkham, *Stored data structures on the Manchester dataflow machines*, in Proc. 13th ISCA, June 1986, pp. 235–242.

[186] A.V.S. Sastry, L.M. Patnaik, and J. Šilc, *Dataflow architectures for logic programming*, Electrotehnical Review, 55 (1988), pp. 9–19.

[187] M. Sato, Y. Kodama, S. Sakai, and Y. Yamaguchi, *EM-C: Programming with explicit parallelism and locality for the EM-4 multiprocessor*, in Proc. PACT'94, Aug. 1994, pp. 3–14.

[188] ———, *Experiences with executing shared memory programs using fine-grained communication and multithreading in EM-4*, in Proc. IPPS 94, April 1994, pp. 630–636.

[189] M. Sato, Y. Kodama, S. Sakai, Y. Yamaguchi, and Y. Koumura, *Thread-based programming for the EM-4 hybrid dataflow machine*, in Proc. 19th ISCA, May 1992, pp. 146–155.

[190] M. Sato, Y. Kodama, S. Sakai, Y. Yamaguchi, and S. Sekiguchi, *Distributed data structure in thread-based programming for a highly parallel dataflow machine EM-4*, Advanced Topics in Dataflow Computing and Multithreading, (G.R. Gao, L. Bic, and J.-L. Gaudiot, eds.), IEEE Computer Society Press, Los Alamitos, CA, 1995, pp. 131–142.

[191] J. Sérot, G.M. Quénot, and B. Zavidovique, *A functional data-flow architecture dedicated to real-time image processing*, IFIP Trans., A-23 (1993), pp. 129–140.

[192] J.A. Sharp, *Data Flow Computing*, Ellis Horwood Ltd. Publishers, Chichester, 1985.

[193] A. Shaw, Arvind, and R.P. Johnson, *Performance tuning scientific codes for dataflow execution*, in Proc. PACT'96, Oct. 1996, pp. 198–207.

[194] T. Shimada, K. Hiraki, K. Nishida, and S. Sekiguchi, *Evaluation of a prototype data flow processor of the SIGMA-1 for scientific computations*, in Proc. 13th ISCA, June 1986, pp. 226–234.

[195] U. Sigmund and T. Ungerer, *Evaluating a multithreaded superscalar microprocessor versus a multiprocessor chip*, in Proc. 4th Parallel Syst. Algorithms Workshop, April 1996.

[196] ———, *Identifying bottlenecks in multithreaded superscalar multiprocessor*, Lect. Notes Comp. Sc., 1123, Springer-Verlag, Berlin, 1996, pp. 797–800.

[197] J. Šilc and B. Robič, *The review of some data flow computer architectures*, Informatica, 11 (1987), pp. 61–66.

[198] ———, *Efficient dataflow architecture for specialized computations*, in Proc. 12th World Congress on Scientifics Computation, July 1988, pp. 4.681–4.684.

[199] ———, *Synchronous dataflow-based architecture*, Microproc. Microprog., 27 (1989), pp. 315–322.

[200] ———, *MADAME - Macro-dataflow machine*, in Proc. MELECON '91, May 1991, pp. 985–988.

[201] J. Šilc, B. Robič, and L.M. Patnaik, *Performance evaluation of an extended static dataflow architecture*, Comput. Artif. Intell., 9 (1990), pp. 43–60.

[202] B.J. Smith, *A pipelined, shared resource MIMD computer*, in Proc. 1978 ICPP, Aug. 1978, pp. 6–8.

[203] ———, *Architecture and applications of the HEP multiprocessor computer system*, SPIE Real-Time Signal Processing IV, 298 (1981), pp. 241–248.

[204] ———, *The architecture of HEP*, Parallel MIMD Computation: HEP Supercomputer and Its Application, (J.S. Kowalik, ed.), MIT Press, Cambridge, MA, 1985, pp. 41–55.

[205] D.F Snelling, *The design and analysis of a Stateless Data-Flow Architectures*, Tech. Report UMCS-93-7-2, University of Manchester, Department of Computer Science, 1993.

[206] D.F Snelling and G.K. Egan, *A comparative study of data-flow architectures*, Tech. Report UMCS-94-4-3, University of Manchester, Department of Computer Science, 1994.

[207] A. Sohn, C. Kim, and M. Sato, *Multithreading with the EM-4 distributed-memory multiprocessor*, in Proc. PACT'95, June 1995, pp. 27–36.

[208] S.P. Song, M. Denman, and J. Chang, *The PowerPC 604 RISC microprocessor*, IEEE Micro, 14 (Oct. 1994), pp. 8–17.

[209] V.P. Srini, *An architectural comparison of dataflow systems*, IEEE Computer, 19 (March 1986), pp. 68–88.

[210] J. Strohschneider, B. Klauer, and K. Waldschmidt, *An associative communication network for fine and large grain dataflow*, in Proc. Euromicro Workshop on Parallel and Distr. Processing, 1995, pp. 324–331.

[211] J. Strohschneider, B. Klauer, S. Zickenheimer, and K. Waldschmidt, *Adarc: A fine grain dataflow architecture with associative communication network*, in Proc. 20th Euromicro Conf., Sep. 1994, pp. 445-450.

[212] J.C. Syre, D. Comte, and N. Hifdi, *Pipelining, parallelism and asynchronism in the LAU system*, in Proc. 1977 ICPP, Aug. 1977, pp. 87–92.

[213] N. Takahashi and M. Amamiya, *A data flow processor array system: Design and analysis*, in Proc. 10th ISCA, June 1983, pp. 243–250.

[214] T. Temma, *Dataflow processor for image processing*, Intl. Journal of Mini and Microcomputers 5 (1980), no. 3, 52–56.

[215] T. Temma, M. Iwashita, K. Matsumoto, H. Kurokawa, and T. Nukiyama, *Data flow processor chip for image processing*, IEEE Trans. Elec. Dev., ED-32 (1985), pp. 1784–1791.

[216] M. Thistle and B.J. Smith, *A processor architecture for Horizon*, in Proc. Supercomputing '88, Nov. 1988, pp. 35–41.

[217] S.A. Thoreson, A.N. Long, and J.R. Kerns, *Performance of three dataflow computers*, in Proc. 14th Ann. Comput. Sci. Conf., Feb. 1986, pp. 93–99.

[218] K.R. Traub, G.M. Papadopoulos, M.J. Beckerle, J.E. Hicks, and J. Young, *Overwiev of the Monsoon project*, in Proc. 1991 Intl. Conf. Comput. Design, 1991, pp. 150–155.

[219] P.C. Treleaven, *Principal components of a data flow computer*, in Proc. 1978 Euromicro Symp., Oct. 1978, pp. 366–374.

[220] P.C. Treleaven, D.R. Brownbridge, and R.P. Hopkins, *Data-driven and demand-driven computer architectures*, Computing Surveys, 14 (1982), pp. 93–143.

[221] P.C. Treleaven, R.P. Hopkins, and P.W. Rautenbach, *Combining data flow and control flow computing*, Computer Journal, 25 (1982), pp. 207–217.

[222] D.M. Tullsen, S.J. Eggers, J.S. Emer, H.M. Levy, J.L. Lo, and R.L. Stamm, *Exploiting choice: Instruction fetch and issue on an implementable simultaneous multithreading processor*, in Proc. 23th ISCA, May 1996, pp. 191–202.

[223] D.M. Tullsen, S.J. Eggers, and H.M. Levy, *Simultaneous multithreading: Maximizing on-chip parallelism*, in Proc. 22nd ISCA, June 1995, pp. 392–403.

[224] T. Ungerer and E. Zehendner, *A multi-level parallelism architecture*, Tech. Report 230, Univ. Augsburg, Institute for Mathematics, 1991.

[225] ———, *Threads and subinstruction level parallelism in a data flow architecture*, Lect. Notes Comput. Sc., 634, Springer-Verlag, Berlin, 1992, pp. 731–736.

[226] R. VEDDER, M. CAMPBELL, AND G. TUCKER, *The Hughes data flow multiprocessor*, in Proc. 5th Intl. Conf. Distr. Comput. Syst., May 1985, pp. 2–9.

[227] R. VEDDER AND D. FINN, *The Hughes data flow multiprocessor: Architecture for efficient signal and data processing*, in Proc. 12th ISCA, June 1985, pp. 324–332.

[228] A.H. VEEN AND R. VAN DEN BORN, *The RC compiler for the DTN dataflow computer*, J. Parall. Distr. Comput., 10 (1990), pp. 319–322.

[229] D.W. WALL, *Limits of instruction-level parallelism*, in Proc. 4th Intl. Conf. Arch. Support for Programming Languages and Operating Syst., April 1991, pp. 176–188.

[230] I. WATSON AND J.R. GURD, *A prototype data flow computer with token labelling*, in Proc. National Comput. Conf., June 1979, pp. 623–628.

[231] I. WATSON AND J.R. GURD, *A practical data flow computer*, IEEE Computer, 15 (Feb. 1982), pp. 51–57.

[232] K.C. YEAGER, *The MIPS R10000 superscalar microprocessor*, IEEE Micro, 16 (April 1996), pp. 28–40.

[233] T. YUBA, T. SHIMADA, K. HIRAKI, AND H. KISHIWAGI, *SIGMA-1: A dataflow computer for scientific computations*, Comput. Physics Comm., 37 (1985), pp. 141–148.

[234] A.C. YUCETURK, B. KLAUER, S. ZICKENHEIMER, R. MOORE, AND K. WALDSCHMIDT, *Mapping of neural networks onto dataflow graphs*, in Proc. 22nd Euromicro Conf., Sep. 1996, pp. 51–57.

[235] E. ZEHENDNER AND T. UNGERER, *The ASTOR architecture*, in Proc. 7th Intl. Conf. Distr. Comput. Syst., Sep. 1987, pp. 424–430.

[236] ———, *A large-grain data flow architecture utilizing multiple levels of parallelism*, in Proc. CompEuro '92, May 1992, pp. 23–28.

PARALLEL PROGRAMMING USING VISUAL PATTERNS

A. S. M. SAJEEV*

Abstract. Parallel Programming is significantly more complex than sequential programming because the programmer has the additional tasks of both specifying processes, and their communication and synchronization requirements. In this paper we propose a visual environment in which a non-expert in parallel programming can concentrate on the sequential aspects of a parallel program and specify its communication and synchronization using visual tools. The visual environment provides, as patterns, encapsulations of common communication and synchronization strategies. In addition, an expert parallel programmer can add new patterns to the repository either by defining it completely, or by extending the existing patterns in the repository.

Key words. Parallel programming languages, object-oriented programming, visual programming, programming patterns

1. Introduction. Visual programming languages have the potential to reduce the complexity of programming by providing visual means for program creation [9]. A number of visual programming languages exist, mostly for the sequential domain. Parallel programming is a more complex activity than sequential programming because the programmer has additionally to deal with the creation of processes and communication between them. So, if visual programming is useful in the sequential domain, it is likely to be even more useful in the parallel domain.

We have designed a visual parallel programming language called V4P [12, 13] based on the 4P-paradigm [11, 10]. V4P provides visual support for programmers who are not conversant with parallel programming to concentrate on the sequential aspects of a parallel program and specify its communication and synchronization requirements using visual tools. A key feature of V4P is its facility to store patterns of parallel programming in a repository. *A pattern is a description of communicating objects and classes that are customized to solve a general design problem in a particular context* [4]. Once patterns are specified and stored, other users can use them to create their own parallel programs. V4P has certain built-in patterns; but expert parallel programmers can introduce additional patterns into the environment. This paper demonstrates parallel programming in the V4P environment and, in particular, discusses the specification and use of patterns in V4P.

1.1. Related Literature. Two of the representative visual environments for parallel programming are Enterprise [14] and Meander [15]. In the Enterprise model, programmers are given a fixed number of models as metaphors from a business enterprise. For example, a department is a model similar to a processor farm. The programmer only needs to type in the code for the units of the enterprise. This has advantages similar to that of using patterns in V4P. However, unlike V4P, the Enterprise model does not let the user define any metaphors; they have to program with only those supplied by the system. Meander is perhaps at the other extreme. There programming is always done with nodes and edges. Meander allows composition of graphs to create process modules, but they do not provide the same flexibility as patterns. While patterns are templates that can be reused to create different programs, process modules are parts of a program.

Darwin [8] is a language for distributed systems configurations. Users can specify the configuration of a distributed system. This is similar to patterns in V4P in the sense

* Department of Computer Science and Software Engineering, The University of Newcastle, Callaghan, NSW 2308, Australia (`sajeev@cs.newcastle.edu.au`)

that a pattern specifies a configuration for parallel programs that follow the pattern. The main difference, once again, is that configurations in Darwin are not generic. Furthermore, Darwin is a language separate from the implementation language (which is C++), whereas in V4P patterns are specified in the same language as the user writes code for each node (Object-Pascal).

Algorithmic skeletons [2] have been explored mainly in the functional programming area. Skeletons provide a generic mechanism to specify parallelism, and in that sense provide the same functionality as V4P's patterns.

The rest of the paper is organised as follows. In the next section we describe V4P and its base coordination language 4P. Section 3 gives two examples of using patterns in parallel programming. Section 4 describes the specification of patterns and Section 5 illustrates the use of inheritance in extending patterns. Section 6 gives the conclusions.

2. Visual 4P. V4P provides a flexible object-oriented, visual environment for parallel programming. While it uses nodes to represent objects, and edges to represent communication channels, the power of the language comes from its ability to accept reusable patterns for parallel programming. The aim is to let sequential programmers create parallel programs without having to write code for process creation, communication and synchronization. V4P is based on the 4P paradigm : 4P, by introducing a very small number of constructs lets parallel programs have the 'look and feel' of sequential programs [10].

2.1. Procedures with preconditions as parallel programs (4P). 4P is a coordination language that can be attached to a sequential object-oriented language to get a concurrent object-oriented language. 4P introduces coordination in terms of two features: one, messages between objects which can be synchronous or asynchronous, and two, each method has a guard attached to it: a method invocation is delayed until its guard becomes true.

Two objects communicate synchronously by one object calling a method of another (which is the default), and asynchronously, by an object send-invoking a method of another. In the case of send, the sender continues execution without waiting, while a new thread is spawned to execute the method invocation. Similar mechanisms are used in languages such as SR [1] to distinguish between synchronous and asynchronous communication.

Each method has a guard (by default TRUE). A method invocation is delayed until its guard becomes true. There are three types of guards: Access, Boolean and History. Boolean guards are ordinary boolean expressions. An access guard is used when a method, before its execution, needs to lock an object. An access guard is specified as:

```
Access_guard:Access_type Object_Reference
Accept_type: 'observe' | 'atomic' | 'exclusive'
```

An observe access to an object means the method cannot modify the state of the object, but can read its state (and other methods can access the object only in observe-mode at the same time). We use the keyword atomic to indicate that each access to the object by this method will be atomic. An exclusive access means that the object is not accessible by any other thread until either the guard is evaluated to false or the method execution is complete. The semantics of observe is obvious. The difference between atomic and exclusive access can be illustrated as in the following example. Suppose an object A contains a method m as defined below.

```
[atomic B; exclusive C]  {access guard of method m}
procedure m;
```

```
begin
  B.x; {Assume x is a method of object B}
  C.y; {Assume y is a method of object C}
  {Do something else}
  B.x; {Call B.x again}
  C.y; {Call C.y again}
  ..
end
```

CODE 1. *Illustrating the difference between atomic and exclusive accesses*

The calls from m to method x will be executed exclusively; so will m's call to y. However, after the first call to B.x finishes, the object B may be accessed by other threads, before it becomes once again exclusively available for m to execute the second call to B.x. On the other hand, exclusive access to C would mean that from the start of procedure m, the object C will not be accessible to any other threads. In particular, when the second call to C.y is made, C will be in the same state as at the end of the first call to C.y.

If a method, through its guard, seeks different kinds of accesses to the same object, the access provided could be any one of those sought. For instance, in the above example, if B and C happen to refer to the same object, the access provided to that object could be atomic or exclusive. It is the programmer's responsibility to avoid such non-deterministic situations.

History guards use regular expressions to specify the acceptable state in terms of the history of execution sequences of methods in an object. Sajeev and Schmidt [11] describes them in detail and discusses how they help to solve the inheritance anomaly problem [7] in the 4P paradigm. The bounded buffer example below illustrates the 4P model. We use this buffer in one of the patterns in Section 5. (For the sequential code in this paper, we use Object-Pascal. The reason is that V4P is being implemented in Delphi, and the underlying language of Delphi is Object Pascal.)

```
Interface
uses
  itemUnit; {where TItem class is declared}

const  MAX = 100;
type

  TBuffer = class
  private
    buffer : array [0 .. MAX-1] of TItem;
    slot : integer := 0;
    next : integer := 0;
  public
    function get : TItem;
    procedure put (item : TItem)
  end;

Implementation

[exclusive next; next < slot] {guard}
```

```
function TBuffer.get : TItem;
begin
  get := buffer[next MOD MAX];
  next := next + 1
end;

[exclusive slot; slot - next < MAX]
procedure TBuffer.put (item : TItem);
begin
  buffer[slot MOD MAX] := item;
  slot := slot + 1
end;
```

CODE 2. *Bounded Buffer problem*

The buffer has two methods, get and put. The get method has a guard to delay calls until there is an unconsumed item in the buffer. The exclusive access to the variable `next` ensures that two calls to get will be executed mutually exclusively. Similar is the case for the put method. However, if the buffer is neither empty nor full, an invocation of put and another of get can run simultaneously.

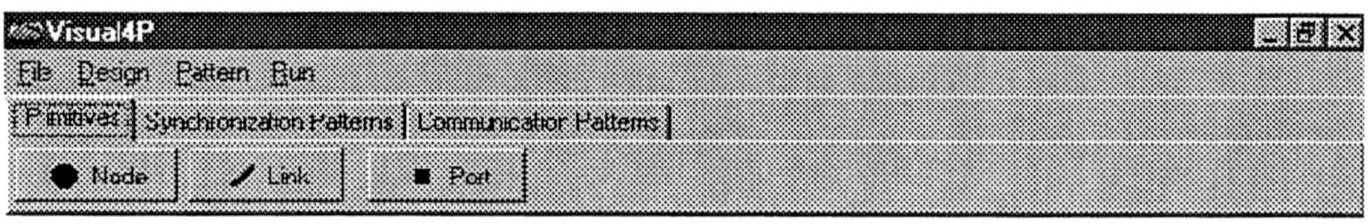

FIG. 2.1. *Visual 4P menu bar*

2.2. Visual Interface to 4P. In V4P, a programmer develops a parallel program by first creating its process communication model visually and then writing usually the sequential code for the different nodes in the model. At the primitive level, the visual representation of a program has a number of nodes. A node may have zero or more ports. Links from other nodes can be connected to a port.

A node is typically a visual representation of an object. A port is internally represented by a method of the object. A port has a guard attached to it; an invocation to the method attached to a port is delayed until its guard holds. Figure 2.1 shows the main menu of the V4P environment.

A programmer may build the program using the primitives (nodes, links and ports), or more easily, using a pattern. Once a pattern is selected, the programmer needs to write the code for each node. Creating process-threads, buffering data for communication etc. are automatically done by the system. Depending on the pattern used, the programmer often does not have to specify the guards, thereby essentially writing a sequential program.

3. Programming using Patterns. In any visual environment for parallel programming the level of support provided to create programs is important. An environment may choose to provide only primitives such as nodes and links. The advantage is that the programmers can then create parallel programs of arbitrary structure. However, they need to do this from scratch every time, and they need to be experts in parallel programming. On the other hand, an environment that provides only high level models like farms and pipes, while reducing the effort on the part of the programmer, makes the environment less flexible: all programs have to conform to the predefined models. Our approach is to provide both primitives and high level models as patterns, but more importantly to allow the creation of more patterns, either as extensions of existing patterns (using the inheritance mechanism of object-orientation) or as entirely new patterns. Thus we envisage two classes of programmers, the expert parallel programmers (referred to as pattern-programmers, in our context) and sequential programmers (referred to as applications programmers).

In this section we will illustrate the use of patterns in parallel programming through examples. The next section will discuss the creation and extension of patterns.

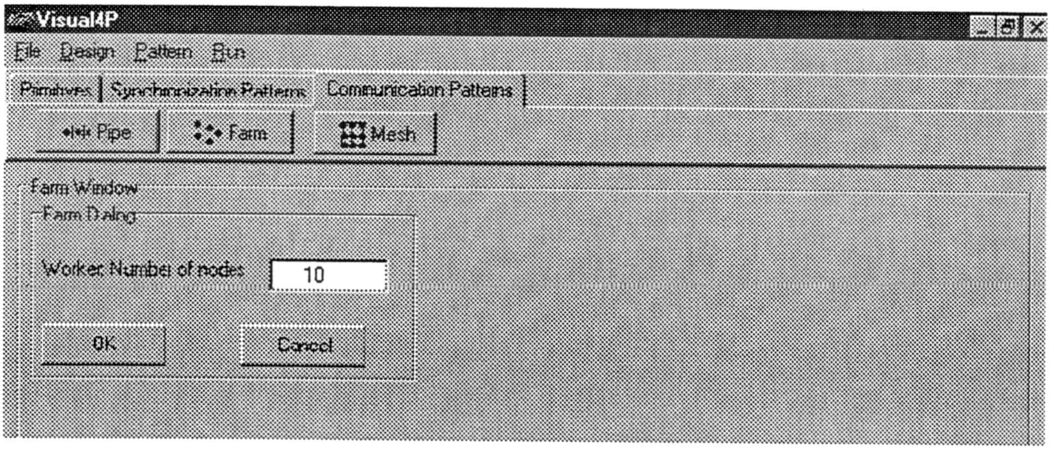

FIG. 3.1. *Farm Window Dialog*

To synthesize a parallel program using patterns, the first step is to choose a pattern, either by double clicking on its icon or by selecting it in the drop down menu. Our first example uses the process farm pattern available in the tab called Communication Patterns (See Figure 3.1). When a user double clicks on its icon, a dialog box appears. It asks for the number of worker nodes. Closing the dialog box, after entering a value for the number of workers, will display a graph for the farm pattern.

The user can now double click on any of the nodes, to get a code editor to enter the class description corresponding to that node. If the code already exists, it could be attached to the node. In the processor farm, it is often the case that each worker is an instance of the same class. Thus all worker nodes will be attached to the same TWorker class. Hence the code can be written once, and then attached to each worker node.

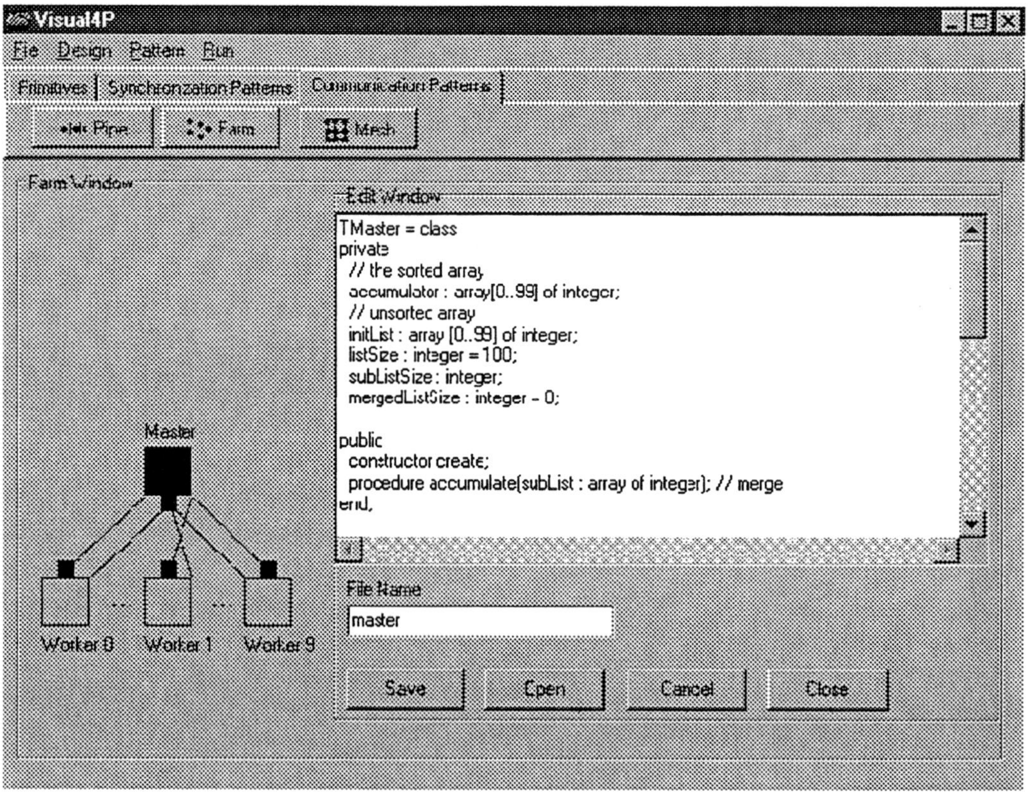

FIG. 3.2. *Farm pattern editing*

3.1. Illustrations. To illustrate the use of the farm pattern we can program parallel sorting as a farm. A master divides the given list of numbers into sublists. Each worker sorts a sublist in parallel with other workers and returns the sorted sublist to the master. The master merges the sorted sublists to get the final output. The master class is defined as:

```
{We assume that the list size is a multiple of the number of workers}
TMaster = class
private
  // the sorted array
  accumulator : array[0..99] of integer;
  // unsorted array
  initList : array [0..99] of integer;
  listSize : integer = 100;
  subListSize : integer;
  mergedListSize : integer = 0;

public
  constructor create;
  procedure accumulate(subList : array of integer); // merge
end;
```

```
constructor TMaster.create;
var i, j : integer;
begin
  {read the numbers}
  subListSize := listSize div worker.size;
  for i := 0 to worker.size-1 do
  begin
    for j := 0 to subListSize-1
      read (sublist[j]);
      worker[i].sort(sublist);
  end;
end;

procedure TMaster.accumulate(subList: array of integer);
var insertPos : integer;
begin
  for i := 0 to high(subList) do
  begin
    insertPos := mergedListSize;
    for j := 0 to mergedListSize-1 do
      if sublist[i] < accumulator[j] then
      begin
        insertPos := j;
        break
      end;
    insert(subList[i], accumulator, insertPos) {inserts subList[i]
       in the accumulator at insertPos position
       --details not shown}
    mergedListSize := mergedListSize + subListSize;
  end
end;
```

CODE 3. *Master class using a farm-pattern*

The worker class is defined as:

```
TWorker = class
public
 procedure solve(subList : array of integer);
end;

TWorker.solve(subList: array of integer);
begin
  sort(subList); // details not shown
  master.accumulate(subList)
end;
```

CODE 4. *Worker class using a farm-pattern*

The code written for both the master and the workers is sequential. The predefined farm-pattern (see next section) has already specified the concurrency requirements, in order to make this code parallel. They are:

- Instantiate the number of workers specified in the dialog box and and the master.
- Send-invoke calls to worker.solve and master.accumulate. That means, the master does not wait for one worker to finish before giving the next chunk of work to the next worker. Similarly, a worker does not wait for the result to be accumulated by the master before terminating (or in a general situation, looking for the next piece of work).
- Delay the execution of the body of the master's accumulate method until there is exclusive access to the accumulator for each worker's invocation.

We will consider another simple example to again demonstrate how the application programmer only needs to write sequential code to synthesize a parallel program with the help of patterns. A bank account provides several services such as checking the account balance, depositing money, withdrawing money etc. In a joint account (held by a company, for instance) there could be simultaneous multiple accesses to the account (through different branches or teller-machines). We do want to restrict that depositing and withdrawing must be done exclusively, even though the balance may be read simultaneously. The pattern to go for is the ReadersWriters pattern defined in the Synchronization patterns tab. Double clicking on the pattern, as before, will display a dialog box. This time it will ask for the number of reader-ports and the number of writer-ports and their names. In this example, there is one reader port: checkBalance and two writer ports: deposit and withdraw. The pattern has only one node for which the user enters the bank-account class specification.

```
TAccount = class
private
  balance : currency;
public
  function getBalance : currency;
  procedure deposit(amount : currency);
  procedure withdraw(amount : currency);
end;

function TAccount.getBalance: currency;
begin
  getBalance := balance
end;

procedure TAccount.deposit(amount: currency);
begin
  balance := balance + amount
end;

procedure TAccount.withdraw(amount: currency);
begin
  if balance >= amount then
    balance := balance - amount
```

```
  {else raise exception -- not shown}
end;
```

CODE 5. *Bank account class using a readers-writers pattern*

As in the previous example, the Account class is purely sequential. The synchronization required is already captured in the Readers-Writers pattern used. The Readers-Writers pattern specifies that there can be multiple access to the object through a reader method, but exclusive access through a writer-method. All that the applications programmer has to do is identify `getBalance` as a reader-method and `deposit` and `withdraw` as writer methods to achieve the required synchronization. Obviously, the ports of the Account object need to be linked with other nodes to create a complete program.

3.2. Discussion. Patterns encapsulate synchronization in terms of method-guards of the 4P paradigm, and communication in terms of send and call invocations of methods. Parallel programming therefore reduces to the act of identifying the right pattern and providing the sequential code for the different nodes of the pattern. The pattern also shows the topology of the program. A visual representation of the topology helps increase the legibility of the program.

We do not believe that all parallel programs can be developed this way. If an appropriate pattern cannot be found, there are two approaches a programmer can take in V4P. One is to define their own patterns, probably inheriting from an existing pattern that is closest to the required behaviour. This approach would create a new pattern that will be reusable in other similar solutions. Alternatively, one could develop the program from scratch. To do this graphically one can use the primitives such as nodes, links and ports in the Primitives tab of the V4P interface, first to develop the topology, and then to attach code (including guards for synchronization) to the nodes.

4. Pattern Specification. In the previous section we saw how patterns can encapsulate the topology and process interactions of parallel programs. V4P provides a uniform and flexible mechanism of pattern specification so that new patterns can be introduced into the environment in a uniform manner. Currently patterns are specified textually and used visually. There is no separate language for specifying patterns; we use the same underlying language: the one used to specify the class descriptions of the nodes.

4.1. Primitives. The primitive classes in the system are TNode, TLink and TPort. The interfaces of these classes are defined as follows:

```
TNode = class
public
  label : String;
end;

TPort = class
public
  owner : TNode; {owner of a port}
  guard : String;
  method : String;
  accessType : TAccessType; {send, call or either}
  label : String;
end;
```

```
TLink = class
{a link connects a node to a port of another node}
public
  head : TNode;
  tail : TPort;
  label : String;
end;
```

CODE 6. *Specification of primitive classes*

The accessType attribute of TPort class is of type TAccessType, defined by:

```
  TAccessType = (accessSend, accessCall, accessDontCare);
```

It specifies whether the invocations at this port are to be sent, called or either.

In the specification of patterns, often one needs to use arrays of nodes, links and/or ports. The interface to TNodeArray is specified below. It uses an enumerated type:

```
TValueTime = (patternDesignTime, programDesignTime, runTime, anyTime);

TNodeArray = class
public
  size : integer;
  node : array [1..size] of TNode;
  procedure setSizeAt(when : TValueTime)
end;
```

CODE 7. *NodeArray specification*

The setSizeAt method tells when the size of the array will be available. If it is specified as programDesignTime then, when a user, while developing a program, chooses a pattern which contains a node-array, a dialog box will appear asking for the number of nodes.

TLinkArray and TPortArray declarations are similar to that of TNodeArray except that they have arrays of TLink and TPort classes respectively.

4.2. Specifying Patterns. A pattern is specified in terms of the kind of nodes it has, the ports for each node, the links between the nodes, and often the guards and methods for each port. If the guards and methods are not attached to a port in a pattern, then the user of the pattern will need to attach them at program—as opposed to pattern—design time. Each component can be labelled by assigning a string to its label attribute.

4.3. Specifying a processor farm pattern. A processor farm generally consists of a master process and several workers. A master divides the task into several subtasks and asks the workers to solve the subtasks. Each worker, after completing its task, will return the result to the master, who will accumulate the partial results to construct the complete result. There are several variations of this pattern. We shall discuss some of them later in the paper. The aspects common to different variations can be abstracted into an abstract farm class. It specifies a master node and an array of worker nodes. The master has a result port and an array of result links to link the result port to the workers (so they can return the results of subtasks). We specify that the result port is attached to a method called accumulator, and the guard for the method is exclusive accumulator (i.e. exclusive access to accumulator). The abstract farm also has an array of problem-ports and problem-links for the master to send subtasks to workers.

```
TAbstractFarm = class(TPattern)
public
  master : TNode;
  resultPort : Port;
  resultLink : TLinkArray;

  worker: TNodeArray;
  problemPort : TPortArray;
  problemLink : TLinkArray;

  constructor create; virtual;
end;

constructor TFarm.create;
var i :integer;
begin
  master.label := 'Master';
  resultPort.owner := master;
  resultPort.method := 'Accumulate';
  resultPort.guard := 'exclusive accumulator';
  resultPort.accessType := accessSend; {send-invoke Accumulate}

  for i := 0 to worker.size-1 do
  begin
    worker[i].label := 'Worker ' + intToStr(i);

    {Establish link between workers and the result port of Master}
    resultLink[i].head := worker[i];
    resultLink[i].tail := resultPort
  end
end;
```

CODE 8. *Abstract farm pattern*

In the common form of processor farm, each worker has a port (problemPort) to receive the problem (i.e., the subtask) it has to solve. This port is linked to the master. A method, called solve, is attached to the port whose invocations (i.e. accessType) will be asynchronous (i.e., accessSend). The processor farm pattern can be specified as a descendant of the abstractFarm. When an instance of the processor farm (TFarm, below) is created, it first executes the parent's create to establish the resultPort and resultLinks. Then it sets up the rest of the ports and links (see the create method below).

```
TFarm = class(TAbstractFarm)
public
  constructor create; override;
end;

constructor TFarm.create;
var i :integer;
begin
```

```
  inherited create; {Execute the parent's create}

  worker.setSizeAt(programDesignTime);

  problemPort.size := worker.size;
  problemLink.size := worker.size;

  for i := 0 to worker.size-1 do
  begin
    problemPort[i].owner := worker[i];
    problemPort[i].method := 'solve'
    problemPort[i].accessType := accessSend;

    problemLink[i].head := master;
    problemLink[i].tail := port[i];
  end
end;
```

CODE 9. *Processor farm pattern*

Processor farm is a predefined pattern in V4P. For new patterns, the pattern-programmer can attach a title (by default, the class name), an icon, and a natural description to the pattern and store it in the pattern repository.

Since we have also used the ReadersWriters pattern in the examples in the previous section, we also show the definition of that pattern here:

```
TReadersWriters = class
private
  lock : integer;
public
  object : TNode;
  readers : TPortArray;
  writers : TPortArray;
  constructor create;
end;

constructor TReadersWriters.create;
var i : integer;
begin
  readers.setSizeAt(ProgramDesignTime);
  writers.setSizeAt(ProgramDesignTime);
  for i := 1 to readers.size do
  begin
    readers[i].owner := object;
    readers[i].guard := 'Observe lock'; {observe access to lock}
    readers[i].label := 'Reader ' + intToStr(i);
    {readers[i].method is left undefined. The pattern-user specifies
    the reader method(s) at program design time through its dialog box}
  end;
```

```
  {Similar to the above loop for writers -- not shown here}
end;
```

CODE 10. *Readers-writers pattern*

5. New patterns by inheritance. A pattern programmer can create new patterns by inheritance from existing patterns. To demonstrate this, we will create an agenda farm as an extension of the farm. An agenda farm has an agenda object where the master will initially keep the agenda items for workers to pick up (instead of directly sending them to the workers). An agenda farm is useful in situations where the workers, while working on a subtask, need to create new subtasks; they can place such subtasks on the agenda for other workers who become free. An agenda farm, apart from workers and a master needs a node for the agenda. An agenda is essentially a buffer. So we use the class TBuffer defined in Section 2 for the agenda. The agenda has two ports: one to deposit the problems (problemPort) and the other for workers to retrieve the problems (getPort). ProblemPort is inherited from TAbstractFarm and getPort is declared within TAgendaFarm.

```
TAgendaFarm = class(TAbstractFarm)
public
  agenda : TBuffer;  {use TBuffer class for agenda}
  getPort: TPort;
  getLink : TLinkArray;
  constructor create; override;
end;

constructor TAgendaFarm.create;
begin
  inherited create;
  {Attach the problemPort to put method of Agenda;
   we need only one problem port}
  problemPort.size := 1;
  problemPort[0].owner := agenda;
  problemPort[0].method := 'put';

  {Attach the getPort to get method}
  getPort.owner := agenda;
  getPort.method := 'get';
  {Since the guards are already defined for put and get in the
    Tbuffer class, they will be automatically  assigned to the
    respective guard fields}

  worker.setSizeAt(programDesignTime);
  getLink.size := worker.size;
  problemLink.size := worker.size + 1;

  {Link problemPort[0] to master}
  problemLink[0].head := master;
  probelmLink[0].tail := problemPort[0];

  {Link problemPort[0], getPort and resultPort to all workers}
```

```
  for i := 0 to worker.size-1 do begin
    problemLink[i+1].head := worker[i];
    problemLink[i+1].tail := problemPort[0];
    getLink[i].head := worker[i];
    getLink[i].tail := getPort
  end
end;
```

CODE 11. *Agenda farm—an illustration of using inheritance*

6. Conclusions. V4P is a visual language which provides patterns for parallel programming. A pattern specifies the process communication structure; the user of the pattern has only to provide the sequential code corresponding to the objects. In other similar visual environments, a user is restricted to the patterns provided by the system. In V4P, however, users can specify patterns of their own and add them to the repository for reuse. Because of the object-oriented environment, patterns can be created as extensions of existing patterns. Furthermore, we do not define a separate language for pattern specification. This paper has shown that creating patterns is a flexible and reusable setting for developing parallel programs.

Currently, pattern development is textual, only pattern use is visual. This is acceptable since we see two classes of programmers: sequential programmers who want to create parallel programs (they can get most benefit from the visual environment), and expert parallel programmers who want to extend the already available patterns in the environment with new patterns (who would not mind textual programming). We are, however, studying ways to provide a visual environment for pattern programming as well.

6.1. Task Partitioning and Load Balancing Issues. Some object-oriented parallel languages classify objects as active and passive. An active object forms a concurrent task, and therefore programmers can perform task partitioning by specifying the active objects in their program. In 4P, however, an object can have multiple threads executing it simultaneously (subject of course to synchronization constraints). In 4P and V4P, programs are designed by composing the solution out of logical classes and instantiation of objects from those classes. A "task" may be spread out over different classes, but each class represents a logical entity in the solution space. From an application programmer's point of view, we believe, this approach will make the programming activity simpler than when he/she needs to think in terms of task partitioning. Programming languages rarely provide constructs for load balancing; it is often left to the underlying implementation. However, in some large-scale problems, load balancing hints from the programmer will be useful. V4P currently does not provide any facilities in this regard. One possibility is to extend the attributes of patterns to include pragma specification to give hints to the compiler (similar to that in Ada language).

Future work will be in three major areas: scalability, performance and pattern discovery.

6.2. Scalability. Object-orientation provides a clean and systematic method to develop large programs as a composition of classes. V4P being an object-oriented language supports this paradigm. However, on the interface side, similar to any visual language, it has to deal with the limitations of (a) screen size and (b) the number of visual objects a user can handle at a time. At the moment, V4P uses ellipses when the number of nodes is larger than what can be displayed on the screen; clicking on the ellipses would hide some of the nodes, and make others appear. This mechanism is not sufficient for a visual environment.

Modularisation is one way of approaching this problem. Statecharts [5] are a good example of illustrating the benefit of modularity in developing large finite state machine (FSM) diagrams in terms of composite state interactions where a composite state in turn can be represented as a FSM. Visualisation researchers have also investigated mechanisms to address scalability of views. Cone trees, perspective walls and fish-eye views [3] are examples of methods proposed to scale up visual systems.

6.3. Performance. Perhaps, the main advantage of parallel programming is improvement in performance. While V4P currently concentrates on ease of programming, efficient optimization techniques need to be used by the compiler so that the resulting programs run faster than their sequential equivalents.

6.4. Pattern discovery. To increase the usefulness of the programming environment, we need to discover patterns of parallel programming [6] from a wide variety of problem domains. Currently, V4P includes common patterns identified in the parallel programming community. Even though the facility for creating user-defined patterns makes the environment flexible, it would be useful for sequential programmers if the environment already had patterns to parallelise problems coming from different domains. It is also important to provide help systems to enable programmers to identify the appropriate patterns for their problems and to use them correctly. V4P, while relieving the applications programmer from thinking in terms of coding process synchronization and communication, requires him/her to think in terms of selecting appropriate patterns for their problems, and though this is at a more abstract level than, for instance, coding synchronization, it still requires education and practice.

Acknowledgements. Discussions with Professors Heinz Schmidt and Bala Srinivasan on various related themes have been very useful. Comments, suggestions and corrections of the guest editor Professor L. M. Patnaik, the anonymous referees and Professor John Crossley are much appreciated.

REFERENCES

[1] G. R. Andrews, *Concurrent programming—principles and practices*, Benjamin-Cummings, 1991.

[2] G. H. Botorog and H. Kuchen, *Algorithmic skeletons for adaptive multigrid methods*, in Lecture Notes in Computer Science, 980, Springer, 1995.

[3] M. Burnett, et al. *Scaling Up Visual Programming Languages*, IEEE Computer, 28, 1995, pp. 45–54.

[4] E. Gamma, R. Helm, R. Johnson and J. Vlissides, *Design patterns: elements of reusable object-oriented software*, Addison-Wesley,1995.

[5] D. Harel and E. Gery, *Executable Object Modeling with Statecharts*, IEEE Computer, 30, July 1997, pp. 31–42.

[6] D. Lea, *Concurrent Programming in Java—Design Principles and Patterns*, Addison-Wesley, 1997.

[7] S. Matsuoka and A. Yonezawa, *Analysis of Inheritance Anomaly in Object-Oriented Concurrent Programming Languages*, In Research Directions in Concurrent Object-Oriented Programming, Agha G., Wegner P., Yonezawa, A (eds.), MIT Press, 1993, pp. 107–150.

[8] J. Magee, N. Dulay and J. Kramer, *Structuring parallel and distributed programs*, IEE Software Engineering Journal, 8, 1993, pp. 73–82.

[9] B. A. Myers, *Visual programming, programming by example, and program visualization: a taxonomy*, Proc. CHI '86, 1986, pp. 59-66.

[10] A. S. M. Sajeev, *Linguistic Support for Regulating Process-Instantiations*, In Parallel Computing and Transputers, D. Arnold, R. Christie, J. Day and P. Roe (eds.), IOS Press, Amsterdam, 1993, pp. 51–57.

[11] A. S. M. Sajeev and H. W. Schmidt, *Integrating concurrency and object-orientation using boolean, access and path guards*, Proc. 3rd Intl. Conf. High Performance Computing, Trivandrum, IEEE Computer Society Press, 1996, 68–72.

[12] A. S. M. Sajeev, *Pattern Specification in a Visual Parallel Programming Environment*, Proc. 5th International Conference on Advanced Computing, Chennai, Dec., Tata-McGraw-Hill, 1997, pp. 243–248.

[13] A. S. M. Sajeev, *A Visual Interface for Parallel Program Development*, Proc. Parallel and Distributed Computing and Networks Conference, Singapore, IASTED Press, August, 1997, pp. 198–201.

[14] J. Schaeffer, D. Szafron, G. Lobe and I. Parsons, *The enterprise model for developing distributed applications*, IEEE Parallel and Distributed Technology, August, 1993, pp. 85–95.

[15] G. Wirtz, *Graph-based software construction for parallel message-passing programs*, Information and Software Technology Journal, 36, 1994, pp. 405–412.

PARALLEL COMPUTING WITH GENERALIZED CELLULAR AUTOMATA

W. A. MANIATTY* , B. K. SZYMANSKI*, AND T. CARACO †

Abstract. *Cellular automata* (CA) are fundamental computational models of spatial phenomena, in which space is represented by a discrete lattice of *cells*. Each cell concurrently interacts with its neighborhood which, in traditional CA, is limited to the cell's nearest neighbors. In this paper we discuss *generalized cellular automata* (GCA), an important but unexplored class of CA, in which the cell's interaction domain extends beyond the nearest neighbors. The computational power necessary to run large scale CA (and GCA) models has only recently been available thanks to parallel processing. This paper focuses on implementation and performance of GCA in biological modeling. In particular, we present results of simulating the spread of epidemics and the creation of spatial infection patterns that are important for disease control.

The simulation system is implemented on three different platforms: the MasPar MP-1 SIMD computer, the IBM SP-2 MIMD machine and a network of workstations (NOW) that consists of Sun SPARCstation 5 and UltraSPARC 2's connected via Ethernet. The system presented in this paper has been specialized for simulating a four species spatially explicit model, however, the implementation may be readily modified to represent other models. Simulation results are presented for simple epidemics and vector-borne diseases spread by parasites.

Key words. parallel algorithms, parallel simulation, cellular automata, parallel computing, epidemics, ecology

AMS subject classifications. 68Q22, 68U05, 92D25, 92D30

1. Introduction.

Many large-scale natural phenomena arise from concurrent, spatially localized interactions of small entities. Examples are fluid dynamics [46], forest fires [14], population dynamics and spread of epidemics [44]. *Cellular automata* (CA) model such phenomena by discretizing space into a lattice of *cells* [9]. Each cell is in one of a finite set of discrete states and interacts with its neighborhood, referred to as the cell's *stencil*. In CA models each cell updates its value as a function of its current state and its stencil. Despite their simplicity, CA display surprisingly complex behavior. Wolfram [47, 48] classifies the qualitative convergence of two-dimensional CA into the following taxonomies: (1) evolving to a homogeneous state, (2) evolving to a simple separated locally periodic structure, (3) yielding chaotic and aperiodic patterns and (4) yielding complex patterns of localized structures. However, very little is known about predicting CA behavior without running them.

Percolation models [39] are closely related to CA. They embed a graph structure onto a problem space, and model a phenomena as a fluid flowing along the edges from *wet* source vertices to *dry* destination vertices. This means that each cell computes its impact on its neighbors (for regular lattices this forms a dual of CA) [1].

Traditionally, CA, as well as percolation models equate stencils with the nearest neighbors only, although, sporadically more diverse models were sometimes considered[2]. However,

---

*Department of Computer Science, Rensselaer Polytechnic Institute, Troy, NY 12180-3590, ({maniattb,szymansk}cs.rpi.edu).

†Department of Biological Sciences, SUNY Albany, Albany, NY 12222.

[1] One of the anonymous reviewers noted that also lattice gas automata (LGA) and lattice Boltzmann models (LBM) have similar features to the GCA models presented in this paper. For a description of LGA and LBM see for example [12, 41].

[2] For example, Ermentrout and Edelstein-Keshet [19] survey several CA models of biological processes, including an epidemiological model where each cell, (i, j) in a $N \times N$ lattice interacts with the nearest

many phenomena, especially those studied in biology, ecology and sociology, have longer range interactions. Often interactions between organisms in nature and between humans in society are of such character and the size of a stencil is an important parameter of such interactions. CA models for such phenomena require stencils that extend beyond the cell's nearest neighbors and which can be varied from simulation to simulation. We refer to CA with extended and variable stencils as *generalized cellular automata* (GCA).

This paper focuses on parallel computing environments for GCA used to model biological systems. We concentrate on epidemiological models and compare and contrast several implementations of the simulation system on various parallel architectures. One of the most important modeling results is the simulation trajectory. We describe the algorithms needed for measuring the simulation trajectory and show their affinity to some classical image processing algorithms. We describe also visualization and interactive simulation tools which we developed to assist users in running and analyzing the simulation.

Ecologists have long recognized that the spatial context of ecological interactions is fundamentally important to understanding population dynamics, community stability, and biodiversity [23, 25]. To simulate the spatial and temporal dynamics of a multi-species ecosystem, the habitat is mapped onto a GCA with each cell's state indicating the presence or absence of species involved in a simulation [44]. A probabilistic model can describe a cell's state transitions as functions of the states of cells within its stencil. The size of the stencil and the location of the affected cell within it are based on the characteristics of the species and the habitat. The implemented model allows diverse analyses [11, 31, 32]. We can examine both direct transmission and the ecologically significant vector-borne disease. The software is parameterized by the modeled species' properties for ease of experimentation. It has been used to investigate the relatively unexplored issue of how systematically varying varying the stencil size and shape impacts outcomes of epidemics [18] and competition [11]. The simulation's results include the number of cells in each state at the end of simulation, the distribution of the species in the habitat, as well as size, frequency and fractal dimensions of species' spatial clusters.

The model presented in [44] is highly data parallel and its implementation requires regular communication patterns, hence it is suitable for many architectures. This model has been implemented on a MasPar MP-1 Single Instruction Many Data (SIMD) machine, an IBM SP2 distributed memory Multiple Instruction Multiple Data (MIMD) computer, and on a network of workstations (NOW). The PEs on the MasPar MP-1 are arranged in a two-dimensional, eight-nearest neighbor, toroidally-wrapped mesh, connected to a master processor, the DPU. The SP2's processors are interconnected through a multistage switch. The NOW consists of Sun SPARCstation 5 and UltraSPARC 2 workstations linked with $10\frac{Mb}{sec.}$ Ethernet using TCP/IP.

There has been a substantial amount of work in the field of parallel CA, with work done in both generalized tools and tools dedicated to particular applications. Lubachevsky [28] developed an asynchronous CA on a SIMD mesh (MasPar MP-1) suited for a subclass of CA applications (such as some Ising models) where the scheduling of state changes does not depend on the stencil. Margolus developed CAM-8 [34], specialized parallel hardware to support CA applications. Di Grigorio et al. implemented CAMEL [16], which executes models expressed in the CARPET programming language on a mesh of transputers. Our simulation tool implements Szymanski and Caraco's four species GCA [44] for ecological and epidemiological modeling on multiple general purpose parallel architectures. It should

neighbors to the *complementary cell* at location $(N-i, N-j)$

be noted that the Szymanski-Caraco model, like many CA models, has state changes that are dependent on stencil content, rendering Lubachevsky's approach unsuitable for this application.

The model used in simulation is discussed in § 2. The implementation of the model, including a brief description of algorithms used, the implementations' performance, and visualization tools are discussed in § 3. The ecological results of some simulations are reviewed in § 4. Finally, conclusions and future directions for this research are given in § 5.

2. GCA and Its Application. Consider a d-dimensional space occupied by discrete entities. We model finite regions of this space on a discrete lattice, Ω, of dimension d with N cells (discrete points). At any time t, each point (cell) is a state drawn from a finite (and usually small) set S. In Ω the distance between cells is measured via a distance metric, L_k, where k specifies the norm used. The presented applications assume that the lattice is rectangular. Let m_i denote the length of the ith dimension (using norm L_k). In our application [32, 44], the space is two-dimensional ($d = 2$) and the distance is measured by infinity norm, i.e. $k = \infty$. In this case, the modeled space can be denoted $\Omega = \prod_{n=1}^{d}\{j|1 \leq j \leq m_n\}$. Each cell, $x \in \Omega$, is then uniquely identified by its integer coordinates: $x = [c_1, \dots, c_d]$ and has a state $s(x, t_i) \in S$ at time $t_i \in T$, where T is a finite time series $T = \{t_1, \dots, t_{stop}\}$. The *configuration* at time t of Ω is the global state $C_t = \bigcup_{x \in \Omega} s(x, t)$. Each cell $x \in \Omega$ has a stencil surrounding it, denoted $\delta_x \subset \Omega - \{x\}$, of cells that can influence state transitions at x. In GCA, δ_x may include elements which are not the nearest neighbors of x. In this paper we consider GCA for which all stencils are equal in size and in their placement around their generating cells. The stencil size is denoted by δ. The biological results of our research indicate that the stencil size fundamentally influences the qualitative and quantitative behavior of CA and the environment that it models [11, 18].

As time advances from t_i to t_{i+1}, the state of each cell x is selected according to the state transition probability function. We assume that this function is independent of the simulation time, so it could be defined as $p : S \times S^{\delta} \times S \rightarrow [0, 1]$, such that $(\forall s_0, s_1 \dots s_\delta \in S : \sum_{s_{new} \in S} p(s_0, \dots, s_\delta, s_{new}) = 1)$. A GCA, then, can be formally defined as the quadruple (Ω, S, δ, p).

2.1. A Four Species Model. Most epidemic models assume that a pathogen is transmitted when an infective host contacts a susceptible host. Recently, however, greater attention has been directed to vector-borne diseases where individuals of a parasitic species sequentially exploit many host individuals, and can transport the pathogen from an infected to an uninfected host. The direct effect of the parasite on the host population is sometimes small, but the indirect effect (via the pathogen) is often severe.

In the most general form the implemented model can simulate a four-species ecosystem composed of two competing hosts, a parasite feeding on both hosts, and a pathogen that employs the parasite as a vector between host individuals [44]. We assume that a vector-borne pathogen can infect individuals of two host species. The host populations compete for space and once an individual of one host species occupies a cell, its mortality (freeing the cell) is independent of other hosts.

A single parasitic species can occupy a cell only if an individual of either host population already occurs at that cell; the parasite's range cannot exceed its host's range. If the parasite exploits both a host individual that is infected with the pathogen and a nearby uninfected host, the parasite may carry the pathogen from the former to the latter host individual. We allow the parasite to transmit the pathogen both within and between host species. The parasite generally will reduce a host individual's survival and reproduction to a lesser extent than will the pathogen. The parasite may prefer to exploit one of the host species. Hence, the model addresses the question of how behavioral selectivity influences the dynamics of an epidemic and so governs a spatial pattern in an interactive biotic community. Assuming that there is one host species means that each cell can be in one of five possible states, $S = \{1, 2, 3, 4, 5\}$, coding of which is shown in Figure 2.1(a).

2.2. Simulating Epidemics with the Four Species Model. A variety of epidemics can be expressed with the model presented in § 2, including simple epidemics discussed in § 2.2.1, vector-borne epidemics presented in § 2.2.2 and general epidemics described in § 2.2.3.

2.2.1. Modeling Simple Epidemics with the Four Species Model. The classic simple epidemic [4] assumes that the individual is either susceptible or infective. Since the simple epidemic excludes recovery, pathogen loss is eliminated. By replacing parasitism of adjacent hosts by contact between individuals, the model described above can provide a stochastic, spatially explicit representation of the simple epidemic [3]. Parameters governing the gain and loss of the parasite allow us to generalize the notion of "contact" between host individuals. The host grid might represent plants, animals with fixed territories, stable home ranges [37], or households in human populations. For this application, the state space is $S = \{1, 2, 3\}$ and its coding is a subset of the coding shown in Figure 2.1(a). The relative frequency of state 1 (empty cells) remains constant in this application according to the simple epidemic assumption that the host population is constant. A site empty at time $t = 0$ remains so and a cell with a host never becomes empty. The only possible transition in this simple model is from state 2 to state 3.

2.2.2. Modeling Vector-Borne Epidemics with the Four Species Model. The model described in § 2 was also a basis for simulation of a vector-borne disease in which the spread of the pathogen from one individual to another involves a *vector*. A host must be exposed to a parasite residing on a "nearby" infected host to acquire the pathogen. Following the assumptions of the simple epidemic, there is neither host nor pathogen mortality. Hence, the initial density and spatial arrangement of hosts are likely to govern the rate of epidemic progress.

2.2.3. Modeling General Epidemics with the Four Species Model. For more general epidemic modeling, it is sometimes necessary to have hosts experience mortality and reproduction. A host's mortality is assumed to be independent of its neighborhood, and have the single step probability of $\mu_i, i \in \{2, 3, 4, 5\}$ which is influenced by the presence or absence of infestation and infection (see Figure 2.1). ρ is the probability (per time interval) that an open cell (in state 1) receives an offspring from an occupied cell within the open cell's stencil. We assume that propagation is independent of the presence or absence of the parasite[3]. Occupied cells reproduce independently of each other.

The environment is represented by a CA with N cells,

with a transition probability function, p. For brevity, we denote by $p(j, k)$ the transition probability from state j to state k which is a function of the states of the cells in the corresponding stencil. Let $\sigma_x(U)$, where $U \subset S$, represent the number of cells in δ_x that are in one of the states in U. Hosts in state j die with probability μ_j. Mortality of a parasite represents recovery from infestation. We assume that it takes place with probability μ_d so the

[3]The general model presented in [44] does consider effects on infestation and infection on reproduction.

state	host	parasite	pathogen
1	absent	absent	absent
2	present	absent	absent
3	present	present	absent
4	present	absent	present
5	present	present	present

(a) State to Species Mapping

Species	Set of states
Host	$\{2,3,4,5\}$
Parasite	$\{3,5\}$
Pathogen	$\{4,5\}$

(b) Species to State Mapping

FIG. 2.1. *State numbering conventions*

	$k=1$	$k=2$	$k=3$	$k=4$	$k=5$
$j=1$	$\overline{\rho}^{\sigma(\{2,3,4,5\})}$	$\overline{p}(1,1)$	0	0	0
$j=2$	μ_2	$\overline{\mu_2}(\overline{\alpha}^{\sigma(\{3,5\})})$	$\overline{p}(2,2)$	0	0
$j=3$	μ_3	$\overline{\mu_3}\mu_d$	$(\overline{\mu_3})(\overline{\mu_d})(\overline{\beta}^{\sigma(\{5\})})$	0	0
$j=4$	μ_4	0	$\overline{p}(4,4)$	$\overline{\mu_4}(\overline{\alpha}^{\sigma(\{3,5\})})$	0
$j=5$	μ_5	0	0	$\overline{\mu_5}\mu_d$	$\overline{p}(5,4)$

TABLE 2.1
State transition probabilities, $p(j,k)$, used in epidemics modeling; for brevity, $\overline{v}$, for $v \in \{p,\mu,\alpha\}$ denotes complementary value $1-v$.

average life time of the parasite is $1/\mu_d$. We also assume that a parasite has the probability α of infesting the neighboring hosts. β denotes the probability of the pathogen infecting the host infested by a parasite carrying the pathogen. The state transition probabilities, $p(j,k)$, are given in Table 2.1. Note that death probabilities are stencil independent, while reproduction, infection and infestation probabilities are dependent on the states of stencil's cells.

3. The Model's Design and Implementation. Performance and utility were our primary design goals. An efficient simulation engine is critical for the system's performance. § 3.1 briefly introduces simultaneous reduction, which is used for computing state transition probabilities efficiently. The simulation trajectory measures, needed for interpreting the simulation's results, motivated the design of interesting parallel algorithms. *Fractal dimension*, which is a measure of spatial complexity, is discussed in § 3.2. The parallel computation of wave front propagation velocity is described in § 3.3. Placement of data and operations executed on a distributed-memory machine can significantly impact the total computation time. Data distribution of the MasPar MP-1 implementation is described in § 3.4. Performance tuning of the MasPar MP-1 implementation is discussed in § 3.5. Data distribution issues for coarse grained distributed memory MIMD (IBM SP2 and NOW) implementations are described in § 3.6. The programming language's impact on portability and performance tuning of the MIMD implementation is discussed in § 3.7. Performance results of the various simulation engines are compared and contrasted in § 3.8. Data visualization and interactive simulation tools which were developed to facilitate understanding of the simulation results, are discussed in § 3.9.

3.1. Simultaneous Reduction. Each cell's state transition probability can be expressed as a function of its current state, and the states of cells in the corresponding stencil,

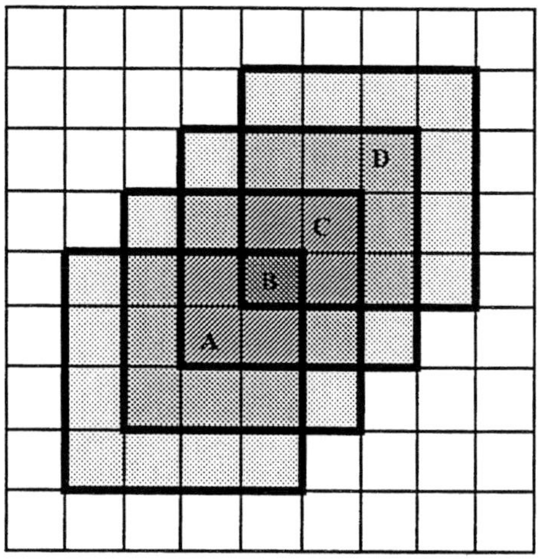

FIG. 3.1. *Overlapping stencils for cells A, B, C, D*

as in § 2. Let n_1 and n_2 stand for the lengths of the sides of the stencil, p_1 and p_2 be the offsets (measured from the lower left corner of the stencil) of the affected cell, and $s_{i,j}$ be the current state of the cell (i, j). Then, the state transition probability of cell (m, q) to a new state s' is defined as:

$$\text{Prob}[s_{m,q} \rightarrow s'] = \sum_{i=m-p_1}^{m+n_1-p_1} \sum_{j=q-p_2}^{q+n_2-p_2} f(s_{m,q}, s_{i,j}) \tag{3.1}$$

This operation is similar to what the image processing community refers to as a *convolution*. Image filtering transforms a discrete input *image* (represented as a two dimensional array of pixels) into an output image by applying a convolution operation at each pixel. This operation often computes a weighted average of the neighborhood about each input pixel [22, 24].

For each cell at every time step of the simulation, the right hand side of equation (3.1) is evaluated. This computation takes a significant portion of the total execution time of the simulation. Equation (3.1) is an example of a reduction computed simultaneously over many overlapping contiguous sections of an array, as shown in Figure 3.1.

Reduction applies associative binary operators across a list of elements [13, 27]. Let A be an N element array, i.e. $A[1..N]$, and $\oplus$ be an associative binary operator. The reduction of A produces a single result defined as follows:

$$r = \mathit{reduce}(A, 1, N, \oplus) = \oplus_{i=1}^{N} A[i] = A[1] \oplus A[2] \oplus A[3] \oplus \cdots \oplus A[N] \tag{3.2}$$

Traditional parallel algorithms for solving reduction focused on reducing either the entire array or disjoint sections of the array using variations of the well known parallel prefix algorithm [13, 27].

Simultaneous reduction applies reduction operators to uniformly sized overlapping contiguous array subsections called *stencils*. The *simultaneous reduction* of $\oplus$ on array $A[1..N]$, with stencil size, s, and result position $p, 1 \leq p \leq s$ is denoted $SPR(A, p, w, \oplus) = spr_1, spr_2,$

$\ldots, spr_N$ where $\forall i 1 \leq i \leq N$ and it produces a vector of result, each of which is defined as:

$$
\begin{aligned}
spr_i &= reduce(A, \max(1, i-p), \min(N, i+s-p), \oplus) \\
&= \oplus_{j=\max(1,i-p)}^{\min(N,i+s-p)} A[j]
\end{aligned} \tag{3.3}
$$

Parallel computation of $SPR(A, p, s, \oplus)$ requires concurrently performing many reduction operations on overlapping array sections to obtain each of the spr_i in (3.3), which is not supported by traditional parallel prefix algorithms for arbitrary p and s combinations. The challenge is to maximize the reuse of partial results of many reductions executed simultaneously.

Functions using stencils to define their inputs are ubiquitous in scientific computations, motivating extensive work on their optimization. Many approaches exploit hardware dependent instructions to effectively compute functions over stencils consisting of nearest neighbors. Bromley et al. described an experimental tool for generating functions of stencils called a *convolution compiler*[4] which generates data parallel codes at compile time for the TMC CM-2 using register allocation, loop unrolling optimizations and minimized data motion (both within and between nodes). Brickner et al. [6, 7] extended that work to develop production level stencil compilers based these techniques for the TMC CM-2 and CM-5. Brickner [6, 7] presents examples using nearest neighbor stencils, however the methods described could be extended to compute functions of larger stencils. The functions that could be compiled by these methods are more general than a simultaneous reduction because the function's use of a particular input value may depend on its relative position within the stencil (i.e. neighboring stencils may use the same value in different ways). As a result, the intermediate values generated during the function evaluation are also position dependent, thereby limiting the efficiency of the stencil computation in a way that is not inherent in simultaneous parallel reduction. It should be noted that many stencil functions used in practice are either simultaneous reductions or can be decomposed into a series of simultaneous reductions yielding more efficient computation.

Bordawekar et al. [5] describe compiler techniques for optimizing arbitrary stencil based functions in distributed computations where an individual processor's problem size could exceed the available memory (so that swapping to secondary storage is required). In [43], we presented algorithms for the simultaneous reduction problem that exploit the associativity and commutativity of binary operators used in reduction to yield optimal solutions for different architectures. As an example, for a linear array of processors, the following *prefix-suffix* algorithm can be used.

For this algorithm, the entire range N of array A is divided into N/n disjoint sections, each of size n. The algorithm consists of two stages:

1. executing the parallel prefix algorithm on disjoint sections of the input array A to obtain the result for each disjoin section in one location, and partial results for overlapping sections in the others, and
2. applying operator $\oplus$ to partial results obtained in the previous step.

The algorithm uses two auxiliary arrays, a prefix array, $P[1..N]$, and a suffix array, $S[1..N]$, defined as follows: for the k-th disjoint section of array A extending from $kn - n + 1$ to kn, the arrays P, S are:

$$(\forall\ kn - n < i < kn) P[i] = \oplus_{j=kn-n+1}^{i} A[j] \text{and} S[i] = \oplus_{j=i}^{kn} A[j] \tag{3.4}$$

[4]The convolution compiler team at TMC won the Gordon Bell Award in 1990.

Once the arrays P and S are known, the solution can be evaluated at the left end[5] of the section as follows:

$$res[i] = \begin{cases} S[i] & \text{if } i = kn - n + 1, \\ S[i] \oplus P[i + n - 1] & \text{otherwise.} \end{cases}$$

The above computation is inexpensive and requires a single communication *shift* for the distance $n - 1$ and a single application of the operator $\oplus$. The cost of evaluating arrays P and S dominates the complexity of this algorithm.

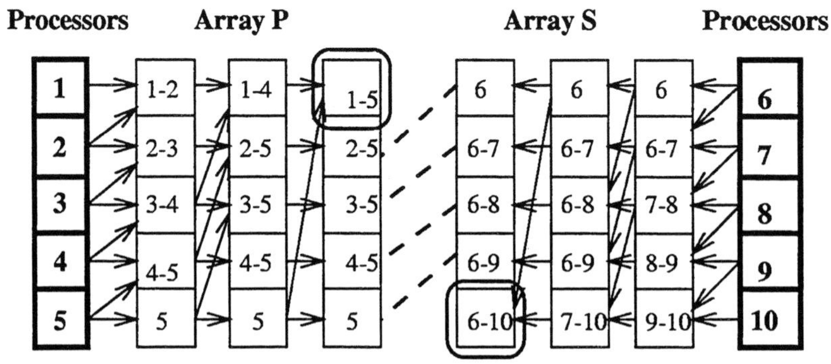

FIG. 3.2. *Prefix-Suffix Algorithm for $n = 5$.*

A SIMD mesh architecture (such as the MasPar MP-1) is sensitive to the stencil's size, $\delta = n_x n_y$, where n_x is the stencil's horizontal length, and n_y is its vertical length. The optimal SIMD mesh algorithm uses $(n_x - 1) + (n_y - 1)$ communication distance, with no more than $2(\log n_x + \log n_y)$ communication latencies, memory and operations cost.

The optimal coarse grained distributed memory MIMD algorithm requires block partitioning as described in § 3.6 and applies a sequential algorithm locally to each block. Assuming that the stencil is smaller than the block size, there are $O(1)$ communication latencies and the communication volume per each processor is $O(\delta\sqrt{\frac{N}{P}})$, where N is the problem size (number of cells in Ω) and P is the number of processors. The operation and memory cost is $O(\frac{N}{P})$. The efficiency of the algorithms was measured on the MasPar MP-1 and reported in [29], and (indirectly as part of the run time) on both the IBM SP2 as reported in § 3.8.2 and a network of workstations (see § 3.8.3).

3.2. Fractal Dimension Computation. The complexity of the spatial patterns arising in the habitat may influence both community dynamics and its control, such as disease control which difficulty increases with the growth of spatial complexity. *Fractal dimension* measures spatial complexity because larger fractal dimension correspond to a more complex spatial patterns. Two-dimensional habitats have fractal dimensions in the interval $[1, 2]$, where 1 corresponds to a line and 2 corresponds to a plane.

We adopted Sugihara's technique for computing fractal dimension of images composed of a lattice of *pixels* (which assume a value of either 0- set off, or 1 set on) in [26, 42]. Computing the fractal dimension involves creating an image from the model's configuration C_t and then processing it.

[5] Right-end placement of the result can be achieved by switching P and S in their roles, i.e., by using the expression $P[i] \oplus S[i - n + 1]$. Hence, the placement of the result at the given offset can always be achieved by a single shift for the distance of at most $n/2$.

In the lattice of the model presented in § 2, cells have values assigned from a set of states S usually of higher cardinality than 2. However, we can distinguish a subset $U \subset S$ of local states that are of interest to the user (e.g., testing for the the presence of a pathogen implies $U = \{4, 5\}$). Fractal dimension computation requires measuring clustering of cells in a state which belongs to U. We will call such cells set on, and the cells which have a state in $S - U$ will be called set off. Hence, a pair (C_t, U) defines an image. The set of all cells set on at time t will be denoted $SetOn(C_t, U) = \{x | s_{x,t} \in U\}$. Two cells in $SetOn(C_t, U)$ are *connected* if they are adjacent, or if they can reach each other by a path through Ω such that all cells on the path are in $SetOn(C_t, U)$. The *image component* (also called a *cluster*) containing $x \in SetOn(C_t, U)$ is the set of cells connected to x in $SetOn(C_t, U)$. The *image component label* of cell $x \in SetOn(C_t, U)$ uniquely identifies which image component x is participating in. The well known *image component labeling problem* [27] consists of computing the image component label for each cell in $SetOn(C_t, U)$. A cell in $SetOn(C_t, U)$ is said to be on the *perimeter* if it is adjacent to some cell not in $SetOn(C_t, U)$. The set of all perimeter cells will be denoted $OnPerimeter(C_t, U)$.

Fractal dimension is the regression of the logarithm of image component perimeter on the logarithm of image component area. Suppose that (C_t, U) has n image components, numbered $1 \le i \le n$. Let c_i denote set of cells in the ith image component, the *area* of c_i be $a_i = |c_i|$ and perimeter of c_i be $perimeter_i = |c_i \cap OnPerimeter(C_t, U)|$. Let $x_i = \ln a_i$ and $y_i = \ln perimeter_i$, with means $\overline{x} = \sum_{i=1}^{n} x_i/n$ and $\overline{y} = \sum_{i=1}^{n} y_i/n$. Fractal dimension, ϕ, can be expressed as:

$$\phi = 2\frac{\sum_{i=1}^{n}(x_i y_i) - n\overline{x}\overline{y}}{\sum_{i=1}^{n} x_i^2 - n\overline{x}^2}.$$

On a SIMD mesh machine, such as MasPar MP-1, computing the image component labels was done in $O(\sqrt{N})$ time using Cypher's algorithm [15]. Then, for each cell a record is created containing the image component, the processor id, and a flag indicating whether the cell is on the perimeter or not. Sorting such records in ascending order using the image component label as the primary key and the processor id as the secondary key on a SIMD mesh takes $O(\sqrt{N})$ messages and operations. As a result, all the members of c_i are placed in contiguous locations in a one dimensional array, so both a_i and $perimeter_i$ can be computed by a segmented scan operator using $O(\sqrt{N})$ messages. The fractal dimension is obtained using reduction operators with a complexity of $O(\sqrt{N})$ in number of operations and messages which is also the overall complexity of the entire computation (see [31] for more details).

Implementation on a coarse grained MIMD architecture is nontrivial. We are adopting Bader and JáJá's image component labeling algorithm [2] and are extending it to compute the area and perimeter of each image component.

3.3. Discrete Voronoi Diagram and Velocity Computation . The well known Voronoi diagram problem was first posed almost ninety years ago by G. Voronoi [45], and after decades of study is still an open area of research. Consider the d-dimensioned space $\mathcal{S}$ of elements (typically called points) using the L_k distance metric and let $\mathcal{P}$ be a distinct finite nonempty subset of $\mathcal{S}$. The *Voronoi diagram* of $\mathcal{S}$ is a partitioning on $\mathcal{S}$ induced by $\mathcal{P}$. For points $a, b \in \mathcal{S}$ the distance between a, b is denoted $\| a - b \|$. Each point $p \in \mathcal{P}$ is assigned its *Voronoi partition*, $VP(p)$ which contains all points of $\mathcal{S}$ for which p is the nearest point in $\mathcal{P}$. Let $d_{\mathcal{P}}(q)$ denote the distance from $q \in \mathcal{S}$ to the nearest point in $\mathcal{P}$, i.e.,

$d_{\mathcal{P}}(q) = \min_{p \in \mathcal{P}} \| p - q \|$. Given a point, $p, p \in \mathcal{P}$, the Voronoi partition about p is:

$$VP(p) = \{q \in \mathcal{S} | \| p - q \| = d_{\mathcal{P}}(q)\} \tag{3.5}$$

When S is a discrete rectangular space with N cells, it corresponds to the lattice Ω described in § 2, with $\mathcal{P}$ being a set of cells in the lattice. Adamatzky [1] defines the *discrete Voronoi diagram* (DVD) as a Voronoi diagram in discrete space and presents solutions for the L_1 and L_∞ norms on fine grained SIMD mesh architectures using a modified breadth first search (BFS). Maniatty and Szymanski present improvements to Adamatzky's algorithms in [33]. The optimal sequential solution for computing DVDs for the L_1 and L_∞ metrics uses a BFS forest with roots at $\mathcal{P}$ and runs in $O(N)$ time.

Informally, *wave front propagation velocity* (called velocity for short) is a measure of the rate at which a phenomena emanates out from a set of initial sources. Use of velocity measurements in population biology began with Fisher's [20] model for the spatial advance of an advantageous gene, and with Skellam's [40] study of the ecological spread of invading species. Recent biological applications include measuring the velocity of epidemics (e.g. rabies in foxes by Murray, et al. [37]), and developing analytical solutions for equations defining such velocities in population dynamics [36]). This fundamental spatio-temporal measurement might have image processing applications, particularly for measuring propagation in digitized time series images.

Let $U \subset S$ be a subset of states. Informally, states in U are meant to identify cells that are a part of pattern of interest (such as the pattern of species presence in epidemiology). Let $\omega_U(t) \subseteq \Omega$ denote the set of cells (discrete points) such that at time t, $\omega_U(t) = \{x | s_{x,t} \in U\}$. Let $v_U(t)$ denote the velocity of the phenomena indicated by U at time t. Informally, velocity measures the maximum observed displacement divided by the time. More formally, velocity is defined as:

$$v_U(t) = \begin{cases} \max_{x \in \omega_U(t)} \left(\frac{d_{\omega_U(0)}(x)}{t} \right) & \text{if } \omega_U(t) \neq \emptyset \wedge t > 0, \\ 0 & \text{otherwise.} \end{cases} \tag{3.6}$$

Velocity can computed using the following algorithm: (i) at $t = 0$, compute the DVD induced by $\omega_U(0)$, labeling each cell with its nearest neighbor in U, (ii) at time t, for each cell $x \in \omega_U(t)$ compute $d_{\omega_U(0)}(x)$, and (iii) compute $\max_{x \in \omega_U(t)} d_{\omega_U(0)}(x)$.

For this section we will concentrate on L_∞ solutions in two dimensional lattices, these techniques can be used for the L_1 norm and can be extended to higher dimension. For a SIMD Mesh architecture (i.e. MasPar MP-1), we adopted a method similar to Adamatzky's DVD algorithm [1, 33], which uses synchronous BFS to compute $d_{\omega_U(0)}(x)$. This algorithm's complexity is $O(\sqrt{N})$ in number of operations and parallel messages, as well as in communication distance. Computing $v_U(t)$ given $d_{\omega_U(0)}$ requires sending messages $O(\sqrt{N})$ distance and involves $O(\log N)$ operations and parallel message passing operations (which is optimal for this architecture).

The same three-step algorithm can be used for block partitioned lattices on coarse grained MIMD architectures (e.g. IBM SP2 and NOW), however, step (i) (solving for $d_{\omega_U(0)}(x)$) via direct application of the synchronized BFS DVD algorithms described in [1, 33]) requires $O(\sqrt{N})$ iterations, each performing $O(N/P)$ operations on P processors, therefore, it is not work optimal. Below, we sketch a work optimal MIMD algorithm which can

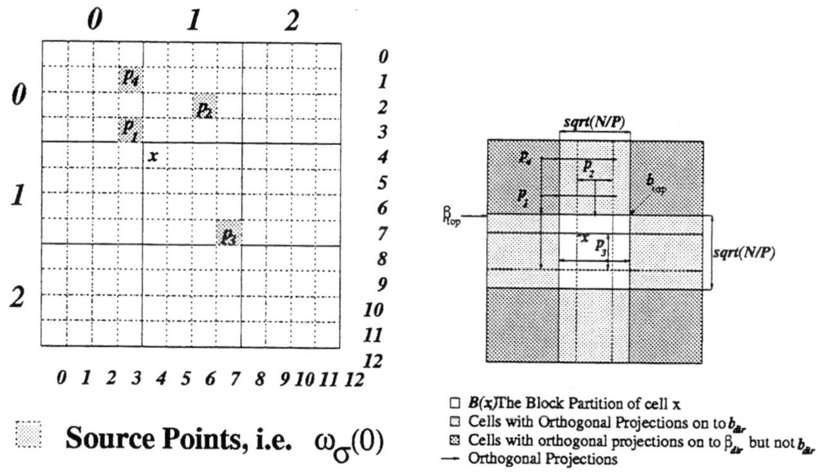

(a) $D_U(x) = \{p_1\}$ (b) Orthogonal Projections

FIG. 3.3. *A coarse grained DVD example using block partitioning with* $\omega_U(0) = \{p_1, p_2, p_3, p_4\}$ *and* p_1 *closest to* x*, as seen in (a). Note that* p_1 *does not orthogonally project onto* b_{dir}*, hence,* β_{dir} *is needed, as per (b).*

be used for either the L_1 and L_∞ distance metrics. In the interest of brevity, only the L_∞ case is discussed below.

The algorithm first computes the DVD induced by $\omega_U(0)$. Consider a cell $x \notin \omega_U(0)$ resident on processor P_x. Let $y \in \omega_U(0)$ be the nearest neighbor to x, and let y reside on processor P_y. Then either (i) $P_x = P_y$ and a sequential BFS application on P_x will correctly compute $d_{\omega_U(0)}(x)$ or (ii) $P_x \neq P_y$ and computing $d_{\omega_U(0)}(x)$ requires remote information from P_y. Let $B(x)$ be the block partition to which x belongs (i.e. the set of cells resident on processor P_x) and $D_U(x)$ denote the set of cells in $\omega_U(0)$ closest to x, i.e. $(\forall y \in D_U(x) :\| x - y \|= d_{\omega_U(0)}(x))$. DVD (and velocity) computation requires handling the case that $D_U(x) - B(x) \neq \emptyset$ (see Figure 3.3). Let $\hat{D}_U(x)$ be the set of cells closest to a partition boundary, $b_{dir}(x)$, where $dir \in \{left, right, top, bottom\}$ (all boundaries can be treated similarly due to symmetry). It can be shown (using the triangle inequality) that $\hat{D}_U(x) \supseteq D_U(x) - B(x)$, and since the number of cells on the boundary is limited, $|\hat{D}_U(x)| \in O(\sqrt{N/P})$. The algorithm computes $\hat{D}_U(x)$ as follows (see Figure 3.3):

1. For each partition boundary, b_{dir} create a $d-1$ lattice subspace $\beta_{dir} \supseteq b_{dir}$, which projects the endpoints of b_{dir} to the partition boundaries.
2. Compute the set of cells generating the minimal orthogonal projections on each β_{dir} via cumulative min or max reductions of the lattice coordinates of the cell. This is necessary because the nearest cell in $\omega_U(0)$ to a cell in b_{dir} might not orthogonally project onto b_{dir}. This requires $O(N/P + \sqrt{N})$ operations (where P is the number of processors) and $O(\log P)$ data communication steps per partition boundary and message size of $O(\sqrt{N})$.
3. Compute the set of cells nearest to each point on b_{dir} boundary using a modified BFS, introducing cells at the "right" time, i.e. according to their distance from β_{dir}. This in turn can be done by sorting the set of cells inducing minimal orthogonal

projections on β_{dir} in $O(\sqrt{N})$ operations via radix sort since, for L_1 and L_∞ norms, the distance from the mesh boundary is $O(\sqrt{N})$ and the distances are integral.

An application of the process used in Step 3 at higher dimension permits correct local computation of the DVD given the boundary information obtained. The modified BFS is done in $O(N/P)$ steps, however the boundary points need to be sorted by distance to their nearest point in the distinguished set to ensure correct processing (again using radix sort in $O(\sqrt{N/P})$ operations), giving a complexity of $O(N/P + \sqrt{N/P})$ operations per processor. The total asymptotic complexity of computing the DVD is therefore $O(N/P + \sqrt{N})$ operations, with $O(\log P)$ message passing operations with message size $O(\sqrt{N})$. Computing the local $d_{\omega_U(0)}(x)$ requires $O(N/P)$ operations and each processor can store those values in $O(N/P)$ storage. The reduction step across all the cells takes $O(N/P + \log P)$ operations, with $O(\log P)$ message passing steps with message size $O(1)$. The asymptotic complexity of computing $v_U(t)$ is therefore $O(N/P + \sqrt{N/P})$ in number of operations, $O(\log P)$ in number of messages, each message of $O(\sqrt{N})$ size. This means that the algorithm is work optimal when $P \ll \sqrt{N}$, an inequality that often hold for coarse grained MIMD systems. To the authors' knowledge the solution presented here is the only work optimal algorithm published to date.

3.4. SIMD (MasPar MP-1) Implementation's Data Distribution. The model was implemented on a MasPar MP-1 SIMD parallel computer, using MasPar's parallelized dialect of C, MPL. The array of processing elements (PEs) of the MasPar is organized in a two-dimensional grid with a master processor, the *data processing unit* (DPU). The DPU is connected to a DECstation 5000 workstation, which is called the *front end*. Each processing element has eight nearest neighbors. Each processing element can communicate with its neighbors directly and in parallel with others using *xnet* operations. There is also a global router which allows communication between any two arbitrary PEs at a much higher communication cost than xnet operations.

The architecture matches the grid-partitioned environment being simulated. Ecological cells map naturally onto the PEs. Local state changes at each cell are programmed as operations on local variables, whereas the global simulation trajectory measures are stored in the front-end processor. Careful algorithm design minimized the amount of data communicated and the number of communication steps. Furthermore, each communication step was designed to have consistent direction along the xnet and minimal distance in our algorithms [31, 43], eliminating contention for communication links and promoting efficient use of the MasPar's interconnection network. The tight synchronization of SIMD architecture execution facilitates the update of the global state at each time step but requires careful design of algorithms to maintain high utilization of PEs.

3.5. Performance Tuning the MasPar MP-1 Implementation. Performance tuning on the MasPar MP-1 was done using the MPPE programming tool to get profiling measurements. The simultaneous reduction operator [43] discussed in § 3.1 can be optimized if the stencil is known at compile time. We designed software to generate unrolled loops and sequences of xnet communication operations during simultaneous parallel reduction. The efficiency is highly dependent on the stencil area (since the number of operations required is nonlinear with regard to stencil area), giving a speedup of about 1.5 for many stencil sizes over run time iterative algorithms for stencil reduction. Initial implementations utilized the DPU to perform all sequential operations, which greatly reduced simulation throughput (especially for input and output operations). By shifting input, output, and sequential tasks to the much faster DECstation front end we were able to get a speed up by a factor of roughly

2. Additional speedups were obtained by code tuning of the parallel sections of the code, in particular by utilizing MasPar MP-1's much faster additions for 8 bit and 16 bit in place of standard 32 bit integers. By selecting the smallest size of integers suitable for counting the number of cells in each state (which has an upper bound of δ), we were able to obtain another speedup of a factor of 1.5 to 2, giving us a total speedup of a factor of 5.

3.6. MIMD Implementation's Data Distribution. This section describes data distribution issues in a coarse grained distributed memory MIMD implementation. This implementation was ported to both the IBM SP2 and a NOW.

The IBM 9076 SP2 is a MIMD parallel supercomputer. Each processing element in the SP2 is an IBM RS/6000 with 64 kilobytes of data cache, 128 megabytes of local memory, and an interface into the high-speed inter-processor switch. The high-speed switch topology is a bidirectional multistage interconnection network. The IBM AIX Parallel Environment on the SP2 provides a single-program-multiple-data (SPMD) programming environment. Several versions were written; preliminary ones were written in the C programming language, whereas the later versions use C++ and utilize the MPI [35] message passing library for communication. When executed, parallel programs are automatically distributed and loaded onto the requested number of processors.

The network of workstations in the Computer Science Department of Rensselaer is quite heterogeneous. We chose a (relatively) homogeneous subset of machines, using seven SPARCstation 5s and two UltraSPARC 2s, preferring the (somewhat slower) SPARCstation 5's for smaller problem sizes in an attempt to keep timings uniform. The nodes all ran Sun's Solaris 2.5 and were networked via a Ethernet using TCP/IP. The MPI chameleon/p4 version was used for message passing, so the software was quite similar to the IBM SP2 version.

The MIMD implementation of the model allocates many cells per processor, to efficiently utilize the few powerful processors available. We use a *a block* decomposition, in which a problem size of $N = n_1 \times n_2$ is contiguously partitioned over P processors with each partition containing $\frac{n_1}{P} \times \frac{n_2}{P}$ elements. Typical problem sizes have $n_1 = n_2 = \sqrt{N}$. The implementation is based on a SPMD approach in which each processor asynchronously executes the same program on different data.

Efficient MIMD programs exploit asynchrony in the underlying problem, since synchronization, especially barrier synchronization, has a large performance penalty. On the surface it would seem that time step driven simulations would have strong synchronization constraints, however the locality of interaction permits us to exploit a certain amount of asynchrony. The MIMD implementation has no barrier synchronization calls. At every time step a processor must wait for all of the inputs from its neighbors, before advancing to the next time step. Thus if one processor were fast, it could get a time step ahead of its neighbor, and then it would have to block on receipt of boundary data. The maximum difference (measured in the time step) between any two processors during the simulation is equal to the diameter of the mesh. Whenever the global simulation trajectory is measured, global synchrony is enforced to support the reduction of the data local to each processor across all processors, thereby eliminating the need for explicit barrier synchronization.

Further speedups were obtained by interleaving communication and computation by:

- using nonblocking MPI message passing routines which support noncontiguous message buffers, thereby reducing the number of copy operations [35],
- interleaving communication and computation by precomputing the partial results of stencil reductions and simulation trajectory measurements that do not require data from neighboring processors during the communications phase (see Figure 3.4).

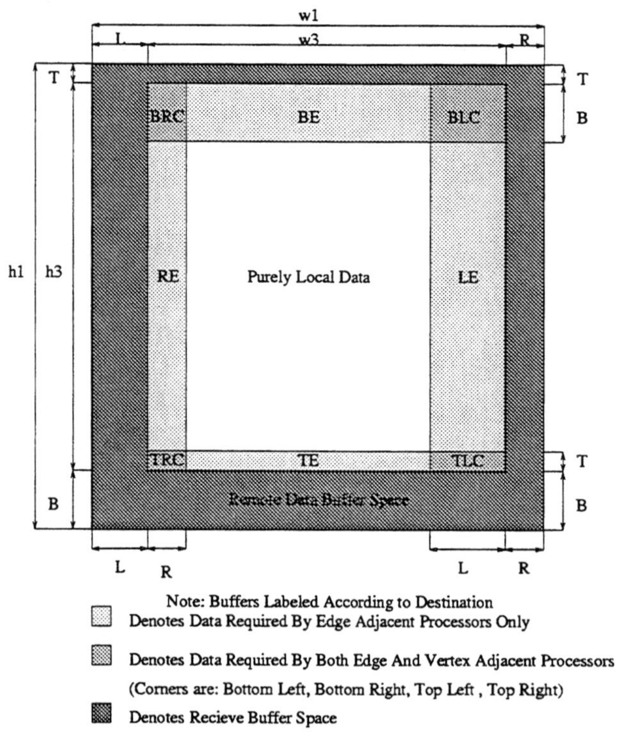

FIG. 3.4. *Stencil size's relation to a partition's buffer allocation*

3.7. MIMD Implementation's Language Issues (IBM SP2 and NOW). We faced several language tool difficulties during the development cycle. Initially C++ and MPI were unavailable on the SP1 which was then our initial target, and we resorted to C and used the MPC message passing protocol. The contiguous buffer required to hold the simulation state was allocated at compile time (for efficient multi dimensional array indexing), its dimensions were computed using preprocessor directives. As a result, when the local problem size or stencil dimensions changed, a recompilation was required. This version was directly ported to MPI. The next phase of development replaced the 2-d arrays storing the simulation state and the 3-d arrays used in stencil reduction with dynamic arrays in C++. Diagnosing errors and performance issues under C++ was challenging, since many development tools did not work well in presence of automated internal naming conventions employed by many C++ compilers (so-called *name space mangling* effect). Early experiences with profilers on the SP2 under MPI were not positive because of name space mangling. In particular, the ability of the SUN collector tool's profiler to decode mangled names was critical in diagnosing a programming error which caused a slow down by a factor of 150 of the C++ version (an inadvertent use of call by value instead of call by reference due to a missing "&" character induced frequent implicit copy constructors for a large array).

3.8. Performance Results of Parallel Simulation. We compare and contrast the computational performance of the SIMD and MIMD implementations. Trajectory measurements were disabled during the performance runs to measure computational performance without impact of I/O subsystem. A summary of the MasPar MP-1 performance is presented in § 3.8.1 and the MIMD IBM SP2 performance is analyzed in 3.8.2.

3.8.1. Performance of the MasPar MP-1 Implementation. Thirty six executions of the model were timed using 32 bit integer and 64 bit floating point arithmetic on the MasPar MP-1 (with 2048 PEs). The simulations differ in both the number of cells in the environment (one PE is allocated to a cell on the MasPar) and the area of influence of each cell (i.e., the size of the stencil). Raw timings of the MasPar MP-1 implementation as a function of both stencil size and number of cells are presented in Figure 3.5. The timings

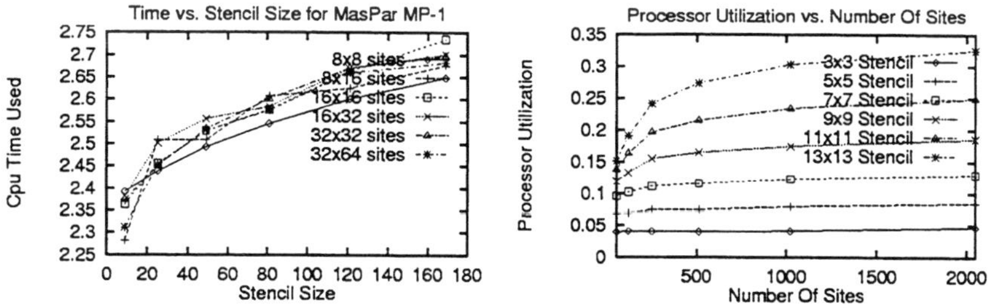

(a) Run Time vs. Stencil Size (b) Processor Utilization

FIG. 3.5. *Performance of the MasPar MP-1 implementation*

indicate that the implementation scales well with respect to the number of processors, but exhibits sensitivity to the stencil size. Let T_{MP-1} be simulation throughput, measured in number of state transition computations per second per processor. It can be determined as follows:

$$(3.7) \qquad T_{MP-1} == \frac{100 \ timesteps \times 2048 \frac{transitions}{timestep}}{2048 \ processors \times 2.25 \ sec.} \approx 44 \frac{transitions}{sec}$$

This value is useful as a standard of comparison of raw speed between different implementations of the simulations.

Utilization of MasPar processors is obtained from MasPar's advertised speed and speed measured at simulation runs. It is plotted as a function of the number of cells and as a function of the stencil size in Figure 3.5. For the largest stencil and the maximal number of cells, simulation sustained a high utilization, for SIMD architecture[6] of 32.6%. Utilization in SIMD architectures is limited by the way conditional flow of control is executed. Processors not taking a branch have to wait for branch completion, when they are reactivated. There is a nine-way branch in computing the state transition probability inherent in the nine-state ecological model. Increased efficiency of computation over larger stencils and environments is the result of sublinear (logarithmic or square root) complexity of several data sampling algorithms in terms of stencil size.

3.8.2. Performance of the IBM SP2 Implementation. Performance measurements were done for various numbers of processors, problem sizes, and stencil sizes. Stencil sizes were selected so that their areas would vary by (roughly) an order of magnitude. All of the performance graphs presented use a block decomposition. We begin with the traditional

[6]Parallel computation on SIMD TMC machine with utilization of 10% won Gordon Bell Prize [17] and with 30% utilization on MasPar the SuParCup93 Award [30].

parallel speedup measure, where the speedup is defined as a ratio of a sequential implementation's run time to a parallel implementation's run time. It is plotted in Figure 3.6. The

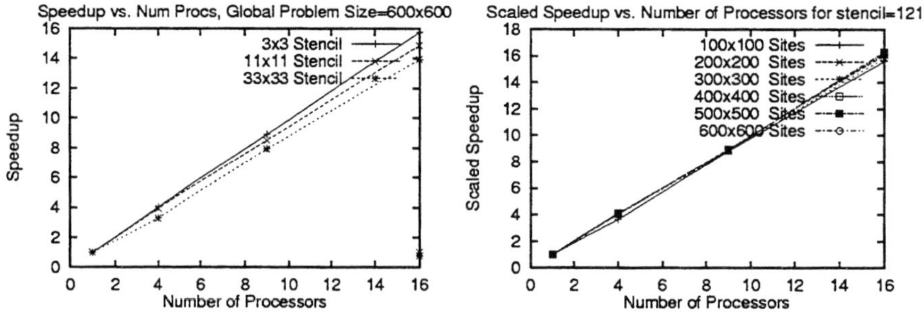

(a) Raw Speedup Vs. P

(b) Scaled Speedup Vs. P

FIG. 3.6. *Speedup on IBM SP2 vs.* P = *number of processors*

effect of scaling the workload over processors (i.e. the problem size is proportional to the number of processors) on run time is shown in Figure 3.7. Scaled workload performance measure [21] scales the problem size (and therefore workload) along with the number of processors. It is shown in Figure 3.6 for the fixed size stencils of $\delta = 121 = 11 \times 11$. The workload increases linearly with the number of processors. The observed speedup is roughly linear with respect to the number of processors, and multi-processor performance improves with the problem size per processor. This improvement results from an increase of the computation to communication ratio caused by faster growth of the computation on each processor than communication volume with the growth of the problem size.

Comparing throughput of architectures can give us insights into their relative performance. Let T_{SP2} be simulation throughput, measured as the number of state transition computations per second per processor, then:

$$T_{SP2} = \frac{100 \ \mathit{timesteps} \times 5.76 \times 10^6 \frac{\mathit{transitions}}{\mathit{timestep}}}{16 \ \mathit{processors} \times 300 \ \mathit{sec.}} = 1.2 \times 10^5 \frac{\mathit{transitions}}{\mathit{sec.}} \tag{3.8}$$

The SP2 speed relative to the MasPar MP-1 is $\frac{T_{SP2}}{T_{MP-1}} = 2700$.

3.8.3. Performance on a Network of Workstations. We employed a benchmarking structure similar to the one used on the IBM SP2, to facilitate comparisons of results. Runs were done for the identically scaled workload sizes as on the IBM SP2 (see § 3.8.2) and for number of workstations $P \in \{1, 4, 9\}$. Getting accurate timings on NOW was non-trivial since the machines are in public use, and even if the pool of processors was currently unused the network was subject to load variations during runs. Therefore, if a major load fluctuation was detected during a benchmarking run, it was discarded and restarted.

Traditional speedup vs. the number of processors is shown in Figure 3.8. The scaled speedup (compare § 3.8.2) for the 11×11 stencil is shown in Figure 3.8. The run time (wall clock) for scaled work loads as a function of the number of processors for the 11×11 stencil (similar to § 3.8.2, Figure 3.7) is shown in Figure 3.9.

The NOW implementation is scalable, but to the lesser degree than the IBM SP2 implementation (compare § 3.8.2). On the IBM SP2 the interconnection network can concurrently

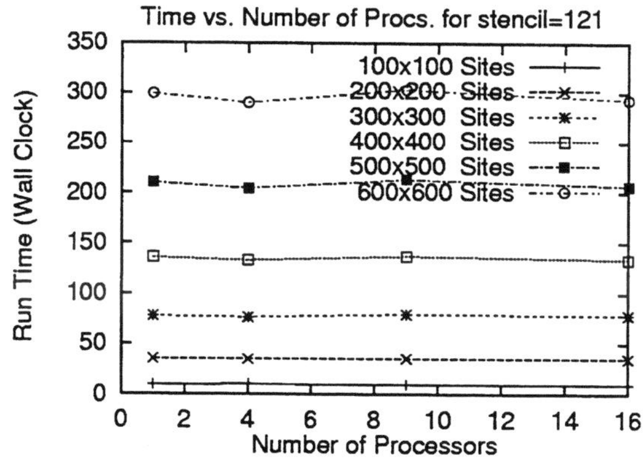

FIG. 3.7. *Run time on IBM SP2 for a scaled workload vs. number of processors*

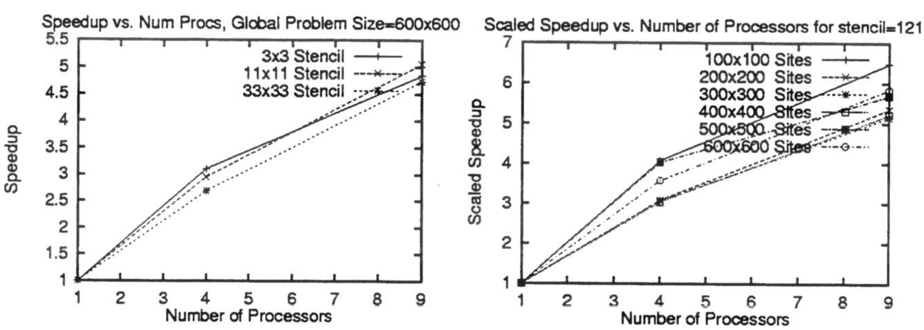

(a) Raw Speedup Vs. P

(b) Raw Speedup Vs. P

FIG. 3.8. *Speedup on NOW vs. P = number of processors*

route many messages between processors. The amount of communication between a processor and its neighbors in each time step is $O(\delta\sqrt{\frac{N}{P}})$ in distributed parallelized systems, where N is the problem size, δ is the stencil area and P is the number of processors. In contrast, the Ethernet connections employed in NOW have smaller bandwidth, larger latency, and they serialize communication. For NOW, serial communication increases as we add processors, so the serialized communication incurs a $O(\delta\sqrt{NP})$ communication volume transfered in $O(P)$ messages, compared to the parallelized $O(\delta\sqrt{\frac{N}{P}})$ communication volume and $O(1)$ messages on the IBM SP2. As previously, the throughput of the NOW is measured in state transitions per second per processor:

$$T_{NOW} = \frac{100\ timesteps \times 3.24 \times 10^6 \frac{transitions}{timestep}}{9\ processors \times 1355\ sec.} = 2.7 \times 10^4 \frac{transitions}{sec.} \tag{3.9}$$

Comparison of relative throughput of a single processor in the NOW and a single MasPar MP-1 PE yields $\frac{T_{NOW}}{T_{MP-1}} \approx 600$. Similar comparison of an IBM SP2 processor to a processor in the NOW yields: $\frac{T_{SP2}}{T_{NOW}} \approx 4.5$.

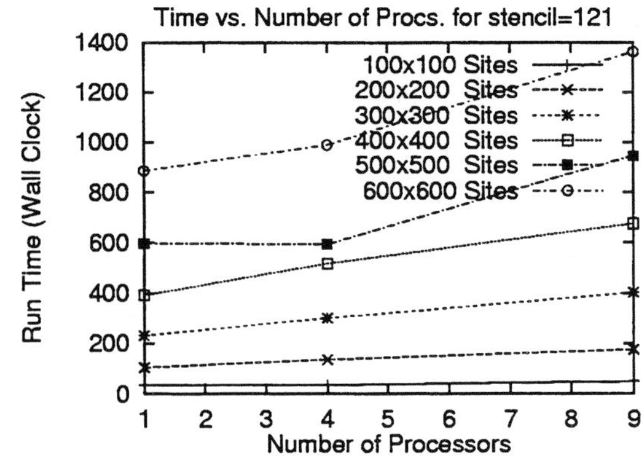

FIG. 3.9. *Run time on NOW for a scaled workload vs. number of processors*

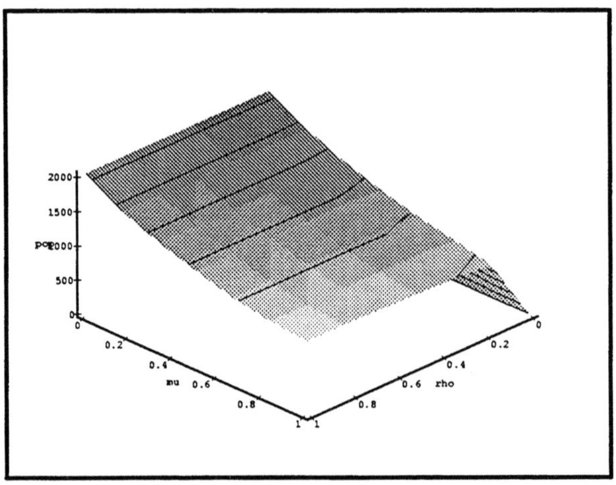

FIG. 3.10. *An animation frame, plotting population (pop) as a function of mortality (mu* $= \mu_2$ *) , and fecundity, (rho* $= \rho_2$*)*

3.9. Visualization and Interactive Tools. Large scale simulations require tools to foster understanding of the model's behavior given the large volume of data generated. Model validation and result interpretation benefit from interactive simulation and post processing of the results of several simulation trajectories for comparison of simulations run under different parameters. Many visualizations of simulation results are possible, including simulation trajectory displays for multi-media presentation of results and comparison of simulation trajectories across various parameter sets. The latter can be used to show a relationship between several parameters or to demonstrate temporal correlation between the runs (e.g. Figure 4.2, see § 4). One such example is shown in Figure 3.10 which displays population densities (along the z axis) obtained using a post processing pass to format the data for input to a visualization tool. Frames (as in Figure 3.10) are displayed in ascending order of time, and may be animated or concatenated together into solids. The surface plot function of *Maple*, a symbolic math package, was used. We also use the University of Florida's *SciAn* data visualization tool. The *TEMPEST Viewer*, called *TV* was our initial interactive visualization tool [32]. TV was written in C and used the *Simple User Interface Toolkit*, *SUIT*, from the University of Virginia. This version runs on SUN workstations using SUN OS and Solaris. Recent availability of Java, with its high level of portability, its accessibility via the world wide web and its ease of user interface development made it practical to create a new interactive visualization tool. *GUST*, the *Graphical User interface Simulation Tool* provides an accessible mechanism for interactively exploring simulation trajectories of our model. A sample GUST window is shown in Figure 3.11.

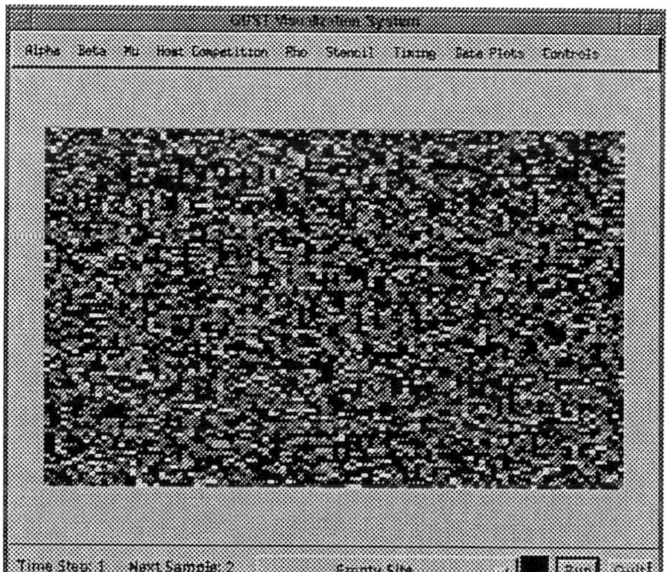

FIG. 3.11. *A sample Gust screen*

We used the Java AWT kit for user interface design. The Gust window contains a MenuBar object which supports pull down menus to access simulation control parameters and permits the user to view data plots of simulation trajectory measures, using Brookshaw's *Graph2D* library [8]. For world wide web access we used a publicly available applet [10], *AppletButton*, from SUN and "launched" the Gust application from the applet. Remote access involves down loading the Gust's byte codes and executing the intermediate representation (byte code) via either an embedded interpreter or a just in time compiler in a browser, making Gust's performance highly browser dependent. Gust can be accessed via the URL `http://www.cs.rpi.edu/research/gust/`.

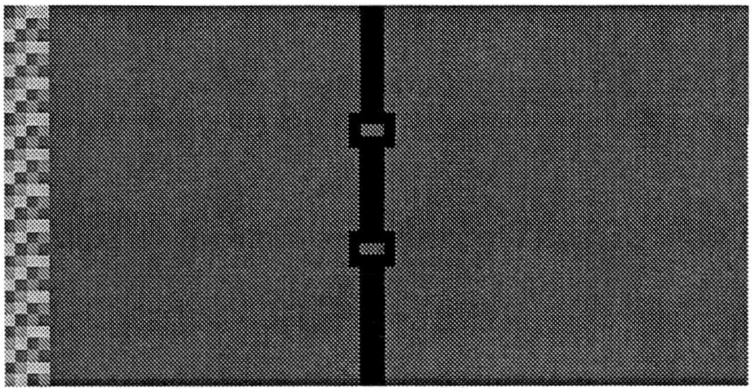

FIG. 4.1. *Tomography of epidemic about to cross the river*

4. Ecological Results. In this section we consider two sets of experiments. The experiment described in § 4.1 runs on the MasPar MP-1 and investigates the transient spatial patterns of a vector-borne epidemic. Another experiment, described in § 4.2, runs on the IBM SP2 to model transient and stable state behavior of a *general epidemic*, that is an epidemic where the disease is spread by direct transmission, and hosts experience mortality, birth, and recovery from the pathogen.

4.1. Simulating the Transient Behavior of a Vector-Borne Epidemic. Each simulation started with the same ecosystem. Hosts without parasite or pathogen occupy most cells (90.2%). A thin barrier that cannot be occupied splits the environment into left and right halves. The two "islands" are ecological "stepping stones" for the parasite and pathogen[7], as seen in Figure 4.1. A few hosts carrying the parasite, pathogen, or both (2% of each state) are at the far left; hence, the epidemic spreads from left to right.

Two simulation results are discussed here:

1. The overall frequency of diseased hosts at each sampling points.
2. The overall biodiversity of the environment at each sampling point.

The extent of infection is an epidemic's most fundamental ecological attribute. The spatial frequency of diseased hosts describes the epidemic's temporal evolution. Community biodiversity increases with the number of distinct ecological (local) states and strongly influences extinction trends. We varied some of the parameters described in § 2.2: the probability of infestation, α, the probability of infection, β, and host recovery from infestation via μ_d. Community biodiversity is used to measure global ecological diversity by quantifying variability by identity [38]. Since the extinction can occur, there are five states in the simulation, numbered according to Figure 1(a). Let f_i be the fraction of cells in state i, $(i = 1, \ldots, 5)$. Let p_i represent the fraction of sites with state i, and S be the number of states satisfying $p_i > 0$.. A community biodiversity index measures the spatial ecological diversity at a given time and since a community biodiversity index should grow as the variance of p_i's decreases [38], we selected the entropy, $H = \sum_{i=1}^{S} f_i \ln f_i$, as its measurement. The simulations were run for 100 time steps, with sampling every 10th step. Patterns emerged in the simulations indicating ecologically significant outcomes [31] as described in Table 4.1. Graphs of average frequency of infected hosts over time and mean community biodiversity over time for the patterns listed in [31] are shown in Figure 4.2.

[7] This is an abstraction of more realistic case of wild fox rabies moving from continental Europe to Great Britain across the English Channel via the tunnel [49].

	Parasite's Progress	Pathogen's Progress
1	No Spread	No Spread
2	Stopped at Barrier	No Spread
3	Saturates Environment	No Spread
4	No Spread	Contained by Parasite
5	Stopped at Barrier	Contained by Parasite
6	Saturates Environment	Saturates Environment

TABLE 4.1
Patterns observed in vector borne epidemics

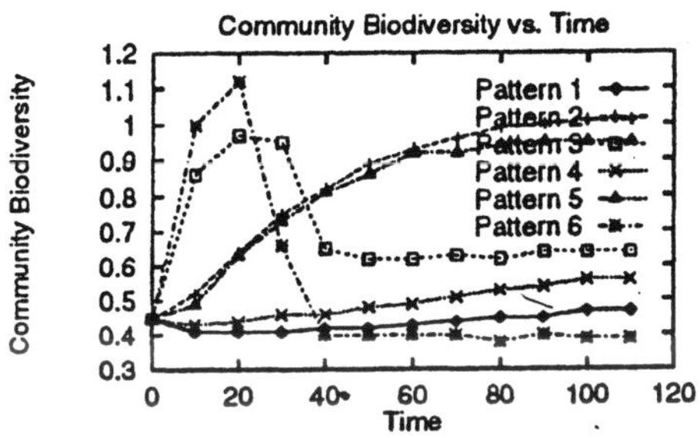

(a) Community Biodiversity vs. Time

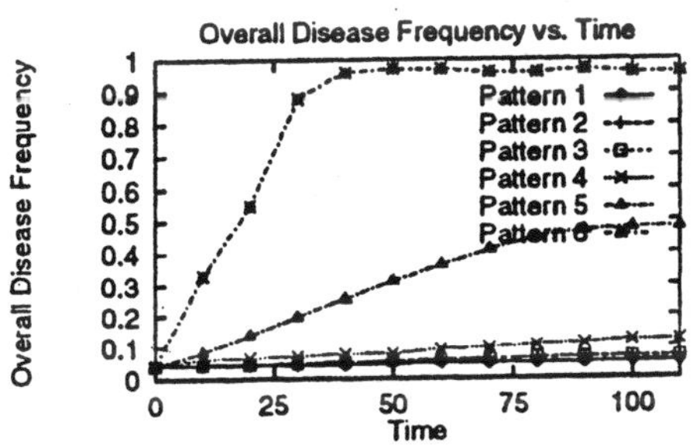

(b) Disease Frequency vs. Time

FIG. 4.2. *Ecological results*

4.2. Simulating Steady State and Transient Behavior of a Spatial Epidemic. Consider a general epidemic where a pathogenic parasite is communicated via direct contact, and exploits a single host species, in which hosts do not experience recovery, i.e. $\mu_d = 0$. Using the notation presented in § 2.2, the set of possible states for each cell in this system is $\{1, 2, 3\}$ (see Figure 2.1) and μ_i, where $i = 2, 3$, denotes mortality of the host in each of the possible states. We assume that $\mu_3 \geq \mu_2$, so that $(\mu_3 - \mu_2)$ is the additional mortality imposed on each diseased individual. All hosts survive or die independently.

We simulated the spatially explicit processes of birth, death and parasite infestation in environments of three sizes ($N \in \{10^4, 10^5, 10^6\}$ cells). We fixed mortality of uninfested hosts at $\mu_2 = 0.1$ throughout, and fixed the parasite attack probability at $\alpha = 0.09$ in all simulations. We varied stencil size ($\delta \in \{25, 2601\}$), host-propagation ($\rho \in \{0.03, 0.09\}$), and the mortality probability for infested hosts ($\mu_3 \in \{0.1, 0.4, 0.7\}$ and $\mu_2 = 0.1$).

To initiate a simulation, susceptible hosts were dispersed across the lattice randomly and independently at a density of 0.25 per cell. Then 1% of the hosts (in the center of the lattice) were designated as infested. Each simulation continued for 2000 iterations. Both species (host and parasite) remained extant in all simulations. Furthermore, densities of both susceptible and infested hosts equilibrated by time 1000 in each simulation. Density variances over the second 1000 iterations all fell in the interval $(10^{-8}, 10^{-4})$, so that variation compared to the mean was extremely small.

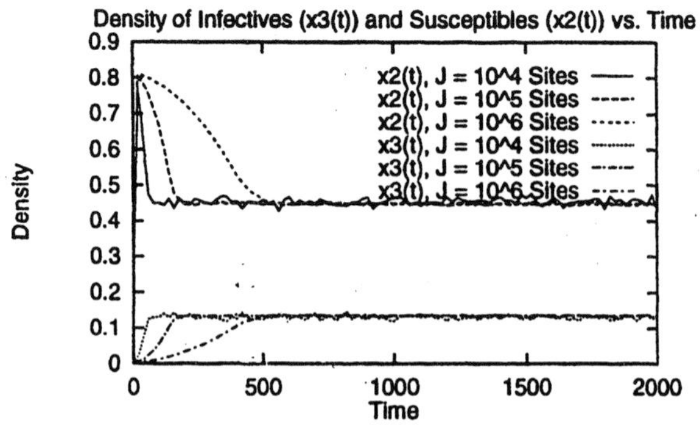

FIG. 4.3. *Host densities vs. time for* $\rho = 0.03, \mu_3 = 0.7, \delta = 5 \times 5$ *case*

Figure 4.3 shows a qualitatively typical result; densities of susceptibles and infested hosts are plotted against time for the three different environment sizes, N. Time required for the densities to reach their long-term averages increases with N. But the levels at which the densities equilibrate are essentially independent of the size of the environment. The latter pattern was anticipated and held for every combination of δ, ρ, μ_3 simulated.

5. Conclusion. Implementation of the generalized cellular automata model described in § 2 posed challenging problems such as, simultaneous reduction operation, computing the fractal dimension, and wave front propagation velocity, which motivated the development of novel parallel algorithms. The results confirmed the important conclusion, reached by many authors, that both the general purpose MIMD machines and NOW performed very well running data parallel simulations. Notwithstanding the good fit of the model of epidemics with SIMD architecture, a single node of an SP-2 was equivalent to about 2700 PE's on a MasPar MP-1 and a single SPARCstation 5 node of the NOW is equivalent to about 600 PE's on a MasPar MP-1. Although the tight synchronization is required in our simulation, the cost of communication and synchronizations is proportional to square root of the data allocated to each processor on the IBM SP-2 and to the square root of the product of the number of processors and global problem size on the NOW, whereas the computation is linearly proportional to the problem size. Hence, our simulations are scalable and the larger the problem analyzed, better the performance of the parallel machines. Thanks to this property we were able to simulate efficiently spatially explicit models which revealed phenomena not present in the homogeneous models of smaller computational complexity. The software described in this paper is in public domain and can be accessed via the URL `http://www.cs.rpi.edu/research/tempest/`.

The distribution and abundance of all species exhibit some degree of spatial variation. Spatial heterogeneity in abiotic factors or biotic processes may govern population dynamics and the resulting characteristics of ecological communities. Despite a long-standing recognition of the importance of spatial variation, analytical and computational models of spatially detailed ecological interactions have only recently become available [23, 25]. Our spatially explicit model addresses the population dynamics of (as many as) four species through simulation of the epidemiological landscape of a carrier-borne disease. Related ecological questions have been approached by modifying the model.

Acknowledgments. The authors thank W. Kaplow and J. Waiveris for their help in developing the previous MIMD implementations of the software and M. Duryea for providing comments on this paper and using the software, the anonymous reviewers and M. Nibhanupudi for comments on the paper. This work was partially supported by NSF grants BIR-9320264 and CCR-9527151, and by fellowship from IBM Corporation. The contents of this entry does not necessarily reflect the position or policy of the U.S. Government—no official endorsement should be inferred or implied.

REFERENCES

[1] A. I. Adamatzky, *Voronoi-like partition of lattice in cellular automata*, Mathematical and Computer Modelling, 23 (1996), pp. 51–66.

[2] D. Bader and J. JáJá, *Parallel algorithms for image histogramming and connected components with an experimental study*, Journal of Parallel and Distributed Computing, 35 (1996), pp. 173–190.

[3] N. T. J. Bailey, ed., *The Mathematical Theory of Infectious Diseases and Its Applications, 2nd. Edn.*, Charles Griffin, London, 1975.

[4] D. J. Bartholomew, *Stochastic Models for Social Processes, 3rd Edn.*, Wiley, New York City, NY USA, 1983.

[5] R. Bordawekar, A. Choudhary, and Ramanujam, *Automatic optimization of communication of out-ofcore stencil codes*, in Proceedings of 10th ACM Intl. Conference on Supercomputing, Philadelphia, PA, May 1996, ACM Press.

[6] R. G. Brickner, *Designing a stencil compiler for the connection machine model cm-5*, Tech. Rep. LA-UR-94-3152, Los Alamos National Laboratory, 1994.

[7] R. G. Brickner, W. George, S. L. Johnsson, and A. Ruttenberg, *A stencil compiler for the connection machine models cm-2/200*, in Proceedings for the Fourth International Workshop in Compilers for Parallel Computers, Delft, The Netherlands, December 1993. Additional information available on line at http://www.c3.lanl.gov/~rgb/CM2_Delft.html.

[8] L. Brookshaw, *Java 2d graph package.* Additional information available on line at http://www.sci.usq.edu.au/staff/leighb/graph/Top.html, April 1997.

[9] A. W. Burks, *Theory of Self-Reproducing Automata, John von Neuman*, University of Illinois, 1968.

[10] M. Campione and K. Walrath, *The Java Tutorial*, Addison-Wesley, Reading, MA, 1996. Additional information available on line at http://www.javasoft.com/nav/read/Tutorial/index.html.

[11] T. Caraco, W. Maniatty, and B. K. Szymanski, *Spatial effects and competitive coexistence*, in Proceedings of the Workshop on Spatioteomporal Models in Biological and Artificial Systems, F. L. Silva and et al., eds., vol. 37 of Frontiers in Artificial Intelligence and Applications, Sintra, Portugal, November 1997, IOS Press, Amsterdam, pp. 9–16.

[12] S. Chen, G. D. Doolen, and K. G. Eggert, *Lattice-Boltzmann fluid dynamics: A versatile tool for multiphase and other complicated flows*, Los Alamos Science, 22 (1994), pp. 100–109. Additional information available on line at http://lib-www.lanl.gov/pubs/la-sci.htm.

[13] T. H. Cormen, C. E. Leiserson, and R. L. Rivest, *Introduction To Algorithms*, McGraw Hill, 1990.

[14] J. Cox and R. Durrett, *Limit theorems for the spread of epidemics and forest fires*, Stoch. Proc. and their Applications, 30 (1988), pp. 171–191.

[15] R. CYPHER AND J. L. C. SANZ, *Algorithms for image component labeling on simd mesh-connected computers*, IEEE Transactions on Computers, 39 (1990), pp. 277–281.

[16] S. DI GRIGORIO, R. RONGO, W. SPATARO, G. SPEZZANO, AND D. TALIA, *High performance scientific computing by a parallel cellular environment*, Future Generation Computer Systems Journal, 12 (1997).

[17] J. DONGARRA, A. H. KARP, K. KENNEDY, AND D. KUCK, *1989 Gordon Bell prize report*, IEEE Software, (1990).

[18] M. DURYEA, J. GARDNER, T. CARACO, B. K. SZYMANSKI, AND W. A. MANIATTY, *Host spatial heterogeneity and extinction of an SIS epidemics*, Journal of Theoretical Biology, (1998). to appear.

[19] G. B. ERMENTROUT AND L. EDELSTEIN-KESHET, *Biologically motivated cellular automata*, Journal of Theoretical Biology, 160 (1993), pp. 97–133.

[20] R. A. FISHER, *The wave of advance of advantageous genes*, Annals of Eugenics, 7 (1937), pp. 355–369.

[21] J. L. GUSTAFSON, *Reevaluating Amdahl's law*, CACM, 31 (1988), pp. 532–533.

[22] R. M. HARALICK AND L. G. SHAPIRO, *Computer and Robot Vision*, vol. I, Addison Wesley, Reading, MA, 1992.

[23] A. HASTINGS, *Spatial heterogencity and ecological models*, Ecology, 71 (1990), pp. 426–428.

[24] R. JAIN, R. KASTURI, AND B. G. SCHUNK, *Machine Vision*, McGraw-Hill, New York, NY, 1995.

[25] P. KAREIVA, *Population dynamics in spatially complex environments: theory and data*, Philosophical Transactions of the Royal Society, London, B, 30 (1990), pp. 175–190.

[26] J. R. KRUMMEL, G. SUGIHARA, R. V. O'NEILL, AND P. R. COLEMAN, *Landscape patterns in a disturbed environment*, Oikos, 48 (1987), pp. 321–324.

[27] F. T. LEIGHTON, *Introduction To Parallel Algorithms and Architectures:Arrays · Trees · Hypercubes*, Morgan Kaufman Publishers, San Mateo, California, 1992.

[28] B. D. LUBACHEVSKY, *Efficient distributed event-driven simulations of multiple-loop networks*, CACM, 32 (1989), pp. 111–123.

[29] B. MANIATTY, B. SINHAROY, AND B. SZYMANSKI, *Efficiency of data alignment on MasPar*, SIGPLAN Notices, 28 (1993), pp. 48–51. Online information available at ftp://ftp.cs.rpi.edu/pub/maniattb/dataalign.ps.Z.

[30] B. MANIATTY, B. SZYMANSKI, AND T. CARACO, *Virtual epidemics - ecological modeling on a parallel machine*, Tech. Rep. CS 93-18, Dept. of Computer Science, Rensselaer Polytechnic Institute, 1992. SuParCup '93 Student Prize award.

[31] W. MANIATTY, B. SZYMANSKI, AND T. CARACO, *Implementation and performance of parallel ecological simulations*, in Proceedings IFIP WG10.3 International Conference on Applications in Parallel and Distributed Computing, Amsterdam, The Netherlands, 1993, Elseveir Science Publishers B.V. Online information available at ftp://ftp.cs.rpi.edu/pub/maniattb/ifips93.ps.Z.

[32] ———, *Tempest: a fast spatially explicit model of ecological dynamics on parallel machines*, in Proceedings of the 1994 International Simulation Conference, San Diego, CA, 1994, The Society For Computer Simulation. Online information available at ftp://ftp.cs.rpi.edu/pub/maniattb/hpc94.ps.Z.

[33] W. A. MANIATTY AND B. K. SZYMANSKI, *Fine-grain discrete Voronoi diagram algorithms in l_1 and l_∞ norms*, Mathl. Comput. Modelling, 26 (1997), pp. 71–78. Also Technical Report 97-3 Department of Computer Science, Rensselaer Polytechnic Institute, Troy, NY 12180.

[34] N. MARGOLUS, *Pattern Formation and Lattice-Gas Automata*, American Mathematical Society, 1996, ch. CAM-8: a computer architecture based on cellular automata.

[35] MESSAGE PASSING INTERFACE FORUM, *MPI: A message Passing Interface Standard*, University of Tennessee, Knoxville, Tennesee, 1995. Additional information available on line at ftp://ftp.mcs.anl.gov/pub/mpi/mpi-1.jun95/mpi-report.ps.Z.

[36] D. MOLLISON, *Dependence of epidemic and population velocities on basic parameters*, Mathematical Biosciences, 107 (1991), pp. 255–287.

[37] J. D. MURRAY AND W. L. STEWARD, *On the spatial spread of rabies among foxes with immunity*, Journal of Theoretical Biology, 156 (1992), pp. 327–348.

[38] E. C. PIELOU, *Ecological Diversity*, Wiley-Interscience, New York, NY, 1984.

[39] M. SAHIMI, *Applications of Percolation Theory*, Taylor & Francis, Bristol, PA USA., 1994.

[40] J. G. SKELLAM, *Random dispersal in theoretical populations*, Biometrika, 38 (1951), pp. 196–218.

[41] S. SUCCI, G. AMATI, AND R. BENZI, *Challenges in lattice Boltzmann computing*, Journal of Statistical Physics, 81 (1995), pp. 5–16.

[42] G. SUGIHARA AND R. M. MAY, *Applications of fractals in ecology*, Trends in Ecology and Evolution, 5 (1990), pp. 79–86.

[43] B. SZYMANSKI, W. MANIATTY, AND B. SINHAROY, *Simultaneous parallel reduction*, Parallel Processing Letters, 5 (1995). RPI Dept. of Computer Science Tech Report CS 92-31.

[44] B. K. SZYMANSKI AND T. CARACO, *Spatial analysis of vector-borne disease: A four species*

model, Evolutionary Ecology, 8 (1994), pp. 299–314. Online information available at ftp://ftp.cs.rpi.edu/pub/szymansk/eec.ps.

[45] G. M. Voronoi, *Nouvelles applications des paramètres continus à la théorie des formes quadratiques. deuxième Mémoire: Recherches sur les parallélloèdres primitifs*, J. Reine Angew. Math., 134 (1908), pp. 198–287.

[46] S. Wolfram, *Cellular automata fluids: Basic theory*, Journal of Statistical Physics, 45 (1986), pp. 471–526. Also in Wolfram's Cellular Automata and Complexity.

[47] ———, *Cellular Automata and Complexity*, Addison Wesley, Reading, MA, 1994. Online information available at http://www.wolfram.com/s.wolfram/books/ca-reprint/.

[48] S. Wolfram and N. H. Packard, *Two-dimensional cellular automata*, Journal of Statistical Physics, 38 (1985), pp. 901–946. Also in Wolfram's Cellular Automata and Complexity.

[49] S. Yachi, K. Kawasaki, N. Shigesada, and E. Teramoto, *Spatial patterns of propagating waves of fox rabies*, Forma, 4 (1989), pp. 3–12.

A FUNCTIONAL APPROACH TO RADIX-r FFTS*

DOROTHY BOLLMAN †, JAIME SEGUEL‡, AND JOHN FEO§

Abstract. We show that each member of a well-known family of radix-r FFTs can be expressed as the composition of functions chosen from a set of four "basis" functions. Thus, a complete library of radix-r FFTs can be developed by programming the four basis functions and composing them to obtain various FFTs. We illustrate this by develeping implementations in the functional language Sisal. We compare performance of these FFTs on a Cray C-90. Based on observations of these results we develop an implementation of an FFT of size 2^k which is seemingly optimal for the Cray C-90. We discuss language features of particular benefit for programming FFTs and suggest some enhancements that would further streamline the programming.

1. Introduction. In recent years, functional languages have emerged as one of the principal technologies for addressing the challenges of high performance computing. Their mathematical foundation and implicit parallelism make them especially useful to scientists studying parallel algorithms. Functional languages include many high-level constructs not found in conventional programming languages which, when used properly, simplify programming. Consequently, they minimize programming costs and encourage algorithm development. Functional programs are easy to understand, modify, and maintain and are portable, parallel, and fast as well. There is growing evidence that these languages can execute as efficiently as more traditional languages such as Fortran. In this work we study functional implementations of a class of algorithms that play an indispensable role in many scientific and engineering applications.

The *discrete Fourier transform* (DFT) of an n-point data vector x can be expressed as the product of an $n \times n$ matrix by x. Computing the DFT of an n-point vector from its definition thus requires naively $O(n^2)$ operations. In 1960, Good [10], and independently by Thomas [17] in 1963, laid the foundations of what is known today as the Good-Thomas prime factor algorithm. In 1965, Cooley and Tukey [7] published the well-known Cooley-Tukey algorithm. Both algorithms reduce the arithmetic complexity of computing the DFT of an n-point vector to $O(n\ log\ n)$. The family $\mathcal{F}$ of these algorithms have given rise to a whole family of DFT algorithms that have come to be known as *fast Fourier transforms* (*FFTs*).

FFTs of size $n = r^k$ are typically expressed in terms of FFTs of size r. In such a case, r is called the *radix*. Eight well-known variations of the radix-r FFT algorithm are: Cooley-Tukey, Gentleman-Sande, Pease (decimation in time and frequency), Korn-Lambiote (decimination in time and frequency), Stockham, and Transposed Stockham. The family $\mathcal{F}$ of these algorithms, all of $O(n\ log\ n)$ complexity, differ from one another in data flow characteristics and have varying degrees of performance efficiency depending on the target architecture.

It is unfortunate that most of the FFT literature is characterized by a complete lack of uniformity in either mathematical or algorithmic notation. Because of this, the differences and similarities between various FFTs have not been fully understood or appreciated. A major step forward in alleviating this situation is the use of tensor products, which in re-

*The authors thank Cray Research Incorporated for the dedicated computer time they provided in support of this work. The work of the first two authors was supported by NSF grants HRD9450448 and CDA94117362.

†Mathematics Dept., Univ. of Puerto Rico, Mayaguez, PR 00681 (bollman@jacobi.upr.clu.edu)

‡Mathematics Dept., Univ. of Puerto Rico, Mayaguez, PR 00681 (jseguel@jacobi.upr.clu.edu),

§ Tera Computer Company, Seattle, WA 98102 (john@tera.com).

cent years have become a widely used tool for unifying, designing, analyzing, and modifying FFT algorithms. One can express an algorithm that takes into account the architecture of the target machine as a formula in tensor notation and then translate the formula into a computer implementation. Performance of the code can then identify opportunities for optimization that in turn leads one to use the laws of tensor algebra to modify the original algorithm. However, there is still a considerable gap between the algorithmic and mathematical notation. There is almost no commonality among FFT implementations found in the literature, even for those based on algorithms expressed in tensor notation. Changes in an algorithm are most often explained in terms of line by line changes in the code or by replacing a whole program by another one when in fact the real difference is that the two algorithms simply differ in a functional argument.

In this work we identify four "basis" functions that are common to all radix-r FFTs in the sense that each member of $\mathcal{F}$ can be expressed as a composition of the basis functions. These basis functions serve to unify and aid the understanding of the relationships between the various radix-r FFTs. They also greatly simplify the programming effort. We can build a complete library of radix-r FFTs by simply programming the four basis functions and then composing them to obtain the various FFTs. We illustrate this idea for a family of commonly used radix-r FFTs which we implement in the functional language Sisal, compare their performance on a Cray 90 and based on observations from these results, we develop an implementation of an FFT of size 2^k, a "hybrid Stockham" algorithm, that is seemingly optimal for the C-90.

We chose Sisal as the implementation language not only because it offers the advantages of a functional language, as described above, but for several other reasons as well. First, FFT algorithms written in Sisal have been shown to execute faster than Cray FFT library routines on the Cray C-90 and scale almost linearly with the number of processors [3, 5, 8]. Secondly, Sisal syntax is similar to the mathematical notation of the algorithm, which simplifies the programming effort. Moreover, the use of a functional language is entirely consistent with our *functional* view of radix-r FFTs as compositions of functions from some fixed set of basic functions. It is usually easy to express the composition of functions in a functional language and we can do so without fear of side effects. Unfortunately, there is a problem here with Sisal, whose present version does not permit either functional arguments or values. We comment further on this shortcoming in Section 9 and suggest language enhancements that could further streamline the programming.

The specific organization for the rest of this work is as follows. In Sections 2 and 3 we review some well-known results that are needed in the rest of the work. In Section 2, we establish the definitions and notation and in Section 3, we give the tensor formulas for the members of $\mathcal{F}$. In Section 4 we show that each of these algorithms can be expressed in terms of just four basic functions, which we term the "basis" functions. In Section 5, we give Sisal "templates" for the basis functions, which are essentially recipes that give us, for any given radix r and functional parameters, the Sisal code for these functions. In Section 6, we illustrate the use of the templates for $r = 3$ and give performance results for Sisal implementations of the members of $\mathcal{F}$ on a Cray-90. In Section 7, we develop implementations and give performance results for the radix-4 case. The best performing implementations in this latter case are the Stockham algorithms. In Section 8, we take advantage of the best features of the previously considered FFTs to develop a high performance "hybrid" Stockham FFT for size 2^k. In Section 9, we discuss some functional language features that would simplify the programming of the FFT algorithms. In the last section, we summarize and present some conclusions.

2. Preliminaries. In this section, we review basic notation and definitions that will be used later for tensor formulations of FFT algorithms. Throughout this work, N denotes the set of nonnegative integers and N' denotes the set of positive integers. For each $n \in N$, we denote the *set* $\{0, 1, \cdots, n-1\}$ by N_n and the *vector* $[0, 1, \cdots, n-1]$ by V_n. In the interest of economizing space, we shall many times write column vectors as row vectors whose components are separated by commas. Thus, for example,

$$[1, 2, 3] = \begin{bmatrix} 1 \\ 2 \\ 3 \end{bmatrix} \tag{2.1}$$

2.1. Tensor product. The tensor product of an $m \times m$ matrix $A = (a_{ij})$, $i, j = 0, ..., m-1$, by an $n \times n$ matrix B is the $mn \times mn$ matrix

$$A \otimes B = (a_{ij}B). \tag{2.2}$$

For example,

$$\begin{bmatrix} 1 & 2 \\ 3 & 4 \end{bmatrix} \otimes \begin{bmatrix} 5 & 6 \\ 7 & 8 \end{bmatrix} = \begin{bmatrix} 1\begin{bmatrix} 5 & 6 \\ 7 & 8 \end{bmatrix} & 2\begin{bmatrix} 5 & 6 \\ 7 & 8 \end{bmatrix} \\ 3\begin{bmatrix} 5 & 6 \\ 7 & 8 \end{bmatrix} & 4\begin{bmatrix} 5 & 6 \\ 7 & 8 \end{bmatrix} \end{bmatrix} = \begin{bmatrix} 5 & 6 & 10 & 12 \\ 7 & 8 & 14 & 16 \\ 15 & 18 & 20 & 24 \\ 21 & 24 & 28 & 32 \end{bmatrix}$$

Equivalently, we can define the tensor product as

$$A \otimes B = [a_{ij}b_{kl}] \tag{2.3}$$

where both the row indexing set $\{(i, k) : 0 \le i \le m-1,\ 0 \le k \le n-1\}$ and the column indexing set $\{(j, l) : 0 \le j \le m-1,\ 0 \le l \le n-1\}$ are ordered lexicographically.

The tensor product is associative, and satisfies the equation

$$(A \otimes B)(C \otimes D) = AC \otimes BD \tag{2.4}$$

whenever the matrix products AC and BD are defined. It also satisfies the equation

$$(A \otimes B)^T = A^T \otimes B^T \tag{2.5}$$

where T denotes transposition. A special case of (2.4) is

$$A \otimes B = (A \otimes I_n)(I_m \otimes B) \tag{2.6}$$

where I_n and I_m denote the $n \times n$ and $m \times m$ identity matrices, respectively.

The two products that appear on the right side of (2.6) play important roles in FFTs and in fact have special significance for vector-parallel machines such as the Crays. The product $u = (I_m \otimes B)x$ where B is a square matrix of size n and x is a vector of size mn is a *parallel* operation since the action of

$$I_m \otimes B = \begin{bmatrix} B & & & \\ & B & & \\ & & \cdot & \\ & & & \cdot \\ & & & & B \end{bmatrix} \tag{2.7}$$

on x can be performed by applying B (in parallel) to each subvector X_i, $i = 1, 2, \cdots, m$ of length n of x. On the other hand, the product $u = (A \otimes I_n)x$ where A is a square matrix of size m is a *vector* operation since

$$(A \otimes I_n)x = \begin{bmatrix} a_{0,0}X_0+ & \cdots & +a_{0,m-1}X_{m-1} \\ . & \cdots & . \\ . & \cdots & . \\ . & \cdots & . \\ a_{m-1,0}X_0+ & \cdots & +a_{m-1,m-1}X_{m-1} \end{bmatrix} \tag{2.8}$$

where + denotes vector addition.

2.2. Stride permutations. The permutation defined by

$$p(mn, m)(i) = \begin{cases} mi \text{ modulo } mn - 1, & \text{if } 0 \le i \le mn - 2 \\ mn - 1, & \text{if } i = mn - 1. \end{cases} \tag{2.9}$$

is called a *stride permutation* and m is the *stride.*

Let $P(m, n)$ be the matrix representing $p(m, n)$. It is easy to see from the definition that

$$P(m, n)P(m, r) = P(m, nr) \tag{2.10}$$

where n and r are divisors of m. Additionally,

$$P^T(mn, m) = P^{-1}(mn, m) = P(mn, n). \tag{2.11}$$

and

$$A \otimes B = P(mn, n)(B \otimes A)P(mn, m), \tag{2.12}$$

This last identity is known as the *Commutation Theorem.*

2.3. Catenation. If x and y are vectors of sizes m and n, respectively, then $x \parallel y$ is the vector of size $m + n$ defined by

$$(x \parallel y)[i] = \begin{cases} x[i] & \text{if } 0 \le i \le m - 1 \\ y[i - m] & \text{if } m \le i \le m + n - 1 \end{cases}$$

It is convenient to extend the definition of $\parallel$ so that for scalars c and d $c \parallel d = [c, d]$ and for any vector x, $x \parallel c = x \parallel [c]$ and $c \parallel x = [c] \parallel x$. For example,

$$[1, 2] \| [3, 4, 5] = [1, 2, 3, 4, 5].$$

In the interest of economizing space, we shall many times write column vectors as row vectors whose components are separated by commas. Thus, for example,

$$[1, 2, 3] = \begin{bmatrix} 1 \\ 2 \\ 3 \end{bmatrix} \tag{2.13}$$

Catenation is clearly associative. If $x_0, x_1, \cdots, x_{n-1}$ are vectors then we define

$$\|_{i=0}^{n-1} x_i = x_0 \parallel x_1 \parallel x_1 \parallel \cdots \parallel x_{n-1} \tag{2.14}$$

2.4. Direct sum. If B_i, $i = 0, 1, \cdots, m-1$, are square matrices of size n_i, then the *direct sum* of $B_0, B_1, \cdots, B_{m-1}$ is the block diagonal matrix

$$\bigoplus_{i=0}^{m-1} B_i = \begin{bmatrix} B_0 & & & & \\ & B_1 & & & \\ & & \cdot & & \\ & & & \cdot & \\ & & & & B_{m-1} \end{bmatrix} \tag{2.15}$$

From the definition of tensor product, we know that

$$I_m \otimes B = \bigoplus_{i=0}^{m-1} B. \tag{2.16}$$

A useful property of direct sums is

$$\bigoplus_{i=0}^{m-1} B_i \bigoplus_{i=0}^{m-1} C_i = \bigoplus_{i=0}^{m-1} B_i C_i \tag{2.17}$$

where the B_i and C_i are square matrices of size n_i.

3. Radix-r FFTs as tensor expressions. Matrix expressions of FFTs based on tensor products appeared as early as 1968 in Pease's [14] work, but it was not until the work by Johnson *et al* [12] that tensor notation began to replace "butterfly" diagrams in the description and modifications of FFT algorithms. Complete treatments of tensor representations of FFTs are given in [18] and [19].

3.1. The discrete Fourier transform.. The discrete Fourier transform (DFT) of a complex n-dimensional vector $x = (x_l)$ is the complex vector $\hat{x} = (\hat{x}_k)$ determined by the linear system

$$\hat{x}_k = \sum_{l=0}^{n-1} x_l \omega_n^{kl}, \quad 0 \le k \le n-1; \tag{3.1}$$

where $\omega_n = e^{2\pi i/n}$ and $i = \sqrt{-1}$. In matrix terms, (3.1) is written as

$$\hat{x} = F_n x \tag{3.2}$$

where $F_n = [\omega_n^{kl}]$ is the $n \times n$ complex matrix representation of (3.1).

Clearly, the arithmetic complexity of computing $\hat{x}$ from x using (3.2) is $O(n^2)$. However, in 1965 Cooley and Tukey [7] showed that the DFT can be computed in time $O(n \log n)$. Subsequently, variations of the Cooley-Tukey algorithm, which vary in vector size and data flow, have appeared in the literature. These algorithms together with the original Cooley-Tukey algorithm are generically known as *fast Fourier transforms* (FFTs). In the next section we describe a family of these FFTs in terms of tensor notation. All of these algorithms are based on the "basic splitting equation," derivations of which can be found in e.g. [19], follow from this equation:

$$F_{rs} = (F_r \otimes I_s) T_s^{rs} (I_r \otimes F_s) P(sr, r), \tag{3.3}$$

where

$$T_s^{rs} = \bigoplus_{i=0}^{r-1} (D_s^{rs})^i, \tag{3.4}$$

$$D_s^{rs} = diag(1, \omega_{rs}, \omega_{rs}^2, \cdots, \omega_{rs}^{s-1}), \tag{3.5}$$

and

$$(D_s^{rs})^i = diag(1, \omega_{rs}^i, \cdots, \omega_{rs}^{i(s-1)}). \tag{3.6}$$

3.2. A family of radix-r FFT variants. In the rest of this work, we consider transforms of length $n = r^k$. If $k \geq 3$, equation (3.3) can be applied recursively. For example,

$$F_{r^3} = (F_r \otimes I_{r^2}) T_r^{r^3} (I_r \otimes F_{r^2}) P(r^3, r) \tag{3.7}$$

and

$$F_{r^2} = (F_r \otimes I_r) T_r^{r^2} (I_r \otimes F_r) P(r^2, r). \tag{3.8}$$

Substituting (3.8) in (3.7) and applying (2.4), we have

$$F_{r^3} = (F_r \otimes I_{r^2}) T_r^{r^3} (I_r \otimes F_r \otimes I_r)(I_r \otimes T_r^{r^2})(I_{r^2} \otimes F_r)(I_r \otimes P(r^2, r))P(r^3, r) \tag{3.9}$$

The permutation represented by the matrix $(I_r \otimes P(r^2, r))P(r^3, r)$ is called *digit-reversal* and denoted by $R(r^3)$. In general, the digit-reversal $R(r^k)$ is a permutation such that for any vector x of size r^k, the result of applying it to x is a vector whose i-th element, $i = 0, 1, \cdots r^k - 1$, is $x[j]$ where j is the integer determined by expressing i in base r and reversing the base r digits.

In what follows, we denote $T_{r^{i-1}}^{r^i}$ by T^{r^i}, $D_{r^{i-1}}^{r^i}$ by D^{r^i}, and the matrix product $A_k A_{k-1} \cdots A_1$ by

$$\prod_{i=1}^{k} A_i.$$

Furthermore, we assume that $I_1 = [1]$ and T^r is the identity matrix. With these conventions, (3.9) assumes the form for a general $n = r^k$

$$F_{r^k} = \left\{ \prod_{i=1}^{k} \left[I_{r^{k-i}} \otimes (F_r \otimes I_{r^{i-1}}) T^{r^i} \right] \right\} R(r^k) \tag{3.10}$$

which is the matrix expression for the radix-r Cooley-Tukey (CT) FFT.

Note the succint way in which the tensor notation bares the idea of the algorithm. Formula (3.10) says that in order to compute the FFT of a vector x of length r^k, we perform a digit-reversal permutation on x. Then for each stage $i = 1, 2, \cdots, k$, apply the "twiddle factor" T^{r^i} to each of r^{k-i} blocks of length r^i, followed by r^{k-i} (parallel) applications of the "butterfly" operations $F_r \otimes I_{r^{i-1}}$ to each resulting block.

The factor $I_{r^{k-i}} \otimes (F_r \otimes I_{r^{i-1}}) T^{r^i}$ in (3.10) determines the FFT data-flow since its central member F_r is a core procedure to which all data is directed. Not surprisingly, all

FFT variants aim at modifying this factor. The main tools for such modifications are the stride permutations.

The formula

$$(3.11) \qquad F_{r^k} = \left\{ \prod_{i=1}^{k} P(r^k, r)(I_{r^{k-1}} \otimes F_r)P(r^k, r^{k-1})(T^{r^i} \otimes I_{r^{k-i}})P(r^k, r) \right\} R(r^k)$$

was originally proposed by Pease [15] and the variant

$$(3.12) \qquad F_{r^k} = \left\{ \prod_{i=1}^{k} (F_r \otimes I_{r^{k-1}})(T^{r^i} \otimes I_{r^{k-i}})P(r^k, r) \right\} R(r^k)$$

was first described by Korn-Lambiotte [14]. These two variants are clearly algebraically equivalent since by the Commutation Theorem

$$P(r^k, r)(I_{r^{k-1}} \otimes F_r)P(r^k, r^{k-1}) = F_r \otimes I_{r^{k-1}}.$$

Because of the presence of $I_{r^{k-1}} \otimes F_r$, the Pease algorithm can be thought of as a parallel algorithm, whereas the Korn-Lambiotte algorithm can be thought of as a vector algorithm because of the presence of $F_r \otimes I_{r^{k-1}}$.

Each of the above algorithms, which we call PDT and KLDT, respectively, is given in its "decimation in time" (DT) form, since the digit-reversal permutation acts on the input vector. In the "decimation in frequency" (DF) versions, digit-reversal is applied to the output vector. The DF forms are obtained from the DT forms by taking the transpose of each side of the given formula. Thus we have the DF variants:

Gentleman-Sande (GS) (The DF form of Cooley-Tukey):

$$(3.13) \qquad F_{r^k} = R(r^k) \left\{ \prod_{i=1}^{k} \left[I_{r^{i-1}} \otimes T^{r^{k-i+1}}(F_r \otimes I_{r^{k-i}}) \right] \right\}$$

Pease DF (PDF):

$$(3.14) F_{r^k} = R(r^k) \left\{ \prod_{i=1}^{k} P(r^k, r^{k-1})(T^{r^{k-i+1}} \otimes I_{r^{i-1}})P(r^k, r)(I_{r^{k-1}} \otimes F_r)P(r^k, r^{k-1}) \right\}$$

Korn-Lambiote DF (KLDF):

$$(3.15) \qquad F_r^k = R(r^k) \left\{ \prod_{i=1}^{k} P(r^k, r^{k-1})(T^{r^{k-i+1}} \otimes I_{r^{i-1}})(F_r \otimes I_{r^{k-1}}) \right\}$$

The Stockham algorithms avoid a separate ordering phase by distributing digit-reversal throughout the combine phase. The Stockham algorithm (S) is given by

$$(3.16) \qquad F_{r^k} = \prod_{i=1}^{k} \left[(F_r \otimes I_{r^{i-1}})T^{r^i} \otimes I_{r^{k-i}} \right] (P(r^i, r) \otimes I_{r^{k-i}})$$

and the transposed Stockham (TS) by

$$F_{r^k} = \prod_{i=1}^{k} \left[I_{r^{k-i}} \otimes (F_r \otimes I_{r^{i-1}}) T^{r^i} \right] (P(r^{k-i+1}, r^{k-i}) \otimes I_{r^{i-1}}) \tag{3.17}$$

4. Functional FFTs. Each of the radix-r, size r^k FFTs in the previous section is of the form

$$\{\prod_{i=1}^{k} step_i\} R(r^k), \tag{4.1}$$

$$R(r^k)\{\prod_{i=1}^{k} step_i\}, \tag{4.2}$$

or

$$\prod_{i=1}^{k} step_i. \tag{4.3}$$

Let CT_i, GS_i, PDT_i, PDF_i, $KLDT_i$, $KLDF_i$, S_i, and TS_i denote the i-th step of the Cooley-Tukey, Gentleman-Sande, decimation-in-time Pease, decimation-in-frequency Pease, decimation-in-time Korn-Lambiote, decimation-in-frequency Korn- Lambiote, Stockham, and transposed Stockham algorithms, respectively. That is,

$CT_i = I_{r^{k-i}} \otimes (F_r \otimes I_{r^{i-1}}) T^{r^i}$,

$GS_i = I_{r^{i-1}} \otimes T^{r^{k-i+1}} (F_r \otimes I_{r^{k-i}})$,

$PDT_i = P(r^k, r)(I_{r^{k-1}} \otimes F_r) P(r^k, r^{k-1})(T^{r^i} \otimes I_{r^{k-i}}) P(r^k, r)$,

$PDF_i = P(r^k, r^{k-1})(T^{r^{k-i+1}} \otimes I_{r^{i-1}}) P(r^k, r)(I_{r^{k-1}} \otimes F_r) P(r^k, r^{k-1})$,

$KLDT_i = (F_r \otimes I_{r^{k-1}})(T^{r^i} \times I_{r^{k-i}}) P(r^k, r)$,

$KLDF_i = P(r^k, r^{k-1})(T^{r^{k-i+1}} \otimes I_{r^{i-1}})(F_r \otimes I_{r^{k-1}})$,

$S_i = ((F_r \otimes I_{r^{i-1}}) T^{r^i} \otimes I_{r^{k-i}})(P(r^i, r) \otimes I_{r^{k-i}})$,

$TS_i = (I_{r^{k-i}} \otimes (F_r \otimes I_{r^{i-1}}) T^{r^i})(P(r^{k-i+1}, r^{k-i}) \otimes I_{r^{i-1}})$.

Let $\mathcal{F}$ be the set consisting of CT_i, GS_i, PDT_i, PDF_i, $KLDT_i$, $KLDF_i$, S_i, and TS_i. We shall single out a family of functions $\mathcal{G}$ that serves as a "basis" for $\mathcal{F}$ in the sense that the i-th step of each member of $\mathcal{F}$ can be expressed in terms of compositions of members of $\mathcal{G}$. We shall see that there are four basic functions g_1, g_2, g_3, g_4, that suffice for the basis $\mathcal{G}$.

4.1. A family $\mathcal{G}$ of four basic functions. In what follows we regard r as a fixed positive integer ≥ 2, $m, s, n \in N'$, where $mrs = n$, $x \in C^n$, and $index : N_m \times N_r \times N_s \rightarrow N_n$. It will be convenient to establish notation for denoting subvectors of a vector $x \in C^n$. By $x[index]$ or $x[index(\_, \_, \_)]$ we shall mean the vector whose i-th component is $x[index(l, h, j)]$ where (l, h, j) is the i-th component in the lexicographical ordering of $N_m \times N_r \times N_s$. For each $l \in N_m$, $x[index(l, \_, \_)]$ is the subvector of x whose i-th component is $x[index(l, h, j)]$

where (l, h, j) is the i-th element in the lexicographical ordering of $N_r \times N_s$. We define $x[index(\_, h, \_)]$, $x[index(\_, \_, j)]$, $x[index(l, h, \_)]$, $x[index(l, \_, j)]$, and $x[index(l, h, \_)]$ similarly.

For example, if $x = [x_0, x_1, \cdots, x_7]$, $m = r = s = 2$, and $index(l, h, j) = 4l + 2h + j$, then $x[index(0, \_, \_)] = [x_0, x_1, x_2, x_3]$, $x[index(1, \_, \_)] = [x_4, x_5, x_6, x_7]$, $x[index(0, 0, \_)] = [x_0, x_1]$,
$x[index(0, 1, \_)] = [x_2, x_3]$, etc.

Let $D_2, \cdots, D_r \in C^s \times C^s$ be diagonal matrices. Define

$$g_1(s, l, x, D_2, D_3, \cdots, D_r, index) = F_r \begin{bmatrix} x[index(l, 0, \_)] \\ D_2 x[index(l, 1, \_)] \\ \vdots \\ D_r x[index(l, r-1, \_)] \end{bmatrix}, \tag{4.4}$$

and

$$g_2(s, l, x, D_2, D_3, \cdots, D_r, index) = DF_r \begin{bmatrix} x[index(l, 0, \_)] \\ x[index(l, 1, \_)] \\ \vdots \\ x[index(l, r-1, \_)] \end{bmatrix}, \tag{4.5}$$

where D is the block diagonal matrix $diag(I_s, D_2, \cdots, D_r)$, and

$$g_3(m, s, x, D_2, D_3, \cdots, D_r, index) = F_r \begin{bmatrix} x[index(\_, 0, \_) \\ (D_2 \otimes I_m) x[index(\_, 1, \_) \\ \vdots \\ (D_r \otimes I_m) x[index(\_, r-1, \_)] \end{bmatrix} \tag{4.6}$$

Finally, for $m \in N'$, $l \in N_m$ and $f : N_n \to C^{rs}$, define

$$g_4(m, l, f) = \|_{l=0}^{m-1} f(l) = f(0) \| f(1) \| \cdots \| f(m-1) \tag{4.7}$$

where $\|$ denotes vector concatenation.

Factors that occur in the members of $\mathcal{F}$ can be expressed in terms of these four functions. In the following examples, as well as in the subsequent discussion, we assume the lexicographical ordering for tuples of arguments of $index$.

Examples:

If $x \in C^{rs}$, then

$$(F_r \times I_s) T_s^{rs} x = g_1(s, 0, x, D_s^{rs}, (D_s^{rs})^2 \cdots, (D_s^{rs})^{r-1}, sh + j) \tag{4.8}$$

and

$$T_s^{rs}(F_r \otimes I_s) x = g_2(s, 0, x, D_s^{rs}, (D_s^{rs})^2 \cdots, (D_s^{rs})^{r-1}, sh + j) \tag{4.9}$$

where $(h, j) = (0, 0), \cdots, (r-1, s-1)$.

If $x \in C^n$, then

$$(F_r \otimes I_{ms})(T_s^{rs} \otimes I_m) = g_3(s, m, x, D_s^{rs}, (D_s^{rs})^2, \cdots, (D_s^{rs})^{r-1}, msh + lm + j) \tag{4.10}$$

where $(h, l, j) = (0, 0, 0), \cdots, (r-1, s-1, m-1)$. If B is an $s \times s$ matrix and $x \in C^{ms}$, then

$$(I_m \otimes B) x = g_4(m, l, Bx[index(sl + \_]). \tag{4.11}$$

4.2. $\mathcal{G}$ is a basis for the family $\mathcal{F}$ of radix-r FFTs . Our goal is to express the above tensor formulas in terms of the functions in $\mathcal{G} = \{g_1, g_2, g_3, g_4\}$. This is straight forward for CT_i and GS_i :

$$CT_i x = (I_{r^{k-i}} \otimes (F_r \otimes I_{r^{i-1}})T^{r^i})x \tag{4.12}$$
$$= g_4(r^{k-i}, l, f_l) \tag{4.13}$$

where

$$f_l = g_1(r^{i-1}, l, x, D^{r^i}, (D^{r^i})^2, \cdots, (D^{r^i})^{r-1}, lr^i + hr^{i-1} + j)$$

and where (l, h, j) varies lexicographically over $N_{r^{k-i}} \times N_{r-1} \times N_{r^{i-1}}$.

$$GS_i x = (I_{r^{i-1}} \otimes T^{r^{k-i+1}}(F_r \otimes I_{r^{k-i}}))x \tag{4.14}$$
$$= g_4(r^{i-1}, l, f_l) \tag{4.15}$$

where

$$f_l = g_2(r^{k-i}, l, x, D^{r^{k-i+1}}, (D^{r^{k-i+1}})^2, \cdots, (D^{r^{k-i+1}})^{r-1}, lr^{k-i+1} + hr^{k-i} + j))$$

and where (l, h, j) varies lexicographically over $N_{r^{i-1}} \times N_{r-1} \times N_{r^{k-i}}$.

There is a problem with implementing the Pease algorithms in Sisal since the tensor formula for each has a permutation factor on the left. Permutations which occur on the left of tensor formulas represent scatter operations, which have no direct implementation in Sisal 12.9.2 Of course one way to implement a scatter operation is by means of a separate permutation phase, a potentially expensive option that we will not consider here. On the other hand, by algebraically manipulating the DF form of the Korn-Lambiote formula, we obtain a Pease variant which can be readily implemented.

$$KLDF_i x = P(r^k, r^{k-1})(T^{r^{k-i+1}} \otimes I_{r^{i-1}})(F_r \otimes I_{r^{k-1}})x \tag{4.16}$$
$$= P(r^k, r^{k-1})v_D \circ P(r^k, r^{k-1})(F_r \otimes I_{r^{k-1}})x \tag{4.17}$$

where $D = T^{r^{k-i+1}} \otimes I_{r^{i-1}}$. We can show that

$$P(r^k, r^{k-1})v_D = v_{D'} \tag{4.18}$$

where

$$D' = \bigoplus_{l=0}^{r^{k-i}-1} (I_{r^{i-1}} \otimes (D_r^{r^{k-i}})^l) \tag{4.19}$$

Hence

$$KLDF_i x = v_{D'} \circ P(r^k, r^{k-1})(F_r \otimes I_{r^{k-1}})x \tag{4.20}$$
$$= v_{D'} \circ (I_{r^{k-1}} \otimes F_r)P(r^k, r^{k-1})x \tag{4.21}$$
$$= (\bigoplus_{l=0}^{r^{k-i}-1} (I_{r^{i-1}} \otimes (D_r^{r^{k-i+1}})^l))(I_{r^{k-1}} \times F_r)P(r^k, r^{k-1})x \tag{4.22}$$
$$= (\bigoplus_{l=0}^{r^{k-i}-1} (I_{r^{i-1}} \otimes (D_r^{r^{k-i+1}})^l))(\bigoplus_{l=0}^{r^{k-i}-1} (I_{r^{i-1}} \otimes F_r)P(r^k, r^{k-1}))x \tag{4.23}$$

$$(4.24)\qquad = \Big(\bigoplus_{l=0}^{r^{k-i}-1} (I_{r^{i-1}} \otimes diag(1, \omega^{l}_{r^{k-i+1}}, \cdots, \omega^{(r-1)l}_{r^{k-i+1}})F_r)P(r^k, r^{k-1})x$$

$$(4.25)\qquad = g_4(r^{k-i}, l, g_4(r^{i-1}, j, X_l, diag(1, \omega^{l}_{r^{k-i+1}}, \cdots, \omega^{(r-1)l}_{r^{k-i+1}})F_r X_{lj}))$$

where

$$(4.26)\qquad X_{l,j}(x) = \begin{bmatrix} 1 \\ \omega^{l}_{r^{k-i}} \\ \omega^{2l}_{r^{k-i}} \\ \vdots \\ \omega^{(r-1)l}_{r^{k-i}} \end{bmatrix} \begin{bmatrix} x[lr^{i-1}+j] \\ x[lr^{i-1}+r^{k-1}+j] \\ \vdots \\ x[lr^{i-1}+(r-1)r^{k-1}+j] \end{bmatrix}$$

Because of the presence of $I_{r^{i-1}} \otimes diag(1, \omega^{l}_{r^{k-i+1}}, \cdots, \omega^{(r-1)l}_{r^{k-i+1}})F_r$ in this new expression for $KLDF_i$ we call the resulting algorithm a DF form of the Pease algorithm.

The DT form of Korn-Lambiote can be expressed in terms $\mathcal{G}$ as follows:

$$(4.27)\qquad KLDT_i x = (F_r \otimes I_{r^{k-1}})(T^{r^i} \otimes I_{r^{k-i}})P(r^k, r)x$$

$$(4.28)\qquad = g_3(r^{i-1}, r^{k-i}, x, D^{r^i}, \cdots, (D^{r^i})^{r-1}, h + lr^{k-i+1} + jr)$$

where (h, l, j) varies lexicographically over $N_{r-1} \times N_{r^{i-1}} \times N_{r^{k-i}}$.
Finally, the Stockham algorithms are easily expressed in terms of $\mathcal{G}$ as follows:

$$(4.29)\qquad S_i x = ((F_r \otimes I_{r^{i-1}})T^{r^i} \otimes I_{r^{k-i}})(P(r^i, r) \otimes (I_{r^{k-i}})x$$

$$(4.30)\qquad = ((F_r \otimes I_{r^{i-1}}) \otimes I_{r^{k-i}})(T^{r^i} \otimes I_{r^{k-i}})(P(r^i, r) \otimes (I_{r^{k-i}})x$$

$$(4.31)\qquad = (F_r \otimes I_{r^{k-1}})(T^{r^i} \otimes I_{r^{k-i}})(P(r^i, r) \otimes I_{r^{k-i}})x$$

$$(4.32)\qquad = g_3(r^{i-1}, r^{k-i}, x, D^{r^i}, (D^{r^i})^2, \cdots, (D^{r^i})^{r-1}, r^{k-i}h + r^{k-i+1}l + j)$$

where (h, l, j) varies lexicographically over $N_{r-1} \times N_{r^{i-1}} \times N_{r^{k-i}}$.

$$(4.33)\qquad TS_i x = (I_{r^{k-i}} \otimes (F_r \otimes I_{r^{i-1}})T^{r^i})(P(r^{k-i+1}, r^{k-i}) \otimes I_{r^{i-1}})x$$

$$(4.34)\qquad = g_4(r^{k-i}, l, g_1(r^{i-1}, l, x, D^{r^i}, (D^{r^i})^2, \cdots, (D^{r^i})^{r-1}, lr^{i-1} + hr^{k-1} + j))$$

where (l, h, j) varies lexicographically over $N_{r^{k-i}} \times N_{r-1} \times N_{r^{i-1}}$.

5. Sisal implementations for $\mathcal{G}$. By the results of the previous section, each of the radix-r, size r^k FFTs we have considered can be expressed up to a permutation in the form $\prod_{i=1}^{k} step_i$, where $step_i$ is either g_3 or a simple composition of g_4 with either g_1 g_2, g_4. Thus, we could easily obtain a package for radix-r, size r^k FFTs in a given target language by simply programming the functions $\mathcal{G}$ and then appropriately compose them to obtain each of the FFTs. Let us consider this possibility in Sisal.

Some explanation of Sisal is necessary. The function header gives the name of the function, the names and types of its parameters and the types of its results. Sisal functions can return one or more results of possibly different types. Array types in Sisal are devoid of size or bound information. The || operator is array catenation. There are two types of for expressions in Sisal, the "forall" expression and the "initial for" expression. The first type, illustrated in the pseudo code of the templates below, initiates instances of independent loop bodies that can be executed in parallel or vectorially on architectures that support these capabilities.

There are two problems with implementing the members of $\mathcal{G}$ in Sisal. First, Sisal, 12.9.2 treats functions as second class objects. They cannot be passed as arguments nor returned as values of functions. A later version that has not been released, Sisal 90, allows functions as arguments. For the present, however, the functions *index* and f used in defining the members of $\mathcal{G}$ cannot be used as parameters in Sisal functions.

Second, implementations of the members of $\mathcal{G}$ require the return of r values in their interior **for** loops and this number must be fixed. That is, Sisal functions of radix-r FFTs cannot contain the radix as a paramenter.

Since we cannot implement the members of $\mathcal{G}$ as proper Sisal functions, we instead give Sisal forms for their implementations. These forms which will serve as "templates" in the sense that for a given value of r and given functional parameters, appropriate sustitutions into the bodies of these forms (as well as appropriate changes to the pseudo function headings) will yield proper Sisal constructs that comprise the corresponding Sisal functions.

Arguments for g_1, g_2, and g_3 include $r-1$ diagonal matrices $D_2, D_3, \cdots, D_r$, which we implement by $r-1$ one-dimensional arrays containing the diagonals.

```
TEMPLATE 1
 function g1(s,l,x,D2,D3, ... ,Dr,index)
  let
   comps1,comps2,...,compsr:=
     for j in 0,s-1
      comp1,comp2, ... ,compr :=
       Fr(x[index(l,0,j)],x[index(l,1,j)]*D2[j],..,
                              x[index(l,r-1,j)]*Dr[j])
     returns array of comp1
             array of comp2
                    .
                    .
                    .
             array of compr
     end for
  in
   comps1||comps2||...||compsr
  end let
 end function
```

The **for** expression in this template computes a vector $[comp1, comp2, \cdots, compr]$ for each value of j and returns the vector $[comps1, comps2, \cdots, compsr]$, where each *compsi* is the concatention of the *compi*s. The template for g_2 is similar except in this case, instead of F_r we use H_r, an r-valued function such that

$$H_r(y_2, \cdots, y_r, z_1, z_2, \cdots, z_r) = [1, y_2, \cdots, y_r]^T \odot F_r(z_1, z_2, \cdots, z_r). \tag{5.1}$$

```
TEMPLATE 2
 function g2(s,l,x,D2,D3,...,Dr,index)
```

```
  let
   comps1,comps2,...,compsr :=
     for j in 0,s-1
      comp1,comp2,...,compr :=
       Hr(D2[j],...,Dr[j],x[index(l,0,j)],x[index(l,1,j)],...,
                                         x[index(l,r-1,j)])
     returns array of comp1
             array of comp2
                   .
                   .
                   .
             array of compr
     end for
  in
   comps1||comps2||...||compsr
  end let
 end function
```

```
TEMPLATE 3
 function g3(m,s,x,D2,D3,...,Dr,index)
  let y1,y2,...,yr :=
   for l in 0,s-1
    comps1,comps2,...,compsr :=
     for j in 0,m-1
      Fr(x[index(l,0,j)],x[index(l,1,j)]*D2[l],...,
                          x[index(l,r-1,j)]*Dr[l])
     returns array of comp1
             array of comp2
                   .
                   .
             array of compr
     end for
   returns value of catenate comps1
           value of catenate comps2
                  .
                  .
           value of catenate compsr
   end for
  in
   y1||y2||...||yr
  end let
 end function
```

The use of the above three templates for given values of r and *index* requires replacing each occurrence of r and $index(a, b)$ by their values and eliminating accompanying ellipses. Similarly, for a given function f, the template for g_4, which follows, requires the replacement of $f(l)$ by the body of the function that computes $f(l)$.

```
Template 4
 function g4(m,l,f)
```

```
  for l in 0,m-1
   comps := f(l)
  returns value of catenate comps
  end for
 end function
```

6. Sisal implementations for radix 3, size 3^k. We illustrate the use of the templates given in the previous section by deriving Sisal implementations of the members of $\mathcal{F}$ for a fixed radix, $r = 3$. Development of implementations for other radices is of course similar.

Having fixed r, it is essential to optimize the computation of $F_r x$, the DFT of size r. It is easy to show that $F_3 x$ can be computed with 16 real operations.

Since Sisal 12.9.2 does not contain the complex data type, one must develop Sisal functions for complex arithmetic in terms of ordered pairs of reals. For the representation of complex vectors it is convenient to use pairs of one-dimensional real arrays. However for purposes of clarity, we shall avoid the cumberson notation of user-defined complex operations and pairs of real arrays by assuming the existence of a **complex** type. Operations on complex numbers will be represented by the usual symbols (as was done in the previous section).

By the results of Section 4, CT_i, GS_i, and TS_i are compositions of g_4 with g_1 or g_2 (i.e., values of g_4 with functional arguments g_1 or g_2) and their implementations consist of two nested **for**s. Denoting the control variable of the outer **for** by l and that of the inner **for** by j, each function *index* is of the form $l * a + h * b + j$, where for $r = 3$, $h = 0, 1, 2$. We thus have the following implementations for g_1 and g_2.

```
function g1(s,l,a,b:integer;x:array[complex];
          D2,D3:array[complex] returns array[complex])
 let
  comps1,comps2,comps3 :=
   for j in 0,s-1
    comp1,comp2,comp3 := F3(x[l*a+j],x[l*a+b+j]*D2[j],
                                  x[l*a+2*b+j]*D3[j])
   returns array of comp1
           array of comp2
           array of comp3
   end for
 in
  comps1||comps2||comps3
 end let
end function

function g2(s,l,a,b:integer;x:array[complex];
          D2,D3:array[complex] returns array[complex])
 let
  comps1,comps2,comps3 :=
   for j in 0,s-1
    comp1,comp2,comp3 := h3(x[l*a+j],x[l*a+b+j]*D2[j],
                                  x[l*a+2*b+j]*D3[j])
   returns array of comp1
```

```
            array of comp2
            array of comp3
    end for
  in
   comps1||comps2||comps3
  end let
end function
```

Implementations of the composition of g_4 with g_1 and g_4 with g_2 are respectively:

```
function parg1(m,s,a,b:integer;x: array[complex];
               D2,D3:array[complex] returns array[complex])]
 for l in 0,m-1
  comps := g1(s,l,a,b,x,D2,D3)
 returns value of catenate comps
 end for
end function
```

```
function parg2(m,s,a,b:integer;x:array[complex];
          D2,D3:array[array[complex]] returns array[complex])
for l in 0,m-1
 comps := g2(s,l,a,b,x,D2,D3)
returns value of catenate comps
end for
```

The implementation of g_3 also involves two nested **for**s and in this case each instance of *index* needed to implement $KLDT_i$ and S_i is of the form $l * a + h * b + j * c$, where l and j are the control variables of the outer and inner **for**s, respectively and $h = 0, 1, 2, 3$. Thus for our purposes, we can implement the function g_3 as follows:

```
function g3(m,s,a,b,c:integer;x:array[complex];
           D2,D3:array[complex] returns array[complex])
let y1,y2,y3 :=
 for l in 0,s-1
  comps1,comps2,comps3 :=
   for j in 0,m-1
    comp1,comp2,comp3 :=F4(x[l*a+j*c],x[l*a+b+j*c]*D2[l],
                                  x[l*a+2*b+j*c]*D3[l])
   returns array of comp1
           array of comp2
           array of comp3
   end for
 returns value of catenate comps1
         value of catenate comps2
         value of catenate comps3
 end for
in y1||y2||y3
end let
end function
```

For DFTs of size 3^k, CT_i, S_i, and $KLDT_i$ require twiddle factors given by $T^{3^i} = \bigoplus_{h=0}^{2}(D^{3^i})^h$ and GS_i, $KLDF_i$, and TS_i require twiddle factors given by $T^{3^{k-i+1}} = \bigoplus_{h=0}^{2}(D^{3^{k-i+1}})^h$. In the following implementations we assume that $D2$, and $D3$ are one-dimensional arrays that contain D and D^2 (where D is either D^{3^i} or $D^{3^{k-i+1}}$), respectively.

```
function CTi(i,k:integer;x,D2,D3:array[complex]
             returns array[complex])
pargl(exp(3,k-i),exp(3,(i-1),exp(3,i),exp(i-1),x,D2,D3)
end function

function GSi(i,k:integer;x,D2,D3:array[complex]
             returns array[complex])
parg2(exp(3,i-1),exp(3,k-i),exp(3,k-i+1),exp(3,k-i),x,D2,D3)
end function

function TSi(i,k:integer;x,D2,D3:array[complex]
             returns array[complex])
pargl(exp(3,k-i),exp(3,i-1),exp(3,i-1),exp(3,k-1),x,D2,D3)
end function
```

An implementation of $KLDF_i$ can be obtained by successively substituting appropriate functional arguments two times in Template 4 and making appropriate changes in variable names to obtain:

```
function KLDFi(i,k:integer;x,D2,D3:array[complex]
               returns array[complex])
for l in 0,exp(3,k-i)-1
 comps:=
  for j in 0,exp(3,i-1)-1
   ccomps:=
    array[0:h3(D2[l],D3[l],x[l*exp(3,i-1)+j],
                          x[l*exp(3,i-1)+exp(3,k-1)+j],
                          x[l*exp(3,i-1)+2*exp(3,k-1)+j])
  returns value of catenate comps
  end for
returns value of catenate comps
end for
end function
```

Implementations of $KLDT_i$ and S_i are as follows:

```
function KLDTi(i,k:integer;x,D2,D3:array[complex]
                          returns array[complex])
g3(exp(3,k-i),exp(3,i-1),exp(3,k-i+1),1,3,x,D2,D3)
end function

function Si(i,k:integer;x,D2,D3:array[complex]
                       returns array[complex])
g3(exp(3,k-i),exp(3,i-1),exp(3,k-i+1),exp(3,k-i),1,x,D2,D3)
end function
```

To complete the implementations of radix r FFTs it remains only to determine implementations for (4.1)-(4.3). A vector $x[i]$, $i = 0, 1, \cdots, n-1$, can be digit-reversal permuted, i.e., $R(r^k)x$, by precomputing a vector of digit-reversed indices, *index* and then computing

$x[index[i]]$, $i = 0, 1, \cdots, n-1$. Fast methods for computing *index* on shared-memory machines can be found in [15]. If *index* contains r^k digit-reversed indices, then $R(r^k)x$ can be computed in Sisal by

```
function permute(n:integer;index:array[integer];
                  x:array[complex]returns array[complex])
for i in 0,n-1
returns array of x[index[i]]
end for
end function
```

The composition of (4.1) can be implemented by

```
for initial
 i:=1;
 y:=x;
 while i<=k  repeat
  y:=step(old i,old y)
  i := old i +1
returns value of y
end for
end function
```

The *for initial expression* in the above code is a sequential loop expression that retains functional semantics. The loop's first iteration is the code between the keywords **for initial** and **while**. The code between the guard and the returns clause is the loop's body and is executed repeatedly while the guard is true. Each execution of the body computes a new value of y in terms of its value in the previous iteration. The value of **old** *name* is the value of *name* in the previous iteration. Since both **old** name and *name* co-exist for the entire execution of the loop body, the computation maintains referentialtransparency.

Thus, the implementation of any of the radix r FFTs presented here can be obtained by making an appropriate application of the function *permute* and replacing $step_i$ by either CT_i, $KLDT_i$, S_i, GS_i, $KLDF_i$, or TS_i in the above Sisal form. For example, an implementation of the radix-3 Cooley-Tukey algorithm for vector size 3^k is given by the following Sisal function, where we assume that $DD2$ and $DD3$ are two-dimensional arrays whose i-th rows contain the diagonals of D^{3^i} and $(D^{3^i})^2$, respectively.

```
function CT(k:integer;index:array[integer];
            x,DD2,DD3:array[complex] returns array[complex])
for initial
 i:=1;
 y:=permute(exp(3,k),index,y);
 while i<=k repeat
  y:=CTi(old i,k, old y,DD2[old i],DD3[old i]);
  i:=old i+1
returns value of y
end for
end function
```

Actually, in practice it is more efficient to define CT_i with a different set of parameters in order to amoritize the cost of exponentiation. For example, we could define

```
function CTi(p,q,p1:integer;x,D2,D3:array[complex]
                            returns array[complex])
parg1(q,p1,p,p1,x,D2,D3)
end function
```

and then define

```
function CT(k:integer index:array[integer];
          x,DD2,DD3:array[complex] returns array[complex])
let n := exp(3,k);
 in
  for initial
   i := 1;
   p1 := 1;
   p := 3;
   q := n/3;
   y := permute(n,index,x);
   while i <= k repeat
    y := CTi(old p,old q,old p1,old y,DD2[old i],DD3[old i]
    i := old i+1;
    p1 := old p;
    p := 3 * old p;
    q := old q/3
  returns value of y
  end for
end let
end function
```

Similar assertions can be made for GSi, TSi, KLDFi, KLDTi, Si and the iterative **for** loops to compose them.

Execution times for radix 3 and 1, 2, 4, and 8 processors are given in Tables 1, 2, and 3.

Table 1. C-90 execution times in seconds for radix-3 FFTs of size 3^{12}

	1 CPU	2 CPU's	4 CPU's	8 CPU's
Cooley-Tukey	1.196	0.607	0.334	0.168
Gentleman-Sande	1.190	0.604	0.316	0.170
DF Pease	1.432	0.799	0.455	0.316
DT Korn-Lambiote	0.953	0.490	0.255	0.155
Stockham	0.939	0.495	0.272	0.147
Transposed Stockham	1.191	0.605	0.366	0.177

Table 2. C-90 execution times in seconds for radix-3 FFTs of size 3^{13}

	1 CPU	2 CPU's	4 CPU's	8 CPU's
Cooley-Tukey	3.610	1.831	0.946	0.518
Gentleman-Sande	3.580	1.818	0.929	0.495
DF Pease	4.597	2.538	1.422	0.974
DT Korn-Lambiote	2.873	1.470	0.756	0.439
Stockham	2.834	1.435	0.732	0.417
Transposed Stockham	3.595	1.814	0.921	0.490

Table 3. C-90 execution times in seconds for radix-3 FFTs of size 3^{14}

	1 CPU	2 CPU's	4 CPU's	8 CPU's
Cooley-Tukey	10.843	5.510	2.828	1.534
Gentleman-Sande	10.769	5.483	2.811	1.496
DF Pease	14.654	8.038	4.562	2.984
DT Korn-Lambiote	8.659	4.411	2.283	1.244
Stockham	8.563	4.333	2.214	1.172
Transposed Stockham	10.809	5.448	2.814	1.532

As can be seen from these results, DF Pease performs up to 2.5 times slower than the other five implementations. This is due to short vector lengths. For the other five implementations, execution times are within 30% of each other and speedup is nearly linear, at least up to four processors. The Stockham implementation is the winner for any number of processors and DF Korn-Lambiote is a close second. The difference in times between these two implementations can be attributed to the final ordering phase needed by Korn-Lambiote. Another advantage of the Stockham algorithm (as well as the transposed Stockham algorithm) is that avoidance of the final ordering phase also eliminates the permutation vector *index*, thus resulting in an economy of n integer words.

7. Radix-4, size 2^k. The most commonly used FFTs are those of size 2^k. Radix-2 FFTs of size 2^k are easily obtained following the development of the previous section. Execution times for radix-2 are given in Tables 4, 5, and 6.

Table 4. C-90 execution times in seconds for radix-2 FFTs of size 2^{19}

	1 CPU	2 CPU's	4 CPU's	8 CPU's
Cooley-Tukey	0.896	0.475	0.230	0.120
Gentleman-Sande	1.194	0.598	0.316	0.158
DF Pease	1.812	0.941	0.545	0.323
DT Korn-Lambiote	0.989	0.499	0.252	0.141
Stockham	0.931	0.470	0.237	0.132
Transposed Stockham	0.858	0.433	0.223	0.115

Table 5. C-90 execution times in seconds for radix-2 FFts of size 2^{20}

	1 CPU	2 CPU's	4 CPU's	8 CPU's
Cooley-Tukey	1.803	0.907	0.459	0.244
Gentleman-Sande	2.390	1.195	0.604	0.322
DF Pease	3.832	1.985	1.109	0.700
DT Korn-Lambiote	1.982	0.999	0.519	0.266
Stockham	1.875	0.942	0.477	0.255
Transposed Stockham	1.726	0.886	0.444	0.235

Table 6. C-90 execution times in seconds for radix-2 FFTs of size 2^{21}

	1 CPU	2 CPU's	4 CPU's	8 CPU's
Cooley-Tukey	3.623	1.821	0.946	0.479
Gentleman-Sande	4.778	2.416	1.242	0.653
DF Pease	7.831	4.242	2.355	1.405
DT Korn-Lambiote	3.987	2.014	1.015	0.563
Stockham	3.767	2.008	0.960	0.511
Transposed Stockham	3.477	1.743	0.890	0.461

As before, there is a noticeable difference between DF Pease and the other implementations for radix 2, while execution times for the other five implementation do not vary from one another by more than 30% and at least up to four processors, have almost linear speedup. However in this case, DF Pease is up to 3 times slower than the other implementations. The fastest implementation is that of the transposed Stockham algorithm. However, the running time of even this algorithm is orders of magnitud slower than the running time of the Cray FFT library routine. We explain why in the next section and we develop a tensor formula for a hybrid algorithm whose performance is equivalent to the library routine.

8. Toward an optimal FFT, size 2^k. In addition to its relative speed, the transposed Stockham algorithm, as well as the Stockham algorithm, also has the advantage as noted in Section 6, that it requires n integer words less storage than the other radix-r algorithms. Given then that the transposed Stockham algorithm is relatively efficient, it is natural to ask if it can be improved even more. An important observation is that vector lengths grow from 1 in the first sequential step to 2^{k-1} in the last. In a vector machine such as the C-90, long vectors must be maintained in order to obtain peak performance. Thus, the transposed Stockham algorithm is much more efficient in its last iterations that its first ones. On the other hand, in the Stockham algorithm, vector lengths decrease from 2^{k-1} in the first iteration to 1 in the last. Thus, Stockham is more efficient in its first iterations that its last ones.

One possibility for maintaining long vector lengths throughout, would be to start with the Stockham algorithm and switch to the transposed Stockham algorithm midway. This idea, which is described in Hockney [11] and which we term the "hybrid Stockham algorithm," has been implemented by Cray Research Inc. in its FFT library routines.

Another possibility for improving performance is to use radix 4 instead of radix 2. This decreases the number of flops as well as the number of sequential steps.

In this section we develop an implementation for the hybrid Stockham algorithm, size 2^k, radix 4. This development is a good illustration of the tensor formulation methodology. That is, having observed the performance of various size 2^k FFTs, we have identified opporunities for optimization. At this stage, we return to a tensor formulation of the algorithm, use laws of tensor algebra to modify it in accordance with the new specification, and then translate the new algorithm to program code.

Now for size 2^k, k even, the Stockham algorithms are just special cases of the general radix-r cases considered previously. For arbitrary k, we can use special cases of mixed-radix versions of the Stockham algorithms [19]. In order to describe these two algorithms, we first define some notation.

Let $n = 2^k$. Define $k_1 = \lfloor k/2 \rfloor$. For k even define $P(n) = R(4^{k_1})$ and $k_2 = k_1$. For k odd define $P(n) = P(n, n/2)(I_2 \otimes R(4^{k_1}))$ and $k_2 = k_1 + 1$. Hence $n = 4^{k_1}$ for k even and $n = 2 \cdot 4^{k_1}$ for k odd.

For k even and each $i = 1, 2, \cdots, k_1$, let $p_i = 4^i$, $q_i = 4^{k_1 - i}$, $r_i = 4$. For k odd and each $i = 1, 2, \cdots, k_2$, let $p_i = 2 \cdot 4^{i-1}$, $q_i = 4^{k_1 - i + 1}$, $r_1 = 2$, and $r_i = 4$, $i \geq 2$. Also define $p_0 = 1$ and $q_0 = n$. Hence $q_i p_i = n$ for all $i = 0, 1, \cdots, k_2$.

The Stockham algorithm for radix-4, size 2^k is given by

$$F_n = \prod_{i=1}^{k_2} S_i$$

where

$$S_i = ((F_{r_i} \otimes I_{p_{i-1}})(T^{p_i}_{p_{i-1}} \otimes I_{q_i})(P(p_i, 4) \otimes I_{q_i})$$

The transposed algorithm for radix -4 is given by

$$F_n = \prod_{i=1}^{k_2} TS_i$$

where

$$TS_i = (I_{q_i} \otimes (F_{r_i} \otimes I_{p_{i-1}})T^{p_i}_{p_{i-1}})(P(sr, s) \otimes I_{p_{i-1}})$$

The midway switch from one Stockham algorithm necessitates a permutation. To explain this, let us start with the identity

$$(P(mr, r) \otimes I_s)P(mrs, m) = P(mrs, mr)(P(sr, s) \otimes I_m)$$

Then,

$$(P(p_i, r_i) \otimes I_{q_i})P(n, p_{i-1}) = P(n, p_i)(P(q_{i-1}, q_i) \otimes I_{p_{i-1}})$$

and

$$S_i P(n, p_{i-1}) = P(n, p_i)(I_{q_i} \otimes (F_{r_i} \otimes I_{p_{i-1}}))T^{p_i}_{p-i-1}(P(q_{i-1}) \otimes I_{p_{i-1}}) \tag{8.1}$$

$$= P(n, p_i) TS_i \tag{8.2}$$

or

$$P(n, q_i) S_i = TS_i P(n, q_{i-1})$$

Thus,

$$F_{2^k} = TS_{k_2}TS_{k_2-1}\cdots TS_1 \tag{8.3}$$
$$= TS_{k_2}TS_{k_2-1}\cdots TS_1P(n,q_0) \tag{8.4}$$
$$= TS_{k_2}TS_{k_2-1}\cdots P(n,q_1)S_1 \tag{8.5}$$
$$= TS_{k_2}TS_{k_2-1}\cdots P(n,q_2)S_2S_1 \tag{8.6}$$
$$\vdots \tag{8.7}$$
$$= TS_{k_2}TS_{k_2-1}\cdots TS_{i+1}P(n,q_i)S_i\cdots S_1 \tag{8.8}$$

Now if we choose $i = \lfloor k_2/2 \rfloor$, vector lengths will never be less than one-half of their maximum lengths. Using the Stockham algorithm for the first half of iterations, where vector lengths decrease, we can switch to the transposed Stockham algorithm for the second half, where vector lengths increase. However, this requires a power-of-two stride permutation, $P(n,q_i)$, of the output vector of the Stockham phase. Such a permutation can seriously degrade performance on a vector machine with an interleaved memory system having a power-of-two number of banks, such as a Cray.

To circumvent this problem, we can insert "gaps" in the output vector of the Stockham phase and then perform a kind of nonpower-of-two stride permutation. The solution is particularly easy to express in Sisal. Step i, S_i, which is implemented by g_3, returns its result, call it y_i, by concatenating vectors of length q_i. With a slight change in g_3, we can insert an extra datum, say 0, at the end of each of these subvectors. We then perform a stride $q_i + 1$ permutation which also simultaneously eliminates the gaps, thus giving the same result as $P(n,q_i)y_i$.

The modified g_3 can be implemented in Sisal as follows:

```
function gapg3(m,s,a,b,c:integer;x,D2,D3,D4:array[complex]
                returns array[complex])
% Returns the same result as g3(m,s,a,b,c,x,D2,D3,D4 except
  a zero is inserted at end of each subvector of length m
for l in 0,s-1
 comps1,comps2,comps3,comps4 :=
   for j in 0,m-1
    comp1,comp2,comp3,comp4 :=
     F4(x[l*a+j*c],x[l*a+b+j*c],x[l*a+2*b+j*c],
                x[l*a+3*b+j*c],D2[l],D3[l],D4[l])
   returns array of comp1
                    comp2
                    comp3
                    comp4
   end for
returns value of catenate array_addh(comps1,0.0d0)
        value of catenate array_addh(comps2,0.0d0)
        value of catenate array_addh(comps3,0.0d0)
        value of catenate array_addh(comps4,0.0d0)
end for
end function
```

Now

$$TS_{i+1}P(n,q_i) = (I_{q_{i+1}} \otimes (F_{r_i} \otimes I_{p_i})T_{p_i}^{p_{i+1}})(P(q_i,q_{i+1}) \otimes I_{p_i})P(n,q_i) \tag{8.9}$$
$$= g_4(q_{i+1},l,f), \tag{8.10}$$

where $f = g_1(p_i, X_l, D_{p_i}^{p_{i+1}}, (D_{p_i}^{p_{i+1}})^2, (D_{p_i}^{p_{i+1}})^3, l{+}hq_{i+1}{+}(q_i{+}1)j))$, and $(l,h,j) = (0,0,0), \cdots, (q_{i+1}-1, 3, p_i)$.

A Sisal implementation of the complete hybrid version of Stockham's algorithm, whose details we omit, is straightforward. Its body consists of an iterative **for** loop whose control variable i ranges from 1 to k_2. Steps $i = 1, i-1$ are the same as in the implementation of Stockham, step i is an application of *gapg*3, step $i+1$ is an application of *parg*1 and steps $i+2, k_2$ are the same as in the implementation of the transposed Stockham algorithm.

Table 7 gives running times for the hybrid Stockham algorithm. Table 8 compares the hybrid Stockham algorithm with the transposed Stockham algorithm (the fastest radix-2 FFT) for size 2^{21}.

Table 7. C-90 execution times in seconds for hybrid Stockham

size	1 CPU	2 CPU's	4 CPU's	8 CPU's
2^{19}	0.086	0.051	0.036	0.028
2^{20}	0.177	0.105	0.068	0.055
2^{21}	0.383	0.221	0.144	0.114
2^{22}	0.789	0.460	0.318	0.234

Table 8. Comparison of C-90 execution times in seconds for size 2^{21}

Algorithm	1 CPU	2 CPU's	4 CPU's	8 CPU's
Transposed Stockham	3.477	1.743	0.890	0.461
Hybrid Stockham	0.383	0.221	0.144	0.114

We thus see that the hybrid Stockham implementation is order of magnitudes faster that the transposed Stockham algorithm (the fastest radix-2 FFT). In fact, it is 9 times faster for one processor and 4 times faster for eight processors. Speedup for this algorithm is degraded by the interruption of data flow casued by the permutation needed between the two stages of the algorithm.

In a previous Sisal implementation of the hybrid Stockham algorithm on a Cray Y-MP/864, the third author and Cann [8, 5] showed that the Sisal implementation was from 22% (for 1 CPU) to 46% (for 8 CPUs) faster than the FORTRAN version taken from the signal processing library provided by Cray Research. Their study also showed that memory usage of the Sisal implementation was no more than the FORTRAN library routine. The Sisal implementation maintained only two copies of the data vector. The algorithm alternated between the two copies and there was no extraneous allocation of memory or copying of data.

9. Useful language features. Several high-level language features that have simplified the programming of the FFTs developed in the previous sections are iterative and parallel loop expressions and array operations. However, there are several other features that would greatly enhance expressibility of the language that are not present in Sisal 12.9.2. The promotion of functions to first class objects would eliminate the need for templates. The use of polymorphism would greatly streamline the programming. Index arrays would eliminate redundant address calculations, separate access and computations, and tend to reduce the number of loops in programs. Some of these features have been included in a new Sisal 90, but the optimizing compiler for this version has not been released.

In this section, we discuss the above features and how their inclusion in the implementation language would simplify the programming of radix-r FFTs. Using these new tools, we show how we can develop a basis of polymorphic functions that allows one to express the radix-r FFTs in a notation that would allow an almost automatic translation to the enhanced version of a functional language that we envision.

9.1. Polymorphism. We define a *polymorphic function* to be a family of functions each of which is defined by the same expression, but whose domains and ranges are distinct. For example, let $first : A \times B \to A$ be the function defined by

$$first(a, b) = a \tag{9.1}$$

where A and B are arbitrary sets. Then $first : \mathbf{N} \times \mathbf{N} \to \mathbf{N}$, $first : \mathbf{N} \times \mathbf{C} \to \mathbf{N}$, etc. are all distinct members of this family

Another perhaps more interesting example of polymorphism is given by $V = [10, 20, 30, 40, 50]$ and $index = [[3, 1], [5, 2, 4]]$. Then

$$V[index] = [V[3, 1], V[5, 2, 4]] = [[30, 10], [50, 20, 40]].$$

(Note that we now allow vectors and arrays to have nonscalar components. We do *not* identify the vector $[[30, 10], [50, 20, 40]]$ with $[30, 10, 50, 20, 40]$.

A concept related to polymorphism is *overloading*, which is the use of the same function name to denote distinct functions. For example, $*$ and $+$ are overloaded function names as they are used to denote multiplication and addition in various distinct domains such as the integers, reals, etc.. Concerning these two symbols, we assume the following overloading conventions: When A and B are scalars, $A * B$ denotes scalar multiplication, when A is a scalar and B is a vector $A * B$ denotes scalar-vector multiplication, and when A and B are vectors of the same size, $A * B$ denotes the componentwise or *Hadamard* product.

The following examples illustrate the generality of the polymorphic function defined by $*$.

$$[1, 2, 3] * [4, 5, 6] = [4, 10, 18] \tag{9.2}$$

$$[1, 2, 3] * [[0, 1], [1, 2], [2, 3]] = [[0, 1], [2, 4], [6, 9]] \tag{9.3}$$

$$[[1, 2], 3, [4, [5, 6]]] * [2, [2, 3], [9, 10]] = [[2, 4], [6, 9], [36, [50, 60]]] \tag{9.4}$$

The uses of $+$ are similar. In fact, the overloading of $*$ and $+$ gives rise to all of the polymorphic functions we need for expressing the algorithms for $\mathcal{F}$. The following example illustrates the main idea. Let A be the matrix

$$\begin{bmatrix} a & b \\ c & d \end{bmatrix}$$

By definition, for any vector $x = [x_0, x_1]$,

$$Ax = [a * x_0 + b * x_1, c * x_0 + d * x_1] \tag{9.5}$$

By overloading of $*$ and $+$, x_0 and x_1 can be either scalars or vectors. Thus, for example, if $x = [[1, 2, 3], [4, 5, 6]]$, then

$$Ax = [[a + 4b, 2a + 5b, 3a + 6b], [c + 4d, 2c + 5d + 3c + 6d]]$$

9.2. Tensor sum. A useful tool for expressing index arrays mentioned above is the "tensor sum," which we now define. Let $V = [v_0 \ \cdots \ v_{m-1}]$ and let c be a scalar. Then, the *tensor sum* of V and c, denoted $V \oplus c$, is defined to be the m-point vector

$$V \oplus c = V + c = [v_0 + c \ \cdots v_{m-1} + c]. \tag{9.6}$$

If $U = [u_0 \ \cdots \ u_{n-1}]$ $(n > 0)$, the *tensor sum* [4] is defined to be

$$V \oplus U = \|_{i=0}^{n-1} (V \oplus u_i) \tag{9.7}$$

The *partitioned tensor sum* is defined by

$$V \dot{\oplus} U = [V \oplus u_0, V \oplus u_1, \cdots, V \oplus u_{n-1}] \tag{9.8}$$

For example,

$$[1, 2, 3] \oplus [4, 5] = [5, 6, 7] \ \| \ [6, 7, 8] = [5, 6, 7, 6, 7, 8]$$

whereas

$$[1, 2, 3] \dot{\oplus} [4, 5] = [[5, 6, 7], [6, 7, 8]]$$

Tensor sums can be used to permute vector components. For example,

$$x[2V_2 \oplus V_2] = x[0, 2, 1, 3] = [x_0, x_2, x_1, x_3]$$

On the other hand, partitioned tensor sums can be used to partition a vector into subvectors or to partition and permute. For example,

$$x[V_2 \dot{\oplus} 2V_2] = x[[0, 1], [2, 3]] = [[x_0, x_1], [x_2, x_3]]$$

whereas

$$x[2V_2 \oplus V_2] = x[[0, 2], [1, 3]] = [[x_0, x_2], [x_1, x_3]].$$

Two important relations between the tensor product and tensor sum are given by

$$(I_n \otimes A)x = \|_{i=0}^{n-1} Ax[V_m \oplus mi] \tag{9.9}$$

where A is an $m \times m$ matrix and I_n denotes the identity matrix of size n and

$$(A \otimes I_n)x = \| \ Ax[V_n \dot{\oplus} nV_m] \tag{9.10}$$

where for any vector $A = [A_0, A_1, \cdots, A_{m-1}]$, $\| \ A$ denotes $\|_{i=0}^{m-1}$.

9.3. A polymorphic basis for F. It is easy to show that the radix-r FFTs can be expressed as compositions of polymorphic versions of F_r, Hadamard products, catenations, and tensor sums. For example, the i-th step of the Cooley-Tukey algorithm can be written as

$$CT\_step(i,x) = (I_{r^{k-1}} \otimes (F_r \otimes I_{r^{i-1}})T^{r^i})x \tag{9.11}$$

$$= \|_{i=0}^{r^{k-1}-1} F_r(v_{T^{r^i}}[V_{r^{i-1}} \dot{\oplus} r^{i-1}V_r] * x[V_{r^{i-1}} \dot{\oplus} r^{i-1}V_r \oplus r^i l]). \tag{9.12}$$

The availability of polymorphic functions greatly simplifies programming effort. The core function F_r is a good example. Since the computation of F_r consists of a series of addition, substraction, and multiplication and these operations are defined on arrays as well as scalars, the same program code should serve for both F_r and $(F_r \otimes I_n)$.

10. Conclusions. In this paper we have identified four basic function that unify the radix-r FFTs and greatly simplify their programming. We have discussed implementations in the functional language Sisal. The code is clean, modular, and parallel. We have made extensive use of parallel **for** expressions and array operations. We have compared the performance of six commonly used FFTs on a Cray C-90. The speedup of all these implementations is almost linear, at least up to four processors. Taking into account the best features of the six algorithms, we developed an FFT implementation for size 2^k that is seemingly optimal for the C-90. We have discussed language features that are most beneficial to FFT programming and have suggested some features that might be taken into account in the design of functional or perhaps, object-oriented languages.

REFERENCES

[1] D.H. Bailey, *A High-performance fast Fourier transform algorithm for the Cray-2*, J. Supercomputing 1 (1987), pp. 43-60.

[2] D. H. Bailey, *A high-performance FFT algorithm for vector supercomputers,* International J. Supercomputer Applications 2 (1988), pp. 82-87.

[3] D. Bollman, F. Sanmiguel and J. Seguel, *Implementing FFT's in Sisal*, Proc. of the Second Sisal User's Conference, Lawrence Livermore National Laboratory, San Diego, CA (1992), pp. 59-65.

[4] D. Bollman, J. Seguel, and J. Feo, *Fast digit-index permutations*, Scientific Prog., 5(2) (1996), pp. 137-146.

[5] D. Cann, *Retire Fortran? A Debate Rekindled,* Comm. ACM, 30(8) (1992), pp. 81-89.

[6] W. T. Cochran, et al. *What is the Fast Fourier Transform?*, IEEE Trans. Audio Electroacoust., AU-15(2) (1967), pp. 45-55.

[7] J.W. Cooley and J.W. Tukey, *An Algorithm for the Machine Calculation of Complex Fourier Series*, Math. Comp., 19 (1965), pp. 297-301.

[8] J. Feo and D. Cann, *Developing a high-performance FFT algorithm in Sisal for a vector supercomputer*, Proc. of the Third Sisal User's Conference, Lawrence Livermore National Laboratory, San Diego, CA (1993), pp. 164-171.

[9] W.M. Gentleman and G. Sande, *Fast Fourier transforms for fun and profit*, Proc. 1966 Fall Joint Computer Conference AFIPS 29, 563-578.

[10] I.J. Good, *The interaction algorithm and practical Fourier analysis*, J. Royal Statist. Ser. B, 20 (1958), pp. 361-372.

[11] R. W. Hockney and C.R. Jesshope, *Parallel Computers 2*, Adam Hilger Ltd., Bristol, England, 1988.

[12] J. Johnson, R. Johnson, D. Rodriguez, and R. Tolimieri, *A Methodology for Designing, Modifying and Implementing Fourier Transform Algorithms on Various Architectures*, Circuits, Systems and Signal Processing, 9 (1990), pp. 449-500.

[13] D.G. Korn and J.J. Lambiotte, *Computing the Fast Fourier Transform on a Vector Computer*, Math. Comp., 33 (1979), pp. 977-992.

[14] M.C. Pease, *An Adaptation of the Fast Fourier Transform for Parallel Processing*, J. ACM, 15 (1968), pp. 252-265.

[15] J. SEGUEL AND D. BOLLMAN, *Fast digit-reversal algorithms on a shared-memory machine*, Parallel Computing 20 (1994), 93-99.

[16] S. SKEDZIELEWSKI, *Sisal* in Parallel Functional Languages and Compilers, B. Szymanski, ed., ACM press, 1991, pp. 105-157.

[17] L.H. THOMAS, *Using a computer to solve problems in physics*, in Applications of Digital Computers, Ginn and Co., Boston, MA, 1963.

[18] R. TOLIMIERI, M. AN, AND C. LU, *Algorithms for Discrete Fourier Transform and Convolution*, Springer-Verlag, New York, 1989.

[19] C. Van Loan, *Computational Frameworks for the Fast Fourier Transform*, SIAM, 1992.

VISUALIZATION OF DO-LOOP PERFORMANCE USING AVS

OSCAR NAÍM* AND ANTHONY J.G. HEY†

Abstract. Performance visualization is the use of graphical display techniques for the analysis of performance data in order to improve understanding of complex performance phenomena. Performance visualization systems for parallel programs have been helpful in the past and they are commonly used in order to improve parallel program performance. However, despite the advances that have been made in visualizing scientific data, techniques for visualizing performance of parallel programs remain *ad hoc* and performance visualization becomes more difficult as the parallel system becomes more complex. Massively parallel processors can produce a huge amount of performance data and sophisticated methods for representing and displaying this data are required.

The use of scientific visualization tools (e.g. AVS, Application Visualization System) to display performance data is becoming a very powerful alternative to support performance analysis of parallel programs. One advantage of this approach is that no tool development is required and that every feature of the data visualization tool can be used for further data analysis.

In this paper the Do-Loop-Surface (DLS) display, an abstract view of the performance of a particular do-loop in a program implemented using AVS, is presented as an example on how a data visualization tool can be used to define new abstract representations of performance, helping the user to analyze complex data potentially generated by a large number of processors[1].

1. INTRODUCTION. Performance is a critical issue in current massively parallel processors. However, the delivery of adequate performance is not automatic and performance tools are required in order to help the programmer to *understand* the behaviour of a parallel program. In recent years, a wide variety of performance visualization tools have been developed for this purpose using different visualization techniques to understand complex performance processes (e.g. Express Tools [27], SIMPLE [20], PA-Tools [26], ParaGraph [15, 14], TOPSYS PATOP [3], and Pablo [28]. A more detailed survey of Performance Tools is contained in reference [21]).

Performance visualization is the use of graphical display techniques to present an analysis of performance data for an improved understanding of complex performance phenomena [18]. Performance visualization systems for parallel programs have been helpful in the past and they are commonly used in order to improve parallel program performance [32, 15, 28]. However, despite the advances that have been made in visualizing scientific data, techniques for visualizing performance of parallel programs remain *ad hoc* and performance visualization becomes more difficult as the parallel system becomes more complex.

Visualization is now recognized as a fundamental element in scientific computing. As high performance computing allows us to solve ever larger problems, and as measurement technology yields ever more data to be studied, so our ability to analyze and understand this data relies more and more on visual processing. One of the advantages of visualization is that it is a way of seeing the unseen [4]. *"Imagination or visualization, and in particular the use of diagrams, has a crucial part to play in scientific investigation"* (Rene Descartes, 1637)[2]. A good summary of the history of visualization is presented by Brodlie in [4].

*Oscar Naím: Computer Sciences Department, University of Wisconsin, Madison, Wisconsin 53706, USA. E-mail: naim@cs.wisc.edu

†A.J.G. Hey: Department of Electronics and Computer Science, University of Southampton, Southampton S017 1BJ, UK.

[1]The initial version of this paper was published in Conference Proceedings [24]. Copyright release to use the material has been obtained.

[2]However, it is important to give a warning about the misuse of visualization. Fred Brooks says that *"The purpose of visualization is to inform, not to impress. If you do inform, then you will impress"* [4].

Popular views like space-time/Feynman diagram (ParaGraph [15, 14]) or event time lines (Express Etool [27]) often provide some insight about program behaviour. Unfortunately, for these tools to be truly useful in the domain of large scale parallel machines they must include abstract high level views [31]. Massively parallel processors can produce a huge amount of performance data. However, data visualization environments can represent large amounts of data in a visual and meaningful form. This data forms a multidimensional data set which can be viewed via different graphical displays and can answer a variety of questions specified by the user. The different types of performance data and the different needs and preferences of users make it difficult to develop a tool that is all-encompassing [34].

This situation motivates the use of AVS (Application Visualization System) [1], a scientific data visualization tool, in order to support performance analysis of parallel programs by using visual abstract representations of the performance of the program (*Do-Loop-Surface* displays [22, 25]). One advantage of this approach is that no tool development is required and that every feature of the data visualization tool can be used for further data analysis. AVS also has its own built-in analysis capabilities. Many analysis functions are available, the methods are scalable with respect to data set sizes and extensible in terms of applying additional analysis (or programming user-specific analysis), and support multiple domains of analysis (e.g. temporal, spatial, and frequency domains). The objective of multiple-domain analysis methods is to selectively focus on a particular aspect of the performance while hiding the contributions from other aspects [34].

The purpose of this paper is to demonstrate the usefulness of AVS for performance analysis of parallel programs, over a potentially large number of processors, by using Do-Loop-Surface displays (DLS), an abstract view of the performance of a particular do-loop in a program. Several case studies are also discussed as well as a brief summary about the related work in this field.

2. RELATED WORK.

In this section, several papers related to the use of scientific data visualization for performance analysis are briefly discussed.

Rover and Wright in [30] present VISTA, a framework to capture, process, and display performance information. In general, the views specific to VISTA are based on applying the techniques of scientific data visualization and multidimensional graphics to program performance visualization. VISTA is applicable to a large class of scalable programs and machines, specifically SPMD and data-parallel programs executing on distributed memory computer systems, and it is presented via a hierarchy of views. At least two levels of observation can be identified in VISTA: microscopic (lower- level) and macroscopic (higher-level). A microscopic perspective highlights the individual components of the system, and specific behaviour is presented in detail. A macroscopic view reflects the overall behaviour of the collection of components. The activity of any component becomes part of an aggregate activity of the system. These levels form a useful hierarchy which must be exploited for larger systems. A key and essential area of study is analyzing the microscopic versus macroscopic performance of large systems, where there is little experience [30].

The examples presented by Rover [30], have shown how visualization is "more than a pretty picture". One has reason, however, to appreciate it for the pretty pictures. This aspect of visualization is largely what gives the user a *macroscopic*, qualitative feel for program performance. This information is valuable, although it does not directly guide the

There are many ways to confuse or impress the users with a nice picture without telling them any useful thing. One have to be very careful when using visualization in order to understand the images we see (e.g. Globus and Raible [11] give 14 ways to say nothing with Scientific Visualization).

user to correct problems and improve performance. Additionally, parallel and distributed graphics resources for scientific visualization can be applied to performance visualization [30].

The work done by Couch in [5] deals with the problem of scalability. In that paper, global context is described by scalable execution views that do not change in format, size, meaning, or clarity as processors are added to an execution. Couch also states that one way to produce a scalable view is to categorize processors by behaviour and display category statistics. Categorical views are particularly useful when there is an inverse mapping for an arbitrary view region to the subset of processors whose behaviour was described in the region. The execution visualization tool *Seeplex* implements this form of category management to provide scalable execution views [5]. Seeplex manages view relationships using a data-flow visualization environment in the spirit of scientific visualization systems such as AVS. Two important issues are also addressed by Couch. The first one is that a scalable view is less useful if one cannot trace back from view features to raw data. The second one is that "*..visualization takes much time, effort, and experience to provide results. We hope to be made obsolete by an automatic analysis method that avoids the global search problem and all its difficulties. However, we do not think this likely*" [5].

Other systems like Paradyn [19], do not use scientific visualization tools directly, but gives us the possibility to provide data to commercial data visualization packages such as AVS.

Finally, another interesting research effort is the approach to parallel program analysis by LeBlanc, Mellor-Crummey and Fowler [17], which is based on a multiplicity of views of an execution. A synchronization trace, capture during execution, is used to construct a graph representation of the behaviour of the program. The user then manipulates this representation to create and tune visualizations using an integrated, programmable toolkit. They also state that tools should be structured so that a programmer can select views of a program execution in some reasonable sequence, where each view takes into consideration previous views and the programmer's current needs. One of the views presented in this work done by LeBlanc, Mellor-Crummey and Fowler, analyzes a similar surface (equivalent to a Do-Loop-Surface) displaying data transfer time, worker processes and rounds of computation. For a Gaussian Elimination experiment, they concluded that the display helped them to find an explanation of a particular performance problem. Although there are similarities between this visualization and the DLS displays, we believe that the DLS displays have several new features such as the use of a Scientific Data Visualization Tool (AVS), providing further data analysis capabilities. Additionally, the idea of using this type of display for performance analysis is evaluated more deeply in this paper.

3. AVS: A DATA VISUALIZATION TOOL. AVS, Application Visualization System [1], is a data visualization environment designed to analyze scientific and engineering data in areas like fluid dynamics, computer-aided engineering, and molecular modeling. AVS users can construct their own visualization applications, by combining software components into executable flow networks. The components, called modules, implement specific functions in the visualization cycle (filtering, mapping, and rendering). The flow networks are built from a menu of modules by using a direct-manipulation, visual programming interface called AVS Network Editor. With this editor, the users can create their own visualizations by selecting a group of modules and drawing connections between them (see figure 1).

The user views, organizes, and further processes the output of a network through one of the AVS subsystems. These subsystems are:

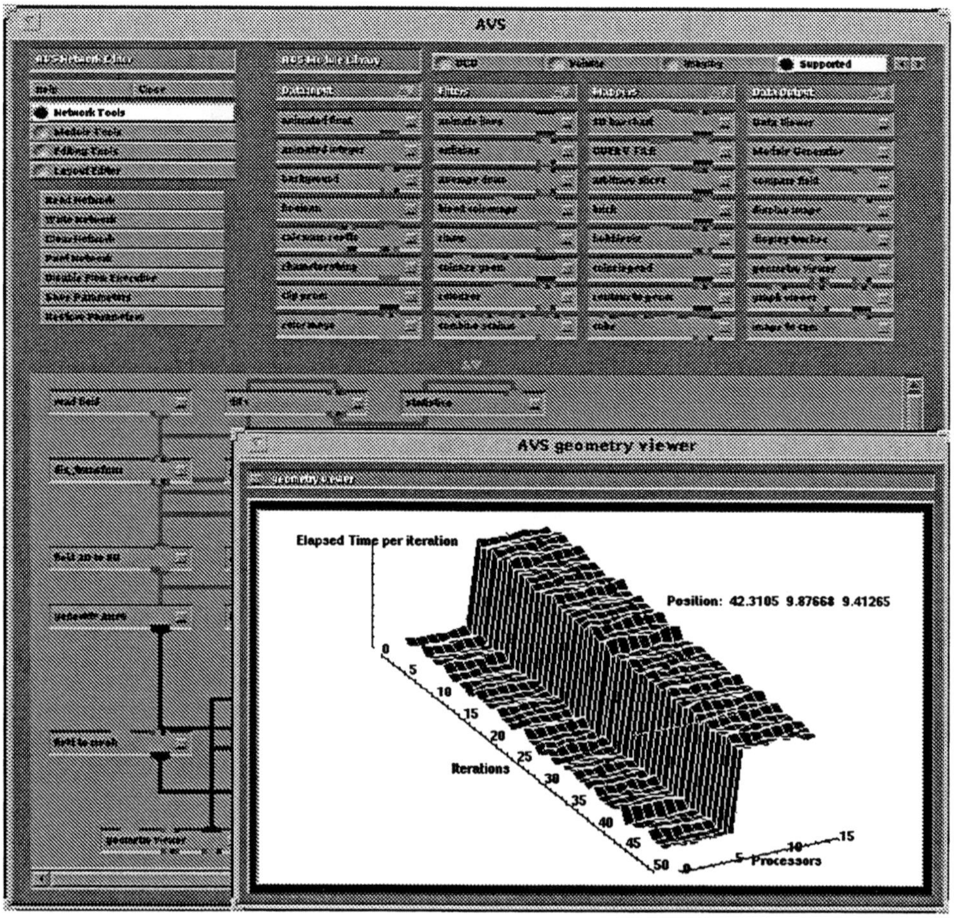

FIG. 1. *AVS Data Network generating a Do-Loop-Surface display.*

- The Geometric Viewer: displays 3D geometric objects.
- The Image Viewer: displays 2D images.
- The Graph Viewer: creates XY and contour graphs of data.

AVS also includes a set of modules for construction of networks, although it is possible for the user to create his own modules by using the AVS Module Generator. This module generator can be used to automatically create module code in C or FORTRAN and it has a visual interface. Modules are software building blocks with well-defined interfaces. Modules take typed data as inputs and produce typed data as outputs. The basic data types in the system are oriented toward scientific data manipulation and graphic display. These types are:

- 1D, 2D, and 3D grids of numbers with scalar values or vectors of byte, integer, or floating-point values at each grid point.
- unstructured cell data.
- geometric data.
- images.
- molecular data.

AVS implements two basic strategies for translating numerical data into colour pictures. In the pixel-based method, data points become pixels, more or less directly. In the geometry-based method, the numerical data is converted to descriptions of 3D geometric objects. There are, in turn, turned into colour images by the machine's low-level graphics software and rendering hardware. For more detailed information about AVS, see [1].

3.1. AVS and Performance Visualization. Performance visualization of parallel programs is important because it helps the user to understand complex performance phenomena. In a single picture, it is possible to see what is happening for the whole execution of a program. Also, for a human being it is easier to recognize visual patterns than to extract the same information from plain numbers.

There are many tools designed for scientific visualization, such as AVS. These tools are used fundamentally to analyze data in areas such as chemistry, fluid dynamics, and different sort of simulations of real phenomena (e.g. seismic simulation, reservoir simulation, weather prediction). In order to handle complex data, tools such as AVS provide very powerful built in capabilities. One can transform and display data in many ways, rotate figures, zoom in and zoom out as necessary, change colour scales, create different views of the same data, analyze statistics, etc. The main purpose of integrating performance analysis with scientific data visualization is, precisely, to take advantage of these excellent capabilities for data analysis. Once we have produced the required performance data (e.g. by instrumenting the program's source code), we are ready for the analysis process. Nothing else is required. One of the advantages of this approach is that no tool development is necessary. This is important for several reasons: (1) we can spend more time analyzing our performance data; and (2) we do not need to reinvent the wheel. To create a visualization program is not a trivial task at all and this effort may be incorporated to a more productive goal, i.e. the performance analysis process.

Many of the current performance visualization tools (e.g. PABLO [28], ParaGraph [15]) provide several set of views that are useful to understand and improve performance. However, when the number of processors increases up to a large number (e.g. hundreds), most of the visualizations provided by these tools become useless. One of the basic problems is the lack of scalability and that these views do not provide an abstraction of performance. However, having the right representation for performance, one can use a scientific visualization tool in order to visualize data even for a large number of processors (scientific data is usually complex). Therefore, if we can provide an abstract view of performance (and also a useful one), then its scalability will mostly depend on the scalability that the visualization tool provides.

In our experience analyzing performance data, we have found that the Do-Loop-Surface is an abstract view of the performance of a parallel program that fits the features mentioned above. The Do-Loop-Surface (DLS from now on) represents the performance of a particular do-loop in a parallel program by measuring the elapsed time per do-loop iteration for every processor. This creates a surface that is displayed and analyzed using AVS, a scientific data visualization tool. We measure do-loops because it is usually where the main computation of the program takes place and also because it is there where we generally find the most interesting behaviour of the program. It is important to notice that AVS is not used only for displaying DLS's, but also for analyzing them. AVS provides a very large set of modules that analyze data in several ways. Also, custom designed modules can be written for specific data transformations (in order to analyze DLS displays, we have created modules that: controls the number of iterations/processors displayed, e.g. see figure 2; computes the difference between the values of two consecutives iterations/processors; and measure the maximum elapsed time between two particular iterations).

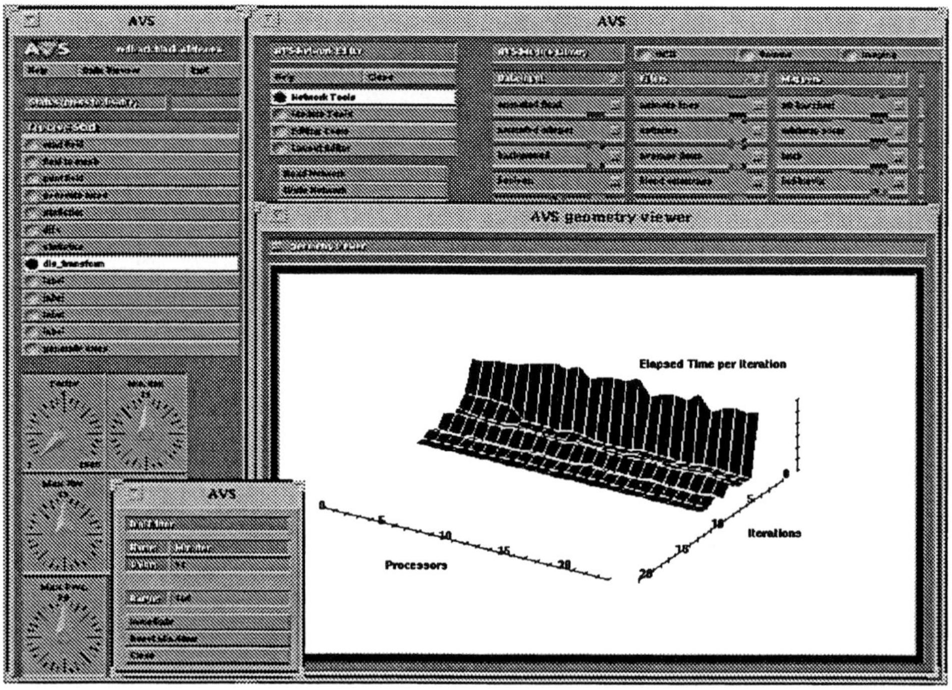

FIG. 2. *The dls_transform module controls the current iterations and processors being displayed. In this figure the first 10 iterations has been deleted.*

4. DO-LOOP-SURFACE. A Do-Loop-Surface or DLS [22, 25], is an abstract view of the performance of a particular do-loop in a program. This surface is created by measuring the elapsed time per iteration for every processor and representing this data as a 3D display. The three axes represent *processors*, *iterations* and *elapsed time per iteration* respectively and we will call *iteration* the execution of each cycle of the particular do-loop being analyzed. By representing a do-loop using a DLS, the user can view a complete execution of this section of the program in a single picture and looking at this display from the right perspective may uncover unknown bottlenecks [3]. A new and evocative vocabulary that explains the particular features of the display is also incorporated (e.g. *mountains, valleys, hilly, flat*). This surface is displayed using AVS [1] (Application Visualization System), which allows rotation of the figure in several ways as well as zooming when necessary and some other interesting transformations.

The main goals of the DLS representation are:

- To provide an abstract view of program performance.
- To provide useful information for the user, allowing detection of unknown bottlenecks using 3D displays.
- To provide scalable views for programs running on a large number of processors.

[3] A *visualization* makes some details of the view manifest, while obscuring others. A view defines *what* information is presented; a visualization describes *how* the information is displayed [17].

By analyzing a DLS, the user can identify performance features like load balance and communication delays[4]. Previous work has shown that DLS displays are also useful in identifying cache/memory effects [23], comparing different communication strategies, and even identifying hardware irregularities (figure 3 illustrates a DLS display that enabled us to discover performance differences in the floating point units of the SPARC-2 chip set on a CM-5. This figure shows that some nodes execute faster than others. Additionally, the figure shows how the user can get information from the display by "clicking" the mouse on the desired position).

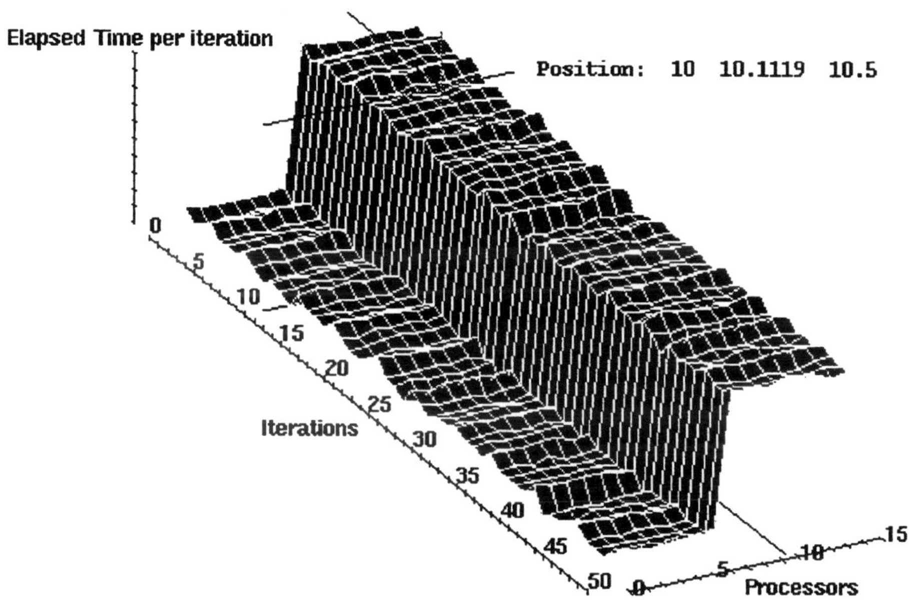

FIG. 3. *DLS display showing differences in execution time of floating point units on a CM-5.*

A do-loop represents one of the most important sections of the program, since it is where the main computation generally takes place. Additionally, a programmer may understand more about do-loop structures than communication directives. A DLS is, therefore, an appropriate structure to visualize. In terms of scalability, a DLS is represented by a single picture that can be zoomed if necessary and a general view of the surface will determine which regions require a more detailed analysis. The DLS displays have been successfully scaled up to 128 processors and we expect they will scale well for a larger number of processors.

4.1. Trace Generation. The DLS displays do not depend on any particular hardware platform or programming style. The only requirements in order to generate a DLS display

[4]Communication delays are very important for message passing systems such as PVM or MPI. These communication delays can be viewed in a DLS by analyzing different patterns for different processors for the same iteration. Of course, from the picture we are not able to distinguish whether these differences are due to computation or communication, unless we know that the program is well balanced. Even then, we might have other factors different than just communications delays (e.g. cache misses) affecting performance, but at least this will show us that *something* is happening. The knowledge that the user has of the application is also very valuable in this case.

are a DLS trace file and AVS. The DLS trace file has been generated in the past by writing a small trace library for the corresponding message-passing system (i.e. PARMACS and PVM). However, for MPI it was easier. The MPI version of Argonne National Laboratory (ANL) comes with a separate environment called MPE (Multi-Processing Environment), which is a software provided by ANL to enhance message-passing programming with MPI, including graphics and profiling capabilities [13]. MPE has a set of profiling routines that are used to create log files of events that occur during the execution of a parallel program. By using this library, one can measure the elapsed time for each iteration on a particular do-loop in a program, which is the information required to display a DLS (figure 4 illustrates how to use MPE to generate the information of a DLS trace file).

```
c
c Definition of the DLS state that we are going to measure. A state
c consist of two events. In our example, these events are 1 and 2
c

  if (myid .eq. 0) then
    CALL MPE_DESCRIBE_STATE(1, 2, "DLSijk", "blue:gray")
  endif
c
c Start generating tracing information
c
  CALL MPE_START_LOG()
  do iter=1,100
c
c First event: beginning of the do-loop
c
    CALL MPE_LOG_EVENT(1, iter, "DLSijk-start")
    do i=1,max_iter
      do j=1,max_iter
        do k=1,max_iter
          c(i,j) = a(i,k)*b(k,j) + c(i,j)
        enddo
      enddo
    enddo
c
c Second event: end of the do-loop
c
    CALL MPE_LOG_EVENT(2, iter, "DLSijk-end")
  enddo

c
c Stop generation tracing information and save it in the file dls.log
c
  CALL MPE_STOP_LOG()
  CALL MPE_FINISH_LOG_("dls.log")
```

FIG. 4. *Generation of DLS trace data using MPE. Note: If a node's trace buffer is full during program execution, then the profiling mechanism will stop recording trace events.*

MPE is currently used it to generate log files for Nupshot, a performance visualization software developed at ANL. Nupshot is an enhanced version of Upshot, also developed at ANL [16]. One of the main advantages of using MPE is that this library can be used with other vendor versions of MPI (since it is based on calls to MPI). In this way, we would be able to generate DLS trace files on any of the platforms supported by MPI. Also, MPE allow us to analyze several do-loops at the same time, making it possible to generate several

DLS's on a single run. The only requirement to display this information as a DLS, is to transform the MPE log-file into the corresponding DLS trace file format required by AVS. For all the advantages that this approach give us, we think that a future freely available version of DLS will be based on MPI only.

5. USING AVS FOR PERFORMANCE VISUALIZATION. The purpose of this section is to describe our experience using AVS for performance analysis purposes. The first experiment consists of the LINPACK benchmark and we analyze it using DLS displays. The second experiment illustrates another use for AVS and the DLS displays comparing the behaviour and performance of different implementations of MPI for the IBM SP2. The final experiment was done in order to test scalability for the DLS displays up to 128 processors. All the experiments shown in this section were performed on an IBM SP2 with 128 processors at Argonne National Laboratory.

5.1. The LINPACK Benchmark. The LINPACK benchmark [6, 13] is a well known numerical code that is often used to benchmark computers for floating-point performance. This program solves the linear system $Ax = b$, where A is a *dense* matrix (i.e. A[i,j] != 0, for every i,j). The problem is solved by computing a factorization of A into PLU, where L is a lower triangular matrix, U an upper triangular matrix, and P is a permutation matrix that represents the exchange of rows used in the *partial pivoting* algorithm (strategy used by this code to improve numerical stability). The matrix A is distributed amongst the processors using the square block scattered decomposition described in [7], which is a practical and general purpose way of decomposing dense linear algebra computations. In problems, such as LU factorization, in which rows and/or columns become inactive as the algorithm progresses, this decomposition provides a good load balance (as it is shown in [7]).

This algorithm was run on an IBM SP2 at ANL. This machine consists of 128 nodes and two compile servers. Each node is essentially an RS/6000 model 370. This model has a 62.5 MHz clock, a 32Kb data cache, and a 32Kb instruction cache. The main features of this system are [12]:

- 128Mb of memory per node.
- 1Gb local disk on each node (400Mb for users and the rest for paging and for the operating system).
- Full Unix on each node (IBM AIX 3.2.5).
- Each node is accessible by Ethernet from the Internet.
- High performance Omega switch for the interconnection network between processors. The SP2 interconnection network is a bidirectional multistage interconnection network. The SP2 method of packet transfer between nodes is related to *wormhole routing* [33]. Latency is 63 micro seconds and bandwidth is 35Mb/s.
- The maximum number of processors for this machine is 128, but 512 systems are available on special request.

Figure 5 shows the execution of the main do-loop of the LU decomposition (subroutine PDLUBR) for 100 processors (with N=6400 and NB=64, where N is the size of matrix and NB the block size used for wrapping). The figure illustrates a clear pattern of *blocks* repeated every 10 iterations and processors. This is due to the fact that the topology used by the algorithm is a grid of 10x10 processes. This is exactly the way the algorithm is designed to work [2]. If you assume that the processors are arranged as a 10x10 grid (10 rows and 10 columns), and the grid is composed of rows and columns, then the factorization of the block is performed by processor columns in a cyclic manner. During the very first iteration processors 0, 10, 20,..., 90 will be involved in the factorization. After factorization, the factored panel (or factored section of the matrix) has to be broadcasted to the rest of the process columns. In this broadcast, processors {0, 1,..., 9}, {10, 11,..., 19},..., {90,..., 99} are involved (i.e. 10 broadcasts occur in parallel). After this step, there is an update operation on the block and this update is done in a processor row, and therefore only processors {0, 1,..., 9} are involved. After this, the updated block is broadcasted to other process rows, so processors {0, 10, 20,..., 90}, {1, 11,..., 91},..., {9, 19,..., 99} are involved in the broadcast (all occur in parallel again). Now the above step is repeated starting with processor 1, that is in the processor column 1.

We can also see how every 10 processors, there is a *drop* in the execution for that particular iteration (creating the diagonal lines of the figure). All these patterns, correspond to the cyclic behaviour of the algorithm. Also, notice how the surface *decreases* as the iterations progress (due to the fact that more rows and columns become inactive as the algorithm move forward). The cyclic patterns can also be seen using Nupshot (figure 6, for 9 processors). However, for 100 processors, it is more difficult to use this sort of display (at least on a single view, see figure 7). For an overall view of performance, the combination AVS-DLS provides a better alternative.

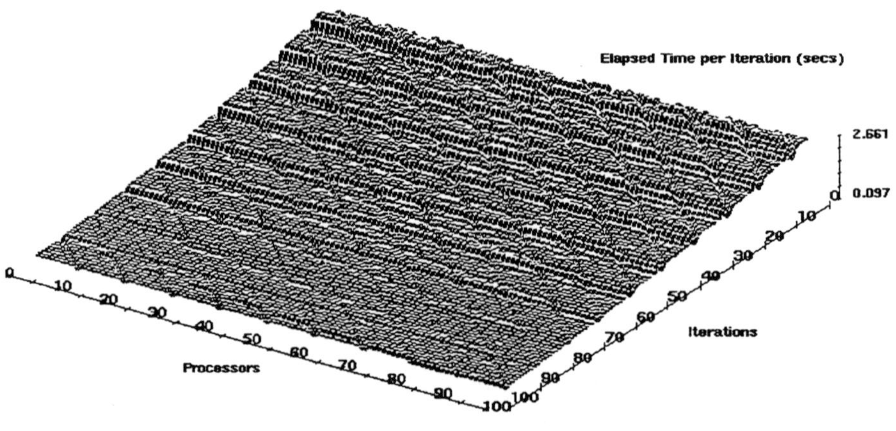

FIG. 5. *DLS display for LINPACK (IBM SP2, 100 processors). Notice the cyclic patterns every 10 iterations/processors. It is also important to say that in this single picture we are displaying the information of 100 iterations for 100 processors.*

5.2. Comparison between ANL-MPI and IBM-MPI. Another interesting experiment was to compare the execution of the two current versions of MPI available for the IBM SP2 at ANL (i.e. IBM-MPI and ANL-MPI). The results can be seen in figures 8 and 9. It is clear from the pictures that both executions are *different*. In a colour picture, we would notice first that the values for the IBM-MPI case are higher than for the ANL-MPI case. Also, the *regularity* of the patterns has been affected. This fact can be deduced by the sequence of peaks present in the first 30 iterations of the algorithm. Nupshot was used in order to confirm this behaviour, and the results are illustrated in figures 6 and 10. The ANL version of MPI proved to be more efficient than the IBM version for this particular application.

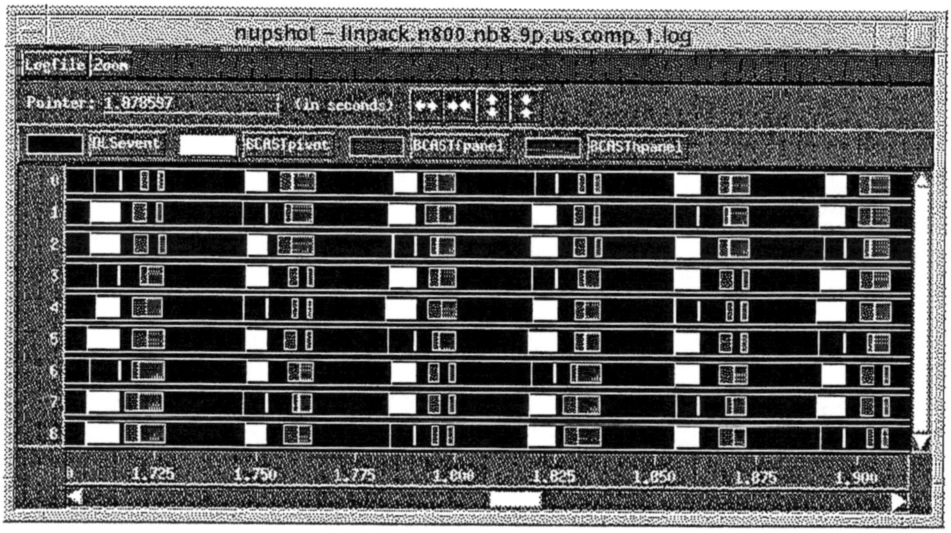

FIG. 6. *Nupshot: section of the LINPACK execution (IBM SP2, 9 processors). Notice the cyclic pattern in communications: first 3 processors, then processors 3 to 5, then processors 6 to 8, and so on. Communications correspond to the three broadcasts inside the main do-loop of the LU factorization of LINPACK.*

5.3. Scalability test using 128 processors. Figure 11 illustrates one of our scalability tests using the full configuration of the IBM SP2 at ANL (128 processors). Additionally, this test allow us to see a very interesting behaviour that we have seen before in similar cases but on different machines (e.g. CM-5): some processors are taking longer (more than 20 percent in some cases) to execute the exact same code. The do-loop we are analyzing consist of statements that do not include any communication at all and they are repeated on every processor. We know that there are a few set of processors that run slower than others (i.e. processors 1, 17, 33, 49, 65, 81, 97, and 113), but we have found that for this particular test some other processors behave different than expected. It seems that either there is also an additional overhead of the operating system that affects the execution of our code or these set of processors are slightly *different* than the others. In terms of scalability, the picture easily represents 128 processors and 100 do-loop iterations. We believe that the DLS displays will scale in the same way as AVS scales. However, for thousands of processors, the trace files will be perhaps too large (especially if the number of do-loop iterations is large too) and the DLS could be more difficult to handle.

6. CONCLUSIONS. Conventional processing, analysis, and display methods for current performance visualization tools typically do not adequately support the evaluation of program performance on parallel systems having more than a few tens of processors [29]. Tools like ParaGraph, do not exploit the analysis capability of the representation. That is the strength of tools such as AVS. The general nature of these tools makes it very convenient to try various image processing functions on the data, after transforming the performance data to images [35].

Scientific and performance visualization share the objectives of representing large multidimensional data sets and analyzing the data to assist visual perception by the human user. Performance analysis is also responsible for showing some link between the visual representations and the logical structure of the program, in addition to showing the phys-

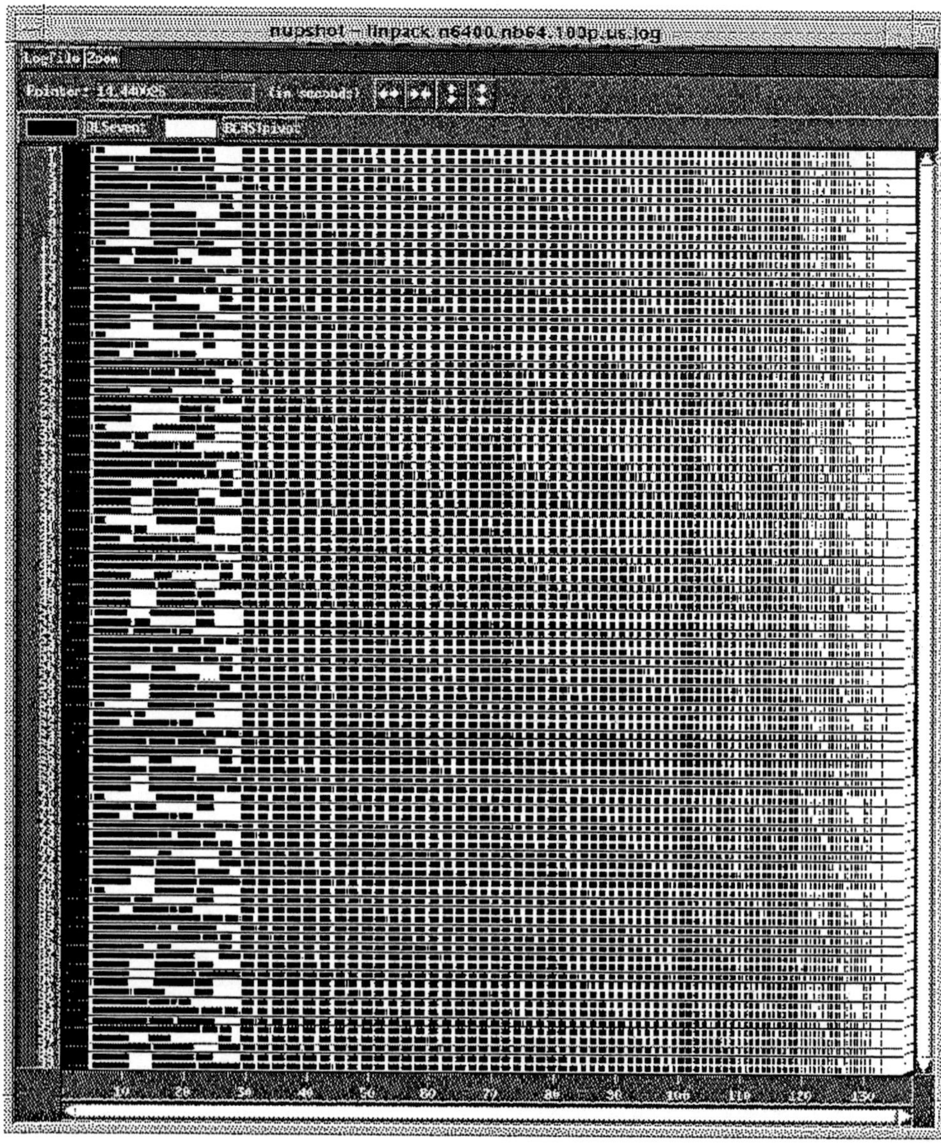

FIG. 7. *Nupshot: section of the LINPACK execution (IBM SP2, 100 processors). The view becomes too complex for a single picture.*

ical interactions among processors. The main contrast between scientific visualization and performance visualization is that the former renders the natural, physical structure of the system under study, and the latter contends with a hierarchy of structures, including higher-dimensional, logical structure, of the system under study [34].

In this paper, the Do-Loop-Surface (DLS) representation of the performance of a particular do-loop in a program has been presented as an alternative to provide an abstract and scalable representation of performance, using a Scientific Data Visualization Tool (AVS [1]). Some advantages and disadvantages of this approach are:

- Advantages:

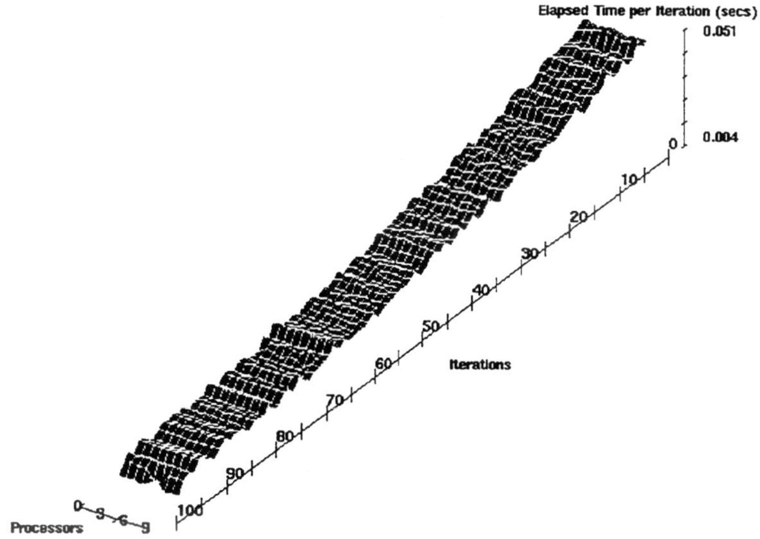

FIG. 8. *DLS: Execution of LINPACK using the ANL version of MPI for the IBM SP2 (mpich).*

  - No tool development is required and every feature of the data visualization tool can be used to find unknown bottlenecks (e.g. rotating a figure may lead the user to discover something that he has not seen before, using a specific module that computes statistics about the data points displayed, etc).
  - Scalability of analysis and display regardless of the amount of data.
  - Extensibility of analysis. As part of our future work, it would be very interesting to take a tool such as Paradyn, which inserts instrumentation dynamically into the application program, and generate the information required by a DLS and pass it to AVS on the fly. In this way, we could use Paradyn to control the amount of data being generated, and AVS to extent the data analysis power of Paradyn.
  - Data importing and exporting capabilities.
  - Extensive image processing capabilities.
- Disadvantages:
  - Fixed data description format that differs from the record structure of raw event data.
  - Specialized programming conventions that make it difficult to write customized code for user-specific functions.
  - Limited options for rapidly developing general graphical displays [35].
  - It is difficult to relate visual data to source code.
  - Visualization is useful, but it is important to give a warning about the *misuse* of visualization.

The DLS display and its implementation by using AVS have shown to be useful to represent and analyze the performance of parallel programs such as the LINPACK Benchmark. In terms of scalability, we are providing results up to 128 processors. The scalability of the DLS displays depends on the scalability provided by AVS. However, we might find troubles

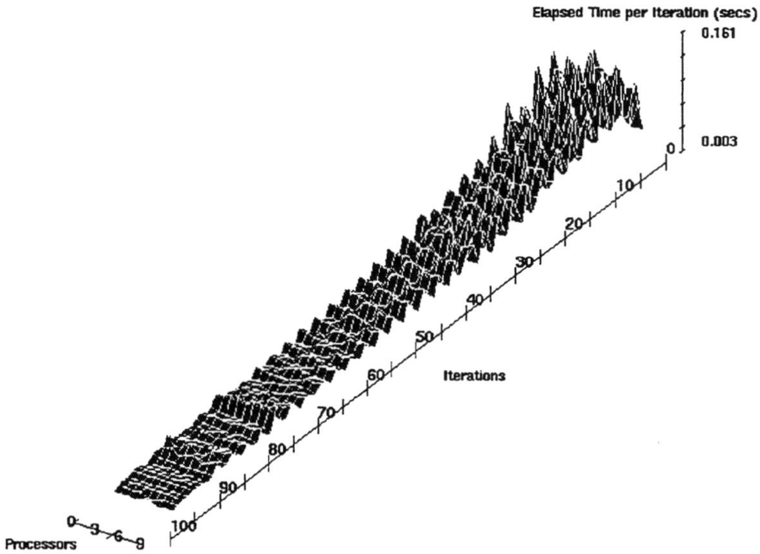

FIG. 9. *DLS: Execution of LINPACK using the IBM version of MPI for the IBM SP2. Notice the differences in terms of regularity that both pictures have. The only thing in common is the fact that the values decreases as the execution progress (which is a feature of the algorithm in general).*

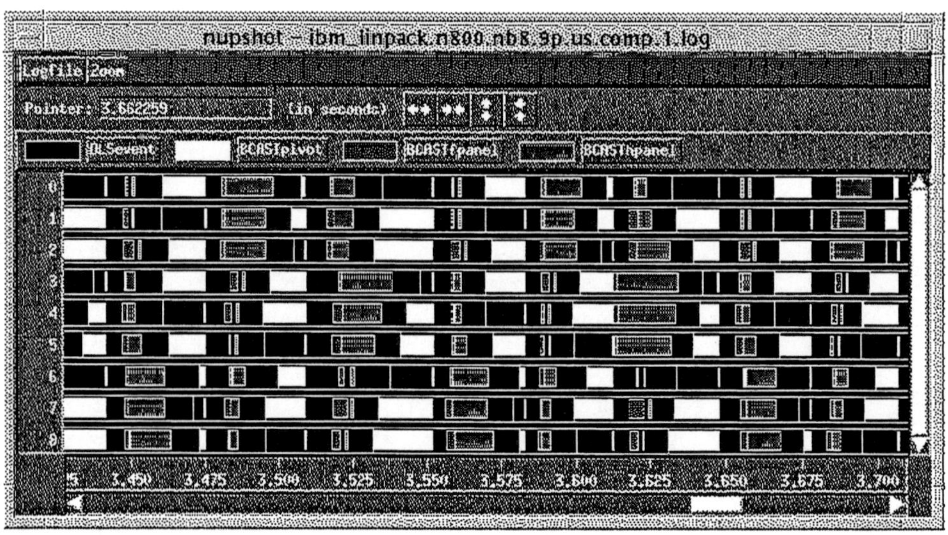

FIG. 10. *Nupshot: Section of LINPACK execution for the ANL version of MPI (IBM SP2, 9 processors). Notice the irregularity in the communication patterns.*

for thousands of processors. For this particular case, it could be possible to select a restricted set of processors and/or iterations, to filter the information during the collection phase, or to collect only the events that we think are performance anomalies. For a very large number of processors, a dynamic notion of performance instrumentation and measurement can be used [19]. In this way, the amount of information produced can be dramatically reduced.

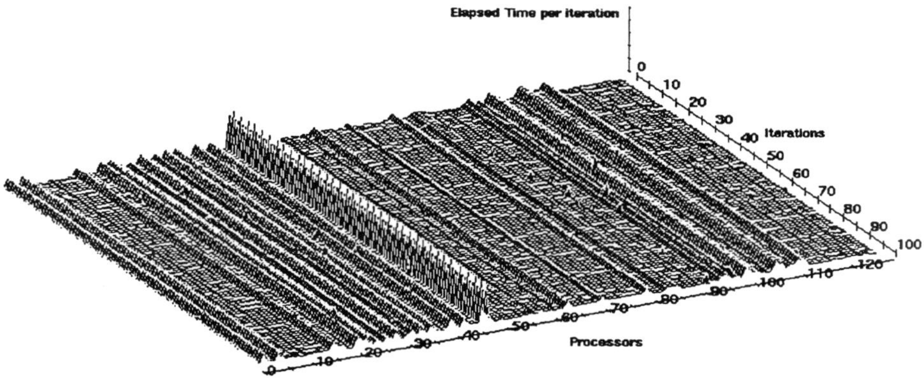

FIG. 11. *DLS: Scalability test (IBM SP2, 128 processors). Notice that some processors take longer to execute the same number of operations (there are no communications inside the do-loop being analyzed).*

DLS is not tided to any particular programming model. At present, a DLS displays the information of postmortem events, but they could also be real time events.

The main purpose of a DLS display is to discover a performance deficiency. It would be ideal, of course, to isolate the cause of the problem since what we really want at the end is to improve performance. However, we do not think that a single tool can do everything and collaborative work between tools with different features and complementary approaches is important[5]. Additionally, if we do not find the problem first, we would not be able to isolate its cause. Therefore, to identify a problem is still important. One could think to collect more information in order to provide a more detailed analysis. In fact, for MPI the DLS trace file is generated from the log file created by the MPE profiling library. This trace file contains more detailed information since it is used by Nupshot, a performance visualization tool. We think that it is a better idea to combine the use of DLS displays with, for example, Nupshot, instead of making the information provided by a DLS more complex. In this way, several views of the performance of a particular program can be viewed and analyzed simultaneously (it could be interesting if we could combined different performance metrics that are displayed separately in one single display).

The Do-Loop-Surface is a contribution towards a better abstract view of the performance of a parallel program, as well as a good example of the advantages that can be gained by using a data visualization tool such as AVS for performance analysis purposes.

"Visualization in its present form is a harmonious blend of several other areas such as computer graphics, art, psychology, statistical analysis, and image processing. Permanent archival and communication systems and image databases also have found their way into certain areas of visualization. It is meeting the demands for increasingly powerful and efficient visual analysis methods in many scientific and engineering disciplines. Virtual reality will make visualization a more fulfilling experience for the human user in the future. Performance visualization can only prosper by integrating these emerging technologies" [35].

[5] An example of collaborative work between DLS and other tools can be found in [8]. This paper illustrates the use of Lebep [10], a parallel benchmark language generator, a Performance Estimator [9] and DLS displays. This paper also shows how the above tools can be used to address the problem of improving application performance from different perspectives.

Acknowledgments. The author(s) gratefully acknowledge use of the Argonne High Performance Computing Research Facility. The HPCRF is funded principally by the U.S. Department of Energy Office of Scientific Computing.

REFERENCES

[1] ADVANCED VISUAL SYSTEMS INC., *AVS User's Guide, Release 4*, May 1992.

[2] BANGALORE, P., *Private electronic mail communication.* Subject: MPI version of LINPACK, March 1995.

[3] A. BODE AND P. BRAUN, *Monitoring and visualisation in topsys*, in Workshop on Performance Measurement and Visualization of Parallel Systems, Moravany, Czecho-Slovakia, October 1992.

[4] K. BRODLIE, *Scientific Visualization - past, present and future*, Nuclear Instruments and Methods in Physics Research - A, 354 (1995), pp. 104–111.

[5] A. COUCH, *Categories and Context in Scalable Execution Visualization*, Journal of Parallel and Distributed Computing, 18 (1993), pp. 195–204.

[6] CWIK, T. AND VAN DE GEIJN, R. AND PATTERSON, J., *Application of Massively Parallell Computation to Integral Equation Models of Electromagnetic Scattering (Invited Paper)*, J. Opt. Soc. Am. A, 11 (1994).

[7] DONGARRA, JACK AND VAN DE GEIJN, ROBERT AND WALKER, DAVID, *LAPACK Working Note 43: A look at Scalable Dense Linear Algebra Libraries*, technical report, University of Tennessee, Oak Ridge National Laboratory, and University of Texas, May 1992.

[8] A. DUNLOP, E. HERNÁNDEZ, O. NAÍM, T. HEY, AND D. NICOLE, *A Toolkit for Optimising Parallel Performance*, Lecture Notes in Computer Science, 919 (1995), pp. 548–553.

[9] A. DUNLOP, A. HEY, AND D. NICOLE, *Parallel performance estimating using memory hierarchy simulation*, Technical Report HPCC94-008, Dept. of Electronics and Computer Science, University of Southampton, Southampton S017 1BJ, UK, 1994.

[10] C. FIGUEIRA AND E. HERNANDEZ, *Benchmarks Specification and Generation for Performance Estimation on MIMD Machines*, in IFIP Transactions in Computer Science and Tecnology, vol. 44, 1994.

[11] A. GLOBUS AND E. RAIBLE, *Fourteen Ways to Say Nothing with Scientific Visualization*, IEEE Computer, (1994), pp. 86–88.

[12] GROPP, WILLIAM AND LUSK, EWING, *Users Guide for the ANL IBM SPx*, MCS, Argonne National Laboratory, January 1995. Draft.

[13] GROPP, WILLIAM AND LUSK, EWING AND SKJELLUM, ANTHONY, *USING MPI: Portable Parallel Programming with the Message-Passing Interface*, Scientific and ENgineering Computation Series, MIT Press, 1994.

[14] M. HEATH, *Recent Developments and Case Studies in Performance Visualization using ParaGraph*, in Workshop on Performance Measurement and Visualization of Parallel Systems, Moravany, Czecho-Slovakia, October 1992.

[15] M. HEATH AND J. ETHERIDGE, *Visualizing the performance of parallel programs*, IEEE Software, (1991), pp. 29–39.

[16] V. HERARTE AND E. LUSK, *Studying Parallel Program Behavior with Upshot*, Technical Report ANL-91/15, Argonne National Laboratory, Illinois, USA, 1991.

[17] T. LEBLANC, J. MELLOR-CRUMMEY, AND R. FOWLER, *Analyzing parallel program executions using multiple views*, Journal of Parallel and Distributed Computing, 9 (1990), pp. 203–217.

[18] A. MALONY AND G. WILSON, *Future directions in parallel performance environments*, in Workshop on Performance Measurement and Visualization of Parallel Systems, Moravany, Czecho-Slovakia, October 1992.

[19] B. MILLER, M. CALLAGHAN, J. CARGILLE, J. HOLLINGSWORTH, B. IRVIN, K. KARAVANIC, K. KUNCHITHAPADAM, AND T. NEWHALL, *The Paradyn Parallel Performance Measurement Tools*, IEEE Computer, 28 (1995), pp. 37–46.

[20] B. MOHR, *SIMPLE: A Performance Evaluation Tool Environment for Parallel and Distributed Systems*, in EDMCC2, Munich, April 1991.

[21] O. NAÍM, *Performance Visualization of Parallel Programs*, PhD thesis, University of Southampton, Department of Electronics and Computer Science, Southampton SO17 1BJ, UK., July 1995.

[22] O. NAÍM AND T. HEY, *Do-Loop-Surface: An Abstract Performance Data Visualization*, Lecture Notes in Computer Science, 797 (1994), pp. 367–372.

[23] ———, *Visualization of cache/memory effects using Do-Loop-Surface displays*, Technical Report HPCC94-003, Dept. of Electronics and Computer Science, University of Southampton, Southamp-

ton S017 1BJ, UK, 1994.

[24] ———, *Visualization of Do-Loop Performance*, Lecture Notes in Computer Science, 1225 (1997), pp. 878–887.

[25] O. NAÍM, T. HEY, AND E. ZALUSKA, *Do-Loop-Surface: An Abstract Representation of Parallel Program Performance*, Concurrency-Practice and Experience, 8 (1996), pp. 205–234.

[26] PALLAS, GMBH, *PA-Tools, Performance Analysis Tools*, 1991.

[27] PARASOFT CORPORATION, *ParaSoft Express. User's Guide*, 1990.

[28] D. REED, R. AYDT, T. MADHYASTHA, R. NOE, K. SHIELDS, AND B. SCHWARTZ, *The PABLO performance analysis environment.* Department of Computer Science, University of Illinois at Urbana-Champaign, 1992.

[29] D. ROVER AND A. WAHEED, *Multiple Domain Analysis Methods*, in Proc. of the 3rd ACM/ONR Workshop on Parallel and Distributed Debugging, May 1993, pp. 53–63.

[30] D. ROVER AND C. WRIGHT, *Visualizing the Performance of SPMD and Data-Parallel Programs*, Journal of Parallel and Distributed Computing, 18 (1993), pp. 129–146.

[31] S. SARUKKAI, D. KIMELMAN, AND L. RUDOLPH, *A methodology for visualizing performance of loosely synchronous programs*, in Scalable High Performance Computing Conference, SHPCC-92, IEEE Computer Society, April 1992, pp. 424–432.

[32] M. SIMMONS AND R. KOSKELA, *Performance Instrumentation and Visualization*, ACM Press, Frontier Series, 1990.

[33] STUNKEL, CRAIG AND ET AL, *The SP2 Communication Subsystems*, tech. rep., IBM Thomas J. Watson Research Center, August 1994.

[34] A. WAHEED, B. KRONMÜLLER, R. SINHA, AND D. ROVER, *A Toolkit for Advanced Performance Analysis*, in International Workshop on Modeling, Analysis, and Simulation of Computers and Telecommunication Systems (MASCOTS'94), Durham NC, January 1994.

[35] A. WAHEED AND D. ROVER, *Performance Visualization of Parallel Programs*, in Visualization '93, San Jose, California, October 1993.

ON DESIGNING AND IMPLEMENTING A COLLABORATIVE SYSTEM USING THE DISTRIBUTED-OBJECT MODEL OF JAVA-RMI

R. R. RAJE* , S. MUKHOPADHYAY* , M. BOYLES* , N. PATEL* , A. PAPIEZ*, AND J. MOSTAFA†

Abstract. As we enter the 21st century, our dependency on the Internet is going to increase each day. This observation has inspired many researchers to invest their efforts into the development of efficient Web-based computing paradigms. Java-RMI is one alternative offered by Sun Microsystems. Using Java-RMI, a software developer can easily design and develop collaborative systems. In this article, we describe the use of Java-RMI in designing a collaborative information classifier, called D-SIFTER. We also present the principles of RMI, the details of our prototype, and some of the results from the preliminary experiments with it.

Key words. Distributed computing, collaborative information filtering, Java-RMI.

1. Introduction. In 1993, the emergence of the World Wide Web (WWW) took the Internet by storm. At that time, the development team at Sun was still working on the design of the new and exciting programming language to be know as Java. Java became the first successful architecture-independent programming language designed specifically with the Internet in mind [1].

Java has many features, as highlighted by its definition [1], "Java: A simple, object-oriented, distributed, interpreted, robust, secure, architecture neutral, portable, high-performance, multi-threaded, and dynamic language." Among these features, Java also gives the programmer the ability to write *applets*, an application that can run through any Java enabled web browser via the WWW. Applets are often fancy, graphically-oriented programs which allow user interactivity.

The net-centric model introduced by Java is an effective paradigm to develop collaborative systems. However, the basic Java model does not support remote object invocations which are desirable to achieve "true" collaborative computing. To address this issue, Sun Microsystems provides an Application Program Interface (API) known as Remote Method Invocation (RMI). RMI has been an integral part of JDK since the 1.1 version.

Distributed information filtering is one such example of a collaborative computing system. In order to explore the suitability of Java-RMI, we have developed a prototype called D-SIFTER (Distributed Smart Information Filtering Technology for Electronic Resources). In this article, we provide an overview of the D-SIFTER design and the details of its Java-RMI implementation. We also briefly describe the results of experiments performed with the D-SIFTER prototype along with conclusions and future research directions.

Before we discuss collaborative information filtering, it is appropriate to mention the principles of RMI. The next section provides a quick overview of RMI. A more comprehensive description of RMI is found in [2] and [3].

2. RMI – Remote Method Invocation. In Java, a remote method invocation occurs when a Java program executing on one machine invokes a method of another Java program executing in an entirely different address space [4]. The necessary interfaces and classes required for the remote invocations are described below.

*Department of Computer & Information Science, Indiana University Purdue University Indianapolis, IN 46202-5132. ({rraje, smukhopa, mboyles, npatel, apapiez}@cs.iupui.edu).

†School of Library & Information Science, Indiana University, Bloomington, IN 47405-1801. (jm@indiana.edu).

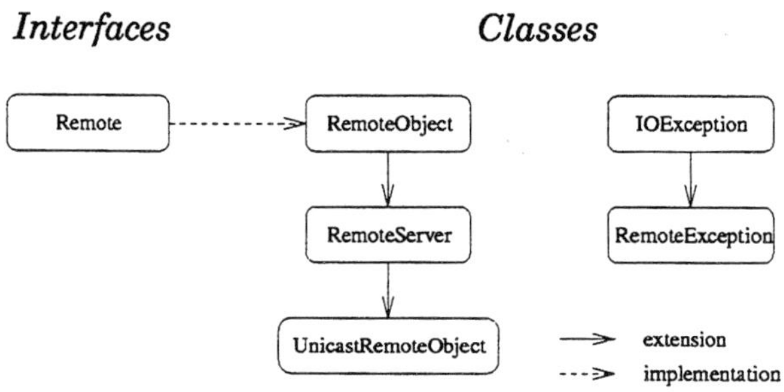

FIG. 2.1. *Class Framework for RMI*

2.1. Class Hierarchy. Figure 2.1 shows the extension and implementation relationships of RMI. More information about the class/interface hierarchy of RMI can be found at the RMI Specification web page, [3]. This hierarchy is the fundamental building block for all classes that will involve remote method invocations. The rest of this section outlines the features of RMI with respect to the above figure.

2.2. Server Stubs and Skeletons. Remote method invocations are handled by two surrogate objects called a *stub* and a *skeleton*. The stub resides on the client machine and the skeleton on the server machine. It should be noted that the terms 'client' and 'server' are associated with each remote call under discussion.

When the client wishes to make a remote call onto the server, it simply calls a method of the stub object (which is local to the machine where the client is residing). It is then the task of the stub object to perform *parameter marshalling* and to assemble the block of bytes that will be sent across the network to the awaiting server machine. Java uses an object serialization mechanism for the parameter marshalling. A detailed description of the object serialization process can be found in [2] and [5].

The skeleton object (residing on the server) receives this block of bytes sent by the stub object. It then disassembles the block, unmarshalls the parameters, calls the desired method of the server program, marshalls the return value from the server method and sends it back to the stub object. The stub unmarshalls the return value or the exception and sends that result to the calling method of the client program.

The stub and skeleton objects give a simple appearance to remote method invocations. RMI takes care of all the low-level network issues, thereby creating an illusion of a local method invocation. The byte-code for the stub and skeleton objects is generated automatically using a program called *rmic* (an integral part of Java-RMI).

2.3. Interfaces & Server Setup. In RMI, the programmer defines an *interface* to express the remote methods to be made available to the clients. Once this interface is created, the programmer of the server class must specify the implementation of these methods. All interfaces for remote objects must extend the `Remote` interface defined within the `java.rmi` package and declare that remote methods throw a `RemoteException`. The `RemoteException` is necessary due to the lack of stability of remote calls.

The server class must then implement this interface so as to export these methods to clients. The server object must also subclass `UnicastRemoteObject` (by using the `extends` keyword) which simply makes the remote object accessible to a calling client.

2.4. Registry Service. The stub and skeleton objects handle the network communication, and the interface allows the programmer to specify which methods a remote client may call. But, how does the client machine know which remote object to use or where on the network to find that remote object? A *bootstrap registry service* is provided with the RMI library for this purpose.

First, the server registers itself with the registry service. Then, prior to a remote method invocation, the client asks the registry service for a stub to the server. The `Naming` object (standard in RMI) is responsible for the actual registration of objects and retrieval of stubs. The client then uses the `lookup` method to retrieve a stub to the server object.

RMI is a natural extension of Java and thus preserves the simplicity of Java. In order to witness RMI's capabilities, effectiveness, and ease-of-use in a networked heterogeneous environment, we designed a prototype (D-SIFTER) from the area of collaborative computing. The next section provides an overview of D-SIFTER.

3. D-SIFTER. A goal of any information filter is to obtain the most successful and accurate classifications for all input documents based upon a knowledgebase provided by the user. In order to maximize this goal, two alternatives exists. The first one aims at making the knowledgebase extra-ordinarily large while the second one exploits the interconnected nature of the World Wide Web by requiring an information filter, having limited knowledge, to collaborate with other similar filters.

The second alternative, *i.e.*, of an interconnected scenario among multiple filters, eliminates the need for a huge central knowledgebase. Each user can have his/her own small knowledgebase and a local filter which will serve that user based on that knowledgebase. In case the knowledgebase turns out to be inadequate, the local filter can collaborate with others over the network. Such a system can elegantly handle the discovery of new keywords and thus the expansion of knowledgebases. Also, a filter can collaborate with multiple filters, thereby obtaining more than one expert-perspective on the classification of documents. Collaboration, however, increases the response time, but this delay is compensated by a better quality of classifications. Due to the inherent heterogeneous characteristics of an interconnected world of filters, Java-RMI was an obvious choice as the implementation paradigm.

D-SIFTER consists of many filters (called agents or clients) each serving their own users and communicating via a common server. The filters communicate with other filters to classify more documents for either itself or for another filter. D-SIFTER builds upon an isolated information filtering system called SIFTER [6, 7] and has four components: the *representation module*, the *classification module*, the *collaboration module*, and the *GUI.* The first two components are identical to the ones in SIFTER. The third and fourth components use Java-RMI and provide the collaborative features.

The representation module is responsible for converting the document into a numeric structure that can be manipulated by the classification module. Once that numeric structure is determined, the classification module then clusters the given document into its appropriate category. For more information on either of these modules, the reader is referred to [8, 6].

We describe the collaboration module in the next subsection and the GUI in Section 5.

3.1. The Collaboration Module. We have developed two versions of D-SIFTER based upon a *single-opinion* and a *multiple-opinion* collaboration model. We have further divided the study of a *single-opinion* model into two different designs: a *user-centric* and a *money-centric* model. The *user-centric* model prioritizes the needs of a user while the a *money-centric* model tries to maximize the gain from providing its services to the other filters. The detailed descriptions of the two variations can be found in [9]. The multiple-opinion model involves a bidding mechanism for filters to communicate and negotiate with each other, thereby achieving a collaborative information classification. More details about the multiple-opinion model are found in [10]. In this article, we will primarily concentrate on the basic single-opinion version of D-SIFTER.

The basic single-opinion version of D-SIFTER achieves the collaboration by using a simple polling method, *i.e.*, the communication between filters is indirect in nature and takes place through the common server. Any number of filters may be connected to the server at any given time, and all filters follow the same basic algorithm for collaboration – *attempt to classify my own documents first, then if there is time, try and help the other remote filters (User-centric).* The formal algorithm is as follows. We use C to denote the local filter.

0. Initially, place all local documents to be classified into an array which serves as the current input document set for C.

1. C attempts to locally classify the next document from the document set. Check to see if the document was your own or remote.
  - *a) If it was your own then*
    - *i) If that classification was successful, present the result to the user.*
    - *ii) If that classification was not successful, then send that document to the server and ask for a remote assistance.*
  - *b) If it was remote then send the result back (either successful or unsuccessful) to the common server with your id on it as a collaborator indicator.*

2. If C has sent a document to the server for remote assistance, check to see if the corresponding result has been posted.
  - *a) If a result has been posted, retrieve that result and present it to the user.*
  - *b) Otherwise, wait until either a result is returned or the time-out period has been reached.*

3. C should then poll the server and see if some other filter has requested assistance for one of its (the other filter's) documents.
  - *a) If such a document exists, retrieve it, delete it from the common server, and place it at the end of C's document set.*

4. Repeat the above steps until the user wishes to disconnect C from the filtering environment.

The *multiple-opinion* model follows a similar algorithm with one major difference. After a filter retrieves a foreign document from the server, it does not delete it. This way the document is still available to other filters.

The time-out period mentioned in Step 2 was an additional constraint we choose to place upon the filters. Its purpose is to protect the user against the unnecessary waste of time reading the classification results of obsolete documents. That is, if the user must wait for more than some period of time, that document is no longer valuable, *i.e*, the user considers it obsolete after some period of time. We consider the time-out period an important part of information filtering; however, due to space limitations this article does not fully explain its purpose and the experiments we conducted measuring the effect of this parameter. For more information, the reader is referred to [9].

The algorithm above clearly shows the need for an ability to execute a method on a different machine. This is exactly what RMI provides. The next section describes the implementation details of the D-SIFTER prototype based on the single-opinion model.

4. Implementation using Java-RMI. Figure 4.1 shows the architecture of D-SIFTER including the Java-RMI components: Server Stub, Server Skeleton, and Registry. It is im-

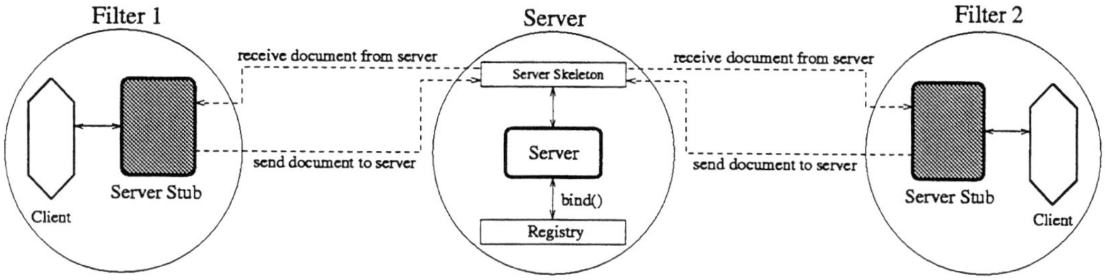

FIG. 4.1. *Architecture of D-SIFTER*

portant to note that Figure 4.1 shows only two filters, but that any number of filters can be connected to the common server.

As Figure 4.1 indicates, the communication between filters is indirect in nature. That is, if a filter wants to collaborate with another filter, it must go through the common server. This indirect communication is achieved as remote calls using RMI. Figure 4.2 shows the actual flow of documents to/from the filters.

Figure 4.2 has four *vector objects* of interest: *input*, *output*, *request*, and *result*. The input and output vectors reside on each filter and store the documents waiting to be classified (local or remote) and present the results from a classification (local or remote) to the user, respectively. The request and result vector are implemented only on the server. Their function is to store the documents that are to be classified remotely by another filter and store the results from another filter's remote collaboration, respectively.

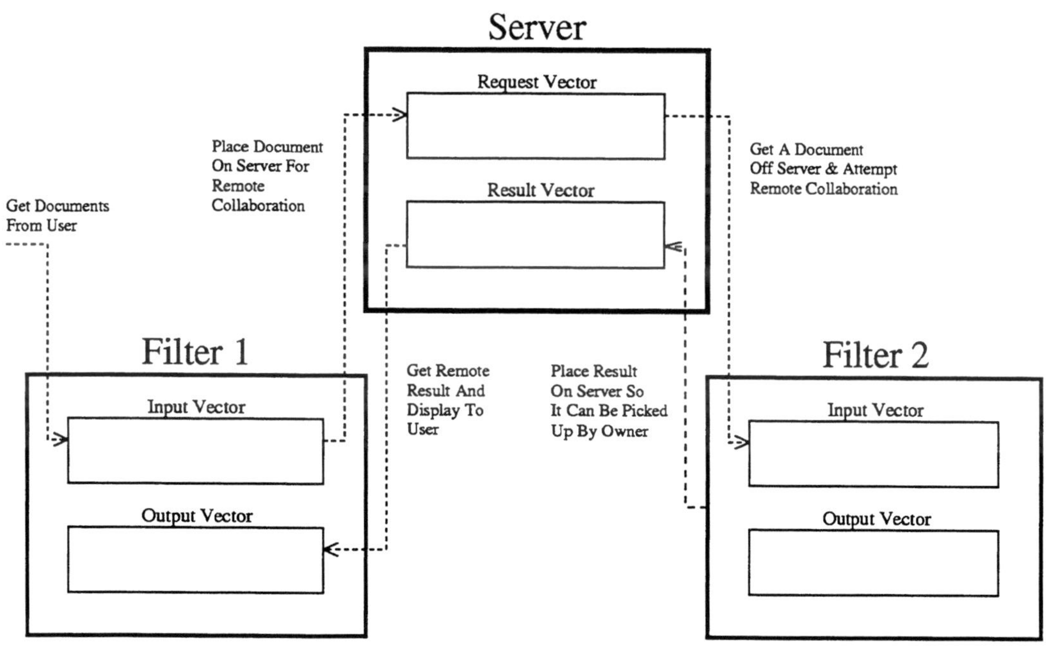

FIG. 4.2. *Communication Flow in D-SIFTER*

In order to invoke remote methods on the common server, we have designed the following remote interface and implementations. The structure of these are based on the RMI principles described in Section 2. Figure 4.3 shows their hierarchy with respect to the RMI hierarchy described in Figure 2.1.

4.1. D-SIFTER Remote Interface. All methods described in the remote interface, `Sift`, are implemented by the server program. These are the methods that a filter may invoke on the server object. The structure of the `Sift` interface is:

```
public interface Sift extends Remote
{
   // return the new filter's id number
   public String get_id() throws RemoteException;

   // place a document on the server
   public void store_document(DocRequest doc) throws RemoteException;

   // remove your document from the server
   public void remove_document(DocRequest doc) throws RemoteException;

   // get the result of the next document you requested assistance on
   public DocResult get_remote_result(String id) throws RemoteException;

   // store your result from an attempted remote agent's document
   public void store_remote_result(DocResult res) throws RemoteException;

   // retrieve another agent's document from the server
   public DocRequest get_doc_request(String id) throws RemoteException;
}
```

4.2. D-SIFTER Server. An instance of this class is the server object. All methods defined in the remote interface, `Sift`, must be implemented here. The class `SiftServer` contains the implementation code for the server program:

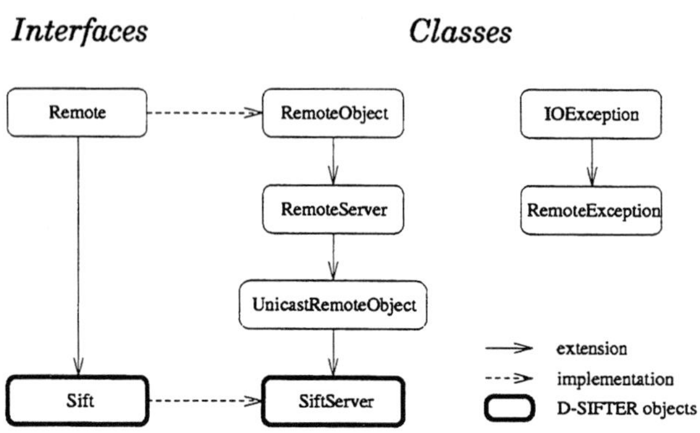

FIG. 4.3. *D-SIFTER Hierarchy*

```
public class SiftServer extends UnicastRemoteObject implements Sift
{
   private String name;
   private Vector request;
   private Vector result;

   public SiftServer(String s) throws RemoteException
   {
      super();
      name = s;

      // Vectors used to store incoming documents and their results
      request = new Vector();
      result = new Vector();
   }

   public synchronized String get_id() throws RemoteException
   {
      // Code to return newest filter's id
         ...
   }

   public synchronized void store_document(DocRequest theDoc)
    throws RemoteException
   {
      // Code to place a local document onto the server
         ...
   }

   public synchronized void remove_document(DocRequest theDoc)
    throws RemoteException
   {
      // Code to remove your document from the server
         ...
   }

   public synchronized DocResult get_remote_result(String id)
    throws RemoteException
   {
      // Code to retrieve the result of the remote classifications
         ...
   }

   public synchronized void store_remote_result(DocResult doc_result)
    throws RemoteException
   {
      // Code to place a document on the server to await assistance
```

```
        ...
   }

   public synchronized DocRequest get_doc_request(String id)
    throws RemoteException
   {
      // Code to retrieve a another filter's document from the server
         ...
   }

   public static void main(String args[])
   {
      // Code to create and install security manager,
      // to create an instance of SiftServer, and
      // to bind a new instance to the registry service
         ...
   }
}
```

Notice the use of the synchronized keyword. This is necessary in order to ensure that no two filters access the server at the exact same time. This is a built-in Java feature that handles concurrency and preserves the data coherence.

The DocRequest and DocResult classes contain the information and flags necessary for each document such as the *title*, *author*, *classification category*, etc. It is this data contained within the instances of the DocRequest and DocResult objects that gets passed among the collaborating filters.

4.3. D-SIFTER Filter. The class SifterApplet contains the following code (common for all filters). In the current version of D-SIFTER, all filters are homogeneous. The filter is implemented as an applet so that the user can interact with it through a familiar browser. The skeleton for the filter code is given below.

```
 public class SifterApplet extends Applet implements Runnable
{
   public synchronized void init()
   {
      // Code used to initialize the applet window
         ...
   }

   public boolean action(Event ev, Object obj)
   {
      // Code used to handle all events within the applet
         ...
   }

   public void run()
   {
      // Code for main driver of filter loop.
```

```
        // The actions performed here are those described in the algorithm above
        // This is the location of all remote method invocations of the D-SIFTER
           ...
    }

    // Code for all local methods

    public void sifter(DocRequest doc) throws IOException
    {
        // Code used to call core SIFTER modules
           ...
    }
}
```

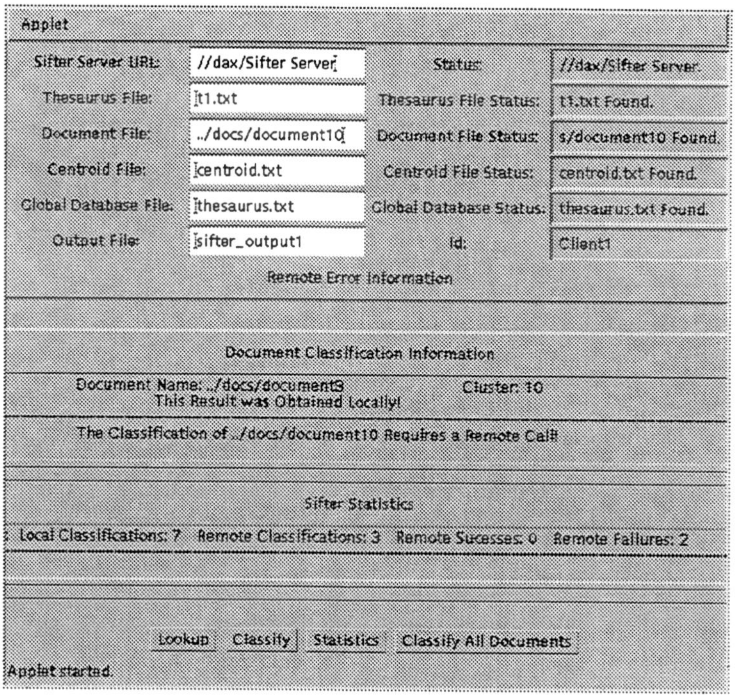

FIG. 5.1. *GUI for D-SIFTER Program*

5. GUI of D-SIFTER. Figure 5.1 shows the graphical user interface of D-SIFTER. The interface is implemented using AWT, Java's API for graphics, and the standard event handling model supported by Java.

The fields in the first column are required as inputs from the user. D-SIFTER displays the appropriate information about these input parameters in the second column.

Below the top fields, there are three message panels. These message panels convey information such as remote errors, document classification information, and some of the current statistics. The buttons at the bottom of the program allow the user to *lookup* a server and connect to it, *classify* the specified document, and show the current *statistics*. The *Classify All Documents* button is mainly being used for testing purposes. It causes the program to classify all 1064 documents used in our experiments.

Now that we have looked at the implementation details of D-SIFTER, below we describe some of our experiments along with their results.

6. Experiments & Results. We conducted several experiments using both models (single- and multiple-opinion) with the D-SIFTER prototype. Here we discuss the results we obtained from experiments conducted on both models. For more information on these and other experiments, see [9]. Our experiments involved measuring the increase in the number of successful classifications when filters were allowed to collaborate. Our experimental environment consisted of three filters executing on Sun Sparc machines, connected via Ethernet, with the Solaris 2.3 operating system.

6.1. Single-Opinion Experiments. Table 6.1 shows the number of successful classifications with and without remote collaboration allowed for 1064 documents from the domain of computer science.

TABLE 6.1
The number of successful classifications for each filter with and without collaboration.

Filter	No collaboration	With collaboration
1	676	866
2	350	800
3	636	893

This simple experiment demonstrates the potential of RMI for designing collaborative systems. As seen from Table 6.1, due to collaboration, Filter 2 increased its classification abilities by 44%. This is a remarkable gain considering the ease with which the isolated filter program was converted into a distributed environment using RMI.

Another experiment we conducted using D-SIFTER was the study of the "time-out" parameter. This experiment showed us that once the "time-out" period reached a *peak value* for each filter, the number of successful classifications did not increase but reached a steady value. More detailed information regarding the "time-out" parameter can be found in [9].

6.2. Multiple-Opinion Experiments. In a multiple-opinion experiment all filters are attempting to classify each document that was posted on the server. This kind of collaboration always results in a maximum number of successful classifications possible. Table 6.2 shows the number of successful classifications with and without remote collaboration allowed for all 1064 documents.

TABLE 6.2
The number of successful classifications for each filter with and without collaboration.

Filter	No collaboration	With collaboration
1	676	998
2	350	998
3	636	998

All three filters can successfully classify 998 documents. This is exactly the number of documents that would be classified by a single filter with a global thesaurus. The remaining 66 documents were impossible to classify by any of the knowledgebases available to filters. Although this approach maximizes the number of successful classifications, it has certain disadvantages. It requires the collaboration of all possible filters and thus is expensive in terms of time.

6.3. Bidding Mechanism and Multiple-opinion Version. We incorporated a market-based economic model, which allows multiple filters to post their bids, in the multiple-opinion version of D-SIFTER. The presence of multiple filters require addressing many interesting issues such as: *Why (or when) should an filter bid? How much time should the requesting filter wait? How much should an filter bid? How should the requesting filter decide which remote collaborator to choose?*

We have used the notion of a bidding function based upon the current financial state (expressed in terms of information dollars – an entity assigned to each filter at the beginning) and the history of document classification. More details about the exact scheme used in this version and the results of the experiments with it are described in [10].

6.4. Performance and Scalability. The performance of the D-SIFTER, measured in terms of the execution time, will always vary based on the network traffic and the hardware used. Our experiments were conducted during the time of a low network traffic and were run on Sun Sparc machines connected via Ethernet. The average time, taken by each filter to classify 1064 documents, was about 50 minutes. The scalability issue has not been studied in depth yet. We run preliminary experiments with several collaborating filters and did not encounter any difficulties. It is essential, however, for any collaborative system to support unlimited number of users. RMI itself does not post any constraints on the numbers of clients calling remote methods. The use of RMI in implementation of D-SIFTER provides basis for potentially unlimited number of collaborating filters.

6.5. An Experiment Using an Asynchronous Version of RMI (ARMI). Currently, RMI is synchronous in nature. While this is satisfactory for many applications, time-critical applications may benefit from an asynchronous mechanism for remote invocations. We have added an asynchronous flavor to RMI called ARMI, see [11]. ARMI is built upon RMI and hence uses the underlying communication paradigm offered by RMI. ARMI allows an overlap of local and remote computations.

As D-SIFTER has inherent asynchronous characteristics, it was logical to develop another prototype using ARMI. Our initial experiments with this prototype indicated that the total time required to classify all 1064 documents was reduced by 13.9 minutes.

7. Future Work. We see many possibilities for enhancement of D-SIFTER developed with RMI version 1.1.1. Currently, RMI is only runnable through the Appletviewer browser (provided with JDK) on Sun workstations and Windows NT machines. However, recently, Sun has announced that the newest version of JDK (1.2) will also work using HotJava and Netscape with the proper plug-in. Also, JDK releases for other machines (such as SGI, HP, and Dec) are now available. We are eager to make the D-SIFTER system truly heterogeneous by running it on different architectures and through different browsers.

Other future directions include conducting additional performance analysis using ARMI, enhancing the graphical user interface, as well as studying the possibilities of allowing dynamic objects for collaborative systems implemented using RMI.

8. Conclusion. We have presented an overview of Java-RMI along with the detailed design of D-SIFTER. During the design and implementation of D-SIFTER, we found RMI to be an effective and easy to use paradigm for collaborative computing. This observation is based on the relatively short development time required for the D-SIFTER prototype. Our results indicate that the collaborative environment of filters achieve a superior performance over the isolated filter. We believe that RMI due to its easy semantics will turn out to be an effective mechanism for other collaborative domains such as interactive visualization and distributed software engineering environments.

Acknowledgments. Snehasis Mukhopadhyay, one of the authors, was supported by the NSF CAREER grant # ECS-9623971 during the course of the research reported in this paper.

REFERENCES

[1] David Flanagan. *Java in a Nutshell.* O'Reilly & Associates, Inc., 1996.

[2] Gary Cornell and Cay S. Horstmann. *Core Java Second Edition.* Sunsoft Press, 1997.

[3] Sun Microsystems. RMI Specification. *www.javasoft.com/products/jdk/1.1/docs/guide/rmi/spec/rmiTOC.doc.html.*, 1997.

[4] Karanjit S. Siyan and James L. Weaver. *Inside Java.* New Riders Publishing, 1997.

[5] Sun Microsystems. Serialization Specification. *www.javasoft.com/products/jdk/rmi/serial/index.html*, 1997.

[6] W. Lam, S. Mukhopadhyay, J. Mostafa, M. Palakal. Detection of Shifts in User Interface for Personalized Information Filtering. *Proceedings of 19th International Conference on Research and Development in Information Retrieval*, Zurich, Switzerland, August 18-22, 1996.

[7] Sifter Research Group. SIFTER. *xtasy.lib.indiana.edu/jmdocs/resfilter.html*, 1998.

[8] J. Mostafa, S. Mukhopadhyay, W. Lam, M. Palakal. A Multi-level Approach to Intelligent Information Filtering: Model, System & Evaluation. *ACM Transactions on Information Systems*, 15(4):368–399, 1997.

[9] Raje, R., Mukhopadhyay, S., Boyles, M. and Papiez, A. An Economic Framework for a Web-based Collaborative Information Classifier. *Proceedings of the International Association of Science and Technology for Development, SE'97 Conference*, pages 362–366, San Francisco, November 2-4, 1997.

[10] Raje, R., Mukhopadhyay, S., Boyles, M., Papiez, A., Patel, N., Palakal, M. and Mostafa, J. A Bidding Mechanism for Web-Based Agents Involved in Information Classification. *WWW Journal, Special Issue on Distributed World Wide Web Processing: Applications and Techniques of Web Agents*, In Press, 1998.

[11] R. Raje, J. Williams, M. Boyles. An Asynchronous Remote Method Invocation (ARMI) Mechanism for Java. *Concurrency: Practice and Experience*, 9(11):1207–1211, November 1997.

AN APPLICATION FRAMEWORK FOR DYNAMIC DISTRIBUTED SOFTWARE ARCHITECTURES

G. R. RIBEIRO-JUSTO* AND P. R. F. CUNHA†

Abstract. There are compelling reasons to combine the concepts of an architecture description language with those of an object-oriented framework to provide support for the development of reusable and extensible software architectures. This paper presents *C++CL*, an object-oriented framework for developing reconfigurable distributed software architectures, which follows that approach. The reconfigurability of *C++CL* enables us to develop distributed systems, which require changes to take place during run time without having to shut the system down. Examples of systems of this kind are evident in banking, industrial control and telecommunications and are becoming more common in many other areas. The main focus of the paper is to show how *C++CL* supports re-usability and the evolution of distributed systems through the use of inheritance and the modelling of architectural styles. Inheritance can be applied not only to the components of an architecture but to the description of the architectural configuration itself. An architectural style, similarly to a pattern, defines an architecture-based solution to a family of problems. The combination of those two concepts provides powerful support for re-usability of architecture descriptions.

Key words. software architecture, architecture description languages, software evolution, distributed systems, object-oriented design

1. Introduction. With the cost and complexity of software systems constantly growing, the need for managing and reusing software components has become paramount. To achieve this software designers require models, methods and description languages which enable them to describe and evaluate the components of their designs in a different manner to that currently used. The main principle is to focus on components and their interaction, the *software architecture*, in order to identify *where* and *how* components can be reused. The architecture of a software system can establish the level at which the designer can specify how the system can evolve by replacing and adding components or modifying component interactions.

Software architectures have played an important role in the development of distributed systems for some time. Distributed software designers have recognised for some time the importance of the concept of software architecture in abstracting certain aspects of the design, such as functional behaviour, enabling them to focus on issues such as communication between components and the distribution of components on the network.

Another important area where software architectures have played a major role is that of dynamic or evolving systems. Unlike serial software where a fault usually shuts down the whole system, an important property of a distributed software is its *robustness* and *availability* in case of faults, as certain components may fail but others can still work. A system where the architecture can change during its execution is usually referred to as a *dynamic* system [19]. Although, any distributed system can incorporate such a property, there are applications where such a property is an essential requirement. For example, embedded systems used in manufacturing, nuclear and power station monitoring systems and banking systems.

In order to describe the software architecture or design structure of a system, appropriate notations different from those used to describe the data structures and the algorithms

*Cavendish School of Computer Science, University of Westminster, 115 New Cavendish St, London, W1M 8JS, UK (justog@wmin.ac.uk).

†Department of Informatics,Federal University of Pernambuco, 50732-970, Recife, Brazil (prfc@di.ufpe.br).

is necessary. Module interconnection languages (MILs) [20, 11, 12, 5] have presented an initial solution to the separating of the computation (programming-in-the-small) from the structure (programming-in-the-large). The system structure is the part of the design where the components and their relationships are defined. However, despite many successful applications of various MILs, there are limitations in their notations, especially in terms of describing reusable and extensible software architectures [29]. As explained in [27], the lack of extensibility and reuse is a serious problem in the development of distributed systems. More recently, new architecture description languages (ADLs) have been proposed [21] but they focus mainly on formal notations such as Wright [3], ASDL [25] and ZCL [14], which provide high-level abstractions to specify and reason about software architectures.

A solution to the problem of building reusable and extensible software components is the use of (object-oriented) application frameworks [10, 27]. An application framework basically combines a collection of classes and objects which embodies an abstract design for a family of problems. A survey of frameworks for parallel and distributed computing can be seen in [4].

An architectural application framework, which combines the concepts of application frameworks and software architectural styles, then becomes a very promising approach to the development of extensible and reusable software. Evidence is presented, for example, in [1]. The authors describe key results of their experiences in developing large and complex flight simulation software based on architectural components defined within an application framework.

C++CL is an application framework for (*reconfigurable*) distributed software architectures. The reconfigurability of *C++CL* enables us to develop distributed systems, which require changes to take place during the system execution without having to shut down the system. Examples of these systems are evident in banking, industrial control and telecommunications, and are becoming more common in many other areas [15, 7]. The main focus of the paper is to show how *C++CL* support re-usability and the evolution of distributed systems through the use of inheritance and the modelling of architectural styles [23]. Inheritance can be applied not only to the components of an architecture but to the description of the architecture configuration itself. An architectural style, similarly to a pattern, defines an architecture-based solution to a family of problems [23]. The combination of those two concepts provides powerful support for re-usability of architecture descriptions.

The paper is structured as follows. In the next section, we compare our work with other related works. In Section 3, we enumerate the requirements a framework for reconfigurable software architectures should have and in Section 4 *C++CL* is described in detail. Section 5 gives an overview of *C++CL* reconfiguration model, and compares it with other approaches. Section 6 presents three examples of the use of the framework, focusing on re-usability. Finally in Section 7, we present the main conclusions about and further directions of the work described in the paper.

2. Related Work. Much of the work carried out in the field of distributed software architecture has focused on the development of MILs, especially for developing dynamic reconfigurable distributed systems [19, 11, 12, 18]. These descriptions mainly allow components to interact via port objects as with *C++CL* and components can correspond to C++ objects but in many cases such as in [6] the behaviour of a component is defined in the class constructor, which limits the derivation of new components. More recent ADLs, such as the Olan configuration language [6], extend some of the concepts used in traditional MILs. It provides special broadcast events and handlers which are triggered when a particular event is received. It allows modules to share variables known as attributes. Dynamic configuration is modelled as in Darwin [18]. One interesting aspect of Olan, however, is the use of object-oriented concepts in the configuration language. A composite component class is the unit of structuring where instances are created and bound. Although Olan uses the concept of class it does not support inheritance. In other words, it is object-based and not object-oriented as *C++CL*.

Another important key distinction between *C++CL* and most ADLs relates to the fact that these descriptions are defined by a programming language rather than an application framework such as *C++CL*. In this sense, *C++CL* shares properties of an ADL such as UniCon [28]. Although UniCon provides a larger number of components and connectors it does not support the description of reconfigurable distributed architectures. Also, UniCon provides a limited mechanism for defining new connector types (in addition to the collection of built-in types), and has no means of describing architectural styles.

In terms of application frameworks, much of the work has focused on frameworks for distributed multi-media, which are more concerned with modelling a wide range of media types and formats [9] and do not follow an architectural approach. An exception is Djinn [22], which is aimed at supporting multi-media groupware programming, but models distributed applications as a collection of interacting objects known as components which produce and consume media type and events through ports. It also supports a certain type of composite components. However, the ports basically support event and stream communication, and dynamic reconfiguration is limited. A recent issue of the communication of the ACM describes a number of lessons learned and experiences gained with the use of application frameworks, including some for distributed applications [27]. None of them, however, follow an architectural approach.

Aesop [29], a system for developing style-specific architectural environments, provides a generic object model for architectural representations. The extension of a generic architectural model with types can provide a direct way to enrich the number of architectural elements. The philosophy is similar to that applied to *C++CL*. However, the aim of Aesop is to support the architectural representation whilst *C++CL* aims to support the development of architectural-based applications. Also, *C++CL* is more domain-specific as it is targeted at reconfigurable distributed applications.

Another approach is the use of formalism to specify and reason about distributed software architectures. Several formalisms have been proposed, ranging from generic frameworks like ASDL[25], special specification languages like Wright [3] and also a logical framework [2] which includes the concept of component version and module family, where all modules satisfy the same specification but can have different implementations. *C++CL* certainly differs from the formal approaches as it is not a formal framework but it still shares many of the concepts and the framework structure, in particular those of ASDL.

ZCL [14] is a formal framework specified in Z and based on *C++CL* which enables us to formalise and analyse evolving distributed software architectures. ZCL gives a formal semantics to *C++CL*.

3. Framework Requirements. The key concepts of software architectures are the components, connectors and the (architectural) configuration, where the instances and interconnections of the components and connectors are defined. The various ADLs provide different notations and support to describe and manage software architectures. A taxonomy of ADLs have been presented in [21]. The taxonomy describes the essential (modelling) features of an ADL. In this section, the main concepts of Medvidovic and Taylor's taxonomy are used to define the requirements of a framework aimed to support the development of software architectures.

3.1. Components. Components are the basic units of the software architecture. Their properties determine how they can be combined into systems or composite components. In a distributed environment, a primitive component type usually takes the form of a *process* or *task* which can execute independently and can be allocated to any location within the distributed platform (network). Another important property of an ADL is its support for component evolution, which is usually defined in terms of sub-typing and refinement. Medvidovic and Taylor found very few ADLs which provide such capabilities. Composite components built in a hierarchical manner generating new component types also represent an important concept. The properties of a composite component are derived from the properties of their sub-component types together with any additional constraint defined by the composite component type.

3.2. Component Interface. The interface of the component is one of its essential elements, which defines the types of interaction (or protocols) the component can participate in. The interaction type is primarily defined by the component type. Usually component types specify their interaction constraints in their interface by defining a set of *ports*. Each port can specify a different protocol. For example, a task component type can define a port for synchronous communication and a port for asynchronous communication.

3.3. Connectors. In traditional MILs, the interactions are usually defined by binding the ports of the components. In new ADLs, however, the interactions are explicitly defined by using elements called *connectors* [29]. The main advantage of a connector is to provide a much higher level of abstraction than port bindings. Very few ADLs model connectors as first-class objects and even fewer allow connector evolution through sub-typing [21]. In many cases, a set of pre-defined connectors are provided. Connectors become particularly important when developing dynamic configurations, where connections between many components may be required. A high-level connector can be responsible for managing those linking, simplifying the development of the software architecture.

3.4. Configurations. An *architectural configuration* is used to define the structure or topology of an architecture; that is, it provides the ability to instantiate and compose components in various ways and check the consistency of their interconnection. Most ADLs assume the configuration to be static but, evolution of an architecture is a desirable and essential property. ADLs can provide support for incremental evolution by allowing the replacement of components and connectors. This evolution can happen even at run time.

3.5. Architectural Style. An important issue in the emerging field of software architecture is to identify common *architectural styles* used by many current systems and show how they can be combined and re-used [29]. Medvidovic and Taylor's taxonomy [21] does not explicitly include that concept, even though they consider the idea of incomplete configurations, which are supported by some ADLs. Two concepts are essential for describing architectural styles. Firstly, a *generic architecture* [24], which can have parameters that denote an indeterminate type or object. Specific instances of the architecture can be derived by giving values for those parameters. Secondly, *constraints* are used to define semantic restrictions of the configuration. An architectural style can then be defined in terms of its *vocabulary* (the component and connector types, defined as parameters, that can be used in the configuration of that style) and its *constraints*, predicates which must hold to any configuration in that style [3] .

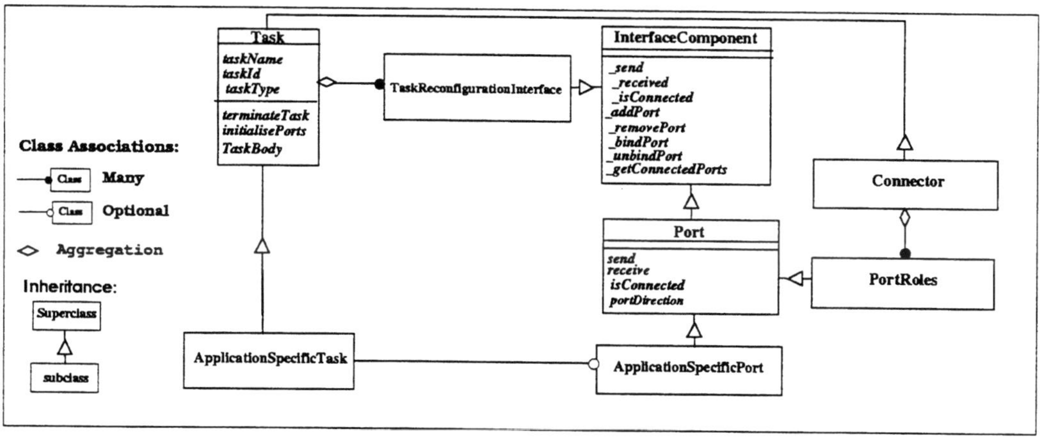

FIG. 4.1. *Portion of the OMT object diagram for C++CL basic classes: class Task, class Port and class Connector.*

4. The *C++CL* Framework. *C++CL* is based on an MIL called CL[11, 12], which has introduced the notion of *planned* reconfiguration. The idea of a planned reconfiguration is to set reconfiguration expressions, that if satisfied during the execution, would automatically trigger reconfiguration activities.

4.1. Components. A *Task* represents a simple abstraction for the concept of process. In the current version of the framework, a task is viewed as a PVM process [31] which provides portability on a wide range of parallel and distributed platforms. Each *Task* performs some computation defined by its *body* which depends on the application domain. It is important to point out that the *body* of the task is seen as the main service provided by the class *Task*, similar to the method *run()* in the Java^{tm} Thread library [16], and not as a built-in service. The behaviour of a *Task* can be easily extended or restricted. For example, a configuration can be defined as a special type of *Task* by extending the operations the *body* can perform. Fig. 4.1 shows an Object Modelling Technique (OMT)[26]) diagram for components (tasks), ports and connectors within our framework.

4.2. Interface. A task interaction type is defined by its ports. The class *Port* defines primitive types of ports. The basic attribute of a port is the *direction* of its interaction which could be input, output or both. The attribute *data type* indicates which type of data the port can handle. As in [25], the class *Port* is generic and the data type is application dependent. The third important aspect of a port is the type of *service* it offers. *C++CL* provides a set of services, like Darwin [20], such as synchronous and asynchronous, request-reply, streams and multi-cast. Application-specific ports can be derived from primitive ports, as illustrated in [13].

4.3. Task and Port Reconfiguration. The class *InterfaceComponent* defines an abstraction for a general kind of communication and configuration server. The implementation of this class depends very much on the (distributed) platform where the application will execute. This means that it abstracts the details of the platform from the other classes in the framework. This is the only class which should be modified if the framework is to be ported to a new platform.

It handles conventional messages, and also special messages for configuration and reconfiguration. These messages can update information stored in the *InterfaceComponent*, can generate new messages and can also be used to interrupt the execution of processes.

Fig. 4.1 shows that each *Task* uses the class *InterfaceComponent* to generate an interface object (*TaskReconfigurationInterface*) used to handle configuration messages which can start or interrupt the execution of that *Task*. It also has information about any communication activity in the *Task* and is therefore used by a connector to manage the operations of its ports.

4.4. Composite Components. A composite component is where an (architectural) configuration is defined. It is usually referred to as a *configuration* (component). A configuration performs very special operations on the system structure. These operations correspond to the services provided by the class *Configuration*. Each operation directly corresponds to an operation in an MIL, like CL, or a formal model like ASDL [25]. For example, the operation *Instance* creates an instance of a component type, and the operation *Link* connects two ports (defining a simple form of connector). Overloading is a good mechanism to implement different forms of the same operation. For example, an instance can be created in a default node. In this case, the operation `Instance (int component)` means that only the component from which the task is created is required. In general , however, the operation `Instance (int component, int node)` is used, as it is necessary to specify on which node the instance will be created.

In order to check consistency of the architectural configuration, especially in the presence of dynamic changes (evolution), a configuration component must store information about its *state*. This information is maintained by the *ConfigurationTable* class. The *ConfigurationTable* is an important part of a configuration component. It is used to keep track of the state of the configuration in terms of hardware and software. The configuration component cannot perform its operations without checking its state. It does not only work like an information repository but it is also responsible for maintaining integrity and consistency of the configuration state. It uses primitive classes which represent abstractions for these architectural entities as illustrated in Fig. 4.2. The main entities are: *ImportedComponent* (a task or configuration type from which instances can be created and usually refers to executable files which can be loaded in different nodes of the configuration); *Node* (a logical node or domain where instances execute); *Instance* (an executable task or configuration created from an *ImportedComponent* at a particular node whose execution is controlled by its parent configuration) and *Link* (a direct connection between ports of two instances which can also represent a bind between a port of an instance and a port of a configuration).

4.5. Configuration Interface. The class *ConfigurationPort* is very similar to the class *Port* except that there are restrictions on the operations which it can perform. A *ConfigurationPort* cannot be used to send or receive messages and only sub-configurations can use them. A sub-configuration uses them to *bind* (external) ports to its sub-components (tasks or sub-configurations). They are similar to ASDL virtual ports [25]. A composite component which contains (configuration) ports can be used in another composite component as a primitive component. The only restriction is that a system should have a *topmost* composite component without ports and which is not part of any composite component. Fig. 4.2 shows a class diagram for a composite component.

4.6. Connectors. The concept of link between two ports employed by many architecture description languages is too primitive when developing complex and especially dynamic software architectures. For this reason, new languages now use the concept of *connector* to provide high-level abstractions for describing relationships or interconnections between

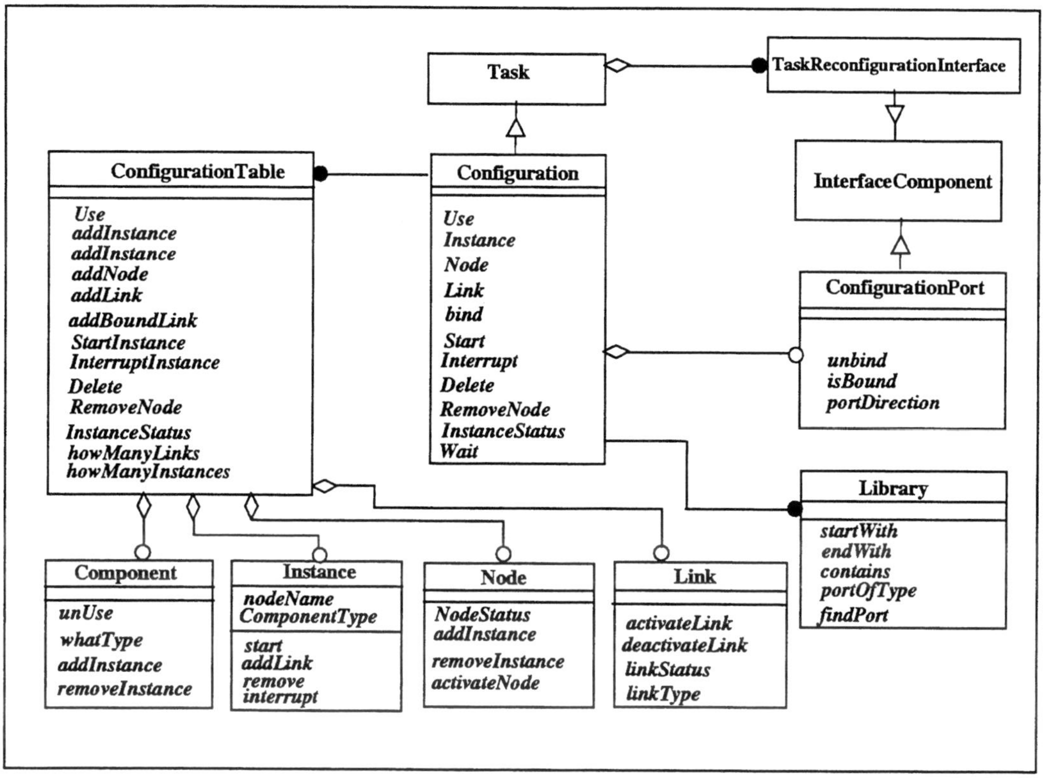

FIG. 4.2. *Portion of the OMT object diagram for the C++CL configuration elements: configuration, configuration port, configuration table and library.*

software components [29]. Connectors can be designed in *C++CL* in various manners. A connector can be designed as a special task which does not perform user-defined computation and has access to the *InterfaceComponent* (see Fig. 4.1). A connector usually manages the connection between more than two tasks and to do so it uses the *InterfaceComponent* to send or receive special messages which enable it to configure ports of the connected tasks. That concept of connector differs from other ADLs, as a connector (task) still denotes a computation unit [21]. Another solution is to define a connector as a special object used in a composite component. In this case, the connector simply manages the links between the ports and is not defined as a separate task. The final approach used in *C++CL* is to create implicit connectors, which are defined as part of a style. This approach is illustrated in Section 6.

4.7. The Library. In addition to the configuration table, *C++CL* maintains a repository of components and connectors (the *Library* class) used to provide a semantic support similar to that described in [30]. The *Library* class is a key object in the specification of architectural constraints and generic software architectures. The *Library* provides a set of *query* operations to select and check attributes of component, connector and interface types. For example, to select all components of type `task`, named *Lecturer* that contain a port of type `INT` with direction `EntryPort`, we can use the expression: `taskName("Lecturer") && portOfType(INT, EntryPort)`.

5. The *C++CL* Reconfiguration Model.

5.1. General Requirements. Etzkorn [8] defines four major requirements and objectives for supporting dynamic reconfiguration. The preservation of systems consistency means that changes should not happen arbitrarily and may only take place in a certain state, called *reconfiguration state.* Since changes should only take place in reconfiguration states, it may take some time from the moment the change is submitted and the time it is executed. However, the program should be designed to guarantee a minimal delay in the execution of the change. The minimal disturbance requirement is a major difference between static and dynamic reconfigurable systems. In the former, the whole system must be shut down whilst in the latter only the parts affected by the changes should be disturbed. The rest of the system should continue to run, even though some degradation may occur. Separation of the application functionality and reconfiguration concerns is required to avoid the modification of the behaviour of the program's components (tasks or processes).

Another important aspect of a reconfiguration model is the degree to which the application is designed to take into account future changes. Etzkorn [8] suggests the classification of the model into two categories: *active* and *passive* change management. Active change management [20] suggests the definition of abstract reconfiguration states (which are application independent) where tasks can be requested by the management system to reach and send an acknowledgment. The management system then waits for acknowledgment from all tasks involved in the change, and guarantees that a reconfiguration state will be reached. The disadvantage of this approach is that extra functionality must be added to each task to reach a reconfiguration state. In the passive approach, the reconfiguration states are application dependent. This means that the designer of a change program must specify a change according to the behaviour of the tasks. The development of the change program becomes an extra part of the design. In terms of the change management system, it means that it must be capable of evaluating "reconfiguration state specifications" which refer to the behaviour of the application tasks. This requires, therefore, some form of *synchronisation* between the reconfiguration program and the respective tasks.

5.2. General Aspects of the C++CL Model. The first aspect to consider is in which category, according to Etzkorn classification [8], the *C++CL* model should be placed. In general terms, the model should be classified as *passive.* The reason being that there is a notion of an explicit configuration state defined in a task. A designer developing a *C++CL* reconfiguration program must have knowledge of the tasks' behaviour to make sure that the consistency of the application is not affected. On the other hand, we must recall that every *C++CL* task contains an interface object (*TaskReconfigurationInterface* of type $InterfaceComponent$), which is responsible for receiving and executing reconfiguration operations upon a task. Reconfiguration operations are usually executed when a task tries to use one of its ports or perform any configuration query function, that is, any operation which invokes its interface object. Hence, a configuration state is defined when a task uses its interface. In fact, the designer can explicitly define configuration states in a task by calling some interface operations which block the task until a configuration message is received from its parent configuration (the configuration which creates that instance of the task). In summary, even though the *C++CL* model is mainly passive, it allows active reconfiguration to be defined.

In terms of Etzkorn's requirements for reconfiguration support, the *C++CL* satisfies all of them. By guaranteeing that a task can only be reconfigured when it accesses its interface, the *C++CL* model preserves the internal state of the task and avoids the loss of any outgoing

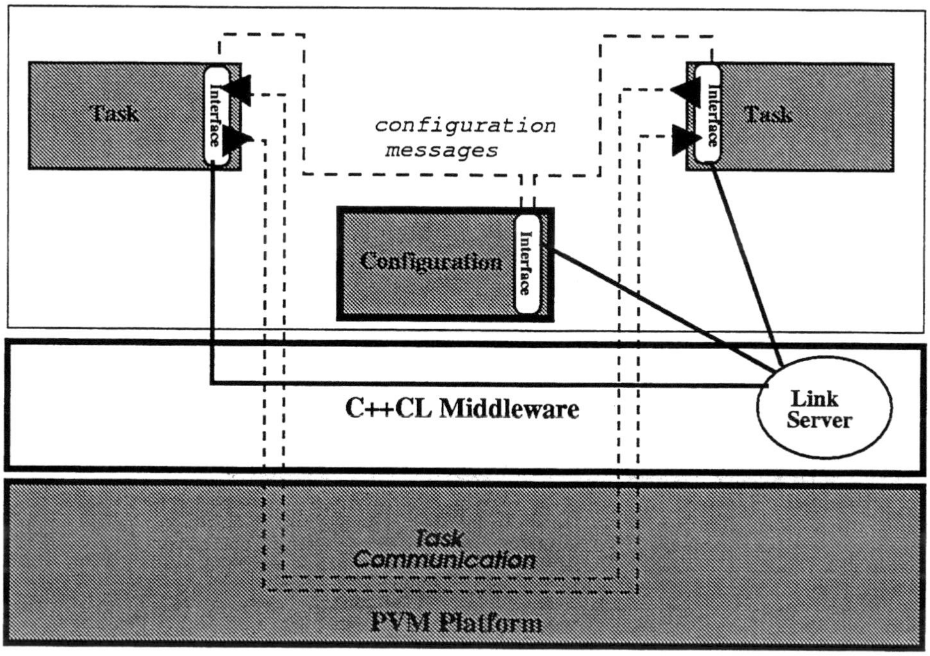

FIG. 5.1. *Overview of the C++CL reconfiguration model, illustrating the relationships between its principal elements.*

message. Unfortunately, incoming messages are locally buffered. If the task does not receive them, they will be discarded. However, we can use the *C++CL active link* connector which implements a model similar to [8] where the user has the option to preserve the pending messages in a link. The time taken for a reconfiguration to be carried out will depend on how the configuration was designed but *C++CL* tries to keep the delay to a minimum. In the *C++CL* model, only the tasks and configurations involved in the reconfiguration are affected. The remaining tasks and configurations continue their normal execution, leading to the minimal disturbance of the system. Finally, as in most reconfiguration models, *C++CL* tasks and configurations are clearly separate.

5.3. Reconfiguration States. A reconfiguration state is specified by the designer with respect to the state of the configuration at a certain time. The state of the configuration is stored in the configuration table of the configuration. It contains information about task instances, their status and location, links between instances' ports, and the status of the hardware. One important aspect of *C++CL* is that in a hierarchical configuration, each sub-configuration has its own configuration table. A parent (higher-level) configuration cannot access information about the internal structure of a (child) sub-configuration. This approach differs from [18, 17] where during elaboration sub-configurations (group modules) are flattened, destroying the hierarchical structure. The *C++CL* model is, therefore, completely *distributed* and modular in the sense that the configuration information is stored by the various sub-configurations.

However, to avoid a long interconnection path between sub-configurations when a configuration port is bound or unbound during a reconfiguration, a *Link Server* has been defined in the *C++CL* middleware as illustrated in Fig. 5.1. The configuration stores the necessary

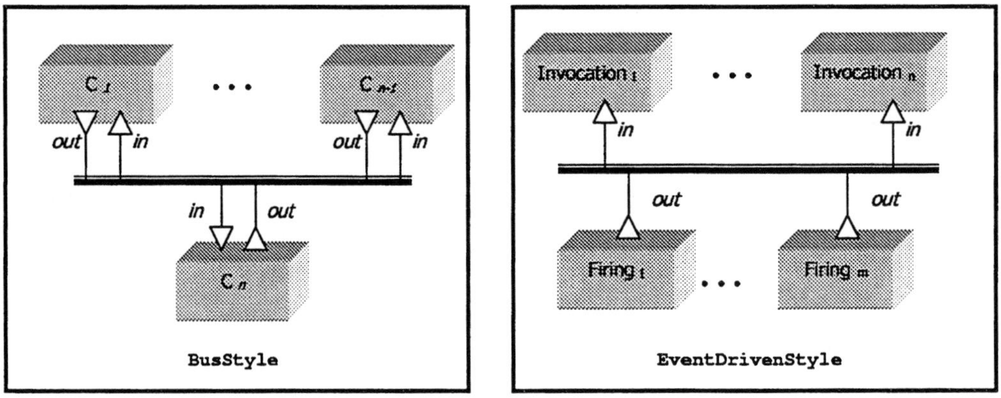

FIG. 6.1. *Graphical representation of a Bus style and Event-Drive style, using the concept of a high-level Bus connector.*

information about the link and sends a request to the *Link Server* to send a reconfiguration message to the tasks bound to that link. The reason is that in order to reduce overhead, the task instances communicate directly using the distributed platform primitives (for example, *PVM* primitives), as illustrated in Fig. 5.1. *C++CL* has, therefore, little impact on the normal performance of the application.

The designer can specify configuration expressions to determine or define conditions for reconfiguration. The *Wait* operation (defined as a method of the class *Configuration*), blocks a configuration component until a configuration condition is satisfied (an event is triggered) or a timeout occurs.

6. Case Studies.

6.1. The Bus Style. Components

In a *bus style*, each component type has at least *one input* and *one output* port. A component uses its input port to receive data from the other components and through its output port it *broadcasts* a message to the other components. No constraints are imposed on the way each component produces (outputs) or consumes (inputs) data. The main constraints of the bus style is that each component should have the capability to both consume and produce data. The other important constraint relates to the fact that any data output by one component is broadcast to all the other components. This is defined through a bus connector, which is an important element of the style. Fig. 6.1 illustrates the bus style. Observe that each component of the style can be of a different type. This means that the style accepts a list of component types as a parameter. To use the bus style in a dynamic environment, two reconfiguration operations are provided. Firstly, an '*add component*' operation permits component instances to be added to the configuration. The '*remove component*' operation corresponds to the reverse operation. A maximum number of instances that can be created is also defined as a parameter for the style.

Architectural styles in *C++CL* are derived from the *Configuration* class. In the interface of the new class, the parameters of the style are defined in the class constructor and operations correspond to (public) methods. Fig. 6.2 presents part of the *C++CL* code for the bus style. Observe that the list of component type names is defined as a parameter using the *C++CL* pre-defined (generic) `List` class. Another parameter, which specifies the maximum number of component types, was also added.

Several parameters were defined for the `AddComponent` method. They correspond to the name of the instance being created, the name of the component type being instantiated, the location in the network where the instance is to be created and the names of the input and output ports, which will play the roles required by the bus style. To remove an instance, however, only the name of the instance is needed.

The constraints of the style are usually checked in the class contructor as Fig. 6.2 shows. The bus style constraint specifies that any component type can be used provided it has at least one input port and one output port compatible with the bus connector. The repository object `theLibrary` is used to define a composed query, which returns (in an `Array` object) all task components of the given name, containing the required input (`EntryPort`) and output (`ExitPort`) ports. If the returned `Array` object has size zero, this indicates that the query has failed, namely, the given component does not satisfy the style constraint. Otherwise, the component type is imported applying the *C++CL* `Use` operation.

The `addComponent` method, illustrated in Fig. 6.2, first checks if a new instance can be added, as the style specifies a maximum number of instances. A new instance is created using the *C++CL* `Instance` operation. Observe that the *C++CL* method `whatComponentId` only returns the id of the given component if that component has been correctly imported (as defined in the class constructor).

In this version of the bus style, we make use of an implicit connector. This means that the style configuration is responsible for managing the links amongst the component instances' ports. Basically, the output port of the new instance is linked to the input port of all the other instances. Similarly, the output ports of all existing instances must be linked to the input port of the newly created instance. The execution of the new instance is explicitly defined using the *C++CL* operation `Start`. To remove an instance in *C++CL* its execution must be first interrupted (applying the `Interrupt` operation). The *C++CL* operation `Delete` disconnects all the instance's ports and deletes the instance from the architectural configuration.

6.2. The Event-Driven Style. In the *event-driven* style, two categories of component types are identified. The first category corresponds to the components that can *fire* (produce) events. The second category consists of the components that are invoked after events have happened. The *firing* (event) component types are therefore required to possess one output port through which events are fired. The *invocation* components, on the other hand, must contain one input port to be notified of events. The event-driven style makes use of a special connector, which broadcasts any event produced by a firing component to all invocation components. Fig. 6.1 illustrates the event-driven style.

A *C++CL* version of the event style is outlined in Fig. 6.3. Each category of components is specified by a *C++CL* `List` object. The style also requires the maximum number of instances that can be created from a component of each category. Similarly to the bus style, to support dynamic reconfiguration the event-driven style provides methods to add and remove instances of components of each category. For simplicity, only the `addInvocationComponent` method is illustrated in Fig. 6.3. Observe that, unlike the bus style, the *C++CL* method `whatComponentId` is not sufficient to guarantee that the given component type has been imported, as there are two categories of component types.

6.3. Heterogeneous Software Architectures. Not all systems can be designed according to a single architectural style. This means that more than one architectural style

```
class BusStyle: public Configuration {

   private:
      int _removeInstance( char*);

      // Style parameters
      int _maxNumberOfElements, noInstances;

      // Define array of instances
      int *instances;

   protected:
      void TaskBody (char** =0);

   public:
      BusStyle ( int MaxNumberOfElements,
         List<char*> componentNames ) ;
      // Define composition rules for style

      void addComponent ( char* instName,
         char* component, int where,
         char* input, char* output);
      void removeComponent
         ( char* instName );
};


BusStyle::BusStyle ( ··· )
{
   ...

   // Check the consistency of the components
   for ( int i=0; i< componentNames.size(); i++ ) {

   // check if each component name is valid
   //and it contains the required ports

   Array *component =
      (*theLibrary- >taskName((*componentNames[i])))&&
      ((*theLibrary- >portOfType(styleType, ExitPort)) &&
      theLibrary- >portOfType(styleType, EntryPort));

      if ( component- >_size <= 0 )
         cerr << "Component does not satisfy the style";
      else
         // Import the style component(s)
         Use ( task, (*componentNames[i]));

      // Create a family of instances
      instances = new int[_maxNumberOfElements];
}


void BusStyle::addComponent ( ··· )
{
      if ( noInstances >=_maxNumberOfElements )
         return; // can't add new instance

      instances[noInstances] = Instance (instName,
         whatComponentId(component), where);

      // Add the links - implict connector
      for ( int i=0; i < noInstances; i++ ) {
         Link ( instances[noInstances], 0, ExitPort,
            instances[i], 1, EntryPort);
         Link ( instances[i], 0, ExitPort,
            instances[noInstances], 1, EntryPort);
      }
      Start (instances[noInstances]);
      noInstances++;
}

void BusStyle::removeComponent ( char* instName )
{
      ...

      int instId = _removeInstance( instName );
      if ( instId <0 )
         return; // Instance name not valid

      Interrupt  ( instId );
      Delete ( instId ); //All links are deleted
      ...

}
```

FIG. 6.2. *The C++CL interface and implementation of the Bus style, with the C++CL keywords written in bold letter.*

may be required to design parts of a system. We refer to an architecture of this kind as heterogeneous. In this section, we illustrate how heterogeneous architectures can be defined using *C++CL*. Assume a college application where individual lecturers communicate with their students, providing on-line (teleconference-based) tutorials. At the same type, the lecturers may receive information from the college management and part of this information may be forwarded to the students even during a tutorial. In this simple application, we can identify two styles. One relates to the interaction between a lecturer and the students and the other relates to the interaction between a lecturer and the management. Since the interaction between a lecturer and the students can occur in both ways and also amongst the students, the bus style could be applied to model those interactions. The interaction between the lecturers and the management, on the other hand, is assumed to occur in only one way, so the event-driven style could be applied to model it. Fig. 6.4 illustrates a solution for the college application using an instance of the bus style (we call this sub-configuration `LecturingConfiguration`) and one instance of the event

```
class EventDrivenStyle: public Configuration {

  private:
    int _removeInstance( char*);
    // Style parameters
    int _maxFiring, _maxInvocation,
      noFiringComp, noInvocationComp;

  // Categories of component types
    List<char*> firingComponents;
    List<char*> invocationComponents;

    // Define array of instances
    int *firingInst, *invocationInst;
    _removeInstance ( char* instName,
      int instances[], int *noInstances );

  protected:
    void TaskBody (char** =0);

  public:
    EventDrivenStyle ( int MaxFiring,
      List<char*> FiringComponents,
      int MaxInvocation,
      List<char*> InvocationComponents);

    // Define the composition rules for the style

    void addFiringComponent ( char* instName,
      char* component, int where, char* output );
    void addInvocationComponent ( char* instName,
      char* component, int where, char* input);
    void removeFiringComponent (char* instName);
    void removeInvocationComponent (char* instName);
};
```

```
...
addInvocationComponent ( ··· )
{
  if ( noInvocationComp >= _maxInvocation )
    return; // can't add Invocation instance

  Boolean found =false;
  // Are the invocation components valid?
  for ( int i=0; (i< invocationComponents.size())
      && ! found; i++ ) {

    if ( strcmp ( component,
      (*invocationComponents[i]))==0 )
    found = true;
  }

  // not a valid InvocationComponent
  if ( !found ) return;

  invocationInst[noInvocationComp] =
    Instance (instName,
      whatComponentId(component),where);

  // Connect the new invocation component
  for (int i=0; i < noFiringComp; i++ )
    Link ( invocationInst[i], 0, ExitPort,
      invocationInst[noInvocationComp], 1,EntryPort);

  Start (invocationInst[noInvocationComp]);
  noInvocationComp++;
}
```

FIG. 6.3. *The C++CL interface and implementation of the Event-Driven style, with the C++CL keywords written in bold letter.*

style (we call this sub-configuration `DepartmentManagementConfig`). Observe that a component *gateway* connects the instances of the respective styles. That component separates the two sub-configurations. Another important point relates to the fact that, since both sub-configurations will communicate with the gateway component, configuration ports must be added to them.

To illustrate how to derive a new configuration class from a defined style, we present a version of the `DepartmentManagementConfig` class in Fig. 6.5. The new configuration extends the style configuration and declares a `ConfigurationPort` called `out` of the type defined by the user. The constructor of the new class uses the repository object to check if the lecturer component given as a parameter contains an output port, as required by the configuration`DepartmentManagementConfig`, and creates the configuration port object. Since the configuration `DepartmentManagementConfig` does not define a style but a specific configuration, the method `TaskBody` must be declared, specifying the behaviour of the configuration. In this example, the behaviour basically defines that the instances of *Lecturer* type are added as invocation components and a firing component of type *Head* is also created. In addition, the configuration binds the lecturer output port to the configuration port.

We finally illustrate the configuration of a specific application using *C++CL* by presenting a version of the college configuration in Fig. 6.6. The description of the software architecture is defined in the body of the class (`TaskBody`). In general, an architecture is created by importing the required component types, creating instances from them and linking the instances' ports. Finally, the execution of each instance is started. Observe that these steps are followed for simple configurations, which do not present a complex dynamic behaviour.

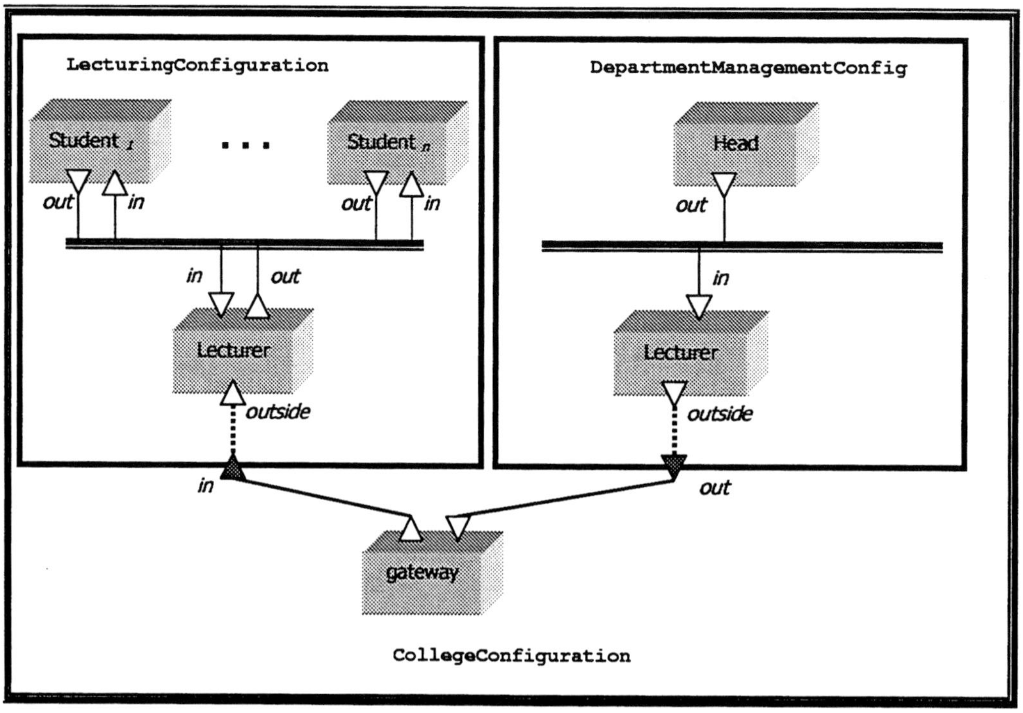

FIG. 6.4. *An example of a heterogeneous software architecture which combines instances of a Bus style and an Event-Driven style.*

7. Conclusions and Future Work. There are compelling reasons to combine the concepts of an architecture description language with those of an object-oriented framework to provide support for the development of reusable and extensible software architectures. This paper presented *C++CL* an object-oriented framework for developing distributed software architectures, the key aspect of which is to demonstrate how that approach can be applied in practice to support the development of reconfigurable distributed software architectures. Our approach is also applicable to the development of architectural styles. Many ADLs support the development of reusable components but few can support reusable architecture descriptions, and more importantly architectural styles. We can claim that our work is original in that respect. Another important result of the paper is to show that the use of a library of components is important in developing generic and extensible architectures. The reason is that the architecture description can refer to component attributes and not necessarily to the component names themselves.

Our work is progressing in various ways. Firstly, the reconfiguration middleware, currently implemented in PVM and TPC/IP, is being ported to CORBA. This will allow us to combine a wide range of components. The architecture description language has been revised in order to provide high-level notation to support the development of generic architectures. Basically, we are making more use of features of the library of components. Another direction is to support specific architectural styles. We are extending our framework to support the development of distributed multi-agent and multi-media applications. Those types of architecture require special types of connectors, for example for continuous media and knowledge messages respectively, and parameters to model attributes such as quality of service of a communication and mobility of the agents.

REFERENCES

[1] G. D. ABOWD, L. BASS, L. HOWARD, AND L. NOTHROP, *Structural modeling: An application framework and development process for flight simulators*, Tech. Report CMU/SEI-93-192, Software Engineering Institute, Carnegie Mellon University, August 1993.

[2] P. S. C. ALENCAR AND C. J. P. DE LUCENA, *A logical framework for evolving software systems*, Formal Aspects of Computing, 8 (1996), pp. 3–46.

[3] R. ALLEN, *A Formal Approach to Software Architecture*, PhD thesis, School of Computer Science, Carnegie Mellon University, May 1997.

[4] R. AMSTRONG, R. A. BALANCE, D. FORSLUND, L. CURFMAN-MCINESS, D. MEIRON, AND J. REYNDERS, *Frameworks for parallel computing*, in Parallel Object Oriented Methods and Applications (POOMA), 1995.

[5] M. R. BARBACCI, C. B. WEINSTOCK, D. L. D. ANDM. J. GARDNER, AND R. LICHOTA, *Durra: a structure description language for developing distributed applications*, Software Engineering Journal, 8 (1993), pp. 83–94.

[6] L. BELLISSARD, S. B. ATALLAH, F. BOYER, AND M. RIVEILL, *Distributed application configuration*, in Proceedings of 16th International Conference on Distributed Computing Systems, IEEE CS Press, May 1996, pp. 579–585.

[7] E. H. DURFEE, D. L. KISKIS, AND W. P. BIRMINGHAM, *The agent architecture of the University of Michigan digital library*, Software Engineering Journal, 144 (1997), pp. 52–60.

[8] G. ETZKORN, *Change programming in distributed systems*, in Proceedings of International Workshop on Configurable Distributed Systems, IEE, Great Britain, 25-27 March 1992.

[9] S. J. GIBBS AND D. C. TSICHRITZIS, *Multimedia Programming: Objects, Environments and Frameworks*, Addison-Wesley, 1995.

[10] R. JOHNSON AND V. RUSSO, *Reusing object-oriented designs*, Tech. Report UIUCDCS-R-91-1696, Department of Computer Science, University of Illinois at Urbana-Champaign, May 1991.

[11] G. R. R. JUSTO AND P. R. F. CUNHA, *Dynamic configuration as a paradigm to develop flexible and robust system*, in Proceedings of ICYCS'91, Beijing, China, 1991, Int. Academic Press, pp. 46–50.

[12] ———, *Programming distributed systems with configuration languages*, in Proceedings of the International Workshop on Configurable Distributed Systems, IEE, London, 1992, pp. 118–127.

[13] ———, *An application framework for dynamic distributed software architectures*, in Proceedings of 5th International Conference on Advanced Computing (ADCOMP'97), Tata McGraw-Hill, India, December 1997.

[14] G. R. R. JUSTO, V. C. DE PAULA, AND P. R. F. CUNHA, *Formal specification of evolving distributed software architectures*, in Proceedings of Ninth Workshop on Database and Expert Systems Applications (DEXA'98) and International Workshop on Coordination Technologies for Information Systems (CTIS'98), DEXA'98, IEEE CS Press, August 1998, pp. 548–553.

[15] R. LADDAGA AND J. VEITCH, *Dynamic object technology (introduction to special issue)*, Communications of ACM, 40 (1997), pp. 36–38.

[16] D. LEA, *Concurrent Programming in Java: Design Principles and Patterns*, Addison-Wesley, 1996.

[17] J. MAGEE, N. DULAY, S. EISENBACH, AND J. KRAMER, *Specifying distributed software architectures*, in Proceedings of 5th European Software Engineering Conference, Spring-Verlag, 25-28 September 1995, pp. 137–153.

[18] J. MAGEE, N. DULAY, AND J. KRAMER, *A constructive development environment for parallel and distributed programs*, in Proceedings of the 2nd Int. Workshop on Configurable Distributed Systems, SEI, Carnegie Mellon University, IEEE Computer Society Press, March 1994.

[19] J. MAGEE, J. KRAMER, AND M. SLOMAN, *Constructing distributed systems in CONIC*, IEEE Transactions on Software Engineering, SE-15 (1989), pp. 663–675.

[20] J. N. MAGEE, N. DULAY, AND J. KRAMER, *Structuring parallel and distributed programs*, in Proceedings of the International Workshop on Configurable Distributed Systems, IEE, Great Britain, 25-27

March 1992, pp. 102–117.

[21] N. MEDVIDOVIC AND R. TAYLOR, *A framework for classifying and comparing architecture description languages*, in Proceedings of 6th European Software Engineering Conference, ACM Press, September 1997, pp. 60–76.

[22] S. MITCHEL, *DJINN: A programming framework for distributed multimedia groupware applications*, tech. report, Department of Computer Science, Queen Mary and Westfield College, University of London, July 1996.

[23] R. T. MONROE, A. KOMPANEK, R. MELTON, AND D. GARLAN, *Architectural styles, design patterns and objects*, IEEE Software, (1997), pp. 43–52.

[24] M. MORICONI AND R. A. REIMENSCHNEIDER, *Introduction to SADL 1.0: a language for specifying software architecture hierarchies*, tech. report, SRI International, 1997.

[25] M. D. RICE AND S. B. SEIDMAN, *Using Z as a substrate for an architectural style description language*, Tech. Report CS-96-120, Department of Computer Science, Colorado State University, September 1996.

[26] J. RUMBAUGH, W. BLAHA, F. PREMERLANI, AND W. LORENSEN, *Object-oriented Modeling and Design*, Prentice Hall International, 1991.

[27] D. C. SCHMIDT AND M. E. FAYAD, *Lessons learned building reusable OO application frameworks for distributed software*, Communications of ACM, 40 (1997), pp. 85–88.

[28] M. SHAW, R. DELINE, D. V. KLEIN, T. L. ROSS, D. YOUNG, AND G. ZELESNIK, *Abstractions for software architecture and tools to support them*, IEEE Transactions on Software Engineering, 21 (1995), pp. 314–335.

[29] M. SHAW AND D. GARLAN, *Software Architecture: Perspectives On an Emerging Discipline*, Prentice Hall, 1996.

[30] N. SINGH, *Unifying heterogeneous information models*, Communications of ACM, 41 (1998), pp. 37–44.

[31] V. S. SUNDERAM, *PVM: A framework for parallel distributed computing*, Concurrency: Practice And Experience, 2 (1990), pp. 315–339.

```
class DepartmentManagementConfig:
   public EventDrivenStyle{

   private:
   // Declare the configuration's ports
      ConfigurationPort<StylePortType> *out;
      int noLecturer;
   protected:
      void TaskBody (char** arg=0);

   public:

      DepartmentManagementConfig (
         List<char*> headComponent,
         int noLecturers,
         List<char*> lecturerComponents);
};
      ...
DepartmentManagementConfig ( cdots )
{
   ...

   // Check if lecturer component is valid
   Array *component =
      (*theLibrary- >taskName(lecturer) &&
      theLibrary- >portOfType (portType, ExitPort) );

   if ( component- >_size <= 0 ) {
      cerr << "Lecturer component not valid"<<endl;
   }
   else {
      // Create the configuration port
      out = new ConfigurationPort<StylePortType> (
         ConfigurationExitPort );
   }
}
      ...
TaskBody (··· )
{
      ...

   // Create the configuration
   for (int i=0; i < noLecturers; i++ )
   {
      cout << "Enter lecturer name: ";
      cin >>name;
      addInvocationComponent(
         name, "Lecturer", i, "in");
   }

   cout < "Enter Department Head Name: ";
   cin >>name;
   addFiringComponent(
      name, "Head", where, "out");

   // Bind the lecturer component entry port
   // to the configuration port
   Bind ( out, "Lecturer", "outside");
}
```

FIG. 6.5. *The C++CL interface and implementation of a composite configuration derived from the Event-Driven Style and using configuration ports.*

```
class CollegeConfiguration: public
    Configuration {

  protected:
    void TaskBody (char**);
  public:
    CollegeConfiguration ( char* name, int arg ) :
        Configuration ( name, arg ) {} ;
};

void
CollegeConfiguration::TaskBody (char** argv)
{
  int DepartmentType, LecturingType,
    GatewayType;

// Import the modules
  DepartmentType = Use ( configuration,
    "DepartmentManagementConfig");
  LecturingType = Use ( configuration,
    "LecturingConfiguration");
  GatewayType = Use ( task, "gateway");

  // Create the instances
  Instance ( "department", DepartmentType );
  Instance ( "lecturing", LecturingType);
  Instance ( "gateway", GatewayType);

  // Link the instances
  Link ("department", "out", "gateway", "in");
  Link ("gateway", "out", "lecturing", "in");

  // Start the execution
  Start ( "department" );
  Start ( "lecturing" );
  Start ( "gateway" );
}
```

FIG. 6.6. *The C++CL interface and implementation of a heterogeneous configuration derived from the Bus style and Event-Driven style.*

A FRAMEWORK FOR PERFORMANCE-BASED PROGRAM PARTITIONING[1]

RAM SUBRAMANIAN AND SANTOSH PANDE*

Abstract. Most of the reported work in the Parallelizing Compilers literature focuses on analyzing program characteristics such as the dependences, loop structures, memory reference patterns etc. to optimize the generated parallel code [3, 2, 7, 8, 14, 10]. Unfortunately, parallelizing compilers have very little or no knowledge of the actual run time behavior of the synthesized code on the underlying hardware due to the complex behavior of the underlying hardware and software subsystems. This interaction could significantly affect the performance of the generated code and must be considered during program partitioning phases of the compiler.

In this paper, we present an efficient and accurate performance model based program partitioning approach for parallel architectures. We introduce the concept of `behavioral edges` for capturing the interactions between computation and communication through parametric functions. We present an efficient algorithm to identify behavioral edges, modify costs using the behavioral edges and adapt the schedule to improve schedule length. The program partitioning phase uses the static estimates computed using the behavioral edges and partitioning is iteratively performed using the ordering on PDG based on computed intervals. A significant performance improvement (factor of 10 in many cases) is demonstrated by using our framework.

1. Introduction and Motivation. Parallelizing Compilers play a key role in translating sequential or parallel programs written in high level language into the object code for highly efficient concurrent execution on a multi-processor system. When the object code executes on the underlying hardware and software subsystems, a complex interaction occurs amongst a number of underlying hardware subsystems at different levels. These interactions could be from a much finer level such as the the multi-function pipelines within a CPU, to a more coarser level such as at the interconnection network, cache and/or at the memory hierarchy level. Most of the reported work in the parallelizing compilers literature focuses on analyzing the program characteristics such as the dependences, loop structures, memory reference patterns etc. to optimize the generated parallel code. This is evident from the theory of loop parallelization [3] and other techniques for detecting, transforming and mapping both the loop and task parallelism [2, 7, 8, 14, 10, 17, 21, 22, 15, 27]. Unfortunately, parallelizing compilers have very little or no knowledge of the actual run time behavior of the synthesized code on the underlying hardware due to the complex (sometimes unpredictable) behavior of the underlying hardware and software subsystems. More precisely, most optimizing parallel compilers do not have the performance estimation capability to match their sophisticated program analysis and restructuring ability. Due to this reason, the actual performance of the code may be different (often worse) than the anticipated one at compile time.

The execution efficiency of the object code (in terms of its speed) is critically dependent upon the underlying model of computation anticipated by the compiler while generating the code [26, 23, 24, 25]. Such limitations of the parallelizing compilers can lead to two implications. Any nonconformance of the actual run time model to the static one anticipated by the compiler can lead to heavy performance penalties. On the other hand, if the compiler uses a very conservative model of computation, several potential opportunities for parallelization could be lost. An excellent example of this scenario is that most parallelizing compilers tend to choose a higher level of granularity than is really necessary to keep the synchronization and communication overheads low. This could lead to a significant performance loss. Thus, it is important that the program partitioning be driven by the run time performance model of the architecture and the underlying real machine.

The present approaches to performance enhancement involves the use of a separate performance evaluation tool to gather the performance statistics of the executing code. In important performance modeling approaches such as Paradyn [31] or Pablo [32], the performance evaluation of an executing program is done through a dynamic instrumentation or through a trace driven technique respectively. Thus, the user is responsible for guiding the estimator tool to elicit the performance data and gain insight into the potential bottlenecks. Thus, this approach demands a highly advanced user who is very familiar with the performance bottlenecks of his/her program and also has an intimate

---

*Department of ECECS, P.O. Box 210030, University of Cincinnati, Cincinnati, Ohio 45221–0030, E-mail : rsubrama@ececs.uc.edu, santosh@ececs.uc.edu (correspondence)

[1]This work is supported by the National Science Foundation grant no. CCR-9696129 and DARPA contract ARMY DABT63-97-C-0029

knowledge of the underlying architecture. Such a level of intimate knowledge of the program as well as the architecture is obviously the compiler's (not user's) domain. Based on this motivation and due to the fact that the program partitioning should be driven by the run time performance model of a program, we propose a compiler framework based on static analysis of programs for accurate and efficient performance-based partitioning.

1.1. A case for performance based partitioning. We now introduce the motivation behind our work through an example, Figure 1.1. The node computation costs and the edge communication costs are shown next to each node and edge respectively. The node and edge costs are found using operations count and the sizes of the messages and assuming a certain cost model. Typical cost models for message passing use a fixed start-up cost and a component proportional to size of message. We first show how to find optimal partitioning assuming an ideal architecture in which cost of each message is independent of any other concurrent messages.

A task graph G(V,E) is a directed acyclic graph (DAG) such that each node $v_i \in V$ represents a task and the directed edge $e(v_i, v_j) \in E$ represents the precedence constraint from v_i to v_j, that corresponds to the actual data dependence edge. The computation cost of node v_i is denoted by $t(v_i)$ and the communication cost of edge $e(v_i, v_j)$ is denoted by $c(v_i, v_j)$.

In order to minimize the completion time, it is desirable to schedule the successor of a node on the same processor so that we save on the communication cost on the edge that connects the two nodes. We, however, still continue to pay communication costs on the other edges. The completion time found by using this strategy is given by

$$t(v_i) + \min_{j:e(v_i,v_j)\in E} \{ \max_{k:k\neq j, e(v_i,v_k)\in E} (t(v_j), t(v_k) + c(v_i, v_k)) \} \tag{1.1}$$

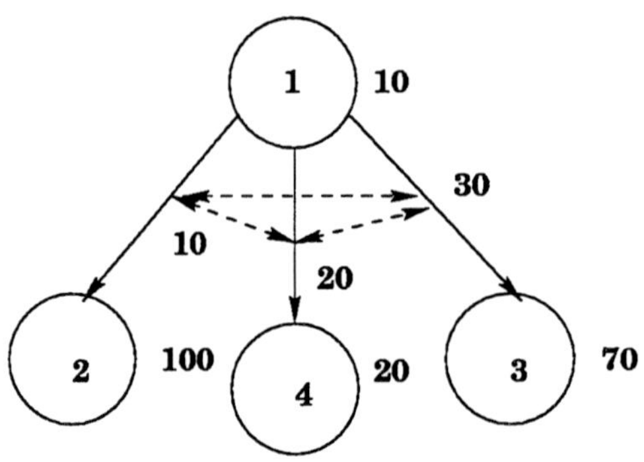

FIG. 1.1. *An Example Graph*

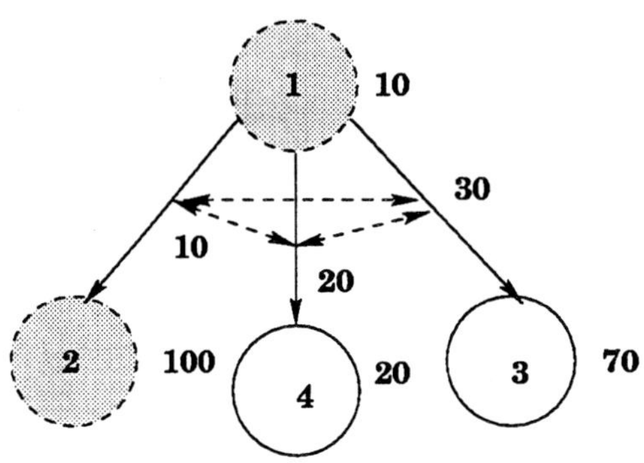

FIG. 1.2. *Partition on Ideal Architecture*

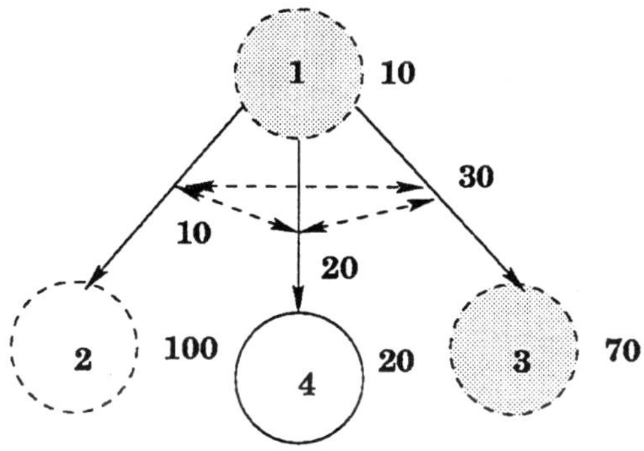

FIG. 1.3. *Partition on Real Machine : One Communication Channel, Shortest Message First Protocol*

Using the ideal architecture (in which the cost of each message is independent of any other concurrent messages), the optimal partition found using the above strategy is given in Figure 1.2. However, on a real machine, the costs of concurrent messages could affect each other. The behavior is shown by dashed lines in Figure 1.1. For example, if there is only one communication channel available per processor, it will be time-multiplexed between different concurrent messages which will have an influence on costs of communication. Assuming a shortest message first protocol, the longer messages will have more delays than indicated on ideal architecture. Under this condition, the optimal partition changes to the one shown in Figure 1.3. The actual completion time of the partition shown in Figure 1.2 on this real machine is 130 as against 110 as predicted; whereas the completion time of partition shown in Figure 1.3 found using actual message-passing protocol used (shortest message first) is 120. This shows that a more sophisticated performance based model must be used to perform program partitioning.

The organization of this paper is as follows: Section 2 presents an outline of our approach, section 3 presents our solution methodology, section 4 explains our algorithm, section 5 includes results and discussion, section 6 contains related work, followed by conclusions in section 7.

2. Outline of Our Approach. Accurate modeling of run time behavior of a program on a given architecture is a very complex task. The involved complexities are on both sides: the program as well as the architecture. A typical program consists of compile time unknown variables and dependencies, unknown branch conditions, unknown depths of recursions and unknown memory access and communication patterns. On the architecture side, complexities could be due to unknown latencies and cache behaviors, unpredictable network conflicts and hot spots. Since an architecture has a number of sub-component systems that interact in a complex (often non-deterministic) manner, developing an accurate behavioral model of the complete system is almost impossible. We thus propose a unified approach that tends to bring the program behavioral model and the architectural behavioral model as close as possible for accurate performance estimation as follows:

- Through an extensive compiler analysis, we first derive an accurate static estimate of the performance for possible cases. We also perform many analyses in this process that determine which parts of the program are most sensitive to the architectural variances and to what degree. A given program may use the underlying architectural components only in a given manner – our goal is to capture most *sensitive* and *dominant* program components.
- After deriving the static estimates using the analysis phase we carry out performance-driven program partitioning. The goal is to minimize the program completion time by accounting for the accurate computation and communication costs and their interplay discovered by the above framework.

Following is an outline of the solution methodology of our approach:

- We develop Augmented Program Dependence Graph intermediate form that can represent a detailed execution behavioral description of the program on a given parallel architecture. We introduce a concept of *behavioral edges* that represents the dependencies and the interactions of the computation or communication as decided by the underlying architecture. Using this representation we will be able to get a detailed and accurate estimate for the computation and the communication costs incurred by the program.

- Next, we develop an extensive framework for sensitivity and dominance analysis for determining the *most critical and sensitive* program components that determine the overall program completion time. The goal is to gain an insight into the program components that are critical to performance through static analysis.
- We finally develop an extensive framework for efficient performance-based program partitioning method for the task parallelism represented in the augmented PDG.

We now describe a framework for accomplishing the above objectives.

3. Solution Methodology.

3.1. Intermediate form for performance analysis. Traditionally the parallelizing compilers use a hierarchical representation using the Program Dependence Graph (PDG) whose vertices represent the computation and edges reflect the data and control dependences denoting the partial order on the program execution. The PDG is thus, a tuple, G(V,E,C(V), C(E)), where, V is the set of nodes, E is the set of edges, C(V) is the set of node computation costs and C(E) is the set of edge communication/synchronization costs. These costs are primarily based on the operation counts and the number of data items to be communicated. Thus, it can be seen that these models are simplistic and are a major source of error. In order to reflect the performance costs, the representation must be made more accurate and elaborate. For example, a communication cost for data-flow on the PDG edge can not be simply a symbolic constant but it is crucially dependent on a number of other factors such as:

- Buffer set-up delays: There are a number of hard-ware and software overheads involved on both send and receive ends for setting up the buffers, copying data into buffers and returning from a software trap to initiate or complete the communication. These overheads themselves are dependent on the state of the system at both sending and receiving end. In addition, these overheads depend on the type of communication and are different, for example, for point to point and multi-cast type communications.
- Network set-up delays: Depending on the switching and message passing protocol, the set up delays could exist to establish a given hardware path. These delays could be dependent on the state of the network at that point.
- Transmission delays: Finally, once a path is set up, the message may take a variable amount of time depending on the underlying packet switching and routing algorithm. Again, these delays could depend on the state of other traffic in the network at the given point of transmission.

Thus, it can be seen that even to model a basic step such as communication, there are enormous challenges involved. We first develop an elaborate model of each architectural component and based on this model, add several annotations to the basic PDG to reflect the complex inter-dependent behaviors. In the above particular example, the communication on the edge is represented by a function of different parameters. In order to capture the dependences of these parameters on each other, we introduce an extra set of edges called **behavioral edges** that denote the direction and degree of the interaction. If the behavior is symmetrically influenced then the edge will be undirected otherwise it will be directed. The degree of interaction is captured by a partial function of all the involved variables. The behavioral edges could thus, be of four types which could denote:

- Interaction of computation on computation : An example of this scenario is the one in which, potential merge of two computation nodes denoting two loop nests may lead to the referenced data not fitting into cache and consequent increase in the loop execution cost.
- Interaction of computation on communication : An example of this scenario is the one in which directly storing the data to be sent in the communication buffer will speed up the communication, however, it may slow computation due to non-use of cache.
- Interaction of communication on computation : An example of this scenario is one in which an incoming message may lead to a context switch and slow down the computation.
- Interaction of communication on communication : This could occur due to the sharing of the underlying network between two concurrent messages.

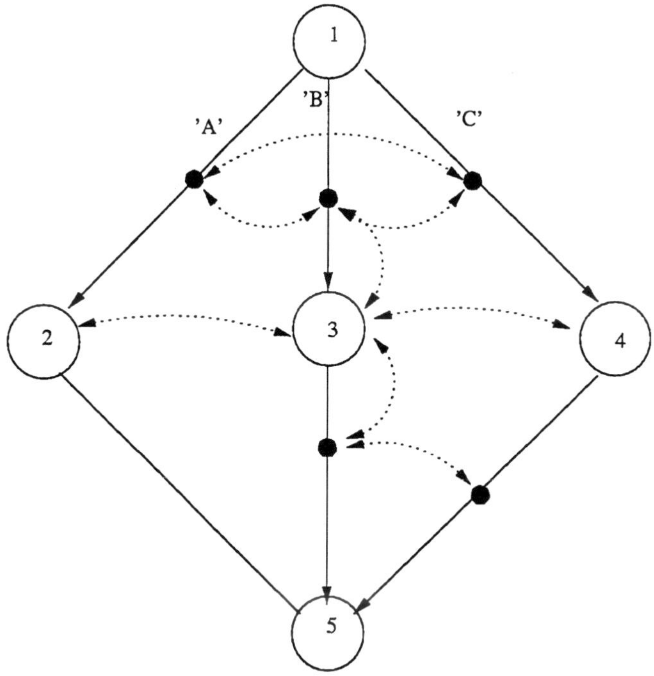

FIG. 3.1. *An Example Augmented PDG*

Thus, an edge could have a source or sink on a PDG computation node or on a PDG precedence edge. These edges designate the behavioral interactions between the respective entities through a parametric function involving all the variables involved in the interaction. For example, if communication on a PDG precedence edge is affected by communication on another PDG precedence edge, we will add a behavioral edge between the two. This edge will bear a partial function involving the number of available channels, buffers, network delays, sizes of the messages and the routing parameters that reflects the interactions of these two communications. If the interaction is symmetric, the edge added will be bidirectional with the same function, otherwise, it will be unidirectional and there will be two such edges and two partial functions. The partial functions map the original cost on an edge or a node to an appropriately modified cost using the underlying parameters and the other interacting costs. For example, a partial function $f(a,b,c)$ on a behavioral edge going from precedence edge $e1$ to $e2$, designates the modification in the cost of edge $e2$ due to the cost of edge $e1$ and the underlying parameters a, b and c. Thus, we augment the PDG to include the behavioral edges with the partial functions. The augmented PDG is thus, a tuple $G(V, E, C(V), C(E), B(f))$, where $B(f)$ denotes a set of behavioral edges with the respective partial functions. Thus, through this elaborate model of augmented PDG, we capture the interactions of computation and communication. In the next subsection, we develop an example to illustrate the Augmented PDG.

3.2. Augmented PDG Example. The solid lines in Figure 3.1 represent the precedence constraints on the computation and the dotted ones represent the behavioral edges between two nodes or two precedence edges or between a node and an edge. In this example, the communication costs on edges (1,2), (1,3) and (1,4) are inter-dependent since it occurs concurrently. This is designated by three behavioral edges. Similarly, the incoming communication on node 3 can perturb its ongoing computation and thus, there is an edge between edge (1,3) and node 3. Similarly the cache performance of computation at node 2 will be affected if merged with 3 and the same is true with the merger of nodes 3 and 4. This is designated by the respective behavioral edges between these nodes. However, no such performance degradation possibly occurs for nodes 2 and 4 and hence there is no edge. Similarly, maybe the outgoing communication on edge (3,5) can be improved if the data is directly written in the communication buffer and thus, there is a behavioral edge between the node 3 and edge (3,5). There is also a behavioral edge between edge (3,5) and (4,5) to denote the interaction of communication between them.

3.3. Machine specialization. The next phase performs the specialization of the PDG to the actual underlying machine on which the code will be executing. The goal of this phase is to eliminate redundant behavioral edges by specializing the PDG. For example, on a general cache-based architecture, there will be a behavioral edge between two computation nodes due to the fact that the sizes of data may not fit in a cache due to limited cache size. This behavioral edge has to be added in the PDG due to unknown cache size and unknown sizes of base and derived data types in the architectural model since the exact machine of implementation is unknown. But once the exact machine of implementation is known, one may be able to remove some of the redundant behavioral edges. For example, in above case, if the data sizes are compile time known and cache size is sufficiently large on a given machine, the corresponding behavioral edge between two computational nodes is redundant and could be removed. Another example of this scenario is if we assume that there is a behavioral edge between two communication edges. Such an edge could be present due to the conservative assumption that the underlying network can not support two such simultaneous permutations for data transfers on two edges. After specializing to a given machine, if it is determined that the network can support such simultaneous permutations, this behavioral edge can be removed.

General algorithm for specializing PDG to a given machine and removing redundant behavioral edges is as follows:

1. Apply machine parameters to the behavioral edge functions.
2. Attempt to solve the behavioral edge function in closed form and compare the solution to the constraints imposed by the machine.
3. If the constraints are met, remove the behavioral edge.
4. Propagate the results of closed form and the behavioral edge removal to the other functions and iterate to transitively remove the edges.
5. Finally compute the model edge costs using the machine parameters.

3.4. Sensitivity and Dominance Analysis. The next important phase is the identification of critical program components that are quite sensitive to the architectural uncertainty and are also dominant so that overall program completion time is decided by their execution cost.

At the end of step 5 of the algorithm in previous section, we will have an accurate closed form solution for static costs for some computation nodes and some communication edges. However, for many others, we will be unable to determine the performance estimates due to the non-deterministic architectural parameters. This problem is especially crucial for communication due to unpredictable network latencies and other delays that are hard to model analytically. We now develop a framework for studying the impact of the imprecise communication latencies on partitioning.

When a task v_i is scheduled on a processor $p(v_j)$ on which a predecessor task v_j is scheduled, no communication is needed between v_i and v_j. The schedule time is given by,

$$stime(v_i, p(v_j)) =$$

$$\max_{k:k\neq j,(v_k,v_i)\in E}((stime(v_j, p(v_j)) + t(v_j)), (stime(v_k, p(v_k)) + t(v_k) + c(v_k, v_i))) \tag{3.1}$$

The completion time of a node v_i on processor $p(v_i)$ is given by,

$$ctime(v_i, p(v_i)) = stime(v_i, p(v_i)) + t(v_i) \tag{3.2}$$

The *flexibility* of an edge is a measure of the allowable cost increase in it without affecting the schedule time of the destination node. Thus,

$$flex(v_j, v_i) = stime\ (v_i) - ctime\ (v_j) \tag{3.3}$$

An edge (v_j, v_i) is said to be *purged* in a schedule S, if both v_j and v_i are allocated to the same processor and thus, there is no communication between them. The set of all *purged* edges in the schedule is denoted by S_p.

An edge (v_j, v_i) is said to be a *dominant* edge of a schedule S if increasing the cost of the edge results in an equal increase in the schedule time of the destination node v_i. The set of all *dominant* edges in the schedule is denoted by S_d. It is obvious from their definition that the sets of purged edges and dominant edges are disjoint. Our aim is to find the *dominant* edges. Next, we derive some properties of the graph using the terms defined above.

Lemma 1

In a schedule S, for an edge (v_j, v_i), $flex(v_j, v_i) = 0 \quad (v_j, v_i) \in S_p$ and there is no other path from v_j to v_i.

Proof:
If:
Assume $flex(v_j, v_i) = 0$ which implies that $stime(v_i) = ctime(v_j)$.
This is possible only if v_j and v_i are allocated to the same processor which means that $(v_j, v_i) \in S_p$. $stime(v_i) = ctime(v_j)$ also implies that there is no other path from v_j to v_i. We will prove this by contradiction. If we assume that there is another path from v_j to v_i through $v_{j'}$, it would lead to the schedule time of v_i being greater than that of v_j at least by an amount equal to $t(v_{j'})$, contradicting $stime(v_i) = ctime(v_j)$.
Only if:
Since there is no other path from v_j to v_i, the schedule time of v_i must be equal to completion time of v_j. Hence (v_j, v_i) is a purged edge. □

Lemma 2

In a schedule S, an edge (v_j, v_i) such that $(v_j, v_i) \notin S_p$, $(v_j, v_i) \in S_d \iff flex(v_j, v_i) = c(v_j, v_i)$.

Proof:
If :
Assume $flex(v_j, v_i) = c(v_j, v_i)$. Increasing the cost of the edge (v_j, v_i) will result in increase in schedule time of v_i (derived immediately from equations 3.3 and 3.1) which means that $(v_j, v_i) \in S_d$.
Only if:
Assume $(v_j, v_i) \in S_d$ which implies that increasing the cost of edge (v_j, v_i) results in increasing the schedule time of node v_i. From equations 3.1 and 3.3 this is possible only if, $flex(v_j, v_i) = c(v_j, v_i)$.
□

We can use the conditions mentioned in the above lemmas for computing the *purged* and the *dominant* edges of the graph from schedule to schedule.

Suppose, we have generated a schedule S_1 for a certain cost model and the actual machine model is different for which we would need to generate schedule S_2 due to increase in communication costs on the edges due to constrained machine resources (such as the limited number of communication channels etc. as shown in earlier example). Depending on the magnitude of cost increase on each of the incoming edges, following three scenarios are possible in order to determine new schedule S_2 of a node v_i:

1. The new schedule time of the node v_i remains the same even after the cost increases on its input edges : schedule S_2 of v_i remains the same as S_1.
2. The new schedule time of the node v_i is determined by a dominant edge (v_j, v_i) in the schedule S_1; the schedule time of v_i in schedule S_2 is increased by $\epsilon(v_j, v_i)$, where, $\epsilon(v_j, v_i)$ is cost increase for edge (v_j, v_i). In this case, merely the schedule time of v_i increases, the processor assignment is still the same. Thus, only schedule regeneration is needed.

3. The new schedule time of the node v_i is determined by an edge (v_k, v_i), where, (v_k, v_i) is not a dominant edge in schedule S_1. In this case, rescheduling may be needed to allocate v_i to a different processor, to preserve the properties of the schedule.

We now address the first of these conditions below. The following theorem summarizes the conditions when the schedule for a node v_i remains the same as the old one.

Theorem 1

Let $\epsilon(v_j, v_i)$ be the increase in the communication cost of an edge (v_j, v_i). If $\epsilon(v_j, v_i) \leq flex(v_j, v_i) - c(v_j, v_i)$, for $(v_j, v_i) \notin S_p$, the schedule will be invariant assuming there is no dominant edge (v_j, v_i) incident on node v_i.

Proof:

Since (v_j, v_i) can not be a dominant edge, two cases are possible:
Case I : (v_j, v_i) is a purged edge: Increasing the cost of purged edge does not affect the schedule since the schedule time of v_i is not affected.
Case II: (v_j, v_i) is not a purged edge:
Since $\epsilon(v_j, v_i) \leq flex(v_j, v_i) - c(v_j, v_i)$, it is clear that the schedule time for the node v_i does not change. Thus, the schedule (processor assignment to node v_i) remains invariant. □

This phase allows us to determine the conditions under which the dominant parts of the program could affect overall partitioning decisions.

3.5. Program Partitioning. The key goal here is to partition the PDG using the results of the previous analysis. The program partitioning can be driven by two goals:

- Partition to optimize the execution of the dominant and the sensitive program components only since any degradation in them could affect the overall performance.
- Partition to optimize the PDG as a whole.

We perceive that the problem is very hard (NP-Hard) to optimize the complete PDG in general. Thus, we first focus on optimizing the performance of the dominant and sensitive program components that determine the overall program completion time. A possible solution methodology involves, first dividing the set of nodes and edges into a forest of graphs that cover the original graph. Each entity in the connected components of the graph carry a set of behavioral edges connecting them. Thus, *independent* partitioning decisions could be taken for the disjoint graphs in the above representation. For determining the partition decisions within a connected component, an ordering must be determined. This could be achieved by performing a topological sort on the behavioral edges in conjunction with the precedence edges of the original PDG. The partitioner then assumes independent parameters in the topological (top-down) order and first carries out a locally optimized partitioning. Using the behavioral edge, the cost impact of this partition is propagated down to determine the partitioning of the sink of the behavioral edge and the associated behavioral function.

The outline of the partitioning algorithm is as follows:

- Take transitive closure of the behavioral edges, find the set of reachable nodes from the sinks of the behavioral edges and take their transitive closure. Repeat this process to divide the graph into a forest of graphs. Independent partitioning decisions could be taken for each of these graphs.
- Within a connected component, perform a topological ordering on behavioral edges and original graph edges.
- Perform partitioning in the topological order as above and propagate the results top down. That is, we first carry out partitioning at the source of a behavioral edge and propagate the parameters through the behavioral edge to carry out partitioning at its sink.

For example, in figure 3.2, we could take independent partitioning decision for sub-graph consisting of nodes 1, 2, 3 and 4 and the corresponding edges. However, since there is a behavioral edge between edges (3,5) and (4,5), we have to first take partitioning decision for sub-graph of nodes 3,4

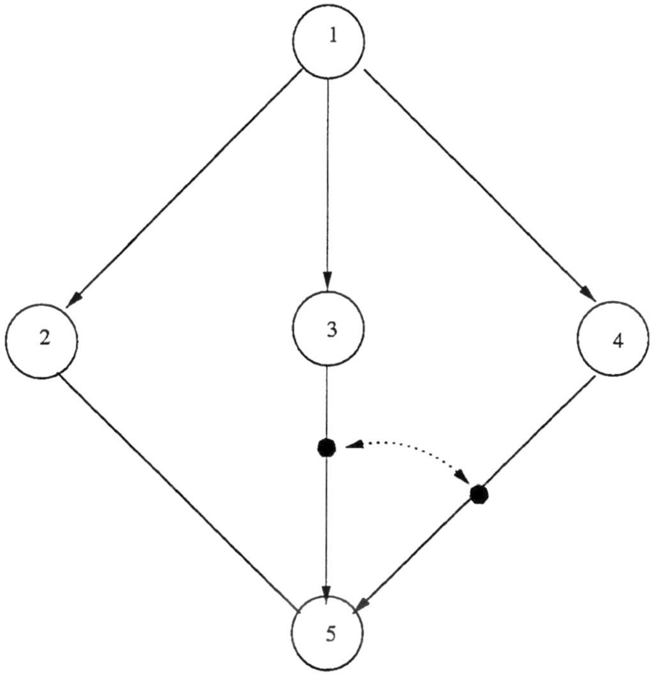

FIG. 3.2. *Partitioning Illustration*

and 5 edges (3,5) and (4,5) and then consider partitioning of graph of nodes 2,3,4 and 5 and the corresponding edges.

4. An Iterative Algorithm for Partitioning. One of the most important reasons for changes in schedule times of different nodes at run times, is the change in the communication costs of the edges. As mentioned before, edge costs vary dramatically depending on the communication models of the underlying architecture. Concurrent communication may be affected by shortest message first, First Come First Served (FCFS) protocols etc. Each of these schemes potentially affect the edge costs and hence affect the task schedules.

We have developed an algorithm to study the effect of behavioral edges between edges of the PDG, where there is a potential for concurrent communication. In our algorithm, pairs of concurrent communication edges are identified and a bidirectional behavioral edge is associated with each pair. The effect of the underlying communication model (shortest message first model or FCFS model) is used to determine the communication costs of these edges. For example, assume that the underlying architecture cannot support concurrent message passing but supports a shortest first communication model. Let an edge e_1 in the PDG be connected to edges $e_2, e_3, \ldots, e_i$ by means of behavioral edges. If edge cost $c(e_1)$ is the least among the above edges, e_1 would be communicated first and the communication costs of the rest of the edges will increase by $c(e_1)$. The increase in edge costs would, in turn, worsen the schedule. A re-computation of the schedule has to be done under this circumstance, and the new schedule could affect the behavioral edges, in turn. A two way dependence exists between the schedule and the edge costs. Thus, this algorithm iteratively refines the dependence between behavioral edges and schedule, by computing a schedule using behavioral edges and uses this schedule in turn to compute the effect of cost changes due to behavioral edges. In this way the algorithm arrives at a stable schedule. A given scheduling algorithm thus, can be used as an input to our iterative algorithm, which it will invoke to compute the schedule. Other inputs to our iterative refinement algorithm are the task graph G, message passing model M, and the convergence limit Ψ [2]. Our algorithm demonstrates an effective method for finding operational

[2]The convergence of this algorithm is slow in some cases; thus, we impose Ψ as a limit imposed on the differences between successive schedule lengths.

behavioral edges, changing costs appropriately and iteratively minimize the schedule for an input task graph.

Algorithm:

```
Iterative_Partition()
Input:
    A ≡ scheduling algorithm
    G ≡ task graph - G(V,E,C(V),C(E)
    M ≡ message passing model (SMF, FCFS)
    Ψ ≡ limit
Output:
    schedule S
Begin
    {Denote cost model of edges as C1}
    C1(E) ← C(E);

    {invoke algorithm A, using C1 to find schedule S1}
    S1 = call_A ( G(V,E,C(V),C1(E)) );

    {Iteratively refine schedule}
    call iter_schedule( G(V,E,C(V),C1(E), S1 );

End Iterative_Partition

iter_schedule()
Input:
    S1 ≡ schedule
    G ≡ task graph - G(V,E,C(V),C1(E)
Output:
    S2 ≡ Final schedule
    L2 ≡ Final schedule length
Denotation:
    { An edge from node i to node j is denoted by (i,j) }
Begin
    {First find behavioral edge pairs from schedule S1. beh_edge_pairs[i] is a list
    of edges connected to edge i by a behavioral edge. List ended with -1 }
    repeat
      for (all edges (i,j) in G) do
        for (all other edges (u,v) in G) do
          { A directed edge (i,j) has behavioral edges to all directed edges (u,v) such
          that node u ≠ j and u is not the successor of node j}
          if ((u ≠ j) ∧ (u ≠ SUCC(j))) then
             if ((ect(i) ≤ ect(u) < last(j)) ∨
                (ect(u) ≤ ect(i) < last(v))) then
                    add edge (u,v) to
                    beh_edge_pairs[(i,j)]
             endif
          endif
        endfor
      endfor

      { SUCC(j) - successor node of node j; ect - earliest completion time of node; }
      { last - latest allowable start time modify costs of edges connected by behavioral edges}
      for (each row r of beh_edge_pairs) do
```

```
      If (M = SMF) then
        sort edges of row r in ascending
             order of costs
      endif

      for (each edge (u, v) in
           beh_edge_pairs[(i, j)]) do
        { If nodes u and v are not assigned to the same processor then modify costs }
        If ( Processor(u) ≠ Processor(v) ) then
          c((u, v)) = c((u, v)) + c((i, j));
        endif
      endfor
    endfor

    {Denote modified cost of edges as C2}
    C2(E) ← C1(E);

    {Use modified costs to compute schedule S2. Invoke algo A, using C2 to find schedule S2}
    S2 = call_A ( G(V, E, C(V), C2(E)) );
    L1 = schedule_length(S2, C2);

    { Using C2 and S1 find schedule length L2 }
    L2 = schedule_length(S1, C2);

  until ((convergence) ∨ (L2 - L1 > Ψ))
End iter_schedule
```

4.1. An Example. An example PDG and its associated schedule is shown in Figure 4.1(a) and Figure 4.1(b) respectively. When this graph is input to the algorithm with costs C1 and the scheme is First Come First Served, the schedule obtained is S1, using a scheduling algorithm A. In the figures shown, P1, P2 and P3 are 3 processors on which the corresponding nodes are scheduled. The arrows between the nodes in different processors represent communication edges. Once schedule S1 is computed, the algorithm identifies behavioral edges between the task graph edges using the schedule S1. These behavioral edges are found depending on whether there exists a concurrent communication amongst the task graph edges. In this case, the behavioral edges found for S1 are shown in Figure 4.2(b). These behavioral edges are used by the algorithm to modify edge costs from C1 to C2. For the example DAG, the edges that have the costs modified are edges $(3,5)$ and $(4,6)$, with new costs of 7 each. The modified costs are also shown in Figure 4.2(b) in bold. Using the new costs C2, a schedule S2 is determined by the scheduling algorithm A, as illustrated in Figure 4.2(c).

The schedule S1 has schedule length 26 and uses 3 processors. This schedule is not the minimum obtainable when the costs of the edges change to C2. The schedule length obtained when S1 operates with C2 costs is 30. The schedule S2 obtained using modified costs C2 has a schedule length of 29, which is 1 less than the length of the schedule that would have resulted from schedule S1 operating with costs C2. When the iteration progresses to completion, the costs are further refined and schedule lengths are minimized. The final schedule length obtained is 26.

4.2. Complexity. We now analyze the complexity of our iterative algorithm. The complexity of finding the pairs of behavioral edges is $O(e^2)$. Each edge in the task graph can be potentially connected by behavioral edges to every other edge in the graph. If there are e edges in the graph, we have a worst case of $(e-1)+(e-2)+\ldots+1 = e(e-1)/2$ behavioral edges. Since the algorithm examines every pair of edges, its complexity is $O(e^2)$. Modifying the costs incurs a worst case complexity of $O(e^2)$. The step of finding out concurrent communication edges using the earliest and latest, start and completion times, reduces the number of actual behavioral edges drastically. This improves the average case of the algorithm to a large extent. The worst case complexity of the

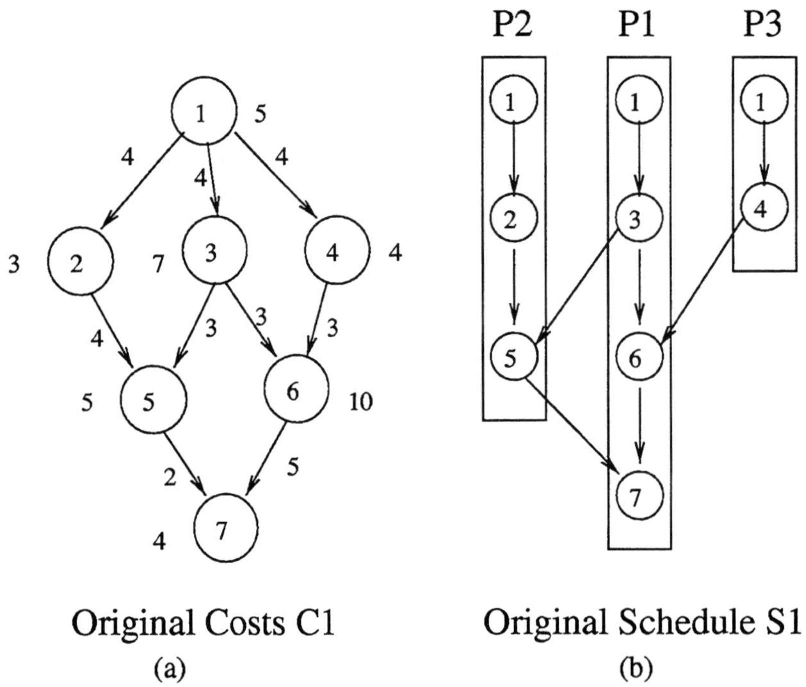

FIG. 4.1. *An Example DAG, with costs C1 and its Schedule S1*

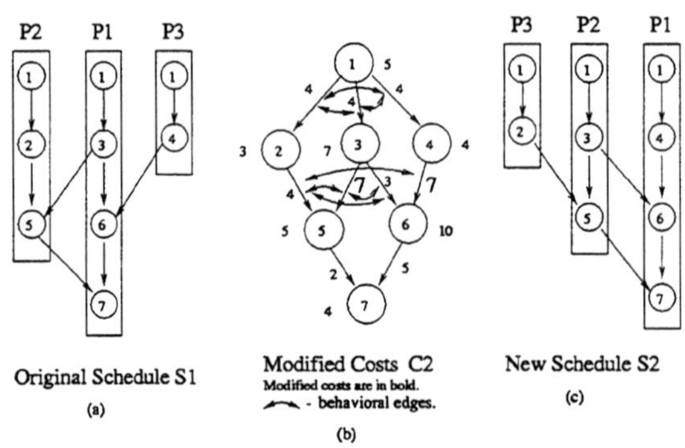

FIG. 4.2. *Illustration of Algorithm*

algorithm is, however, $O(e^2)$ per iteration of the algorithm. Assuming the algorithm converges in k iterations, the overall complexity of the algorithm is $O(ke^2)$.

5. Results and Discussion. In this work, we have used the STDS algorithm developed by Darbha et al. [5] as an input to our iterative algorithm for performance evaluation. We have chosen STDS algorithm due to its relative insensitivity to cost changes as demonstrated in a recent paper by Darbha et. al [6]. Our motivation here is that the use of such a stable algorithm would demonstrate the essential merit of our iterative based approach, by factoring out the effect of sensitivity of the schedule to the underlying algorithm.

The above algorithm was implemented on a SUN SPARC 5. The input to the algorithm were different types of task graphs with different node and edge sizes. Examples of the graphs that were given as input are illustrated in Figure 5.1. These graphs occur in various numerical analysis computations [12]. The cost of each node and each edge for the Mean Value graph was randomly selected so that it lies within a certain specified range. A range of 1 to 20 was empirically selected to be used for our tests. The Cholesky Decomposition graph inputs were constructed in two ways. One, using randomized costs for edges and nodes between a certain range (1-20 in the experiments). The

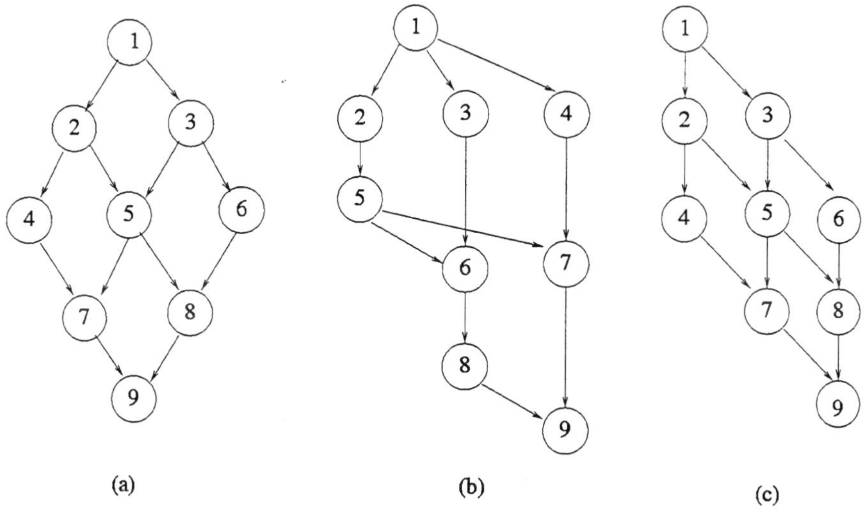

FIG. 5.1. *Examples of Graphs given as input: (a) Mean Value analysis task graph, (b) Cholesky Decomposition task graph, (c) a Laplace Equation solver task graph*

Mean Value Graphs							Laplace solver graphs				
Nodes	Edges	L1	P1	L2	P2	Factor	L1	P1	L2	P2	Factor
49	84	210	12	1548	12	6.37	237	12	1214	12	4.12
100	180	323	27	3687	27	10.41	402	27	3000	27	6.46
144	264	382	33	7110	33	17.60	539	38	4455	38	7.26
225	420	497	58	13437	58	26.00	768	55	6907	55	8.00
324	612	639	76	23287	76	35.00	1050	78	10969	78	9.44
400	760	726	105	37889	105	51.00	1267	100	15952	100	11.59

TABLE 5.1
Table of results: Mean Value graphs, Laplace equation solver graphs

second set of inputs were generated using the depth of the task graph from the root and assigning a decreasing order of costs corresponding to the depth, which accurately reflect certain instances of the Cholesky Decomposition problem. The Laplace Equation task graph inputs were constructed to characterize a typical matrix of $n \times n$ size. The number of nodes and edges in the task graph depends on the size of the problem. The costs of nodes and edges for the Laplace Equation solver were constructed in the same way as for the Cholesky Decomposition graph. The node sizes were varied from 50 to 400 nodes and the average values for the schedule lengths have been tabulated in Table 5.1, Table 5.2 and Table 5.3.

In all tables, L1 and L2 are the schedule lengths as computed by the algorithm. P1 is the number of processors required to schedule the tasks for schedule length L1 and P2 for schedule length L2. The *Factor* column shows the factor of improvement of the new schedule S2 over S1 using the new costs C2, as discussed in the previous section. Table 5.1 shows results for both Mean Value and Laplace Equation solver graph inputs. The algorithm for the Mean Value graph inputs showed divergence and a limit was found necessary to terminate the iterations. It can be seen from the tables that the larger the size of the input, the better is the performance improvement due to our algorithm. This could be attributed to the fact that a larger graph size would increase the possibility of concurrent communication and this effect is captured more efficiently by our algorithm leading to a performance enhancement. The drawback, of course, is that more analysis is needed during each iteration of the algorithm due to large values of e^2. This leads to increase in overall execution time. From Table 5.2 and Table 5.3, an anomaly is seen in the input with 230 nodes. The randomized costs input results in an improvement more than twice that of the fixed costs input. A possible reason could be the existence of a very sensitive and dominant part of the task graph that

Cholesky Decomposition Graphs						
Nodes	Edges	L1	P1	L2	P2	Factor
54	89	193	24	1255	24	5.50
119	209	443	65	5647	64	11.74
152	271	571	88	9193	88	15.10
230	419	875	146	13316	146	14.22
324	599	1243	216	37485	216	29.16
405	755	1561	279	53560	279	33.31

TABLE 5.2

Table of results: Cholesky Decomposition graphs with costs corresponding to the depth of the nodes

Cholesky Decomposition Graphs						
Nodes	Edges	L1	P1	L2	P2	Factor
54	89	204	14	2319	14	10.36
119	209	487	71	5809	71	10.92
152	271	492	96	7629	96	14.5
230	419	705	151	20849	151	28.57
324	599	742	247	18996	247	24.60
405	755	839	317	27494	317	31.77

TABLE 5.3

Table of results: Cholesky Decomposition graphs with randomized costs

could contain numerous concurrent edges.

When the costs of the edges are modified, the schedule also changes and vice versa. Hence, a convergence is not always guaranteed but rather the schedules may oscillate between two values. The reason is that the edge costs are modified using the previous schedule and behavioral edges, and the new schedule is in turn dependent on the modified edge costs. This two way dependence can cause schedules in two iterations to repeat in subsequent pairs of iterations. Let us consider a case in which the final schedules oscillate between two values. In this case,one can still see that the worse schedule of the two could represent the worst case behavior of the underlying communication as far as this graph is concerned. In such a situation, the algorithm could only choose the better of two schedules.

In certain cases, the new schedule S2 results in a large improvement in schedule length over old schedule S1. This is due to the fact that a small change in the costs causes the older schedule S1 to become highly inefficient. Such graphs would be more responsive to our algorithm and the schedules adapt easily to changes to edge costs. Hence, these graphs exhibit a high factor of improvement when scheduled with our algorithm. As can be seen, in all cases, the algorithm adapts schedules and costs to each other using behavioral edges and minimizes schedule length. The improvement in many schedules is of the order of 10.

6. Related Work. The present approaches to performance enhancement involve the use of a separate performance evaluation tool to gather the performance statistics of the executing code. One of the most important performance estimation and evaluation approaches, Paradyn [31], is based on the concept of dynamic instrumentation in which the program's binary code is modified 'on the fly' to insert and detach the instrumentation code as desired by the user. Another important effort in this area is Pablo [32] which uses a more traditional approach of generating a trace through the execution of the program and then provides the analysis of this trace to identify the performance bottlenecks. Wisconsin Wind Tunnel (WWT) project has contributed an important discrete event simulation technique that results in accurate and fast performance estimation through simulation [40].

However, the approaches based on performance tool demand that a user be responsible for guiding the estimator tool to elicit the performance data and gain insight into the potential bottlenecks. Since the compiler is responsible for translating program behavior to its underlying implementation on a given architecture, it would be logical for a compiler to automate the performance instrumentation process for accuracy and efficiency and not the user. The compiler can also perform more realistic program partitioning for high execution efficiency using the result of this analysis as indicated above.

Performance estimation of a parallel program has been the focus of research by parallelizing compiler researchers for a while. Sarkar [20] first developed a framework based on operation counts and profile data to estimate the program execution costs for Single Assignment Languages. This framework was used to guide the program partitioning process of the compiler. Another important effort from Rice University involved development of *Parascope Editor* [33] in which the user annotates the program and is given a feed-back based on performance estimates to help the development process. However, the use of compilation techniques for estimation was a complex program due to limits on static estimation analysis [34] and also due to the complex run time behaviors of the architectures that could not be easily captured. The communication overhead is especially tricky to model and the complexity of modeling its software component has been shown [35]. The effect on message passing or shared memory model on the performance characteristic of a parallel program was analyzed by Chandra and others [36].

Some studies have indicated the potential of compiler analyses for performance prediction. In particular, Wall [34] discusses the relative merits of static estimators vs. profile data and provides a study to determine the utility of profile data gathered during one execution instance on another. Wang [37] proposes a portable framework that estimates the performance costs using symbolic information for super-scalar architectures. Graham et. al. [38] make a case for static estimators by evolving a metric to compare the estimated relative execution frequencies to that derived from the profiles.

However, the above efforts relate to performance estimation on super-scalar architectures only using the behavioral characteristics of the pipelines, caches etc. They do not attempt to address the complex issue of performance modeling and evaluation on multi-processor shared or distributed memory systems. The P3T system based on Vienna Fortran [30] was the first attempt in using the compiler techniques for performance estimation for such systems. However, the approach focussed more on the effect of the compiler optimizations and transformations on the performance rather than on relating it to the behavior of the underlying architectural components. For example, P3T based on Vienna Fortran Compiler (VFC) estimates the effect of loop unrolling, tiling, strip-mining and a whole variety of loop transformations to choose their best ordering on a given architecture. It does not take into account multi-level, asynchronous characteristics of such systems that would lead to complex behavioral patterns and even non-determinism posing extreme challenges in modeling these systems.

The goal of our approach is precisely this: to be able to capture these complex behaviors by specializing them to the program characteristics and machine model. We thus propose a unified approach that tends to bring the program behavioral model and the architectural behavioral model as close as possible for accurate performance estimation. We then propose a framework for highly efficient program partitioning based on an iterative solution.

7. Conclusion. We have proposed an approach based on performance driven program partitioning that accurately accounts for the run time costs for computation and communication. The important implications of our contributions are:

- Through extensive compiler analysis, we are also able to determine the *dominant* and *sensitive* program components that affect the overall performance and are able to weigh in effects of various architectural uncertainty on the overall program execution time. We are also able to focus on key components that directly affect the final program performance. This brings things into focus more precisely that is essential for guiding the compiler partitioning phase.
- We have developed a framework based on behavioral edges and have also developed an iterative algorithm to successively refine the schedule to minimize schedule lengths. Using a performance study undertaken, it can be seen that an improvement of over 10 times is possible for many graphs encountered in numerical computations.

REFERENCES

[1] V. Adve, A. Carle, E. Granston and others, *Requirements for Data Parallel Programming Environments*, IEEE Parallel and Distributed Technology, Special Issue on High Performance Fortran, Fall 1994, pp. 48–58.

[2] J. Anderson and M. Lam, *Global Optimizations for Parallelism and Locality on Scalable Parallel Machines*, Proceedings of SIGPLAN '93 conference on Programming Language Design and Implementation, June 1993, pp. 112–125.

[3] U. Banerjee, *Loop Parallelization*, Kluwer Academic Publishers, 1994 (Loop Transformations for Restructuring Compilers Series).

[4] Z. Bozkus, A. Choudhary, G. Fox, T. Haupt and S. Ranka, *Compiling Fortran 90D/HPF for Distributed Memory MIMD Computers*, Journal of Parallel and Distributed Computing, Special Issue on Data Parallel Algorithms and Programming, Vol. 21, No. 1, April 1994, pp. 15–26.

[5] S. Darbha and D. P. Agrawal, *Optimal Scheduling Algorithm for Distributed-Memory Machines*, IEEE Transactions on Parallel and Distributed Systems, Vol. 9, No. 1, January 1998, pp. 87–95.

[6] S. Darbha and S. S. Pande, *Effect of Imprecise Compile Time Costs on Scheduling Tasks on Distributed Memory Systems*, Frontiers '96: The 6th Symposium on the Frontiers of Massively Parallel Computation, pp. 134-143.

[7] M. Gupta and P. Banerjee, *Demonstration of Automatic Data Partitioning Techniques for Parallelizing Compilers on Multicomputers*, IEEE Transactions on Parallel and Distributed Systems, Vol. 3, March 1992, pp. 179–193.

[8] *High Performance Fortran Forum. High Performance Fortran Language Specification, Version 1.0*, Technical Report, CRPC–TR92225, Center for Research on Parallel Computation, Rice University, Houston, TX, 1992 (revised January 1993).

[9] S. Hiranandani, K. Kennedy and C. -W. Tseng, *Compiling Fortran for MIMD Distributed-Memory Machines*, Communications of ACM, August 1992, Vol. 35, No. 8, pp. 66-80.

[10] S. D. Kaushik, C. -H. Huang, R. W. Johnson and P. Sadayappan, *An Approach to Communication-Efficient Data Redistribution*, Proceedings of 1994 ACM International Conference on Supercomputing, pp. 364–373, June 1994.

[11] C. Koelbel and P. Mehrotra, *Compiling Global Name-Space Parallel Loops for Distributed Execution*, IEEE Transactions on Parallel and Distributed Systems, October 1991, Vol. 2, No. 4, pp. 440–451.

[12] Y. -K. Kwok and I. Ahmad, *Dynamic Critical-Path Scheduling: An Effective Technique for Allocating Task Graphs to Multiprocessors*, IEEE Transactions on Parallel and Distributed Systems, May 1996, Vol. 7, No. 5, pp. 506–521.

[13] A. Rogers and K. Pingali, *Process Decomposition through Locality of Reference*, Proceedings of SIGPLAN '89 conference on Programming Language Design and Implementation, pp. 69–80.

[14] D. Bau, I. Kodukula, V. Kotlyar, K. Pingali and P. Stodghill, *Solving Alignment Using Elementary Linear Algebra*, Proceedings of 7th International Workshop on Languages and Compilers for Parallel Computing, LNCS 892, 1994, pp. 46–60.

[15] A. Gerasoulis and T. Yang, *On Granularity and Clustering of Directed Acyclic Task Graphs*, IEEE Transactions on Parallel and Distributed Systems, Vol. 4, Number 6, June 1993, pp. 686-701.

[16] M. Girkar and C. Polychronopoulos, *Automatic Extraction of Functional Parallelism from Ordinary Programs*, IEEE Transactions on Parallel and Distributed Systems, Vol. 3, No. 2, March 1992, pp. 166-178.

[17] P. Tu and D. Padua, *Automatic Array Privatization*, Proceedings of the Sixth Workshop on Language and Compilers for Parallel Computing, August 1993.

[18] V. Chaudhary and J. K. Aggarwal, *Generalized Mapping of Parallel Algorithms to Parallel Architectures*, Proc. 1990 Int'l Conf. on Parallel Processing, Vol. II, August 1990, pp. 137-141.

[19] V. Sarkar, *Automatic Partitioning Of A Program Dependence Graph Into Parallel Tasks*, IBM Journal Of Research And Development, Vol. 35, No. 5/6, Sept.-Nov. 1991.

[20] V. Sarkar, *Partitioning and Scheduling Parallel Programs for Multiprocessors*, MIT Press, Cambridge, Mass. 1989

[21] A. Agarwal, D. A. Kranz and V. Natarajan, *Automatic Partitioning of Parallel Loops and Data Arrays for Distributed Shared-Memory Multiprocessors*, IEEE Transactions on Parallel and Distributed Systems, Vol. 6, No. 9, Sept. 1995, pp. 943-962.

[22] J. Subhlok and G. Vondran, *Optimal Mapping of Sequences of Data Parallel Tasks*, Proceedings of Principles and Practice of Parallel Programming (PPoPP) '95, pp. 134–143.

[23] S. Darbha and S. S. Pande, *Effect of Imprecise Compile Time Costs on Scheduling Tasks on Distributed Memory Systems*, Proceedings of Frontiers '96: The 6th IEEE/ACM Symposium on the Frontiers of Massively Parallel Computation, pp. 134–141.

[24] S. Darbha and S. S. Pande, *A Robust Compile Time Method for Scheduling Task Parallelism on Distributed Memory Systems*, Proceedings of the 1996 ACM/IEEE Conference on Parallel Architectures and Compilation Techniques (PACT '96), pp. 156–162.

[25] S. S. Pande and K. Psarris, *Program Repartitioning on Varying Communication Cost Parallel Architectures*, Journal of Parallel and Distributed Computing 33, March 1996, pp. 205–213.

[26] S. S. Pande and D. P. Agrawal, *Run Time Issues in Program Partitioning on Distributed Memory Systems*, Concurrency Practice and Experience : Special Issue on Resource Management in Parallel and Distributed Systems, Vol. 7(5) (August 1995), pp. 429–454.

[27] S. S. Pande, D. P. Agrawal, and J. Mauney, *A Scalable Scheduling Method for Functional Parallelism on Distributed Memory Multiprocessors*, IEEE Transactions on Parallel and Distributed Systems, Vol. 6, No.

4, April 1995, pp. 388–399.

[28] S. S. PANDE, D. P. AGRAWAL AND J. MAUNEY, *On Control Flow and Pseudo Static-Dynamic Scheduling Method for Private Memory Machines*, Proceedings of the 1990 International Conference on Parallel Processing, St. Charles, 1990, Vol. II (Software), pp. 300-301.

[29] S. S. PANDE, *A Compile Time Partitioning Method for DOALL Loops on Distributed Memory Systems*, Proceedings of the 1996 International Conference on Parallel Processing, August 1996, Vol. III (Software), pp. 35–44.

[30] T. FAHRINGER, *Estimating and Optimizing Performance of Parallel Programs*, IEEE Computer: Special Issue on Parallel and Distributed Processing Tools, Vol. 28, No. 11, November 1995, pp. 47–56.

[31] B. P. MILLER, M. CALLAGHAN, J. CARGILLE, ET. AL., *The Pardyn Parallel Performance Measurement Tool*, IEEE Computer: Special Issue on Parallel and Distributed Processing Tools, Vol. 28, No. 11, November 1995, pp. 37–46.

[32] D. A. REED, AND OTHERS, *Scalable Performance Analysis: The Pablo Performance Analysis Environment*, Proceedings of Scalable Parallel Libraries Conference, IEEE CS Press, 1993, pp. 104–113.

[33] V. BALASUNDARAM AND OTHERS, *A Static Performance Estimator to Guide Data Partitioning Decisions*, Proceedings of 3rd ACM SIGPLAN Symposium on Principles and Practice of Parallel Programming, 1991, pp. 213–223.

[34] D. WALL, *Predicting Program Behavior Using Real or Estimated Profiles*, Proceedings of the 1991 ACM SIGPLAN Conference on Programming Language Design and Implementation, 1991, pp. 59–70.

[35] V. KARAMCHETI AND A. CHIEN, *Software Overhead in Messaging Layers: Where Does the Time Go?*, Proceedings of the 6th ACM International Conference on Architectural Support for Programming Languages and Systems (ASPLOS VI), pp. 51–60.

[36] S. CHANDRA, J. LARUS AND A. ROGERS, *Where is Time Spent in Message-Passing and Shared Memory Programs*, Proceedings of the 6th ACM International Conference on Architectural Support for Programming Languages and Systems (ASPLOS VI), pp. 61–73.

[37] K. -Y. WANG, *Precise Compile-Time Performance Prediction for Superscalar-Based Computers*, Proceedings of the 1994 ACM SIGPLAN Conference on Programming Language Design and Implementation, pp. 73–84.

[38] T. WAGNER, V. MAVERICK, S. GRAHAM AND M. HARRISON, *Accurate Static Estimators for Program Optimization* Proceedings of the 1994 ACM SIGPLAN Conference on Programming Language Design and Implementation, pp. 84–96.

[39] W. BLUME AND R. EIGENMANN, *Symbolic Range Propagation*, Proceedings of the 9th International Parallel Processing Symposium, April 1995.

[40] S. REINHARDT, M. D. HILL, J. R. LARUS, A. LEBECK AND OTHERS, *The Wisconsin Wind Tunnel: Virtual Prototyping of Parallel Computers*, Proceedings of the 1993 ACM Sigmetrics Conference on Measurement and Modeling of Computer Systems, pp. 48–60, May 1993.

DDSCHED: A DISTRIBUTED DYNAMIC REAL-TIME SCHEDULING ALGORITHM

ANUP K. BHATTACHARJEE*, K. RAVINDRANATH*, A. PAL * AND R. MALL †

Abstract. Modern real-time systems need enormous computing power, for which a uniprocessor system is often inadequate. This work is directed at developing a task scheduling algorithm for distributed systems with the goal of achieving flexibility through dynamic scheduling of tasks in a distributed and adaptive manner. In this paper we present a dynamic soft real-time task scheduling algorithm named DDSCHED for distributed systems. The two main components of DDSCHED are a local scheduler and a distributed scheduling scheme. The local scheduler is designed based on the earliest deadline first(EDF) policy and the concept of window. The implementation uses an efficient data structure to reduce the time complexity from $O(n^2)$ for the basic EDF algorithm to $O(n \log n)$. The distributed scheduling scheme is based on a focus-based heuristic algorithm and a bidding-based algorithm. Our algorithm takes care of the network delays.

Key words. scheduling, real-time system, distributed system, EDF policy.

1. Introduction. Real time systems are characterized by logical as well as temporal correctness. The primary performance metric of a real-time system is the predictability of a task's completion time — which from the operating system designer's point of view, is the proper scheduling of real-time tasks to ensure temporal correctness.

Task scheduling in real-time systems can be static or dynamic. The static scheduling approach calculates schedules for tasks off-line and it requires *a priori* knowledge of task's characteristics. The dynamic approach determines schedules for tasks on the fly and allows tasks to be dynamically generated. The static approach is inflexible and cannot adapt to changing environments, especially where the behavior of the environment is not completely predictable. When new tasks are added to a statically scheduled system, the schedule for the entire system must be recalculated; thus it becomes prohibitively expensive in time. On the other hand, the dynamic scheduling approach ordinarily involves higher runtime overheads than static schedulers. However, it is flexible and can easily adapt to changes in the environment.

Real-time tasks can be of two types: *periodic* and *aperiodic* . Periodic tasks are those which recur at a regular time interval, e.g. the scanning of a transducer (e.g., a thermocouple) to measure the temperature of a process at regular intervals. Aperiodic tasks are associated with asynchronous events like the occurrence of an alarm due to some parameter of a controlled physical system going above a threshold. An aperiodic task can be modeled as a four tuple (A,S,P,D) where A,S,P, and D denote arrival time, start time, computation time and deadline respectively. A periodic task can be modeled as (A,S,P,D,T) such that

$$A_{i+1} = D_i$$
$$D_{i+1} = D_i + T$$

where T, A_i, and D_i are the period, arrival time, and deadline of the ith instance of the periodic task respectively.

*Department of Computer Science and Engineering, Indian Institute of Technology, Kharagpur, 721 302, INDIA.,

†Department of Computer Science, Curtin University of Technology, Perth, Australia

The precedence constraints among a set of tasks specify the relationships among tasks. A task T_i is said to precede task T_j, if T_i must finish before T_j begins. Interrelated tasks communicate with each other in real-time to synchronize as well as to exchange data. In static systems, the set of tasks to be scheduled and the precedence graph of the tasks are known in advance. In dynamic system, new sets of interrelated tasks arrive dynamically, and the precedence graph of a new task set is known only when the task set arrives.

Many of the present generation distributed systems are built around Ethernet technology, and have a nondeterministic communication delay because the CSMA/CD protocol is used for media access control. Though this does not cause problem in normal applications, it may be a bottleneck in real-time applications. Any real-time system based on such a nondeterministic protocol must be designed to overcome this indeterminacy. The emerging networking technologies like Ethernet switching, 100VGAnyLAN (IEEE 802.12 standard), ATM technology, and Fast Ethernet (IEEE 802.3) etc. are expected to make distributed systems more attractive than expensive parallel computing systems [10].

In attempting to use distributed systems in real-time applications, the scheduling policy must take care of meeting task deadlines as well as performing load balancing[9]. Most of the load balancing algorithms do not consider the timing constraints of tasks and cannot be directly applied to hard real-time systems.

In this perspective, our present work was undertaken with the following objectives:

- To design an efficient algorithm for scheduling soft real-time tasks in an environment of computers connected through a local area network(LAN), which may use a non deterministic media access protocol.
- To simulate the algorithm in an existing Ethernet based environment
- To gather statistical data about the performance of the developed algorithm and interpret them.

This paper has been organized as follows. In section 2, we survey some of the important work reported in real-time scheduling area. In section 3, we present our algorithm DDSCHED for real-time scheduling of tasks in distributed system and discuss its simulation. In section 4, we discuss the simulation results. Section 5, concludes the work and outlines future directions of our work.

2. Related Work. A large number of reported work discuss algorithms for scheduling a given set of tasks to achieve the least possible finishing time [1–5,7–9]. Garey and Johnson have proved that optimal scheduling of a task set in multiprocessor systems is an NP-complete problem [6]. Clearly then, a heuristic scheduling algorithm has to be designed in order to reduce the scheduling costs.

Several reported work in the area of scheduling in distributed systems deal with task allocation problems [1,2,3,5]. In a traditional distributed system, the main objectives of any task allocation scheme are to balance the load among processors and to minimize the communication cost for tasks. Task allocation is a difficult problem even without timing constraints. For example, finding an optimal assignment of tasks with an arbitrary communication graph for four or more processors with different speeds is known to be NP-hard. Considerable efforts have been spent on more restrictive allocation problems and on developing heuristic algorithms to find suboptimal solutions using network flow and dynamic programming [1].

The main objectives of any distributed scheduling algorithm are to: maximize the utilization of resources, and to minimize the communication costs. These objectives are at odds with each other, because if more information exchange is allowed, one has greater potential for coming up with better resource utilization at the expense of higher communication overhead.

Stankovic and Ramamritham [9] developed a heuristic algorithm for scheduling mutually independent tasks in distributed hard real-time systems. Their goal is to schedule tasks such that the maximum number of tasks can be guaranteed to be completed before their deadline. Their approach consists of a bidding algorithm and a focused addressing algorithm[9]. In focused addressing, if a task cannot be guaranteed to complete at a node, it is sent to a selected remote node which is estimated to have high surplus processing time. In bidding, a task is sent to a remote node whose selection is based on the bids sent by the nodes for the task. Scheduling decision made in focused addressing is based on inaccurate state information, but it entails low communication delay. The communication delay involved in bidding is high, but the selection is based on relatively accurate state information of the nodes. Their work showed how to combine these two schemes in a distributed hard real-time system taking into account the timing constraints of the task. They simulated the algorithm on a single machine and modelled the communication subnet by defining a delay per packet on the basis of a random variable. The simulation results showed that dynamic and distributed real-time scheduling is feasible, and that a system can benefit substantially from distributed scheduling under a wide range of system conditions and task parameters.

3. The DDSCHED Algorithm. In this section, we describe a new scheduling algorithm named DDSCHED (**D**ynamic **D**istributed Real-Time Adaptive **SCHED**uler) as an adaptive algorithm for implementing a soft real-time scheduler for distributed systems, based on a nondeterministic network protocol. The adaptive function takes into account the nondeterministic delay factor in the underlying network for a distributed system specially if CSMA/CD protocol is the media access protocol. Since Ethernet is an easily available and affordable product, it can be used in a soft real-time environment. We aim to incorporate the estimation of network delay based on the most recent load on the network.

3.1. Basis and Assumptions:. The design of DDSCHED is based on (1) a locally executed guarantee algorithm, which determines whether or not a task can be guaranteed to meet its real-time requirements and (2) a distributed remote scheduling algorithm for interacting across the network for remote scheduling in case the task fails to meet it's real-time constraints.

Our scheme requires the presence of one scheduler per node. These schedulers interact so as to determine where a newly arriving task could be scheduled. Each node in the network runs the scheduler independently, and tasks may arrive at any node.

A set (possibly null) of periodic tasks exists at each node. Since a periodic task recurs at regular intervals, it has to be determined at system initialization time, whether there is enough processing power to execute a given set of periodic tasks. We assume that the set of periodic tasks is static, and is known *a priori*.

Aperiodic tasks may arrive at any node in the network. When a new aperiodic task arrives, the scheduler at that node checks whether the task can be scheduled at that node so as to finish before deadline; if so the task is guaranteed. Otherwise the scheduler on the node interacts with the schedulers on other nodes, using a scheme that combines bidding and heuristic based addressing, in order to determine the node to which the task can be sent to be scheduled.

In a given schedule, if at some time t there is no ready task to be run, we refer to the time span between the completion of the last task to be processed before t and the first task to be processed after t as an *idle time* (or slack time). In order to compare the idle time lengths in schedules produced by different algorithms for a given task set, we use the availability function[4]

$$f_Y^X = \begin{cases} 1 & \text{if the processor is idle} \\ 0 & \text{otherwise} \end{cases}$$

This function is defined with respect to a task set Y and according to the scheduling algorithm X in the time interval[0,t]. So for any interval of time $[t_1, t_2]$, the integral $\int_{t_1}^{t_2} f_Y^X dt$ gives the total amount of time for which the processor is idle. Any algorithm based on EDF principle will feasibly schedule a set of periodic tasks as long as the Liu and Layland criterion, as specified below, is satisfied [8].

Let us define

$$L = LCM(P_1, P_2, \ldots, P_n)$$

where P_i is the period of ith task in a set τ . The tasks have computation times C_1,C_2..,C_n. As Liu and Layland [8] have shown, the necessary condition for periodic task set τ to be guaranteed in time L, on that node is

$$\sum_{i=1}^{n}(C_i * (L/P_i) \leq L)$$

The fundamental property of the schedule produced by any preemptive algorithm and in consequence by an EDF-based algorithm for a set of periodic tasks is its cyclicity. Let us assume that τ is feasibly scheduled by EDF. This means that the processor (in the absence of aperiodic tasks) does exactly the same thing at time $t \geq 0$ that it does at $t + k * L$, $(k = 1, 2...)$. So, generating a feasible schedule over an infinite length is equivalent to producing the schedule in the intervals $[k*L, (k+1)*L]$, $k = 0, 1...$, we will call each of this interval, a window. This window property is used in our algorithm to reduce the overhead of scheduling periodic tasks as time moves ahead, since only the window is shifted with time.

We adopt an EDF-based scheme to implement a priority queue for ready tasks, as ordered by increasing deadline, and then do the feasibility and schedule calculations based on the queue (ties are broken arbitrarily unless a separate priority list is maintained for the tasks in addition to the deadline information).

Once a set of periodic tasks is feasibly scheduled, we compute the largest amount of aperiodic processing that can be done at any priority level during an interval $[0, t], t \geq 0$, so that all previously scheduled task deadlines are met. This is done by focusing on a particular priority level, say i, $1 \leq i \leq n$, and ignoring all periodic and aperiodic tasks with priority lower than i. It is easy to see that any time interval $[0, t]$ will consist of an alternating sequence of level $i-1$ busy periods during which the processor is busy with tasks having priorities higher than i and level $i-1$ inactivity periods during which the processor is not processing any tasks with priority $i-1$ or higher. The total length of the level $i-1$ inactivity periods during $[0, t]$ is available for aperiodic tasks at any priority level. This time cannot be allocated arbitrarily, and sufficient time must be available for each of the jobs of the lower priority tasks to meet their deadlines. This means that if T_{ij} is a periodic task i,such that the jth occurrence requires C_i amount of computation time, then C_i must be available to it during $[S_{ij},D_{ij}]$ to complete where the first factor is its earliest starting time and deadline at jth occurance. Let M_{ij} be the total level of i-1 inactivity during $[0, D_{ij}]$. Then we can compute A_{ij} as the largest amount of time available for aperiodic processing between 0 and the completion time of T_{ij}, and still ensure that all deadlines associated with the periodic task set are met and is given by

$$A_{ij} = M_{ij} - j * C_i.$$

To compute the value M_{ij}, the interval $[0, D_{ij}]$ is subdivided into alternating level i-1 busy periods and level i-1 inactivity periods. We must compute the total length of the idle periods M_{ij}. This is done by starting at time 0, computing the length of the initial busy period, if any, then the length of the idle period and then the length of the next busy period, and so on. These alternating calculations continue until D_{ij} is reached and the sum of the lengths of the idle periods gives L_{ij}.

3.2. Description and Implementation.

3.2.1. Local Scheduler. We now describe the basic scheduling algorithm used in the local scheduler. The dynamic algorithm executes in the following three steps:

step 1 This step is the initialization phase. All the periodic tasks which are known *a priori* are checked, so that the necessary condition is satisfied. This guarantees that sufficient computation power is available to schedule the periodic tasks in the window L (LCM of periods).

step 2 In this step, the schedule is computed for the set of periodic tasks.

step 3 This step is performed for aperiodic tasks. The algorithm finds the subset of tasks which are to be rescheduled because of the current aperiodic task, and reschedules them by performing step 2 of the algorithm.

Details of step 2.

The sets of tasks are ordered by increasing deadlines and scheduled. Given such a set, we select the first task, and schedules it as near to its start time as possible (i.e., at the earliest available time after its start). The slack computation method is used for computation of the idle period. The task is scheduled by accumulating all unused processor time past the task's start time until sufficient slack time is found, as explained previously. If the resulting schedule permits this task to complete before its deadline, then the task is schedulable, else it is not schedulable.

The scheduling information used by the algorithm is recorded in a slot list (Fig. 3.1), which is a doubly linked list, in which each slot represents a time already assigned to tasks. A slot has four fields: slot_start, slot_end and two pointers to maintain the list. The list is ordered by the slot start time(slot_start). Since slots do not overlap in time the total available time between two slots is the interval between first slot's end time(slot_end) and the next slot's start time(slot_start).

These slots are indexed by slot start time using a height balanced binary tree. The key in the tree is the task start time. It is to be noted that each task has one and only one entry in the index tree, but it can have multiple slots in the slot list due to preemption. To speed up the feasibility analysis, the adjacent slots are merged. Fig. 3.1 shows the index tree and the slot lists.

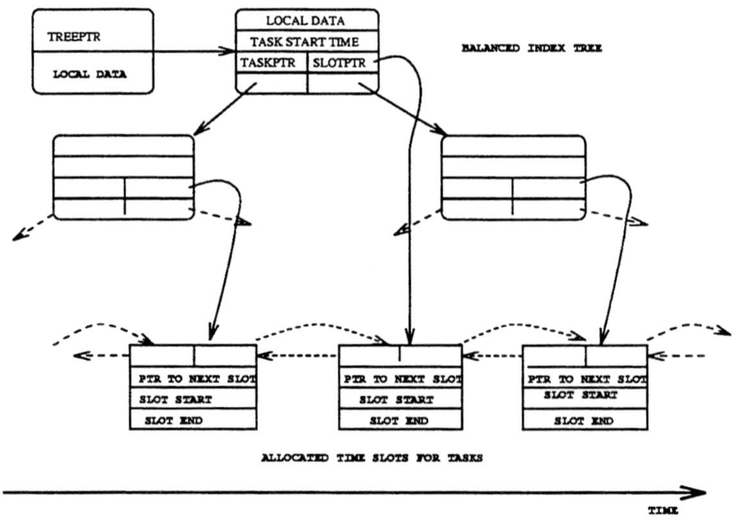

FIG. 3.1. *Index Tree and Slot Lists.*

The tasks are maintained in a priority queue ordered by their deadline. Periodic tasks have changing deadline and this is maintained by the window shifting policy as explained later. The schedulability analysis is done by searching the slot list.

Details of step 3

First a new task T is placed in the EDF list of tasks which records all previously guaranteed tasks. Then a subset of tasks in the updated EDF list is rescheduled. The subset contains those tasks whose schedules conflict with the schedule of T. The chosen subset's size depends on the newly arrived task's start time and end time, and on the tasks already scheduled in the task list. If any of the tasks in the subset is not schedulable, T is considered not schedulable and the local scheduler initiates remote scheduling.

The algorithm is implemented as follows. First we find an interval [i_start,i_end] such that a newly arriving task is entirely contained in the interval based on its start time and deadline. The lower bound i_start is quickly located with the help of the index tree, and then based on the slack time, the other bound i_end is located. The window shifting step is performed before this, based on the task's deadline. This is done as follows.

The task to be scheduled is compared with the current window, if the deadline is outside the window, the new window size is computed. A multiple of current window size and new window size of index tree and slotlist are appended to the existing index tree and slot list. This way, the computation overhead associated with window shift for rescheduling the periodic tasks is minimized. It can be shown that this algorithm has a worst case complexity of O(nlogn) [11] and has been shown to be optimal for uniprocessor scheduling [4].

3.2.2. Remote Scheduler. The remote scheduling mechanism is based on the following schemes.

Heuristic based Scheme (Focused Addressing):
The arrival time (AT) is estimated when the task arrives at the selected node. This takes into account the overhead associated with the network delay and the computation time of the scheduler. If for some node, the estimated surplus between AT and the deadline(D) of the task is factor(FP) times the computation time C of the task, then task T is sent to that node. Here FP is an adaptive parameter and has to be tuned for the system. If a number of nodes satisfy the requirements then one of them is chosen at random and this selected node is referred to as focused node. The chosen node responds to the task in the same way as the original node which had sent the task for remote scheduling.

Bidding Scheme:
If focused addressing fails to schedule a task, the node broadcasts the request for bid(RFB) to all nodes in the system, giving its address so that the response can be addressed to it by the bidders. The main functions of the bidder component on a node are the following

- sending out RFB
- responding to RFB
- evaluating RFBs
- responding to task awards.

On receiving a request for task scheduling from a remote node, the local scheduler does a feasibility analysis and if the task is schedulable, it computes the schedule. The response is sent after this, and the remote node takes action based on the best bid received.

Fig. 3.2 shows a statechart description of the scheduler behavior at each node and Fig. 3.3 shows the process level architecture for the scheme implemented for simulating the algorithm.

In Fig. 3.3, the task NETDELAY is an echo server whose objective is to measure network delay and this task is activated periodically. The clock task CLOCK, as shown in Fig. 3.3, is implemented using the Lamport and Smith algorithm [12] to provide a globally synchronized clock at each node. The communication layer is implemented using UNIX sockets and remote procedure calls (RPC).

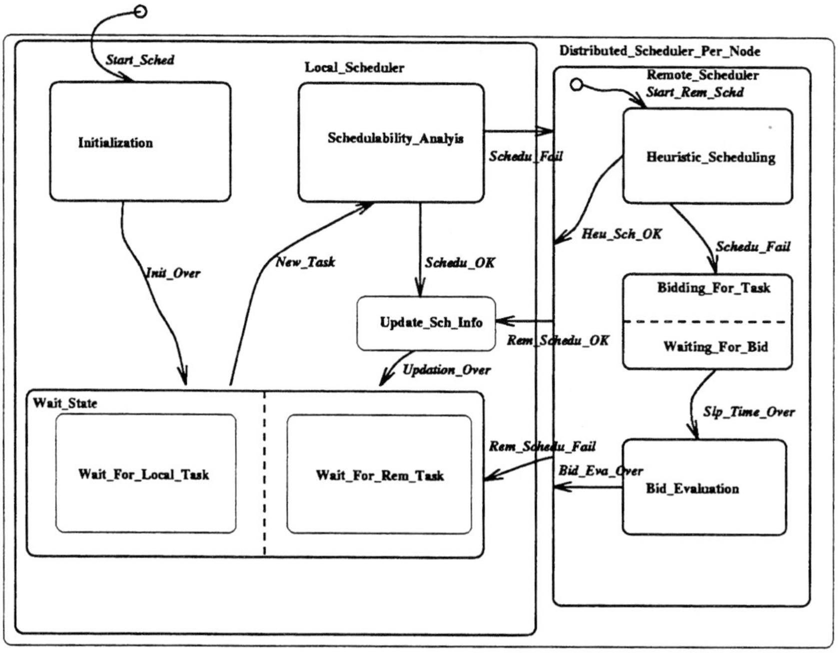

FIG. 3.2. *Process Architecture of the Scheme.*

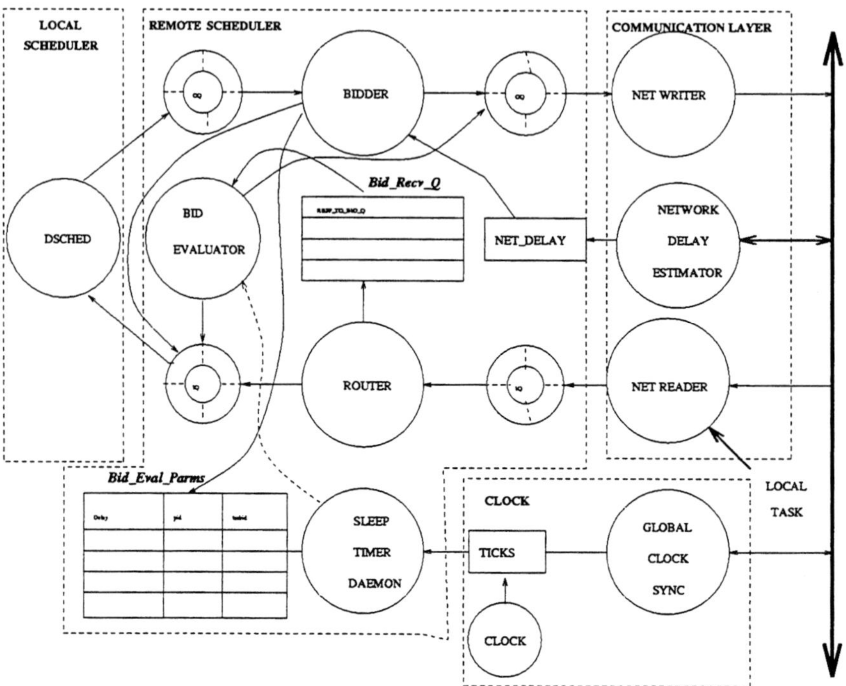

FIG. 3.3. *Process Architecture of the Scheme.*

Algorithm:

```
T: TASK
TaskQ: Priority Task Q
TSL: Slot List
B: Balanced Tree

Initialize all Data Structures
for all periodic tasks do
       T=dequeue(TaskQ)
       Verify and Calculate Schedule
end for

forever(wait for Tasks)
       for all Tasks in TaskQ
       /* check schedulability by dynamicSchedule */
       if(dynamicSchedule(T)==FALSE)
              /* initiate remote scheduling */
              if(remoteSchedule(T)==FALSE)
                     T is not schedulable
              else
                     T is scheduled at remote node
       else
              T is scheduled locally
       endfor
endforever
```

```
Function BOOLEAN dynamicSchedule(Task: T)
    enQueue(TaskQ,T)
    shiftWindow(TaskQ,B,TSL,T)
    Locate an allocated slot SL whose start time is
    nearest to T's start time
    Find an interval [I_START,I_END] such that
           I_START < T.START_TIME and
           I_END - I_START - total Slack = T.RUN_TIME
    for all T in TaskQ in EDF
           if(T.START_TIME lies in [I_START,I_END])
                  if(scheduleTask(TSL,T)==FALSE)
                         deQueue(TaskQ,T)
                         return FALSE
                  else
                         insertInIndexTree(B,T)
                         return TRUE
                  endif
           endif
    endfor
```

4. Performance Studies. The simulated algorithm has been run with the following kinds of input and the performance has been studied:

- Exponential Task Inter-Arrival Time with
  Fixed Task Computation, and
  Normal Distribution of Task Size

In the experimentation, a task's start time is set to be equal to it's arrival time plus a uniformly distributed random number, and the deadline of tasks is defined as: *deadline=start time + computation time + a controlled laxity or slack time.*

4.1. Comparison with basic EDF Algorithm. The heart of DDSCHED is the local scheduler, and therefore it has to be very efficient. Stankovic[9] had used the basic EDF algorithm in the guarantee routine. Fig 4.1 shows a comparison of the performance of DDSCHED with that of the Stankovic's Guarantee algorithm. Here, the Y axis shows the number of tasks currently in the task queue when a new task arrives for scheduling. It can be easily seen that DDSCHED performs better when more number of tasks are in the task queue because of it's O($nlogn$) time complexity. In the algorithm DDSCHED, we reschedule only those tasks in the queue whose deadlines conflict with the newly arrived task's deadline, thus contributing to the better performance.

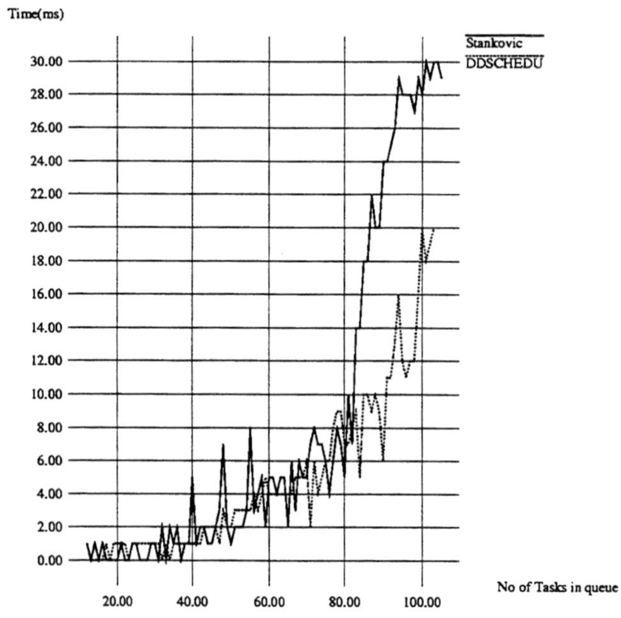

FIG. 4.1. *Comparison of Stankovic's Guarantee Routine and DDSCHED*

4.2. Exponential Inter-arrival Time. Fig. 4.2 shows the percentage of tasks scheduled locally versus task arrival rate (λ). In our experimentation, λ is varied only in one machine (shown as C) and is kept constant in the two other machines (shown as A and B in Fig. 4.2). It can be seen that the number of tasks scheduled locally decreases in the first machine. Fig. 4.3 shows the number of tasks scheduled by remote scheduler. The percentage of tasks scheduled remotely increases initially with λ but slowly decreases later. The decrease occurs due to two reasons:

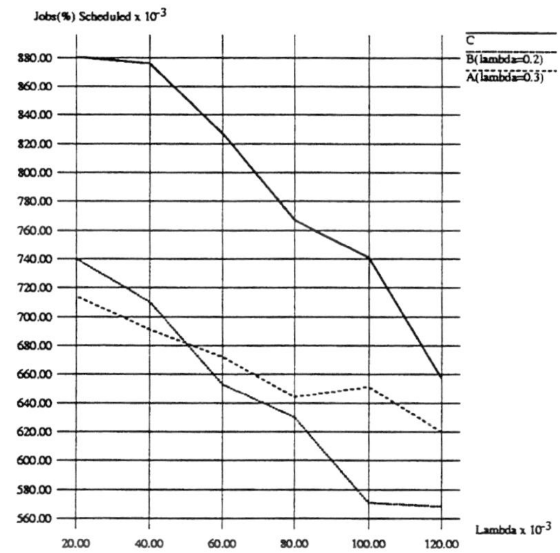

FIG. 4.2. *Tasks Scheduled Locally.*

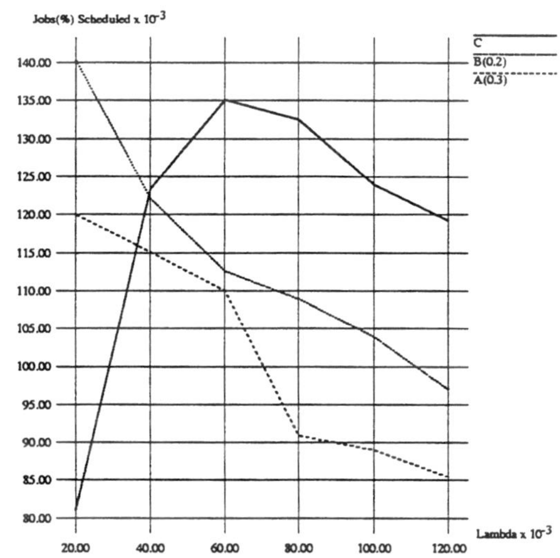

FIG. 4.3. *Tasks Scheduled by Remote Bidding.*

- remote nodes are getting loaded, and
- due to limitation of bid slots some tasks are not bidded and that increases with arrival rate(λ).

The second limitation is due to a limit of number of tasks that can be held for bidding, and can be easily modified by increasing the number of slots. Some of the bidded tasks also timeout(expire their deadline) because of very stringent laxity constraint. Fig. 4.4 shows the effect of laxity and the percentage of tasks scheduled for a given λ ($\lambda = 0.2$) with the task deadline being varied from 10ms to 10000ms. It is seen that percentage of tasks scheduled in the node increase with laxity. So laxity for a task is an important factor for a task to

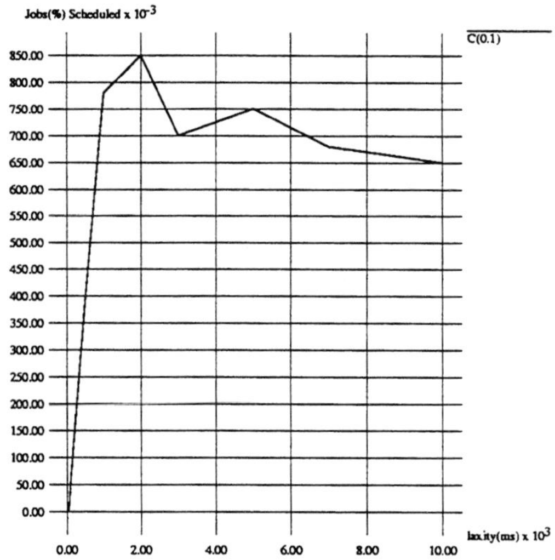

FIG. 4.4. *Effect of Laxity.*

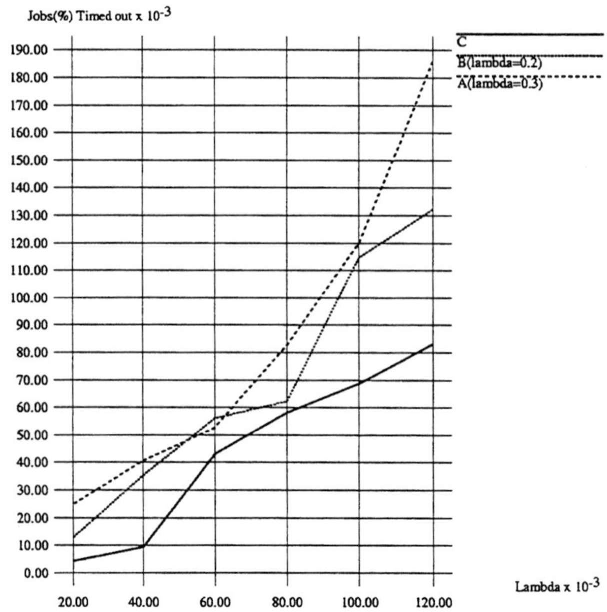

FIG. 4.5. *Effect on Timeout.*

get scheduled in the system. Again it may be observed that there is a fall in percentage of tasks scheduled due to increased laxity because of fixed number of slots.

Fig. 4.5 shows the effect of λ on timeout and it is seen that with higher task arrival rate, more tasks timeout before any bid is received. The steep increase in timeout is also due to the shortage of slots to hold the bidded tasks.

4.3. Effect of Processing Power of a Node. To see how the processing power of a node affects the scheduling of tasks, we simulated the changing processing power of a node by introducing a speed multiplication factor(m_f) in each machine. The inter-task arrival time is exponential with normal distribution of task size($\mu = 1000$ and $\sigma^2 = 100$ units of time). The other two nodes are kept unaffected, and the factor is increased in first node(C) by steps of 1, from 1 (all having same processing power) to 5. Fig. 4.6 and Fig. 4.7 show the effect on percentage of number of tasks scheduled locally and remotely by an increase of processing power of first node at constant λ. The fact that increasing processing power affects both local and remote scheduling can be clearly seen. Figure 4.6 shows that by increasing the processing power, the nodes can guarantee more tasks locally.

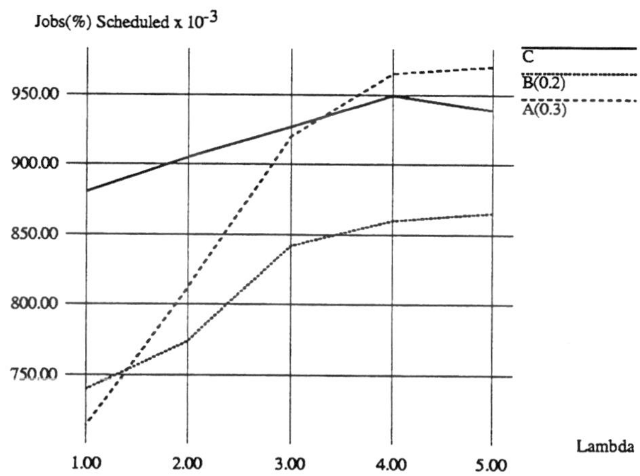

FIG. 4.6. *Effect of Increasing Processing Power on Local Scheduling.*

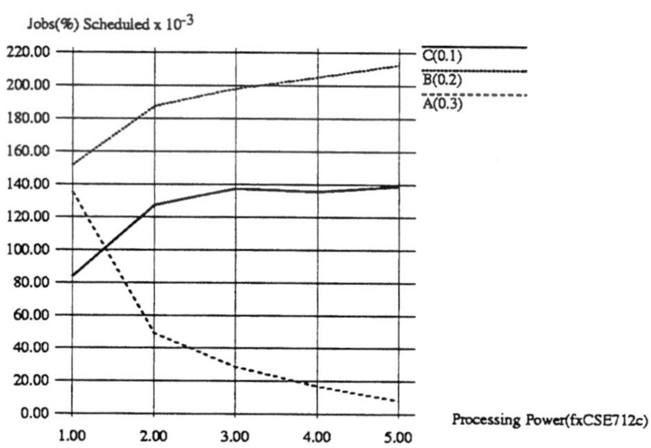

FIG. 4.7. *Effect of Increasing Processing Power on Remote Scheduling.*

5. Conclusion. We have presented an algorithm DDSCHED for scheduling tasks with soft real-time constraints on a loosely coupled computer. We have evaluated its performance and observed the following:

- For a large number of tasks in the task queue, our algorithm DDSCHED is considerably faster than the basic EDF algorithm. The reason for the better performance is due to the strategy to reduce the search domain in the task queue i.e the concept of Window.
- If the task profile is known then the simulated scheduling algorithm can be used to predict the computation requirement in the actual system

Some of the important features of our algorithm are the following:

- DDSCHED is a truly distributed scheduling algorithm, in which all nodes are treated with equal importance.
- The algorithm is designed to schedule periodic as well as aperiodic tasks. The aperiodic tasks may arrive at any time independently at any node.
- We have taken into account the scheduling overhead.
- We have taken network delay into consideration, assuming the underlying network protocol may be non real-time and hence the delay may not be deterministic.
- We have used the features of the focused heuristic and bidding schemes in our scheduling algorithm.

Our current work is directed towards supporting fault-tolerant scheduling of tasks in DDSCHED.

REFERENCES

[1] Stankovic J.A., Spuri M., Natale M.D., and Buttazzo G., *Implications of Classical Scheduling Results for Real-Time System*, IEEE Computer, 6 (1995), pp. 16–25.

[2] Barbara Korousic-Seljak, *Task Scheduling policies for Real-Time Systems*, Microprocessor and Microsystem, 9 (1994).

[3] Burns A., *Preemptive Priority Based Scheduling: An Appropriate Engineering Approach*, Advances in Real-Time Systems, Sang H. Son Ed., Prentice-Hall, 1995, pp. 225–248.

[4] Chetto H. and Chetto M., *Some Results of the Earliest Deadline Scheduling Algorithm*, IEEE Trans. on Software Engineering, 10 (1989), pp. 466–473.

[5] Cheng S.C., Stankovic J.A., and Ramamritham K., *Scheduling Algorithms for Hard Real-Time Systems : A Survey*, Tutorial on Hard Real-Time Systems, IEEE Press, 1988, pp. 150–173.

[6] Garey M.R. and Johnson D.S., *Complexity Results for Multiprocessor Scheduling Scheduling Under Resource Constraints*, SIAM Journal of Computing, 4 (1975), pp. 397–411.

[7] Lehoczky J.P. and Thuel S., *Scheduling Periodic and Aperiodic Tasks Using the Slack Stealing Algorithm*, Advances in Real-Time Systems, Sang H. Son ed., Prentice-Hall, 1995, pp. 175–195.

[8] Liu C.L. and Layland J. , *Scheduling Algorithms for Multiprogramming in Hard Real-Time Systems*, Journal of ACM, 1 (1973), pp. 174–189.

[9] Stankovic J., Ramamritham K., and Cheng S., *"Evaluation of a Flexible Scheduling Algorithm for Distributed Hard Real-Time Systems"*, IEEE Transactions on Computer, 12 (1985), pp. 1130–1143.

[10] Ramamritham K., *Channel Characteristics in Local-Area Hard Real-time Systems*, Computer Networks and ISDN systems, 1987, pp. 3–13.

[11] Schwan K. and Zhou H., *Dynamic Scheduling of Real-Time Tasks and Real-Time Threads*, IEEE Trans. on Software Engineering, 8 (1992), pp. 736–748.

[12] Singhal M. and Sivaratri N., *Advanced Concepts in Operating Systems*, McGraw-Hill, 1994.

COMPARING PARALLEL MULTIDIMENSIONAL INTEGRATION ALGORITHMS

I. GLADWELL* AND M.A. NAPIERALA†

Abstract. We consider the design and implementation of new parallel globally adaptive multidimensional numerical integration algorithms. We describe a pair of algorithms (implemented in MPI on an IBM SP2); one uses a master-slave paradigm and the other is genuinely distributed. Then, we describe modifications of these algorithms to take advantage of a singularity detection scheme. The most obvious competitors for globally adaptive schemes in high dimensions are algorithms based on lattice rules. We compare our globally adaptive strategy with the straightforward implementation of a lattice rule algorithm paying attention to the quality of the respective error estimates. The lattice rule algorithm implementations involve computing new "seeds" for larger numbers of points than used previously, a significant though straightforward computational task.

1. Introduction. Adaptive numerical integration in many dimensions normally requires significantly more memory and computing time than in one dimension (to store and process the data structures). Distributed memory computers can provide potentially more computing power and more memory and cache than even the largest shared memory machines, but it is distributed across the processors and not necessarily usable by algorithms adapted from a shared memory paradigm. We develop globally adaptive multidimensional algorithms for a distributed memory architecture, one with a shared memory flavor and one genuinely distributed. The latter has the ability to fully exploit the distributed memory.

The adaptive algorithms are extensions of the Level algorithms [2, 6]. These algorithms achieve a load balance dynamically; the strategy used involves synchronizing at the end of each "stage", predicting the total work involved globally for the next stage then using this prediction to achieve a "load balance" of the work for individual processors. This global strategy differs from most load balancing strategies used in parallel numerical integration, which exploit the independence of the calculations on individual processors to load balance by sharing work between neighboring processors on the basis of local measures of work remaining. In our global strategy, processors are never idle (except possibly at synchronization) but a global calculation and redistribution is involved at each stage; most local load balancing strategies check regularly for idle processors and redistribute work locally at these checkpoints; some of the algorithms described in [4] lie between these extremes.

Normally when using a shared-memory model on a distributed memory architecture some memory references take significantly longer than others. Machines such as the Meiko CS-2, Thinking Machines CM-5 and IBM SP2 have multilevel switches that make the precise processor connection topology essentially irrelevant to the cost of memory references. On these computers, it is reasonable to assume all inter-processor communications take equal time, and this is our assumption.

We use a message passing model, based on the MPI [9] protocol. This model posits a set of processors that have only local memory but are able to communicate with other processors, that is, are able to exchange information between the respective local memories. Data transfer from the local memory of one processor to the local memory of another requires operations to be performed on both processors. The message passing operations we use are Send, Receive, Broadcast, Gather and Reduce, see Fig. 8. Collective operations (Broadcast, Gather and Reduce) must be executed on both *source* and *destination* processors. For

*Department of Mathematics, Southern Methodist University, Dallas, TX 75275
†Consumer Products Division, Texas Instruments Inc, Dallas, TX 75265.

example, in Reduce, the first argument *local_list* of length *size* identifies a data structure (variable or list) held by each processor, and the argument *operation* can be SUM, MIN, MAX, or be defined by the user. If *operation* is SUM, say, and there are p participating processors with *id*'s $0, 1, \ldots, p-1$ then Reduce(*local_list, global_list, size, SUM, destination*) computes a list *global_list* of size *size* on the process with address *destination*, such that $global\_list_i = \sum_{j=0}^{p-1}(local\_list_i)_j, \quad i = 1, 2, \ldots, size.$

Section 2 describes the parallel implementation of a new adaptive multidimensional algorithm, first in a master-slave implementation and then in a distributed memory form. These algorithms are at the *subdivision* level [11], a grain size suitable for distributed memory architectures. We include devices whereby the subdivision is automatically modified if a singularity is detected. In Section 3, a lattice rank-1 rule algorithm and its parallel implementation is discussed briefly. The performance of these algorithms in sequential and parallel implementations is compared and analyzed in Section 4, including the quality of their error estimates.

Close relatives of our simplest global adaptive algorithms are discussed in [1, 2, 3, 6], including tests on a KSR1 virtual shared memory and a Sequent Symmetry shared memory system. The Level algorithm here is related to, but differs in detail from, the Sword algorithm of [15] and the Fixed Bins Selection Strategy algorithm of [4].

2. Multidimensional Adaptive Algorithms.

2.1. Algorithms $PMDQAG1_{level}$ **and** $PMDQAG2_{level}$**.** We develop two versions of a multidimensional globally adaptive integration algorithm for distributed memory machines. The multidimensional algorithm $PMDQAG1_{level}$, see Fig. 10, resembles our earlier one-dimensional shared memory algorithm $PQAG_{level}$ [6] whereas $PMDQAG2_{level}$ differs in exploiting distributed memory and hence in the algorithm for load balancing.

In $PMDQAG1_{level}$, at initialization, each of the p nodes receives its identifier, *myid*. The initial region of integration is kept globally and is subdivided independently on all processors into m^{dim} pieces (i.e., m pieces in each of dim directions). Throughout, the information about the regions, their integrals and error estimates is kept only in the data structure $LdLEVEL$ on the control node; i.e., the processor with *myid* = *0*. When further subdivision is necessary, the computational nodes receive, through a Broadcast, just the information needed to process their regions of interest. Every computational node selects and subdivides its regions using procedures *Select* and *Sub* [7], see Fig. 9 for more details. Next, the computational nodes evaluate the integration rule and error estimate on the resulting subregions. Simultaneously, the control node subdivides all regions of interest and adds the result to the existing list. The approximate integrals and error estimates for the resulting subregions are calculated by the computational nodes and returned to the control node, which takes care of the updates. If the termination criteria are satisfied, the control node calculates the approximation to the integral and all processors finalize, otherwise the next step of the integration begins. If further subdivision is necessary, the control node decides which regions to subdivide next. The criteria for subdivision are as in [6]: regions in the highest non-empty level of the data structure $LdLEVEL$ are subdivided; parameters in the design and subdivision of are $LdLEVEL$ given in Fig. 7. The information concerning the regions that "reside" on the highest non-empty level is Broadcast to the computational nodes, which calculate their part of work, perform the integration and so on.

Consider a simple two-dimensional example. In Figure 1, the initial region of integration is subdivided into 3^2 pieces: $I_1, I_2, \ldots, I_9$. The regions I_1, I_2 and I_4 are in the highest level of error estimates and are selected for further subdivision; they are the set S of size *lens*

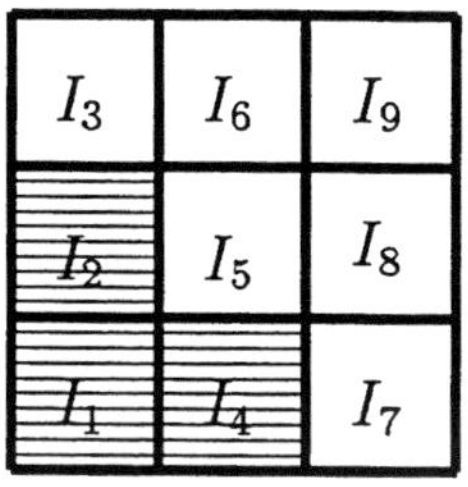

FIG. 1. *After initial subdivision* ($m = 3$)*; shaded 2D subregions to be subdivided*

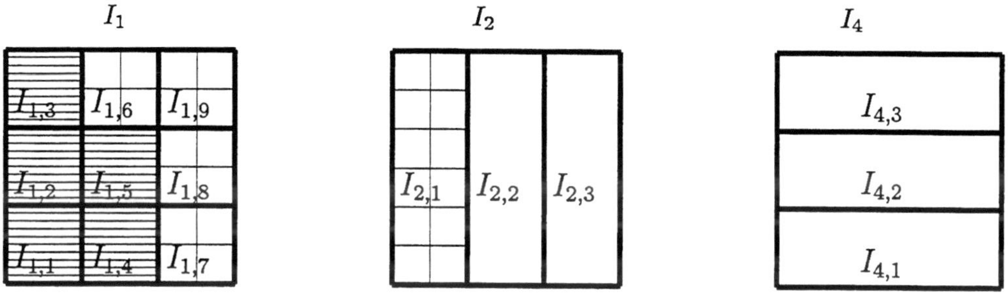

$$S = \{I_1, I_2, I_4\} \quad ND_S = \{2, 1, 1\} \quad DIR_S = \{1, 2, 1, 2\}$$

Node 1 $\quad S_{local} = \{I_1\} \quad ND_{local} = \{2\} \quad DIR_{local} = \{1, 2\} \quad P_{local} = \{I_{1,1}, I_{1,2}, I_{1,3}, I_{1,4}, I_{1,5}\}$

Node 2 $\quad S_{local} = \{I_1, I_2\} \quad ND_{local} = \{2, 1\} \quad DIR_{local} = \{1, 2, 1\} \quad P_{local} = \{I_{1,6}, I_{1,7}, I_{1,8}, I_{1,9}, I_{2,1}\}$

Node 3 $\quad S_{local} = \{I_2, I_4\} \quad ND_{local} = \{1, 1\} \quad DIR_{local} = \{1, 2\} \quad P_{local} = \{I_{2,2}, I_{2,3}, I_{4,1}, I_{4,2}, I_{4,3}\}$

FIG. 2. *Subdivision in 2D;* $p = 3$ *processors*

in Figs. 2 and 3. Figs. 2 and 3 show the processing of I_1, I_2 and I_4 with 3 and 4 computational nodes, respectively. The elements of ND are the numbers of directions of subdivision for each node and those in DIR the actual directions of subdivision, in order. The corresponding values for the individual computational nodes are given the subscript *local* for local array. The system in Fig. 3 is not load balanced. Node 4 will process only 3 regions: $\{I_{4,1}, I_{4,2}, I_{4,3}\}$ while Nodes 1, 2 and 3 each process four regions. For a better balanced system, we may subdivide some regions into more pieces but this type of "load balancing" has only a minor impact, see [7].

The strategy in $PMDQAG1_{level}$ may result in an uneven work load: there is potential for either the control node or the computational nodes to "wait" at synchronization points. For example, the computational nodes may wait when the control node runs *Selection* and takes care of the updates, see Figs. 9 and 10. On the other hand, if the subdivisions in *Sub* take much less time than the calculations in *Integrate*, the control node awaits a signal from the computational nodes.

Algorithm $PMDQAG2_{level}$ uses only collective communication directives, see Fig. 11, and the control node performs the same computations as the other processors. The control node remains in charge of network communication and is responsible for monitoring the

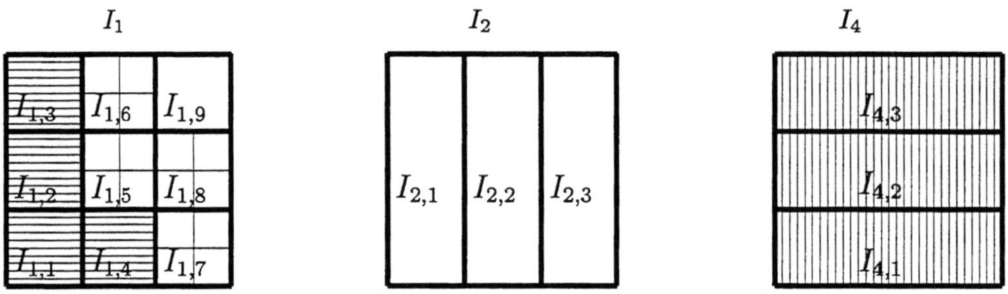

$$S = \{I_1, I_2, I_4\} \quad ND_S = \{2, 1, 1\} \quad DIR_S = \{1, 2, 1, 2\}$$

Node 1 $S_{local} = \{I_1\}$ $ND_{local} = \{2\}$ $DIR_{local} = \{1, 2\}$ $P_{local} = \{I_{1,1}, I_{1,2}, I_{1,3}, I_{1,4}\}$

Node 2 $S_{local} = \{I_1\}$ $ND_{local} = \{2\}$ $DIR_{local} = \{1, 2\}$ $P_{local} = \{I_{1,5}, I_{1,6}, I_{1,7}, I_{1,8}\}$

Node 3 $S_{local} = \{I_1, I_2\}$ $ND_{local} = \{2, 1\}$ $DIR_{local} = \{1, 2, 1\}$ $P_{local} = \{I_{1,9}, I_{2,1}, I_{2,2}, I_{2,3}\}$

Node 4 $S_{local} = \{I_4\}$ $ND_{local} = \{1\}$ $DIR_{local} = \{2\}$ $P_{local} = \{I_{4,1}, I_{4,2}, I_{4,3}\}$

FIG. 3. *Subdivision in 2D; $p = 4$ processors*

termination conditions, so we pick it to be the one with $myid = p - 1$, since in cases of uneven load balancing the processors with highest *id*'s are those that may receive slightly less work. Each processor, including the control node, stores in its local memory its subset of the subregions and all associated information. It determines in its local pool the candidates for further subdivision. They are the regions whose indices reside in the highest non-empty, *top*, level of the local $LdLEVEL$ array. All processors with $highest = max_{all\ processors}(top)$ contain subsets of the subregions for immediate further subdivision; a Gather makes these subregions available globally. Each processor determines its part of the work (in the same way as in $PMDQAG1_{level}$), performs it, and updates the error estimate $errsum$. Using Reduce, the locally held error estimates $errsum$ are accumulated in $totalerrsum$ on the control node and, depending on the size of $totalerrsum$, the algorithm proceeds or terminates. So, the load balancing algorithm is global – it relies on redistributing the work in the highest level of $LdLEVEL$ after a Gather, but the computations are almost all local. Increasing the number of processors, p, can speed up the computation, but also permits solving problems that require greater memory resources as the data structure $LdLEVEL$, which comprises the major memory requirement, is distributed dynamically over all processors.

2.2. Multidimensional Version of QAG_{sing_p}. Next, we modify $PMDQAG2_{level}$ to incorporate singularity detection and treatment in the spirit of the one-dimensional algorithm QAG_{sing_p}, see [6, 14]. Singularities are "detected" by comparing sizes of fourth differences of the integrand. Then, an attempt is made to reduce the impact of the singularity; i.e., to reduce the number of synchronizations due directly and solely to the singularity. We use a mesh graded in the directions of the singularity, the parameters α and p in Fig. 7 determine the grading and subdivision; later, with the same aim we use periodizing transformations in just these directions. The former algorithms are called here $sing_g$ to denote *graded*, in contrast to the latter named $sing_t$ to denote *transformed*. An example of graded subdivision for Fig. 1 with $p = 3$ is given in Fig. 4. Note, all subdivisions in these examples

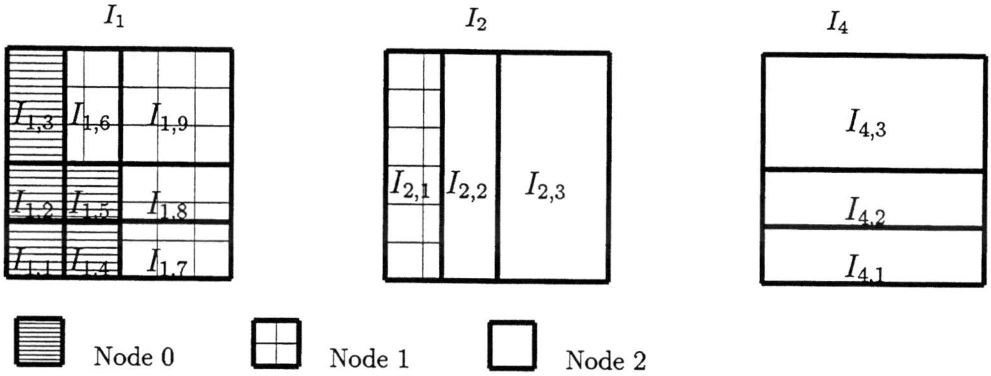

FIG. 4. *Graded subdivision in 2D; $p = 3$ processors*

are graded assuming the boundary faces are 1 and 2 for I_1, 1 for I_2 and 2 for I_3.

The multidimensional "singular" strategy is only considered if each region rn_i in the top non-empty level contains either a_j or b_j for at least one j, $j = 1, 2, \ldots, dim$, which is a direction for subdivision. If n_i is the total number of directions for subdivision for region rn_i then $j \in \{dir_{1,i}, dir_{2,i}, \ldots, dir_{n_i,i}\}$. We apply graded subdivision if one of the following conditions is satisfied:

- *strong condition*: for all regions rn_i, $1 \leq i \leq lens$, scheduled for further subdivision, all the directions for subdivision $dir_{j,i}$, $j = 1, \ldots, n_i$, determined by the fourth difference approximation, are associated with either $a_{dir_{j,i}}$ or $b_{dir_{j,i}}$. This is implemented in algorithm $PMDQAG2_{sing1_g}$;
- *weak condition*: for all regions rn_i, $1 \leq i \leq lens$, scheduled for further subdivision, at least one direction for subdivision $dir_{j,i}$, $j = 1, \ldots, n_i$, is associated with either $a_{dir_{j,i}}$ or $b_{dir_{j,i}}$. This is implemented in algorithm $PMDQAG2_{sing2_g}$.

After the *highest* non-empty level across all the processors is determined and before all regions corresponding to it are gathered, each processor checks if the singularity condition - $lstat$ (strong for $PMDQAG2_{sing1_g}$, weak for $PMDQAG2_{sing2_g}$) is satisfied on its local pool of regions for further subdivision, setting $lstat = 1$ if so, otherwise setting $lstat = 0$. The singularity condition, $stat$, for the global pool is determined using the collective operation Reduce, with *MIN* as the function over all values of the local marker, $lstat$, and is broadcast to all processors. If $stat = 0$ a regular subdivision is used, otherwise a graded subdivision toward the anticipated singularity is used. The grading is as follows:

- in all singular directions ($PMDQAG2_{sing1_g}$),
- only in the directions associated with the singular faces; subdivisions for the remaining directions are not graded ($PMDQAG2_{sing2_g}$).

2.3. Periodization in Adaptive Schemes. In [8, 14] the impact of transformations on the convergence of one-dimensional algorithms is considered. For $S_{dim} = [0,1] \times [0,1] \times \cdots \times [0,1]$, the transformation

$$\int_{S_{dim}} f(x_1, x_2, \ldots, x_{dim}) dx_{dim} \ldots dx_2 dx_1 =$$

$$\int_{S_{dim}} g'(t_1)g'(t_2)\dots g'(t_{dim})f(g(t_1), g(t_2), \dots, g(t_{dim}))dt_{dim}\dots dt_2dt_1$$

where $g'(0) = g'(1) = 0$, $g : [0,1] \to [0,1]$ reduces the power of end-point singularities; so provides an automatic approach to "improving" integrands with end-point singularities before applying an adaptive algorithm. For lattice rule algorithms, periodicity of the integrand in each dimension is a necessity and is ensured by this transformation. Of course, it is not needed for adaptive schemes. When a end-point singularity is detected, we modify the algorithm $PMDQAG2_{sing2_g}$ to $PMDQAG2_{sing2_t}$, using a regular subdivision with the above transformation in the dimensions of the singularities on the interval closest to the singularity only.

3. Parallel Implementation of Rank-1 Lattice Rules. Rank-1 lattice rules approximate the integral

$$\int_{S_{dim}} f(x_1, x_2, \dots, x_{dim})dx_{dim}\dots dx_2dx_1$$

by the sum

$$Q(f, N, z, c) = \frac{1}{N}\sum_{j=0}^{N-1} f\left(\left\{\frac{j}{N}z + c\right\}\right),$$

where $z \in S_{dim}$ is specially chosen to give accuracy in a Fourier series approximation sense, see [17] for details. They are simply adapted to any parallel environment. Because all evaluation points are known in advance, there is practically no need for communication, The algorithm's structure permits coarse grain parallelization. Our MPI version *PLattice*, is based on the sequential algorithm due to Korobov [10] as implemented in the NAG PVM library [13]. In the parallel algorithm, the sum $Q(f, N, z, c)$ should be divided into parts of size inversely proportional to the power of the processors. On a homogeneous network (for example the IBM SP2) it makes sense to choose N/p approximately equal sized parts. The vectors z must be computed for each dimension dim and each value N. For the numerical experiments reported here, computing the vectors z was a major *a priori* task; to the authors' knowledge the vectors for large N have not been computed previously [14]. The pseudo - random vector c_k is computed on the control processor but could be computed in parallel using the pseudo-random generator with the same seed on each processor, hence avoiding communication.

4. Numerical Experiments. We consider algorithms $PMDQAG1_{level}$, $PMDQAG2_{level}$, $PMDQAG2_{sing1_g}$, $PMDQAG2_{sing2_g}$, $PMDQAG2_{sing2_t}$ and *PLattice*. In the following subsections we present: the error estimation results, a one processor implementation comparison for the adaptive schemes and rank-1 lattice rule algorithms on the IBM SP2, and speedup results for adaptive and rank-1 lattice rule algorithms for a variety of numbers of processors. The experiments presented here are for $dim = 4$, with $tol = 10^{-6}, 10^{-7}$, and for $dim = 6$ with $tol = 10^{-3}, 10^{-4}$. The test integrals are:

$$(1) \qquad \int_{S_{dim}} \left(\prod_{i=1}^{dim}\left[1 + 2\pi^2\left(x_i^2 - x_i + \frac{1}{6}\right)\right]\right) dx$$

$$\int_{S_{dim}} \exp\left(-\sum_{i=1}^{dim} |x_i - w_i|\right) dx \tag{2}$$

[16, 18]; in problem (2) $w_i = \frac{1}{2}$ for $i = 1, 2, \ldots, dim$. For $dim = 6$, we also use the singular integrals

$$\int_{S_{dim}} (x_1 + x_2 + x_3)^{-2} (x_4 + x_5 + x_6)^{-2} \, dx, \tag{3}$$

$$\int_{S_{dim}} x_5 x_6 (x_1 + x_2)^{-3/2} (x_3 + x_4)^{-3/2} \, dx; \tag{4}$$

and for $dim = 4$,

$$\int_{S_{dim}} (x_1 + x_2)^{-3/2} (x_3 + x_4)^{-3/2} \, dx. \tag{5}$$

These were specially constructed to test the singularity detection strategies of the new algorithms. Since adaptive multidimensional quadrature codes do not normally include singularity detection it was necessary to construct new test problems. Note, the integrands are constructed with powers in the singular terms appropriate to the overall dimension, *dim*.

The standard polynomial periodization transformation

$$g(x) = 3x^2 - 2x^3 \tag{6}$$

is used in each dimension for the lattice method and for appropriate directions in $PMDQAG2_{sing2_t}$.

4.1. Error Estimation. To compare the quality of the adaptive strategies, and later the lattice rule algorithm, we used the true error, $e = |integral - integral\ estimate|$, in our termination criterion; i.e. we terminated immediately $e < tol$. Error estimation is a weak point for both the adaptive and lattice schemes. In both cases, the error estimates are reliable only if the test integrals are relatively simple. Often, especially for adaptive schemes, the error estimates are much larger than the true error, see Table 1 for a number of examples. Here, the popular Genz-Malik GM(7) rule [5] is used. The higher order McNamee-Stenger formulas [12] are even less efficient or reliable for our problems, and the corresponding results are not presented.

By using a number, q, of samples of the lattice rule with different "seeds" c we can compute a mean for approximating the integral and a standard deviation ε for use as an error estimate. The documentation for the NAG library version of this code recommends using values of q in the range $3 - 5$. Tables 2 - 3 present ε and the true error (the difference between the mean and the true solution) for each of $q = 3$ and $q = 5$. Observe, the errors are sometimes underestimated. We also use an iterated periodization approach (denoted It) [8] with $g(x)$ in (6) for estimating the integral ($r = 1$) and $g(x)$ iterated once to provide a second estimate of the integral for use in the error estimator ($r = 2$). Note, equally we

TABLE 1
Global error estimates; terminated when error < tol

Problem	*dim*	*tol*	PMDQAG1$_{level}$	PMDQAG2$_{level}$	$sing1_q$	$sing2_q$	$sing2_t$
(1)	6	10^{-3}	$0.46 \cdot 10^{-2}$	$0.46 \cdot 10^{-2}$	$0.46 \cdot 10^{-2}$	$0.46 \cdot 10^{-2}$	$0.46 \cdot 10^{-2}$
		10^{-4}	$0.31 \cdot 10^{-2}$	$0.31 \cdot 10^{-2}$	$0.31 \cdot 10^{-2}$	$0.31 \cdot 10^{-2}$	$0.31 \cdot 10^{-2}$
(2)	6	10^{-3}	$0.47 \cdot 10^{-2}$	$0.47 \cdot 10^{-2}$	$0.47 \cdot 10^{-2}$	$0.47 \cdot 10^{-2}$	$0.47 \cdot 10^{-2}$
		10^{-4}	$0.21 \cdot 10^{-3}$	$0.21 \cdot 10^{-3}$	$0.21 \cdot 10^{-3}$	$0.21 \cdot 10^{-3}$	$0.21 \cdot 10^{-3}$
(3)	6	10^{-3}	$0.42 \cdot 10^{-3}$	$0.42 \cdot 10^{-3}$	$0.45 \cdot 10^{-3}$	$0.44 \cdot 10^{-3}$	$0.16 \cdot 10^{-2}$
		10^{-4}	$0.12 \cdot 10^{-3}$	$0.12 \cdot 10^{-3}$	$0.12 \cdot 10^{-3}$	$0.13 \cdot 10^{-3}$	$0.47 \cdot 10^{-4}$
(4)	6	10^{-3}	$0.26 \cdot 10^{0}$	$0.26 \cdot 10^{0}$	$0.24 \cdot 10^{0}$	$0.24 \cdot 10^{0}$	$0.13 \cdot 10^{-1}$
		10^{-4}	$0.61 \cdot 10^{-1}$	$0.61 \cdot 10^{-1}$	$0.23 \cdot 10^{-1}$	$0.23 \cdot 10^{-1}$	$0.54 \cdot 10^{-2}$
(1)	4	10^{-6}	$0.20 \cdot 10^{-3}$	$0.20 \cdot 10^{-3}$	$0.20 \cdot 10^{-3}$	$0.20 \cdot 10^{-3}$	$0.20 \cdot 10^{-3}$
		10^{-7}	$0.92 \cdot 10^{-4}$	$0.92 \cdot 10^{-4}$	$0.92 \cdot 10^{-4}$	$0.92 \cdot 10^{-4}$	$0.92 \cdot 10^{-4}$
(2)	4	10^{-6}	$0.14 \cdot 10^{-5}$	$0.14 \cdot 10^{-5}$	$0.14 \cdot 10^{-5}$	$0.14 \cdot 10^{-5}$	$0.14 \cdot 10^{-5}$
		10^{-7}	$0.18 \cdot 10^{-6}$	$0.18 \cdot 10^{-6}$	$0.18 \cdot 10^{-6}$	$0.18 \cdot 10^{-6}$	$0.18 \cdot 10^{-6}$
(5)	4	10^{-6}	$0.67 \cdot 10^{-2}$	$0.67 \cdot 10^{-2}$	$0.75 \cdot 10^{-2}$	$0.61 \cdot 10^{-4}$	$0.30 \cdot 10^{-3}$
		10^{-7}	$0.63 \cdot 10^{-5}$	$0.63 \cdot 10^{-5}$	$0.15 \cdot 10^{-4}$	$0.15 \cdot 10^{-4}$	$0.69 \cdot 10^{-4}$

could have used the two estimates of the integral in the reverse order but we have no reason to believe the $r = 2$ result is more accurate than the $r = 1$ result, and so have no real justification for using these two approximations to form an error estimate. From [8, 14],

$$(\text{Cost}_{\text{with } q=5}) = \frac{5}{3}\,(\text{Cost}_{\text{with } q=3}) \approx \frac{5}{2}\,(\text{Cost of iterated algorithm}_{\text{with } r=1,2})$$

The numerical results in Tables 2 - 3 show that, generally, using $q = 5$ rather than $q = 3$ samples is not justified. The additional accuracy and slightly smaller error estimates do not justify the additional cost. The new iterated algorithm seems competitive and has a still lower cost. For problem (1), the iterated algorithm is particularly accurate. Such a fluke may occur because just one "sample" is used in computing the integral. The iterated algorithm delivers better accuracy per unit cost than the standard lattice algorithm with $q = 3$ or $q = 5$ samples for problem (1) and for the singular problems (3), (4) and (5). The accuracy delivered for problem (2) is slightly better for the standard lattice algorithm. Using more samples in the lattice rule algorithm does not guarantee a more accurate result, though usually it gives slightly better error estimates. Applying an iterated transformation gives a more accurate result at a lower cost but the error estimate is rather conservative, see the third columns of Tables 2 and 3. In our later comparisons with adaptive algorithms, we use the $q = 3$ results because they are based on an accepted approach to estimating the integral and its error.

Calculating the Korobov coefficients for values of $N > 1,000,000$, as used here, involves a significant one-time computational cost. Hence, in [17] small N rules were designed to be competitive with large N rules. Specifically, an embedded sequence of rank-1 lattice rules was used for integrating problem (1) with $dim = 6$. The results from [17] are presented in Table 4. The embedded sequence technique does not produce as much accuracy per cost as the $q = 3$ samples case, at least for problem (1). In comparing the results from Tables 2 and 4, recall that the number of integrand evaluations in Table 2 is qN and the number in Table 4 is $m(2^6 + 1)$.

Our results do not provide a firm basis for comparison of the adaptive and lattice rule

TABLE 2
PLattice (dim = 6); q = 3, 5 samples and the Iterated algorithm

Problem	N	error	ε $(q=3)$	error	ε $(q=5)$	error	error estimate (It)
(1)	2129	$0.19 \cdot 10^{-1}$	$0.54 \cdot 10^{-1}$	$0.31 \cdot 10^{-1}$	$0.43 \cdot 10^{-1}$	$0.13 \cdot 10^{-1}$	$0.38 \cdot 10^{-1}$
	5003	$0.22 \cdot 10^{-1}$	$0.40 \cdot 10^{-1}$	$0.10 \cdot 10^{-1}$	$0.34 \cdot 10^{-1}$	$0.33 \cdot 10^{0}$	$0.35 \cdot 10^{0}$
	10007	$0.87 \cdot 10^{-2}$	$0.10 \cdot 10^{-1}$	$0.20 \cdot 10^{-1}$	$0.18 \cdot 10^{-1}$	$0.28 \cdot 10^{0}$	$0.34 \cdot 10^{0}$
	20011	$0.23 \cdot 10^{-1}$	$0.73 \cdot 10^{-3}$	$0.72 \cdot 10^{-2}$	$0.12 \cdot 10^{-1}$	$0.17 \cdot 10^{-1}$	$0.21 \cdot 10^{-1}$
	40009	$0.54 \cdot 10^{-2}$	$0.48 \cdot 10^{-2}$	$0.19 \cdot 10^{-2}$	$0.74 \cdot 10^{-2}$	$0.56 \cdot 10^{-1}$	$0.44 \cdot 10^{-1}$
	80021	$0.24 \cdot 10^{-2}$	$0.96 \cdot 10^{-3}$	$0.12 \cdot 10^{-2}$	$0.15 \cdot 10^{-2}$	$0.77 \cdot 10^{-3}$	$0.27 \cdot 10^{-2}$
	160001	$0.17 \cdot 10^{-4}$	$0.11 \cdot 10^{-2}$	$0.48 \cdot 10^{-3}$	$0.52 \cdot 10^{-3}$	$0.12 \cdot 10^{-4}$	$0.16 \cdot 10^{-2}$
	320009	$0.39 \cdot 10^{-4}$	$0.44 \cdot 10^{-3}$	$0.19 \cdot 10^{-3}$	$0.18 \cdot 10^{-3}$	$0.12 \cdot 10^{-5}$	$0.53 \cdot 10^{-3}$
	640007	$0.47 \cdot 10^{-5}$	$0.10 \cdot 10^{-5}$	$0.17 \cdot 10^{-4}$	$0.69 \cdot 10^{-4}$	$0.15 \cdot 10^{-6}$	$0.33 \cdot 10^{-4}$
	1200007	$0.50 \cdot 10^{-4}$	$0.63 \cdot 10^{-4}$	$0.89 \cdot 10^{-5}$	$0.45 \cdot 10^{-4}$	$0.59 \cdot 10^{-7}$	$0.74 \cdot 10^{-4}$
(2)	2129	$0.12 \cdot 10^{-3}$	$0.17 \cdot 10^{-2}$	$0.35 \cdot 10^{-3}$	$0.95 \cdot 10^{-3}$	$0.22 \cdot 10^{-1}$	$0.20 \cdot 10^{-1}$
	5003	$0.18 \cdot 10^{-3}$	$0.29 \cdot 10^{-3}$	$0.18 \cdot 10^{-4}$	$0.36 \cdot 10^{-3}$	$0.72 \cdot 10^{-2}$	$0.76 \cdot 10^{-2}$
	10007	$0.63 \cdot 10^{-4}$	$0.63 \cdot 10^{-4}$	$0.11 \cdot 10^{-3}$	$0.85 \cdot 10^{-4}$	$0.77 \cdot 10^{-2}$	$0.76 \cdot 10^{-2}$
	20011	$0.16 \cdot 10^{-5}$	$0.29 \cdot 10^{-4}$	$0.70 \cdot 10^{-5}$	$0.37 \cdot 10^{-4}$	$0.35 \cdot 10^{-3}$	$0.37 \cdot 10^{-3}$
	40009	$0.18 \cdot 10^{-4}$	$0.51 \cdot 10^{-5}$	$0.23 \cdot 10^{-4}$	$0.10 \cdot 10^{-4}$	$0.38 \cdot 10^{-4}$	$0.41 \cdot 10^{-4}$
	80021	$0.94 \cdot 10^{-5}$	$0.74 \cdot 10^{-5}$	$0.17 \cdot 10^{-5}$	$0.98 \cdot 10^{-5}$	$0.54 \cdot 10^{-4}$	$0.60 \cdot 10^{-4}$
	160001	$0.14 \cdot 10^{-5}$	$0.14 \cdot 10^{-5}$	$0.13 \cdot 10^{-5}$	$0.95 \cdot 10^{-6}$	$0.38 \cdot 10^{-4}$	$0.37 \cdot 10^{-4}$
	320009	$0.24 \cdot 10^{-6}$	$0.48 \cdot 10^{-6}$	$0.11 \cdot 10^{-6}$	$0.40 \cdot 10^{-6}$	$0.12 \cdot 10^{-4}$	$0.12 \cdot 10^{-4}$
	640007	$0.30 \cdot 10^{-6}$	$0.15 \cdot 10^{-6}$	$0.19 \cdot 10^{-6}$	$0.12 \cdot 10^{-6}$	$0.56 \cdot 10^{-6}$	$0.73 \cdot 10^{-6}$
	1200007	$0.85 \cdot 10^{-7}$	$0.60 \cdot 10^{-7}$	$0.54 \cdot 10^{-7}$	$0.53 \cdot 10^{-7}$	$0.81 \cdot 10^{-6}$	$0.92 \cdot 10^{-6}$
(3)	2129	$0.13 \cdot 10^{-1}$	$0.25 \cdot 10^{-1}$	$0.13 \cdot 10^{-1}$	$0.15 \cdot 10^{-1}$	$0.46 \cdot 10^{-1}$	$0.81 \cdot 10^{-1}$
	5003	$0.14 \cdot 10^{-1}$	$0.30 \cdot 10^{-1}$	$0.15 \cdot 10^{-1}$	$0.61 \cdot 10^{-2}$	$0.13 \cdot 10^{-1}$	$0.12 \cdot 10^{-1}$
	10007	$0.14 \cdot 10^{-2}$	$0.18 \cdot 10^{-1}$	$0.52 \cdot 10^{-2}$	$0.45 \cdot 10^{-2}$	$0.37 \cdot 10^{-2}$	$0.30 \cdot 10^{-2}$
	20011	$0.61 \cdot 10^{-2}$	$0.15 \cdot 10^{-1}$	$0.15 \cdot 10^{-2}$	$0.35 \cdot 10^{-2}$	$0.38 \cdot 10^{-4}$	$0.61 \cdot 10^{-2}$
	40009	$0.14 \cdot 10^{-2}$	$0.99 \cdot 10^{-3}$	$0.77 \cdot 10^{-3}$	$0.34 \cdot 10^{-2}$	$0.68 \cdot 10^{-3}$	$0.63 \cdot 10^{-2}$
	80021	$0.14 \cdot 10^{-2}$	$0.18 \cdot 10^{-2}$	$0.77 \cdot 10^{-6}$	$0.20 \cdot 10^{-2}$	$0.17 \cdot 10^{-2}$	$0.26 \cdot 10^{-2}$
	160001	$0.22 \cdot 10^{-2}$	$0.68 \cdot 10^{-2}$	$0.72 \cdot 10^{-3}$	$0.25 \cdot 10^{-2}$	$0.44 \cdot 10^{-3}$	$0.23 \cdot 10^{-2}$
	320009	$0.22 \cdot 10^{-2}$	$0.12 \cdot 10^{-2}$	$0.14 \cdot 10^{-3}$	$0.11 \cdot 10^{-2}$	$0.27 \cdot 10^{-3}$	$0.22 \cdot 10^{-3}$
	640007	$0.23 \cdot 10^{-3}$	$0.13 \cdot 10^{-2}$	$0.11 \cdot 10^{-2}$	$0.83 \cdot 10^{-3}$	$0.47 \cdot 10^{-4}$	$0.11 \cdot 10^{-2}$
	1200007	$0.77 \cdot 10^{-3}$	$0.78 \cdot 10^{-3}$	$0.61 \cdot 10^{-4}$	$0.45 \cdot 10^{-3}$	$0.45 \cdot 10^{-4}$	$0.14 \cdot 10^{-2}$
(4)	2129	$0.11 \cdot 10^{0}$	$0.34 \cdot 10^{-1}$	$0.83 \cdot 10^{-1}$	$0.35 \cdot 10^{-1}$	$0.18 \cdot 10^{-1}$	$0.85 \cdot 10^{-1}$
	5003	$0.19 \cdot 10^{0}$	$0.85 \cdot 10^{-1}$	$0.36 \cdot 10^{-1}$	$0.69 \cdot 10^{-1}$	$0.55 \cdot 10^{-1}$	$0.12 \cdot 10^{0}$
	10007	$0.78 \cdot 10^{0}$	$0.83 \cdot 10^{0}$	$0.47 \cdot 10^{-1}$	$0.25 \cdot 10^{-1}$	$0.67 \cdot 10^{-1}$	$0.44 \cdot 10^{-1}$
	20011	$0.50 \cdot 10^{-1}$	$0.29 \cdot 10^{-1}$	$0.74 \cdot 10^{-1}$	$0.90 \cdot 10^{-1}$	$0.16 \cdot 10^{-1}$	$0.36 \cdot 10^{-2}$
	40009	$0.25 \cdot 10^{-1}$	$0.21 \cdot 10^{-1}$	$0.20 \cdot 10^{-1}$	$0.21 \cdot 10^{-1}$	$0.67 \cdot 10^{-2}$	$0.65 \cdot 10^{-1}$
	80021	$0.43 \cdot 10^{-3}$	$0.61 \cdot 10^{-2}$	$0.76 \cdot 10^{-1}$	$0.81 \cdot 10^{-1}$	$0.33 \cdot 10^{-2}$	$0.33 \cdot 10^{-1}$
	160001	$0.12 \cdot 10^{-1}$	$0.42 \cdot 10^{-2}$	$0.48 \cdot 10^{-2}$	$0.22 \cdot 10^{-1}$	$0.52 \cdot 10^{-2}$	$0.64 \cdot 10^{-2}$
	320009	$0.17 \cdot 10^{-1}$	$0.74 \cdot 10^{-2}$	$0.80 \cdot 10^{-2}$	$0.43 \cdot 10^{-2}$	$0.11 \cdot 10^{-2}$	$0.17 \cdot 10^{-1}$
	640007	$0.15 \cdot 10^{-1}$	$0.58 \cdot 10^{-2}$	$0.44 \cdot 10^{-1}$	$0.46 \cdot 10^{-1}$	$0.12 \cdot 10^{-2}$	$0.10 \cdot 10^{-1}$
	1200007	$0.37 \cdot 10^{-2}$	$0.57 \cdot 10^{-2}$	$0.34 \cdot 10^{-2}$	$0.61 \cdot 10^{-2}$	$0.17 \cdot 10^{-2}$	$0.26 \cdot 10^{-2}$

TABLE 3

PLattice (dim = 4); q = 3, 5 samples and the Iterated algorithm

Problem	N	error	$\varepsilon\ (q=3)$	error	$\varepsilon\ (q=5)$	error	error estimate (It)
(1)	2129	$0.48 \cdot 10^{-2}$	$0.33 \cdot 10^{-2}$	$0.84 \cdot 10^{-2}$	$0.29 \cdot 10^{-2}$	$0.91 \cdot 10^{-3}$	$0.24 \cdot 10^{-2}$
	5003	$0.39 \cdot 10^{-2}$	$0.85 \cdot 10^{-3}$	$0.30 \cdot 10^{-2}$	$0.14 \cdot 10^{-2}$	$0.10 \cdot 10^{-2}$	$0.73 \cdot 10^{-2}$
	10007	$0.10 \cdot 10^{-3}$	$0.20 \cdot 10^{-3}$	$0.19 \cdot 10^{-3}$	$0.31 \cdot 10^{-3}$	$0.18 \cdot 10^{-6}$	$0.65 \cdot 10^{-3}$
	20011	$0.52 \cdot 10^{-4}$	$0.16 \cdot 10^{-3}$	$0.17 \cdot 10^{-4}$	$0.11 \cdot 10^{-3}$	$0.19 \cdot 10^{-5}$	$0.24 \cdot 10^{-3}$
	40009	$0.78 \cdot 10^{-4}$	$0.59 \cdot 10^{-4}$	$0.25 \cdot 10^{-4}$	$0.38 \cdot 10^{-4}$	$0.33 \cdot 10^{-7}$	$0.58 \cdot 10^{-4}$
	80021	$0.90 \cdot 10^{-5}$	$0.29 \cdot 10^{-4}$	$0.12 \cdot 10^{-5}$	$0.21 \cdot 10^{-4}$	$0.11 \cdot 10^{-6}$	$0.77 \cdot 10^{-4}$
	160001	$0.46 \cdot 10^{-5}$	$0.37 \cdot 10^{-5}$	$0.36 \cdot 10^{-5}$	$0.32 \cdot 10^{-5}$	$0.26 \cdot 10^{-9}$	$0.99 \cdot 10^{-5}$
	320009	$0.83 \cdot 10^{-6}$	$0.98 \cdot 10^{-6}$	$0.18 \cdot 10^{-5}$	$0.11 \cdot 10^{-5}$	$0.26 \cdot 10^{-10}$	$0.46 \cdot 10^{-5}$
	640007	$0.64 \cdot 10^{-6}$	$0.58 \cdot 10^{-6}$	$0.13 \cdot 10^{-5}$	$0.49 \cdot 10^{-6}$	$0.10 \cdot 10^{-10}$	$0.30 \cdot 10^{-5}$
	1200007	$0.68 \cdot 10^{-6}$	$0.33 \cdot 10^{-7}$	$0.31 \cdot 10^{-6}$	$0.28 \cdot 10^{-6}$	$0.43 \cdot 10^{-11}$	$0.32 \cdot 10^{-7}$
(2)	2129	$0.81 \cdot 10^{-5}$	$0.12 \cdot 10^{-3}$	$0.56 \cdot 10^{-4}$	$0.97 \cdot 10^{-4}$	$0.40 \cdot 10^{-3}$	$0.49 \cdot 10^{-3}$
	5003	$0.19 \cdot 10^{-4}$	$0.21 \cdot 10^{-4}$	$0.27 \cdot 10^{-4}$	$0.84 \cdot 10^{-5}$	$0.58 \cdot 10^{-3}$	$0.62 \cdot 10^{-3}$
	10007	$0.46 \cdot 10^{-5}$	$0.47 \cdot 10^{-5}$	$0.52 \cdot 10^{-6}$	$0.32 \cdot 10^{-5}$	$0.35 \cdot 10^{-4}$	$0.46 \cdot 10^{-4}$
	20011	$0.13 \cdot 10^{-5}$	$0.78 \cdot 10^{-5}$	$0.26 \cdot 10^{-6}$	$0.25 \cdot 10^{-6}$	$0.80 \cdot 10^{-5}$	$0.26 \cdot 10^{-5}$
	40009	$0.81 \cdot 10^{-6}$	$0.56 \cdot 10^{-6}$	$0.65 \cdot 10^{-6}$	$0.50 \cdot 10^{-6}$	$0.10 \cdot 10^{-5}$	$0.13 \cdot 10^{-5}$
	80021	$0.18 \cdot 10^{-6}$	$0.11 \cdot 10^{-6}$	$0.28 \cdot 10^{-6}$	$0.16 \cdot 10^{-6}$	$0.90 \cdot 10^{-6}$	$0.18 \cdot 10^{-6}$
	160001	$0.91 \cdot 10^{-8}$	$0.68 \cdot 10^{-7}$	$0.50 \cdot 10^{-7}$	$0.46 \cdot 10^{-7}$	$0.57 \cdot 10^{-6}$	$0.68 \cdot 10^{-6}$
	320009	$0.11 \cdot 10^{-7}$	$0.0 \cdot 10^{0}$	$0.61 \cdot 10^{-8}$	$0.0 \cdot 10^{0}$	$0.25 \cdot 10^{-6}$	$0.22 \cdot 10^{-6}$
	640007	$0.27 \cdot 10^{-8}$	$0.34 \cdot 10^{-7}$	$0.54 \cdot 10^{-8}$	$0.0 \cdot 10^{0}$	$0.46 \cdot 10^{-7}$	$0.48 \cdot 10^{-7}$
	1200007	$0.34 \cdot 10^{-8}$	$0.34 \cdot 10^{-7}$	$0.12 \cdot 10^{-8}$	$0.27 \cdot 10^{-7}$	$0.38 \cdot 10^{-8}$	$0.40 \cdot 10^{-8}$
(5)	2129	$0.11 \cdot 10^{1}$	$0.11 \cdot 10^{1}$	$0.69 \cdot 10^{0}$	$0.69 \cdot 10^{0}$	$0.68 \cdot 10^{-1}$	$0.27 \cdot 10^{0}$
	5003	$0.76 \cdot 10^{-1}$	$0.20 \cdot 10^{0}$	$0.20 \cdot 10^{0}$	$0.14 \cdot 10^{0}$	$0.71 \cdot 10^{-1}$	$0.22 \cdot 10^{0}$
	10007	$0.91 \cdot 10^{-2}$	$0.14 \cdot 10^{0}$	$0.10 \cdot 10^{0}$	$0.77 \cdot 10^{-1}$	$0.13 \cdot 10^{-1}$	$0.56 \cdot 10^{-2}$
	20011	$0.24 \cdot 10^{-1}$	$0.39 \cdot 10^{-1}$	$0.49 \cdot 10^{-1}$	$0.49 \cdot 10^{-1}$	$0.16 \cdot 10^{-1}$	$0.57 \cdot 10^{-1}$
	40009	$0.99 \cdot 10^{-1}$	$0.44 \cdot 10^{-1}$	$0.12 \cdot 10^{-1}$	$0.46 \cdot 10^{-1}$	$0.21 \cdot 10^{-2}$	$0.63 \cdot 10^{-1}$
	80021	$0.72 \cdot 10^{-1}$	$0.27 \cdot 10^{-1}$	$0.16 \cdot 10^{0}$	$0.42 \cdot 10^{-1}$	$0.20 \cdot 10^{-2}$	$0.10 \cdot 10^{0}$
	160001	$0.35 \cdot 10^{-2}$	$0.19 \cdot 10^{-1}$	$0.40 \cdot 10^{-1}$	$0.26 \cdot 10^{-1}$	$0.25 \cdot 10^{-3}$	$0.74 \cdot 10^{-1}$
	320009	$0.24 \cdot 10^{-1}$	$0.16 \cdot 10^{-1}$	$0.12 \cdot 10^{-1}$	$0.28 \cdot 10^{-1}$	$0.12 \cdot 10^{-2}$	$0.81 \cdot 10^{-1}$
	640007	$0.22 \cdot 10^{-1}$	$0.93 \cdot 10^{-2}$	$0.96 \cdot 10^{-2}$	$0.19 \cdot 10^{-1}$	$0.62 \cdot 10^{-3}$	$0.21 \cdot 10^{-1}$
	1200007	$0.37 \cdot 10^{-1}$	$0.22 \cdot 10^{-1}$	$0.42 \cdot 10^{-2}$	$0.11 \cdot 10^{-1}$	$0.27 \cdot 10^{-4}$	$0.45 \cdot 10^{-1}$

TABLE 4

Problem (1) (dim = 6); embedded sequence of rank-1 lattice rules, m points

TABLE 4

Problem (1) (dim = 6); embedded sequence of rank-1 lattice rules, m points

m	$2^6 m$	error	error estimate
79	5056	$0.28 \cdot 10^{0}$	$0.59 \cdot 10^{0}$
157	10048	$0.13 \cdot 10^{0}$	$0.30 \cdot 10^{0}$
313	20032	$0.51 \cdot 10^{-1}$	$0.13 \cdot 10^{0}$
619	39616	$0.23 \cdot 10^{-1}$	$0.61 \cdot 10^{0}$
1249	79936	$0.95 \cdot 10^{-2}$	$0.26 \cdot 10^{-1}$
2503	160192	$0.37 \cdot 10^{-2}$	$0.11 \cdot 10^{-2}$
5003	320192	$0.14 \cdot 10^{-2}$	$0.41 \cdot 10^{-2}$

TABLE 5
Adaptive algorithms: subregions/stages

Problem	tol	$PMDQAG1_{level}$	$PMDQAG2_{level}$	$singl_g$	$sing2_g$	$sing2_t$
(1) $dim = 6$	10^{-3}	167277/6	167277/6	167277/6	167277/6	167277/6
	10^{-4}	278741/9	278741/9	278741/9	278741/9	278741/9
(2) $dim = 6$	10^{-3}	51873/5	51873/5	51873/5	51873/5	51873/5
	10^{-4}	209937/6	209937/6	209937/6	209937/6	209937/6
(3) $dim = 6$	10^{-3}	58605/9	58605/9	55989/9	55313/9	33419/22
	10^{-4}	224485/12	224485/12	223813/9	205737/9	161997/30
(4) $dim = 6$	10^{-3}	6281/5	6281/5	5625/5	5625/5	22069/32
	10^{-4}	18377/7	18377/7	22265/10	22265/10	25271/33
(1) $dim = 4$	10^{-6}	18877/7	18877/7	18877/7	18877/7	18877/7
	10^{-7}	76157/9	76157/9	76157/9	76157/9	76157/9
(2) $dim = 4$	10^{-6}	18321/8	18321/8	18321/8	18321/8	18321/8
	10^{-7}	28017/9	28017/9	28017/9	28017/9	28017/9
(5) $dim = 4$	10^{-6}	26545/13	26545/13	25105/12	137049/25	54673/44
	10^{-7}	354801/34	354801/34	353081/30	341017/29	141587/46

algorithms as the error estimation is not reliable in either case, and the aims of the two algorithms are not strictly comparable. There follow some cautious observations based on Tables 1 and 5 for the adaptive algorithms and Tables 2 and 3 for the lattice algorithms. When using Table 5 the number of integrand evaluations is $2^{dim} + 2 \cdot dim^2 + 2 \cdot dim + 1$ times the number of subregions whereas when using Tables 2 and 3 the number of integrand evaluations for $q = 3$, $q = 5$ and the iterated algorithm is 3, 5 and 2 times N, respectively. What is most notable about the results both from the adaptive algorithms and the lattice rule algorithms is that there are a large number of outliers, i.e., unreliable computations. Those we have analyzed seem to be associated with poor error estimation. Generally, the lattice rules perform well when dim is large and the problem is smooth and the adaptive rules perform better for lower values of dim and when there are singularities. However, the failure of of the lattice rules to deliver the accuracies requested for some problems for any value of N for which we have the "seed" vector $\boldsymbol{z}$ and for any strategy makes a direct and fair comparison impossible

4.2. One processor experiments on the ANL SP2. We consider efficiency for one processor implementations for $dim = 4, 6$. In Tables 5-7, we compare the performance of the adaptive schemes and the effectiveness of the singularity detection and treatment strategies.

From Tables 5-7, applying singularity detection and reduction influences performance for the singular problems (3), (4) and (5). It can either improve or, even, slow down convergence. For the singular problem (3) with $dim = 6$ and $tol = 10^{-3}$, the graded singularity reduction strategies in $PMDQAG2_{sing1_g}$ and $PMDQAG2_{sing2_g}$ have little impact on one processor performance; these algorithms are only slightly faster than $PMDQAG2_{level}$. In contrast, the periodization strategy for singularity reduction $PMDQAG2_{sing2_t}$ is much faster. For the same problem with $dim = 6$ and $tol = 10^{-4}$, $PMDQAG2_{sing2_g}$ and $PMDQAG2_{sing2_t}$ are faster than $PMDQAG2_{level}$.

For problem (5) with $dim = 4$ and $tol = 10^{-6}$, algorithms $PMDQAG2_{level}$ and $PMDQAG2_{sing1_g}$ behave similarly. Singularity detection - the weak condition - has a

TABLE 6
Lattice algorithm ($q = 3$): execution time (seconds)

N	(1) $dim = 6$	(2) $dim = 6$	(3) $dim = 6$	(4) $dim = 6$	(1) $dim = 4$	(2) $dim = 4$	(5) $dim = 4$
2129	0.16	0.17	0.19	0.26	0.11	0.12	0.14
5003	0.32	0.40	0.37	0.37	0.22	0.28	0.29
10007	0.64	0.80	0.74	0.74	0.44	0.55	0.57
20011	1.27	1.60	1.47	1.48	0.88	1.10	1.14
40009	2.53	3.17	2.94	2.95	1.75	2.19	2.26
80021	5.06	6.35	5.90	5.90	3.55	4.37	4.53
160001	10.16	12.69	11.73	11.80	7.00	8.74	9.05
320009	20.23	25.41	23.46	23.60	14.00	17.50	18.13
640007	40.50	50.78	46.97	47.26	28.00	34.96	36.20
1200007	75.88	95.23	88.46	88.57	52.48	66.24	68.38

TABLE 7
Adaptive algorithms: execution times (seconds)

Problem	tol	PMDQAG2$_{level}$	$sing1_g$	$sing2_g$	$sing2_t$
(1) $dim = 6$	10^{-3}	140.17	140.25	142.3	140.34
	10^{-4}	233.46	233.2	237.13	233.72
(2) $dim = 6$	10^{-3}	91.61	91.65	92.22	91.74
	10^{-4}	407.44	406.82	409.57	407.10
(3) $dim = 6$	10^{-3}	78.78	75.43	75.14	53.66
	10^{-4}	301.02	300.32	277.88	251.56
(4) $dim = 6$	10^{-3}	9.10	8.16	8.23	48.35
	10^{-4}	27.30	33.36	33.57	56.67
(1) $dim = 4$	10^{-6}	5.50	5.50	5.66	5.56
	10^{-7}	22.43	22.32	22.97	22.45
(2) $dim = 4$	10^{-6}	11.53	11.53	11.74	11.58
	10^{-7}	17.77	17.81	18.13	17.80
(5) $dim = 4$	10^{-6}	14.69	13.91	76.69	37.09
	10^{-7}	195.83	194.63	191.40	86.62

catastrophic effect on the number of regions created for $PMDQAG2_{sing2_g}$. For $tol = 10^{-7}$, $PMDQAG2_{sing2_g}$ performs better and a significant reduction in computing time is observed for $PMDQAG2_{sing2_t}$ (in comparison with the other algorithms). Changing $tol = 10^{-6}$ to $tol = 10^{-7}$, increases the number of subregions for $PMDQAG1_{level}$, $PMDQAG2_{level}$ and $PMDQAG2_{sing1_g}$ by more than a factor of ten and the number of stages (executions of the do while loop) by nearly a factor of three.

For simple integrands at $dim = 6$, the lattice rule algorithms are much more efficient than the adaptive algorithm, see Tables 6 and 7. To achieve the accuracy $tol = 10^{-4}$ for problem (1) only takes 10.16 seconds while the adaptive scheme takes 233 seconds. Similarly for problem (2) takes only 0.80 seconds for the lattice algorithm and over 407 seconds for the adaptive scheme. For harder (singular) problems, the adaptive algorithms are often more efficient than the lattice schemes and in some cases the latter do not return enough accuracy to be used in a comparison.

The adaptive schemes are more effective for $dim = 4$. For problem (1) with $dim = 4$ the adaptive schemes take 5.6 seconds to achieve accuracy $tol = 10^{-6}$. For the lattice rule algorithm with $q = 3$ this accuracy is obtained in 20.23 seconds. This anomalous timing for the lattice rule algorithm is due to the cost of periodization, which is non-negligible if the integrand evaluations are inexpensive. For $tol = 10^{-7}$ it takes the adaptive schemes about 23 seconds. Accuracy of $tol = 10^{-7}$ is not achieved for any lattice scheme with $q = 3$. For problem (5) with $dim = 4$, accuracy $tol = 10^{-6}$ is not achieved for the lattice rule algorithm (the best achieved is $0.27 \cdot 10^{-4}$ for the iterated algorithm) and this problem is inexpensive for the adaptive schemes at 14 - 77 seconds. For problem (5), an accuracy $tol = 10^{-7}$ is achieved for the adaptive schemes in 87 - 195 seconds. Lattice rule algorithms perform very well for some problems for $dim = 4$. For problem (2) with $dim = 4$, an accuracy $tol = 10^{-6}$ is achieved in 1.75 seconds for the lattice rule with $q = 3$ and in 11.5 seconds for the adaptive schemes. Similarly an accuracy $tol = 10^{-7}$ is achieved in 8.74 seconds for the lattice rule, in comparison with 18 seconds for the adaptive schemes.

4.3. Speedup on the ANL SP2. For multiprocessor implementations, we anticipate linear speedups for the lattice rule algorithms for all integrands and all dimensions because they use almost no communication and only collective operations. Table 10 shows execution times for problem (3) for $dim = 4$ and problem (5) for $dim = 6$ using $q = 3$. As anticipated, we achieve linear speedups in both cases.

For the various adaptive algorithms Tables 8 and 9 present timings, and Figs. 5 and 6 present relative speedups. It is tempting to "join the points" in these graphs to predict behavior for other numbers of processors but that could be misleading; the numbers p of processors used was always an integer factor of the total number available and the configuration of these processors was not under our control. The values shown were, however, consistent over a number of "runs". Because these speedups are relative, they are sometimes deceptive, especially for $PMDQAG2_{sing2_t}$ which seems not to speed up significantly as p increases but which is faster than the other algorithms for many problems for the base calculation with $p = 1$. Except for problem (5) with $tol = 10^{-6}$, when the relative speedups would be misleadingly favorable, $PMDQAG2_{sing2_g}$ is over five time slower for $p = 1$ and less than two times slower for $p = 64$ than $PMDQAG2_{level}$ or $PMDQAG2_{sing1_g}$, the relative speedups are similar to those for algorithm $PMDQAG2_{sing1_g}$. Good speedups can be achieved for p relatively large; close to linear for up to $p = 16$ processors. Speedups are better when more subregions and less stages are needed. Then, we have less synchronization points and less, but longer, communications. This is reflected in the poor performance for a larger number of processors of $PMDQAG2_{sing2_t}$ for singular problems, where the number of stages is significantly larger (and so the communications are more frequent) than for other schemes. In general, higher speedups are achieved for smaller tolerances. For example, for $dim = 6$ and for 64 processors higher speedups are achieved for $tol = 10^{-4}$ than for $tol = 10^{-3}$. For problem (5) with $dim = 4$ and $tol = 10^{-7}$, we observe much better speedups than for $tol = 10^{-6}$. The strategy in $PMDQAG1_{level}$ is an exception: for problems (1) and (4) for $dim = 6$, the speedups are better for $tol = 10^{-3}$ than for $tol = 10^{-4}$. When the number of subregions and stages is small, as for problems (1) and (2) with $dim = 4$, (5) with $tol = 10^{-6}$ and $dim = 4$, and (4) with $tol = 10^{-3}$ and $dim = 6$, the cost of interprocessor communication for $PMDQAG1_{level}$ is low relative to the expense of the integrand evaluations and then this strategy is the most efficient.

TABLE 8
Adaptive algorithms: execution times (seconds) dim = 6

Problem	p	PMDQAG1$_{level}$	PMDQAG2$_{level}$	$sing1_g$	$sing2_g$	$sing2_t$
(1)	1		140.17	140.25	142.3	140.34
$tol = 10^{-3}$	2	148.83	70.18	70.27	71.24	70.31
	4	49.68	35.26	35.33	35.84	35.48
	8	24.16	17.93	18.86	18.17	17.89
	16	16.48	9.24	9.23	9.41	9.22
	32	13.67	5.23	5.11	5.19	5.08
	64	11.56	7.86	7.60	7.47	7.60
(1)	1		233.46	233.2	237.13	233.72
$tol = 10^{-4}$	2	242.43	117.20	117.18	118.78	118.19
	4	83.08	59.49	58.84	59.64	58.84
	8	38.05	32.01	30.88	30.19	31.83
	16	22.70	16.85	18.31	15.57	17.25
	32	27.54	15.9	16.00	13.89	14.65
	64	23.69	6.83	6.11	6.58	6.78
(2)	1		91.61	91.65	92.22	91.74
$tol = 10^{-3}$	2	94.52	45.89	45.92	46.24	45.99
	4	32.21	23.18	23.11	23.28	23.17
	8	14.70	11.70	14.06	11.80	11.74
	16	12.56	8.17	10.87	11.09	10.27
	32	6.94	3.42	3.44	3.53	3.46
	64	3.90	2.97	2.69	2.69	2.78
(2)	1		407.44	406.82	409.57	407.10
$tol = 10^{-4}$	2	419.67	204.22	204.86	205.34	204.20
	4	141.61	104.38	102.65	105.15	102.73
	8	62.38	54.10	57.25	53.95	52.03
	16	32.62	26.77	30.32	30.65	30.86
	32	33.24	28.79	26.79	26.81	27.04
	64	17.30	9.04	8.67	8.89	8.82
(3)	1		78.78	75.43	75.14	53.66
$tol = 10^{-3}$	2	82.62	39.55	37.89	37.68	27.27
	4	27.66	21.26	19.08	18.98	13.93
	8	14.24	10.13	12.25	9.69	7.75
	16	6.42	5.47	5.38	5.31	4.84
	32	3.78	3.33	3.25	3.23	3.03
	64	4.99	3.03	3.87	3.77	3.66
(3)	1		301.02	300.32	277.88	251.56
$tol = 10^{-4}$	2	314.35	150.70	150.38	139.09	125.98
	4	107.35	82.02	76.86	69.74	67.69
	8	49.71	38.07	37.97	36.38	34.86
	16	24.73	23.18	19.39	17.95	20.21
	32	16.09	13.73	10.70	11.51	12.23
	64	16.05	9.54	9.00	10.00	13.60
(4)	1		9.10	8.16	8.23	48.35
$tol = 10^{-3}$	2	9.16	4.58	4.12	4.14	24.99
	4	3.47	2.35	2.11	2.18	12.99
	8	1.51	1.27	1.19	1.15	7.30
	16	0.70	0.80	0.74	0.73	4.87
	32	0.43	0.75	0.68	0.67	4.94
	64	0.34	0.96	0.96	0.93	7.04
(4)	1		27.30	33.36	33.57	56.67
$tol = 10^{-4}$	2	29.62	13.88	16.81	16.94	29.06
	4	10.24	6.96	8.54	10.24	15.31
	8	4.83	3.69	4.46	4.56	8.27
	16	2.14	2.07	2.62	2.62	5.48
	32	1.27	1.56	2.04	2.05	4.29
	64	1.26	1.72	2.40	2.40	4.58

TABLE 9
Adaptive algorithms: execution times (seconds) (dim = 4)

Problem	p	PMDQAG1$_{level}$	PMDQAG2$_{level}$	$sing1_g$	$sing2_g$	$sing2_t$
(1)	1		5.50	5.50	5.66	5.56
$tol = 10^{-6}$	2	6.15	2.80	2.85	2.89	2.85
	4	4.44	1.47	1.51	1.52	1.51
	8	1.60	0.85	0.86	0.87	0.88
	16	0.65	0.61	0.61	0.63	0.63
	32	0.50	0.69	0.68	0.67	0.68
	64	0.55	1.10	1.01	1.07	1.04
(1)	1		22.43	22.32	22.97	22.45
$tol = 10^{-7}$	2	23.89	11.26	11.29	11.61	11.30
	4	8.57	5.77	5.78	5.96	5.92
	8	4.60	3.09	3.17	3.23	3.18
	16	2.44	1.91	1.88	1.92	1.88
	32	1.77	1.47	1.48	1.55	1.54
	64	1.24	1.80	1.83	1.83	1.83
(2)	1		11.53	11.53	11.74	11.58
$tol = 10^{-6}$	2	12.66	5.85	5.88	5.99	5.88
	4	4.23	3.03	3.03	3.14	3.05
	8	2.15	1.69	1.68	1.71	1.75
	16	1.17	1.18	1.15	1.12	1.24
	32	0.84	1.01	1.05	1.03	1.02
	64	0.73	1.38	1.33	1.41	1.35
(2)	1		17.77	17.81	18.13	17.80
$tol = 10^{-7}$	2	19.44	9.00	9.04	9.01	9.10
	4	6.54	4.68	4.66	4.80	4.69
	8	3.75	2.55	2.54	2.61	2.64
	16	1.79	1.61	1.66	1.66	1.65
	32	1.25	1.36	1.38	1.39	1.35
	64	1.06	1.79	1.67	1.72	1.64
(5)	1		14.69	13.91	76.69	37.09
$tol = 10^{-6}$	2	16.81	7.42	7.01	39.28	18.86
	4	5.47	3.82	4.13	19.65	10.11
	8	2.69	2.12	3.41	15.72	6.11
	16	1.52	1.45	1.32	5.94	4.21
	32	1.61	1.47	1.31	4.63	6.53
	64	2.17	2.21	3.84	5.23	7.72
(5)	1		195.83	194.63	191.40	86.62
$tol = 10^{-7}$	2	209.51	98.26	97.70	98.50	44.09
	4	72.21	50.80	49.36	48.54	22.41
	8	35.22	25.90	26.05	25.28	12.50
	16	22.50	14.11	13.85	13.60	7.73
	32	14.08	10.55	8.80	8.78	6.62
	64	11.37	9.13	9.43	10.00	11.00

TABLE 4.10
Lattice rule algorithm: Execution times (seconds) ($q = 3$)

Problem	p	$N = 2129$	$N = 80021$	$N = 1200007$
(4.3) $dim = 6$	1	0.19	5.90	88.46
	2	0.091	2.95	44.25
	4	0.055	1.47	22.83
	8	0.023	0.77	11.06
	16	0.011	0.37	5.53
	32	0.0056	0.18	2.76
	64	0.0029	0.09	1.38
(4.5) $dim = 4$	1	0.14	4.56	68.38
	2	0.091	2.28	34.24
	4	0.051	1.14	17.08
	8	0.026	0.57	8.50
	16	0.012	0.28	4.27
	32	0.0041	0.14	2.13
	64	0.0022	0.072	1.09

5. Conclusions. We have developed a number of algorithms for parallel adaptive multidimensional numerical integration for distributed memory machines. A major problem for these algorithms and for the lattice rule algorithms is the inadequacy of the error estimators. If we assume that, in the future, we will be able to find accurate error estimators then in the context of using such estimators, our experiments, based on terminating on size of the true errors, lead to the following conclusions. The one processor implementations of the adaptive schemes are competitive with the lattice rule algorithms for singular problems for high dimensions and superior for singular problems in lower dimensions. They are also competitive with lattice rule algorithms for "relatively" smooth problems in lower dimensions. As anticipated, lattice rule algorithms are significantly more efficient for smooth integrands in higher dimensions and achieve close to linear speedups in multiprocessor implementations. Parallelism on the IBM SP2, a truly distributed machine, is exploitable for adaptive schemes but massive parallelism is not needed. There is insufficient work for many processors, especially if the integrands are inexpensive to evaluate; i.e., the cost of subdividing and distributing the work exceeds the cost of performing it for moderate numbers of processors. Clearly, the performance of the adaptive algorithms will improve for more exp ensive integrands as will the performance of the lattice rule algorithms as the overhead of periodization will be relatively less significant.

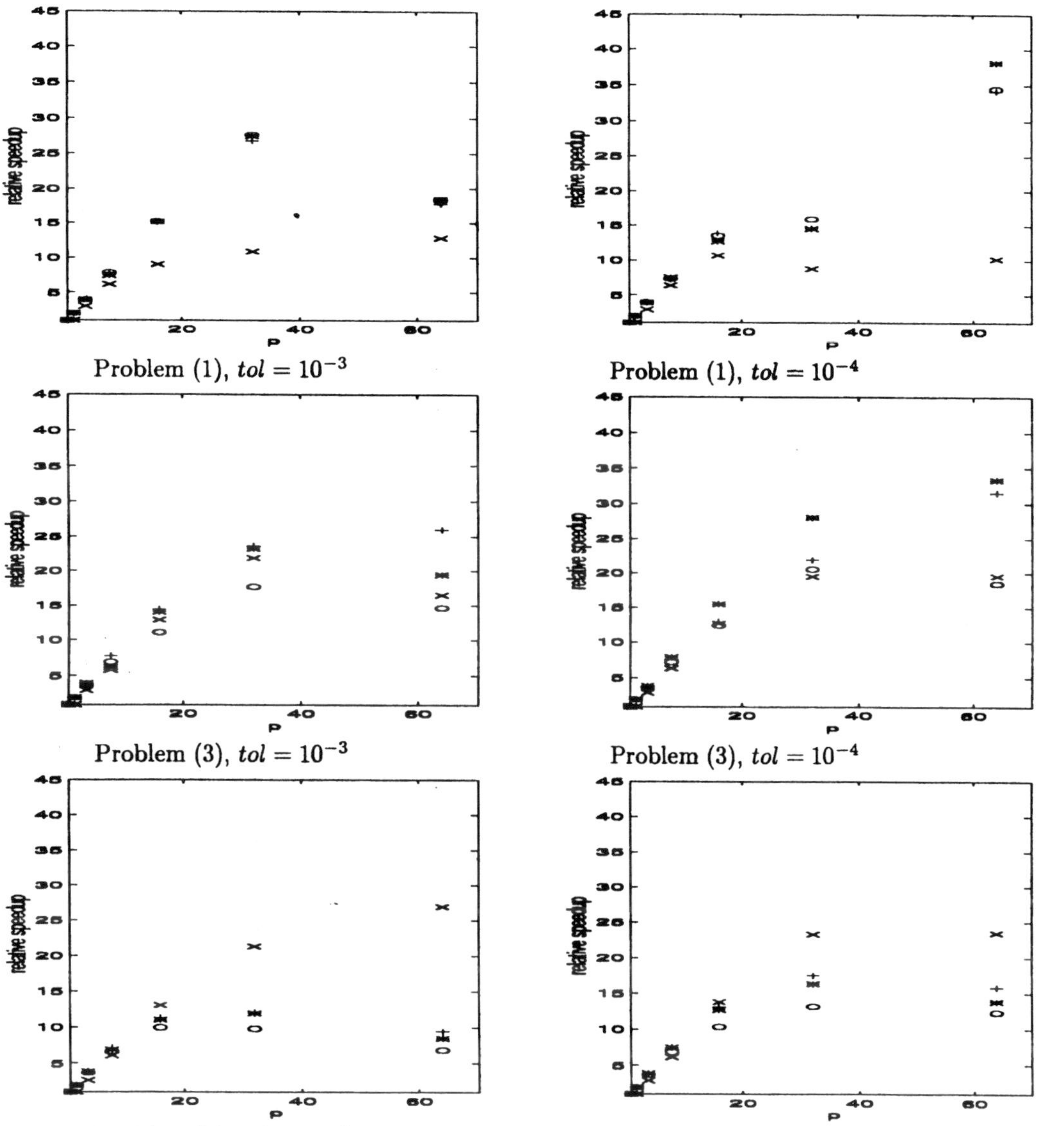

x x x x *PMDQAG1*$_{level}$ + + + + *PMDQAG2*$_{level}$ * * * * *PMDQAG2*$_{sing1_g}$ o o o o *PMDQAG2*$_{sing2_t}$

FIG. 5. *Adaptive algorithms: Relative speedups (dim = 6)*

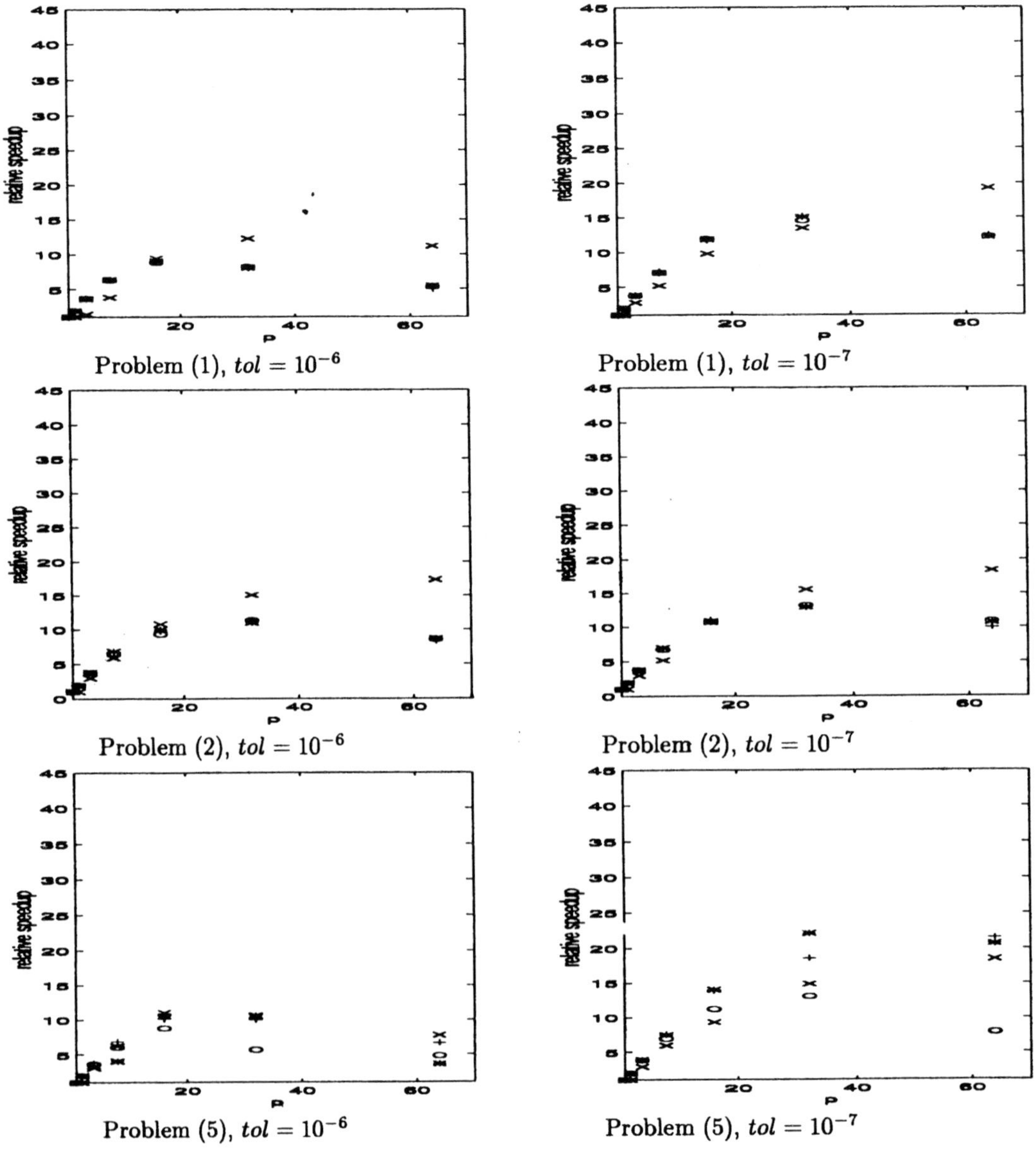

x x x x $PMDQAG1_{level}$ + + + + $PMDQAG2_{level}$ * * * * $PMDQAG2_{singl_g}$ o o o o $PMDQAG2_{sing2_l}$

FIG. 6. *Adaptive algorithms: Relative speedups (dim = 4)*

REFERENCES

[1] Bull, J.M. and Freeman, T.L., *Parallel Globally Adaptive Quadrature on the KSR1*, Advances in Computational Mathematics, 2 (1994), pp. 357-373.

[2] Bull, J.M., Freeman, T.L. and Gladwell, I., *Parallel Quadrature Algorithms for Singular Integrals*, in Proc. IMACS 14th World Congress, Atlanta, (1994), pp. 1136-1139.

[3] Bull, J.M. and Freeman, T.L., *A Comparison of Parallel Algorithms for Multi-dimensional Integration*, in Proc. 8th SIAM Conference of Parallel Processing for Scientific Computation, SIAM, Philadelphia, (1997).

[4] Bull, J.M. and Freeman, T.L., *Parallel Algorithms for Multi-dimensional Integration*, in this issue.

[5] Genz, A.C. and Malik, A.A., *Remarks on Algorithm 006: An Adaptive Algorithm for Numerical Integration over an N-dimensional Rectangular Region*, J. Comput. Appl. Math., 6 (1980), pp. 295-302.

[6] Gladwell, I. and Napierala, M.A., *Reducing Ranking Effects in Parallel Adaptive Quadrature*, in Proc. 6th SIAM Conference of Parallel Processing for Scientific Computation, SIAM, Philadelphia, (1994).

[7] Gladwell, I. and Napierala, M.A., *Testing Parallel Multidimensional Integration Algorithms*, Southern Methodist U. Math Dept., Tech. Rept. 97/05, (1997).

[8] Gladwell, I. and Napierala, M.A., *Recursive Periodization and End-point Singularities*, Southern Methodist U. Math. Dept., Tech. Rept. 97/06, (1997).

[9] Gropp, W., Lusk, E, Skjellum A., *USING MPI, Portable Parallel Programming with the Message-Passing Interface*, The MIT Press, (1994).

[10] Korobov, N. M. *The Approximate Computation of Multiple Integrals*, Doklady Akademii Nauk SSSR, 124 (1959), pp. 1207-1210.

[11] Krommer, A.R. and Ueberhuber, C.H., *Numerical Integration on Advanced Computer Systems*, Thesis/Technical Report, Technical University of Vienna, (1993).

[12] McNamee, J. and Stenger, F., *Construction of Fully Symmetric Numerical Integration Formulas*, Numerische Mathematik, 10 (1967), pp. 327-344.

[13] *The NAG Fortran Parallel Library, Mark 1*, NAG Ltd, Oxford, (1995).

[14] Napierala, M.A., *Univariate and Multivariate, Sequential and Parallel Integration on finite ranges* Ph.D. Thesis, Southern Methodist University, (1996).

[15] Lemme, J.M. and Rice, J.R., *Adaptive Quadrature Algorithms for the ILLIAC IV*, Int. J. Comput. Inf. Sci., 9 (1980), pp. 63-72.

[16] Schmitzberger, P., *Parallel Numerical Integration over General Domains, Deliverable R5Z-3*, RIST, U. of Salzburg, Austria, (1994).

[17] Sloan, I.H. and Joe, S., *Lattice Methods for Multiple Integration*, Clarendon, Oxford, (1994).

[18] Zinterhof, P. and Schmitzberger, P., *Integrate: A Kernel of Fortran and C Package PANNUM for High Dimensional Number Theoretic Quadrature*, RIST Rept., U. of Salzburg, in preparation.

APPENDIX – Pseudocodes for algorithms $PMDQAG1_{level}$ and $PMDQAG2_{level}$

FIG. 7. *Parameters for algorithms* $\mathrm{PMDQAG1}_{level}$ *and* $\mathrm{PMDQAG2}_{level}$

GLOBAL	
dim	dimension of the problem, supplied by user
$[\boldsymbol{a}, \boldsymbol{b}]$	$[a_1, b_1] \times [a_2, b_2] \times \ldots \times [a_{dim}, b_{dim}]$, supplied by user
$f(\boldsymbol{x})$	integrand, supplied by user
ϵ	machine precision
α	"direction" factor for graded subdivision (chosen as $\alpha = \frac{1}{2}$ here)
β	"scaling factor" used in defining widths of the "levels" in data structure *LdLEVEL* (chosen as $\beta = 10$ here)
m	subdivision factor for general subdivision of subregions (chosen as $m = 3$ here)
tol	absolute accuracy requested, supplied by user
p	number of computational nodes
d	$\lceil \log_\beta \frac{tol}{\epsilon} \rceil + 1$ (calculated "threshold" value for data structure LdLEVEL)
OUTPUT	
totalresult	approximation to the integral
totalerrsum	error estimate of the approximation *totalresult*

FIG. 8. *Communication procedures used in algorithms $PMDQAG1_{level}$ and $PMDQAG2_{level}$*

Name	Function
Broadcast	Sends a message to all processors
Gather	Receives a message from all processors
Receive	Receieves a message from an identified processor
Reduce	Receives a quantity from all processors and computes a result fm those quantities
Send	Sends a message to an identified processor

FIG. 9. *Auxiliary Procedures used in algorithms* $\mathrm{PMDQAG1}_{level}$ *and* $\mathrm{PMDQAG2}_{level}$

Name	Function
Integrate	Computes an integral and an error estimate for a specified region
$Integrate_t$	Computes an integral and an error estimate for a specified " singular" region by periodizing transformation (replaces *Integrate* in QAG_{sing_t})
Select	Selects the next regions for subdivision
Selection	Runs on the control node selecting work for the computational nodes
Sub	Subdivides the regions chosen by Select
Update	Updates the integral and global error estimates form the local information computed by Integrate

FIG. 10. *Psuedocode: Algorithm* PMDQAG1$_{level}$

CONTROL NODE

```
tasks = p - 1; controlid = 0; myid = 0
I = {}; Q = E = {}; ND = {}
DIR = {}; LdLEVEL = {}
len = {}; head = {}
S_local = [a_1, b_1] × ... × [a_dim, b_dim]
lens_local = 1; lendir_local = dim
ND_local = {dim}; DIR_local = {1, ..., dim}
FIRST_1 = 1; LAST_1 = m^dim

Call Sub(lens_local, S_local, ND_local, lendir_local,
     DIR_local, FIRST_local, LAST_local, lenp_local, P_local)
Merge P_local with I
errsum = 0
For sender=1, tasks
     Call Receive(message, sender)
     Call Update(sender, lenp_local, error_local, Q_local,
          E_local, L_local, ND_local, lendir_local, DIR_local, leni,
          errsum, Q, E, ND, DIR, LdLEVEL, len, head)
Endfor
If (errsum ≤ tol) Then (todo = done)
Else (todo = more) Endif
Call Broadcast(todo, controlid)
.............................. synchronize ..............................
While (todo = more)
     Call Selection(errsum, leni, E,
          LdLEVEL, len, head, lens, S, ND_S, DIR_S)
     message = {lens, lendirs, S, ND_S, DIR_S}
     Call Broadcast(message, controlid)
.............................. synchronize ..............................
     S_local = S; DIR_local = DIR_S
     ND_local = ND_S = {n_1, ..., n_lens_local}
     FIRST^j_local = 1, LAST^j_local = m^(n_j), j = 1, 2, ... lens,

     Call Sub(lens_local, S_local, ND_local, lendir_local,
          DIR_local, FIRST_local, LAST_local, lenp_local, P_local)
     Merge P_local with I

     For sender=1, tasks
          Call Receive(message, sender)
          Call Update(sender, lenp_local, error_local, Q_local,
               E_local, L_local, ND_local, lendir_local, DIR_local, leni,
               errsum, Q, E, ND, DIR, LdLEVEL, len, head)
     Endfor
     If (errsum ≤ tol) Then (todo = done)
     Else (todo = more) Endif
     Call Broadcast(todo, controlid)
.............................. synchronize ..............................
Endwhile
totalresult = ∑ Q
End Algorithm PMDQAG1_level
```

COMPUTATIONAL NODES

```
tasks = p - 1; controlid = 0
myid = i; i = 1 or 2 or ... or p − 1
S = [a_1, b_1] × ... × [a_dim, b_dim]
lens = 1; lendirs = dim
ND_S = {dim}; DIR_S = {1, ..., dim}
Call Select(tasks, lens, S, ND_S, lendirs, DIR_S, lens_local, S_local,
     ND_local, lendir_local, DIR_local, FIRST_local, LAST_local)
Call Sub(lens_local, S_local, ND_local, lendir_local,
     DIR_local, FIRST_local, LAST_local, lenp_local, P_local)
Call Integrate(lenp_local, P_local, Q_local, E_local,
     ND_local, lendir_local, DIR_local)
error_local = ∑ E_local
message = {lenp_local, lendir_local, error_local,
     Q_local, E_local, L_local, ND_local, DIR_local}
Call Send(message, controlid)

Call Broadcast(todo, controlid)
.............................. synchronize ..............................
While (todo = more)

     Call Broadcast(message, controlid)
.............................. synchronize ..............................
     Call Select(tasks, lens, S, ND_S, lendirs, DIR_S, lens_local,
          S_local, ND_local, lendir_local, DIR_local, FIRST_local, LAST_local)
     Call Sub(lens_local, S_local, ND_local, lendir_local,
          DIR_local, FIRST_local, LAST_local, lenp_local, P_local)
     Call Integrate(lenp_local, P_local, lendir_local,
          Q_local, E_local, L_local, ND_local, DIR_local)
     error_local = ∑ E_local
     message = {lenp_local, lendir_local, error_local,
          Q_local, E_local, L_local, ND_local, DIR_local }
     Call Send(message, controlid)

     Call Broadcast(todo, controlid)
.............................. synchronize ..............................
Endwhile
```

FIG. 11. *Pseudocode: Algorithm* PMDQAG2$_{level}$

CONTROL NODE

```
tasks = p; controlid = p - 1
myid = controlid
I = {}; Q = E = {}; ND = {}
DIR = {}; LdLEVEL = {}
len = {}; head = {}; S = [a, b]
lens = 1; lendirs = dim; ND_S = {dim}
DIR_S = {1, ..., dim}
Call Select(tasks, lens, S, ND_S, lendirs, DIR_S, lens_local, S_local,
      ND_local, lendir_local, DIR_local, FIRST_local, LAST_local)

Call Sub(lens_local, S_local, ND_local, lendir_local,
      DIR_local, FIRST_local, LAST_local, lenP_local, P_local)
Call Integrate(lenP_local, P_local, Q_local, E_local,
      L_local, ND_local, lendir_local, DIR_local)
errsum = sum E_local; Merge P_local with I
Call Update(myid, lenP_local, error_local, Q_local, E_local, L_local,
      ND_local, lendir_local, DIR_local, leni, errsum, Q,
      E, ND, DIR, LdLEVEL, len, head)
Call Reduce(errsum, totalerrsum, 1, SUM, controlid)
.............................. synchronize ..............................
If (errsum <= tol) Then (todo = done)
Else (todo = more) Endif
Call Broadcast(todo, controlid)
.............................. synchronize ..............................
While (todo = more)
      top = highest non-empty level of LdLEVEL
      Call Reduce(top, highest, 1, MAX, controlid)
.............................. synchronize ..............................
      Call Broadcast(highest, controlid)
.............................. synchronize ..............................
      If (top = highest) Then
            Call Selection(errsum, leni, E, LdLEVEL, len, head,
                  len_temp, S_temp, ND_temp, DIR_temp)
      Else S_temp = {}; ND_temp = {}; DIR_temp = {} Endif
      Call Gather(S_temp, S)
.............................. synchronize ..............................
      Call Gather(ND_temp, ND_S)
.............................. synchronize ..............................
      Call Gather(DIR_temp, DIR_S)
.............................. synchronize ..............................
      Call Select(tasks, lens, S, ND_S, lendirs, DIR_S, lens_local,
            S_local, ND_local, lendir_local, DIR_local, FIRST_local, LAST_local)
      Call Sub(lens_local, S_local, ND_local, lendir_local,
            DIR_local, FIRST_local, LAST_local, lenP_local, P_local)
      Call Integrate(lenP_local, P_local, Q_local, E_local,
            L_local, ND_local, lendir_local, DIR_local)
      errsum = errsum + sum E_local; Merge P_local with I
      Call Update(myid, lenP_local, error_local, Q_local, E_local, L_local,
            ND_local, lendir_local, DIR_local, leni, errsum, Q, E, ND,
            DIR, LdLEVEL, len, head)
      Call Reduce(errsum, totalerrsum, 1, SUM, controlid)
      If (errsum <= tol) Then (todo = done)
      Else (todo = more) Endif
      Call Broadcast(todo, controlid)
.............................. synchronize ..............................
Endwhile
result = sum_{i=1}^{leni} Q_i
Call Reduce(result, totalresult, 1, SUM, controlid)
End Algorithm PMDQAG2_level
```

COMPUTATIONAL NODES

```
tasks = p; controlid = p - 1
myid = i; i = 0 or 1 or ... or p - 2
I = {}; Q = E = {}; ND = {}
DIR = {}; LdLEVEL = {}
len = {}; head = {}; S = [a, b]
lens = 1; lendirs = dim; ND_S = {dim}
DIR_S = {1, ..., dim}
Call Select(tasks, lens, S, ND_S, lendirs, DIR_S, lens_local, S_local,

      ND_local, lendir_local, DIR_local, FIRST_local, LAST_local)
Call Sub(lens_local, S_local, ND_local, lendir_local,
      DIR_local, FIRST_local, LAST_local, lenP_local, P_local)
Call Integrate(lenP_local, P_local, Q_local, E_local,
      L_local, ND_local, lendir_local, DIR_local)
errsum = sum E_local; Merge P_local with I
Call Update(myid, lenP_local, error_local, Q_local, E_local, L_local,
      ND_local, lendir_local, DIR_local, leni, errsum, Q,
      E, ND, DIR, LdLEVEL, len, head)
Call Reduce(errsum, totalerrsum, 1, SUM, controlid)
.............................. synchronize ..............................


Call Broadcast(todo, controlid)
.............................. synchronize ..............................
While (todo = more)
      top = highest non-empty level of LdLEVEL
      Call Reduce(top, highest, 1, MAX, controlid)
.............................. synchronize ..............................
      Call Broadcast(highest, controlid)
.............................. synchronize ..............................
      If (top = highest) Then
            Call Selection(errsum, leni, E, LdLEVEL, len, head,
                  len_temp, S_temp, ND_temp, DIR_temp)
      Else S_temp = {}; ND_temp = {}; DIR_temp = {} Endif
      Call Gather(S_temp, S)
.............................. synchronize ..............................
      Call Gather(ND_temp, ND_S)
.............................. synchronize ..............................
      Call Gather(DIR_temp, DIR_S)
.............................. synchronize ..............................
      Call Select(tasks, lens, S, ND_S, lendirs, DIR_S, lens_local,
            S_local, ND_local, lendir_local, DIR_local, FIRST_local, LAST_local)
      Call Sub(lens_local, S_local, ND_local, lendir_local,
            DIR_local, FIRST_local, LAST_local, lenP_local, P_local)
      Call Integrate(lenP_local, P_local, Q_local, E_local,
            L_local, ND_local, lendir_local, DIR_local)
      errsum = errsum + sum E_local; Merge P_local with I
      Call Update(myid, lenP_local, error_local, Q_local, E_local, L_local,
            ND_local, lendir_local, DIR_local, leni, errsum, Q, E, ND,
            DIR, LdLEVEL, len, head)
      Call Reduce(errsum, totalerrsum, 1, SUM, controlid)


      Call Broadcast(todo, controlid)
.............................. synchronize ..............................
Endwhile
result = sum_{i=1}^{leni} Q_i
Call Reduce(result, totalresult, 1, SUM, controlid)
```

PARALLEL ALGORITHMS FOR MULTI-DIMENSIONAL INTEGRATION

J. M. BULL* & T. L. FREEMAN*

Abstract. A central feature of adaptive algorithms for the numerical approximation of definite integrals is the manipulation of the list containing the sub-intervals and corresponding error estimates. Fundamentally different parallel algorithms result depending on whether the list is maintained as a single shared data structure accessible to all processors, or else as the union of non-overlapping sublists, each private to a processor. We describe several variants of these approaches, and compare numerical performances of the algorithms on multi-dimensional problems.

Key words. Multi-dimensional numerical integration, parallel algorithms, globally adaptive algorithms, load balancing.

AMS subject classifications. 65D30, 65Y05

1. Introduction. In this paper, we consider the problem of approximating the definite multi-dimensional integral

$$I = \int_{a_1}^{b_1} \int_{a_2}^{b_2} \cdots \int_{a_n}^{b_n} f(x_1, x_2, \ldots, x_n)\, \mathrm{d}x_1\, \mathrm{d}x_2\, \ldots\, \mathrm{d}x_n$$

to a specified absolute accuracy ϵ. The focus of the paper is the design of algorithms that are suitable for implementation on parallel computers.

In recent years, motivated by different programming models, two approaches to parallel numerical integration have emerged. One is based on adapting the ideas of sequential globally adaptive algorithms to the parallel context by selecting a number of subregions of the range (region) of integration rather than simply the one with largest associated error estimate; see, for example, [2], [3], [10], [13] and [18]. The other approach proceeds by imposing an initial partitioning of the region of integration and treats the resulting subproblems as independent, and therefore capable of concurrent solution. The more sophisticated of these latter algorithms include a mechanism for detecting load imbalance and for redistributing work to neighbouring processors; see, for example, [1], [5], [17] for the one-dimensional case, and [6], [7], [8], [16] for the multi-dimensional case.

The key difference between these approaches is that the former effectively maintains a single list of subregions and is particularly suitable for implementation in a shared-data programming model, whereas in the case of the latter, which is better suited to a message-passing programming model, each processor maintains an independent list of the subregions with which it is dealing and it is the union of these independent lists that corresponds to the single list of the former algorithms. We refer to the two types of algorithm as *single list* and *multiple list* algorithms respectively.

We base the multi-dimensional algorithms in this paper on the adaptive routine D01FCF in the NAG library [19]. The underlying cubature rule pair of this routine is that due to Genz and Malik [12] (see also [11]); it requires $2^d + 2d^2 + 2d + 1$ evaluations of the integrand to estimate an integral over a d-dimensional hyper-rectangle. The routine also returns an estimate of the error in the approximation, and identifies the dimension of the hyper-rectangle in which the integrand is most badly-behaved by computing fourth divided

*Centre for Novel Computing & Department of Mathematics, University of Manchester, Manchester, M13 9PL, U.K. ({markb,lfreeman}@cs.man.ac.uk).

differences of the integrand, so that any further bisections of the hyper-rectangle in the adaptive scheme can concentrate on this 'worst' dimension.

2. Parallel Algorithms. In this section we describe in detail the two classes of algorithms identified in §1.

2.1. Single List Algorithms. The first class, single list algorithms, consists of a family of algorithms that are based on modifying sequential globally adaptive algorithms by the introduction of subregion selection strategies that enable multiple subregions to be subdivided concurrently. Single list algorithms were suggested in the papers of Genz [10] and (in the context of vector processors) Gladwell [13]; they are referred to as dynamic synchronous (DS) algorithms in Bull and Freeman [2]. The essence of the algorithms is a synchronised region selection phase during which a number of subregions that require further refinement are identified, followed by the concurrent application of the numerical integration (cubature) rule to these identified subregions. A generic version of the algorithm is described by the pseudocode given in Fig. 2.1, where p is the number of processors.

Algorithm SL
p-sect region $[a_1, b_1] \times [a_2, b_2] \times \cdots \times [a_n, b_n]$
do while (error $> \epsilon$) and (number of rule evaluations $\leq N_{\max}$)
    SUBREGION SELECTION
    do par
        compute new subregion limits
        apply cubature rule to new subregions
    end do par
    do par
        remove old subregions from list
        add new subregions to list
        update integral approximation and error estimate
    end do par
end do

FIG. 2.1. *Single List Algorithm*

For one dimensional problems the obvious way to achieve the initial p-secting of the region is to divide it into p equal subregions. In several dimensions, the analogous subdivision (dividing the region into p equal subregions in the most badly behaved direction) can have unfortunate consequences. Parts of the region where the integrand is locally well behaved in the selected direction may be subdivided, resulting in an increase in the total number of subregions required to attain the required error tolerance. We have found that the optimal way of generating the initial p-secting, in terms of total execution time to solve the overall multi-dimensional integration problem, is to allow an initial sequential execution of the algorithm, until p active subregions have been generated. In this phase, parallelism may be exploited in concurrent evaluations of the integrand, if desired.

The objective of the subregion selection strategy is to identify sufficient regions with large error estimates to keep all the processors usefully busy. For one dimensional problems we find that when only a few intervals are selected it is worthwhile dividing the selected intervals into several subintervals to generate sufficient work. However for multi-dimensional problems we find that, except in very special circumstances, a multi-secting strategy is counter-productive and thus we adopt a bisection-only approach for our multi-dimensional algorithms. (For moderate p, it is very unusual for a selection strategy to identify fewer then $p/2$ subregions at any stage when dealing with problems in many dimensions; however we find that it is more efficient to accept the load imbalance associated with this unusual situation than to multi-sect some of the selected subregions.) Note that the globally adaptive algorithms that are implemented in sequential libraries, such as the NAG library [19] and QUADPACK [20], select a single subregion at each stage—that with the largest error estimate.

Due to the large numbers of subregions that can be generated by multi-dimensional problems, list updating and subregion selection can become sequential bottlenecks. (This can also be true for one-dimensional problems unless an efficient sorting algorithm, for example heap sorting, is employed—see [14] and §4.) List updating is easily parallelised, since the number of new subregions is known to all the processors and hence their positions in the list can be computed independently. Parallelisation of some of the selection strategies described below is possible by concurrent application of certain tasks to all the subregions in the list.

In [10], Genz proposes simply the selection (and bisection) of the $p/2$ regions with largest error estimates. Gladwell in [13] suggests a region selection strategy that selects all regions that have error estimates above a certain value, such that the sum of the error estimates of the unselected regions is as large as possible without exceeding ϵ. This strategy, unlike that of Genz, is thus independent of the number of processors on the machine. However, both Genz's and Gladwell's strategies are inherently sequential as they require the list of regions (which may become very long in the solution of multi-dimensional problems) to be sorted by error estimates. In [2], we proposed selection strategies for one-dimensional quadrature which avoid the use of sorted information, but these strategies are not so well suited to the multi-dimensional case. Napierala and Gladwell [18] propose their "Level" algorithm as a means of obtaining similar results to Gladwell's strategy, while reducing the cost of ranking the list of regions and allowing the selection strategy itself to be parallelised. A similar strategy (the Adaptive Bins Selection Strategy) is suggested in Bull and Freeman [3]. In both these strategies the regions are sorted into bins according to their error estimates—the aim is to identify sets of regions that have error estimates of approximately equal magnitude. The idea of sorting regions into bins, rather than maintaining an ordered list of regions, was first suggested in the context of globally adaptive quadrature by Rice [21].

The Adaptive Bins Selection Strategy is as follows:

Adaptive Bins Selection

1. Search the list of regions for the largest and smallest error estimates ($E_{\max}$ and $E_{\min}$).

2. Divide the range $[E_{\min}, E_{\max}]$ into b exponentially spaced bins. The ith bin, $i = 1, 2, \ldots, b$, is given by

$$[\exp(\log(E_{\min}) + (i-1)l), \exp(\log(E_{\min}) + il)],$$

where $l = (\log(E_{\max}) - \log(E_{\min}))/b$.

3. Determine the number of regions n_i whose error estimates lie in the ith bin.

4. Find r such that

$$\sum_{i=1}^{r-1} M_i n_i < \epsilon$$

and

$$\sum_{i=1}^{r} M_i n_i \geq \epsilon,$$

where

$$M_i = \exp\left(\log\left(E_{\min}\right) + (i - 1/2)l\right)$$

is the exponential midpoint of the ith bin.

5. Select all regions with error estimates greater than $\exp\left(\log\left(E_{\min}\right) + (r-1)l\right)$, that is all regions whose error estimates lie in bins $r, r+1, \ldots, b$. In other words, select all the regions with large error estimates so that the (approximate) sum of the error estimates associated with remaining regions is less than the required tolerance. (Note that because of the approximate nature of the selection, it is possible that

$$\sum_{i=1}^{b} M_i n_i < \epsilon$$

even though the sum of the error estimates is greater than ϵ. In this case we select all the regions in the largest non-empty bin.)

This selection strategy requires three passes through the list of regions, one to find $E_{\max}$ and $E_{\min}$, one to determine $n_i, i = 1, 2, \ldots, b$, and a final one to find the indices of the selected regions. By allowing separate processors to operate on separate sublists, it is possible to execute each of the three passes in parallel, with a synchronisation point after each pass.

For the experiments in §4 we use $b = 50$. This number of bins is sufficient to obtain a reasonable approximation to the algorithm described by Gladwell in [13]—additional bins give no significant improvements in the number of function evaluations, and increase the cost of the (sequential) search for r in step 4.

Napierala and Gladwell [18] suggest the use of bins with endpoints which depend on ϵ and the machine tolerance but remain fixed throughout the adaptive procedure—this has the advantage that each region needs to be classified only once, but at the expense of the extra storage space required to hold this classification information. In the algorithm described in [18], only intervals in the first non-empty bin are selected. Below we describe a modified algorithm that selects sufficient bins such that the sum of the remaining error estimates is approximately ϵ:

Fixed Bins Selection

1. Divide the range $[\delta, \epsilon]$, where $\delta = \epsilon \times 10^{-K}$ and K is a constant, into b exponentially spaced bins. The ith bin, $i = 1, 2, \ldots, b$, is given by

$$\left[\exp\left(\log\delta + (i-1)l\right), \exp\left(\log\delta + il\right)\right],$$

where $l = \left(\log\epsilon - \log\delta\right)/b$.

2. Determine the number of regions n_i whose error estimates lie in the ith bin. Subregions with error estimates greater than ϵ are assigned to bin $b+1$, and those with error estimates less than δ are assigned to bin 1.

3. Find r such that

$$\sum_{i=1}^{r-1} M_i n_i < \epsilon$$

and

$$\sum_{i=1}^{r} M_i n_i \geq \epsilon,$$

where

$$M_i = \exp(\log\delta + (i - 1/2)l)$$

is the exponential midpoint of the ith bin.

4. If $r \leq b$, then select all regions with error estimates greater than $\exp(\log\delta + (r-1)l)$, that is all regions whose error estimates lie in bins $r, r+1, \ldots, b, b+1$.
Else, if $r = b+1$, then find r' such that

$$\sum_{i=1}^{b} M_i n_i + \sum_{j=1}^{r'-1} e_j^{(b+1)} < \epsilon$$

and

$$\sum_{i=1}^{b} M_i n_i + \sum_{j=1}^{r'} e_j^{(b+1)} \geq \epsilon,$$

where $e_1^{(b+1)}, e_2^{(b+1)}, \ldots, e_{n_{b+1}}^{(b+1)}$ are the error estimates of the regions in bin $b+1$ and $e_1^{(b+1)} \leq e_2^{(b+1)} \leq \ldots \leq e_{n_{b+1}}^{(b+1)}$, and select all regions with error estimates $\geq e_{r'}^{(b+1)}$. (Again it is possible that

$$\sum_{i=1}^{b} M_i n_i + \sum_{j=1}^{n_b+1} e_j^{(b+1)} < \epsilon$$

even though the sum of the error estimates is greater than ϵ. In this case we select all the regions in the largest non-empty bin.)

The natural way to parallelise this Fixed Bins Selection Strategy is to divide the set of newly generated subregions from the previous stage of the algorithm amongst the p processors and classify them concurrently; the information thus generated then must be incorporated into the global lists. By assigning different bins to different processors, this latter step can also be parallelised, although because most of the newly generated subregions tend to lie in a small number of bins this latter parallelisation tends to scale poorly with increasing numbers of processors. A potential difficulty with the strategy is that many subregions might lie in a single bin and 'over-selection' (many more regions are selected than are required to satisfy the error criterion) can result. For the experiments in §4 we use $K = 10$ and $b = 50$.

2.2. Multiple List Algorithms. The alternative approach to parallel numerical integration is to base an algorithm on an initial static distribution of the work; for example, for a machine with p processors the region of integration is divided into p subregions and each sub-integral is assigned to a separate processor. As stated in §2.1, this initial p-secting of the region of integration is best achieved by initial (sequential) applications of the integration rule until a list of p active subregions has been generated. For most integrals, an initial static subdivision of the region of integration alone would lead to an unbalanced computational load and consequently an inefficient parallel computation. To obviate this difficulty a load balancing strategy is usually incorporated into the algorithm; see, for example, de Doncker and Kapenga [7], [8] and Lapegna and D'Alessio [16]. In this section we introduce algorithms of this type and describe a number of load balancing strategies. Note that it is very easy to design load balancing strategies which are non-deterministic, in that the implementation of the algorithm will produce different (though equally valid) results from one run to another. This is true, for example, of the strategy proposed in [7]. We take the view that such strategies are undesirable from a software engineering point of view, and are unlikely to be significantly more efficient than the best deterministic algorithms. We therefore restrict our attention to deterministic algorithms.

The basic multiple list algorithm is described by the pseudocode given in Fig. 2.2.

Algorithm ML:
p-sect region $[a_1, b_1] \times [a_2, b_2] \times \cdots \times [a_n, b_n]$ and
    assign each subregion to a different processor.
do all
    do while (error $> \epsilon$) and (number of rule evaluations $\leq N_{\max}/p$)
        apply k steps of globally adaptive numerical integration
        LOAD BALANCING
    end do
end do all

FIG. 2.2. *Multiple List Algorithm*

Note that the same global error convergence condition is used to terminate both the single list and multiple list algorithms. For the multiple list algorithms, this requires synchronisation of the processors, and is therefore implemented during the synchronised section of code required by the load balancing. Other authors have suggested using a local convergence condition on each processor. However, in the presence of load balancing, a processor should not terminate until all processors have satisfied their local condition, as a terminated processor could be usefully employed in receiving subregions from other processors. In these circumstances, the global condition requires no more synchronisation than the local condition, and as the global condition will generally terminate earlier, there is every reason to prefer it.

It is not obvious what criterion should be used to determine load balance. It is generally true that the larger the error estimate of a subregion, the larger the reduction in total error estimate resulting from its subdivision. Hence the global convergence condition will tend to be satisfied sooner if processors with subregions with smaller error estimates 'help out' processors with subregions with larger error estimates. However since it is not possible to predict the effect on the total error estimate of the subdivision of any given subregion (particularly those with large error estimates, where the integrand is likely to be non-smooth) it is not clear what quantity should be balanced between processors.

The first load balancing strategy is based on that suggested by Lapegna and D'Alessio [16], but uses the total error estimate in a processor's sublist, rather than the largest error estimate (as described in [16]), as the estimator of the load on a processor. (There are arguments in favour of using either as the estimate of the processors' loads; using the largest error estimate has the merit that the set of subregions chosen at any stage is likely to be a good approximation to the set of p subregions with largest error estimates and thus the algorithm should behave in a similar way to Genz's single list algorithm. On the other hand the size of the current local error estimate (the total error estimate of the regions in a given processor's sublist) is a good indicator of the number of function evaluations that will be required to reduce the local error to a given level. In extensive numerical experiments we have found that there is little to choose between these load estimators, with the one based on the total local estimate being slightly more efficient.) Each processor maintains a heap-sorted list of regions (the order being determined by the magnitudes of the corresponding error estimates). The processors are assumed to be logically arranged in a 2-dimensional torus; each processor has exactly four neighbours, labelled North, East, South and West. This processor topology is not intended to reflect the network topology of any machine. For example, on a machine such as the KSR-1 with a single ring network there is no concept of processor locality; see §3 for further details of the architecture of the KSR-1. Indeed for most of the latest generation of parallel architectures, details of the network topology can safely be ignored. The toroidal processor topology is intended to provide enough connectivity to allow sufficiently rapid transfer of work (subregions) between processors, but at the same time limit the amount of communication necessary to achieve this. In [16], it is noted that, for large numbers of processors, a 3-dimensional torus, in which each processor has six neighbours, might be more suitable. Conversely, for small numbers of processors, a ring topology would suffice. Experiments reported in [6] suggest that for up to 32 processors, nothing is gained by using a mesh of dimension higher than two.

The load balancing strategy can be described as follows, where a *stage* consists of k *steps* of adaptive quadrature, followed by load balancing and the global error check (that is, an iteration of the **do while** loop in Fig. 2.2):

Local Error Strategy

1. Choose a neighbour with which to compare loads: if the stage number is odd, choose North, if even, choose East.
2. Transfer the r subintervals with largest error estimates to the neighbour such that the difference in total error estimate is minimised (note that r may be zero.)

It remains to specify the choice of k, the number of steps of adaptive quadrature to apply between each load balancing stage. In §4 we present results for $k = 1$ (we refer to this as the LE (Local Error) Load Balancing Strategy), and for the following scheme (referred to as the RLE (Reduced Local Error) Load Balancing Strategy) which reduces the amount of synchronisation required by increasing k as the algorithm progresses. We let $k = \max\{1, [\gamma s]\}$, where s is the number of steps executed up to and including the one on which the last synchronisation occurred, and $[s]$ denotes the integer closest to s. For example, for $\gamma = 0.1$, load balancing and termination detection occurs at each of the first 15 steps, then at every other step for the next 10 steps, then at every third step, and so on. It can be shown that the number of steps (and hence the number of subregions processed) increases by at most a factor γ compared with the case $k = 1$, but the total cost of the rebalancing and termination detection is considerably reduced. For the results of §4 a value of $\gamma = 0.05$ is used.

The Local Error Strategy described above only balances the load between neighbouring processors. To attempt to balance the load across all the processors, we can iterate the strategy to convergence, as follows:

Iterated Local Error Strategy

1. Let $D_1, D_2, \ldots, D_\nu$, denote the set of directions defining the ν distinct neighbours of each processor. (For example, for a 2×2 grid $\nu = 2$ (each processor has two distinct neighbours) and for a 3×3 grid $\nu = 4$.)
2. Let $j = 1$.
3. Transfer the r subregions with largest error estimates to the neighbour in direction D_j such that the difference in total error estimates is minimised.
4. If no transfers between any processors have occurred in the last ν iterations, then stop; otherwise set $j = (j + 1) \bmod \nu$ and return to step 3.

Bull [4] shows that the above strategy always terminates. The virtue of this strategy is that it achieves load balance, in the sense of approximately equidistributed total error estimates on the processors, at each stage of the algorithm. To achieve this aim some subregions may move substantially across the logical torus of processors within one load balancing step, and the strategy is likely to be computationally more expensive than the Local Error strategy.

In §4 we present results for the above strategy with $k = \max\{1, \lceil \gamma s \rceil\}$ (referred to as the IRLE (Iterated Reduced Local Error) Load Balancing Strategy).

3. The Kendall Square Research KSR-1. We have implemented the algorithms described in §2 on the 32-processor Kendall Square Research KSR-1 computer installed at the University of Manchester. Although no longer in production, the KSR-1 remains a very advanced parallel computer and its non-uniform memory access architecture is typical of many current distributed memory machines, in that it supports virtual shared memory in hardware. Each processor has a peak 64-bit floating point performance of 40 Mflop/s and 32 Mbytes of memory. Up to 32 processors are connected by a uni-directional slotted ring network with a bandwidth of 1 Gbyte/s.

The memory system, called ALLCACHE, is directory-based with full cache coherency. Data movement is request driven; a memory read operation which cannot be satisfied by a processor's own memory generates a request which traverses the ring and returns a copy of the data item to the requesting processor; a memory write request which cannot be satisfied by a processor's own memory results in that processor obtaining exclusive ownership of the data item, and a message traverses the network invalidating all other copies of the item. The unit of data transfer in the system is a subpage which consists of 128 bytes (16 8-byte words). See [9] for a more in-depth discussion of the architecture of the KSR-1. Parallel programming is supported by extensions to Fortran consisting of directives and library calls, in a shared memory (process synchronisation) paradigm. For further details, see [15].

4. Numerical Results. In this section we compare the performances of the implementations described in §2 on a number of test problems. To describe the test problems we first define the test integrands:

$$F_1 = \prod_{i=1}^{d} \left(0.36 + (x_i - 0.3)^2\right)^{-1},$$

$$F_2 = \cos\left(c \sum_{i=1}^{d} i x_i\right),$$

$$F_3 = \prod_{i=1}^{d} x_i^{-0.8}.$$

F_1 has a large peak, and we assume that it is the intended test function in [16], where it is misprinted; it is also a member of Family 2 (Product Peak) in Chapter 11 of [22]. F_2 is oscillatory and is a member of Family 1 (Oscillatory) in Chapter 11 of [22]. F_3 has a singularity at the origin, an important feature not represented in the test problem set of [22].

For all the problems the domain of integration is the d-dimensional unit cube. The problems are defined by selecting the integrand F, the dimension d, and a target number of integrand evaluations I_t. Values of the absolute accuracy ϵ are then chosen so that the NAG routine D01FCF requires approximately I_t integrand evaluations. For the integrand F_2, increasing d dramatically increases the difficulty of the problem, so we include the parameter c (which controls the frequency of oscillations) to offset this effect.

The test problems are defined as follows (we also include the actual value of ϵ used):
Problem 1 $F = F_1$, $d = 6$, $I_t = 10^7$, $\epsilon = 1.469 \times 10^{-4}$,
Problem 2a $F = F_2$, $c = 100$, $d = 2$, $I_t = 10^7$, $\epsilon = 7.084 \times 10^{-9}$,
Problem 2b $F = F_2$, $c = 2$, $d = 5$, $I_t = 10^7$, $\epsilon = 1.114 \times 10^{-5}$,
Problem 2c $F = F_2$, $c = 0.5$, $d = 8$, $I_t = 10^7$, $\epsilon = 7.624 \times 10^{-5}$,
Problem 3 $F = F_3$, $d = 3$, $I_t = 10^7$, $\epsilon = 1.198 \times 10^{-2}$.
Problems 2a, 2b, 2c are chosen to illustrate the effects of increasing the dimension of the problem while keeping the number of integrand evaluations fixed. Note that the integrands used in the test problems are relatively inexpensive to evaluate. For many practical applications, integrand evaluation is likely to be more expensive, with the result that the differences between the best and worst algorithms would be less marked than in the cases presented here.

Table 4.1 shows the number of subregions processed N, the number of function evaluations I, and the execution times (in seconds) required by the NAG routine D01FCF (T_{NAG}) and by a modified version (T_{heap}) which uses heap sorting rather than the much less efficient list insertion of the original code.

TABLE 4.1
Performance of sequential algorithms

Problem	N	I	T_{NAG}	T_{heap}
1	67105	9998645	925.8	100.6
2a	588237	10000029	62130.0	201.9
2b	107529	10000197	2298.0	124.1
2c	24939	10000539	230.2	120.1
3	303031	10000023	17150.0	207.1

Figs. 4.1 to 4.5 show temporal performance (defined as the reciprocal of the execution time) and the number of integrand function evaluations for the parallel algorithms on the five test problems. We present results for six parallel algorithms: three single list algorithms, SLGL which uses the Gladwell selection strategy, SLAB which uses the Adaptive Bins selection strategy, and SLFB which uses the Fixed Bins selection strategy; and three multiple list algorithms, MLLE and MLRLE which use the local error and reduced local error load balancing strategies, and MLIRLE which uses the iterated version of the reduced local error load balancing strategy. The 'Ideal' value of temporal performance is computed as the number of processors p times the temporal performance of the modified sequential algorithm ($1/T_{\text{heap}}$). The 'Ideal' number of function evaluations is simply the number of function evaluations I required by the sequential algorithm. Note that on Problems 2a and 3, for which the algorithms generate very long lists of subregions, results for the single list algorithms on small numbers of processors are omitted. This is because the storage requirements and data access patterns combine to cause significant page capacity misses in the ALLCACHE memory system of the KSR-1. As a result, the code will still execute, but timing results are unreliable. (This problem is peculiar to cache-only memory architecture (COMA) machines, where pages have no fixed home in memory. The single list algorithms tend to result in sparse memory accesses to the large arrays containing the list data. On the KSR-1, a copy of every 16 Kbyte page referenced by a processor must be made resident in that processor's memory, even when only one of the 128 byte subpages on the 16 Kbyte page is actually accessed.)

The behaviour of the algorithms on Problem 1, displayed in Fig. 4.1, is typical. Considering temporal performance, SLAB, SLFB and MLRLE are significantly better than the other algorithms. The number of integrand evaluations required by MLRLE displays a characteristic saw-tooth behaviour. For this algorithm, because of the reduced frequency of synchronisation, convergence can go undetected for a number of extra steps which is bounded but otherwise unpredictable (see §2.2). MLIRLE has a more expensive, and sophisticated, load balancing strategy than MLRLE but any benefit from this is often masked because both algorithms use a reduced convergence testing strategy and as a result convergence is detected on the same step.

MLIRLE therefore does not result in a reduced total number of integrand evaluations and thus is less efficient. MLLE also has a more expensive, because it is more frequent, load balancing strategy; this results in fewer integrand evaluations (very close to the ideal value of 10^7), but the cost of load balancing on every iteration outweighs any gains in the reduced integrand evaluations. The considerable costs associated with heap sorting the long list of subregions mean that, despite using the smallest number of integrand evaluations, SLGL requires more than twice the execution time on 30 processors compared with the best algorithms.

Fig. 4.2 displays the behaviour of the algorithms on Problem 2a. For this particular 2-dimensional problem, the final list of subregions contains over 500,000 items and it is the housekeeping associated with this list that dominates the computation. MLRLE exhibits super-linear speed-ups for up to 30 processors and is the most efficient algorithm for this problem. MLIRLE exhibits super-linear speed-ups for up to 16 processors after which parallel performance begins to tail off. SLAB displays close to ideal (linear) speed-up for up to 30 processors, even though there is an almost 15% increase in the number of integrand evaluations required by SLAB (compared with SLGL), which is caused by the approximate nature of the Adaptive Bins Selection Strategy. SLFB achieves reasonable parallel performance, although not so good as MLIRLE, MLRLE and SLAB; this is at least partly explained by

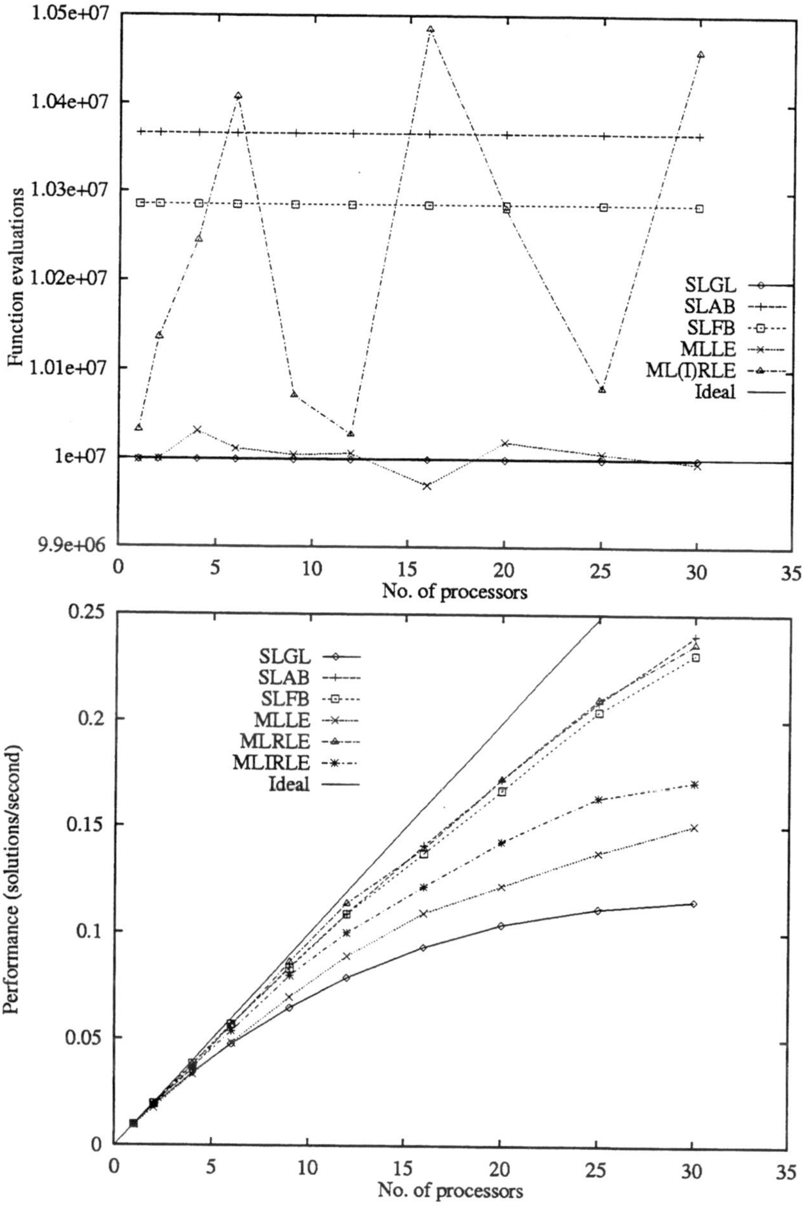

FIG. 4.1. *Problem 1: No. of function evaluations and temporal performance on KSR-1.*

the 20% increase in the number of integrand evaluations required by SLFB (compared with SLGL), which is again caused by the approximate nature of the Selection Strategy. MLLE and SLGL both perform poorly, MLLE because of the large number of synchronised calls of the load balancing algorithm, and SLGL because of the heap sorting of the long list of subregions.

Fig. 4.3 displays the behaviour of the algorithms on Problem 2b which is a 5-dimensional version of the oscillatory problem; for this problem the final list of subregions contains about

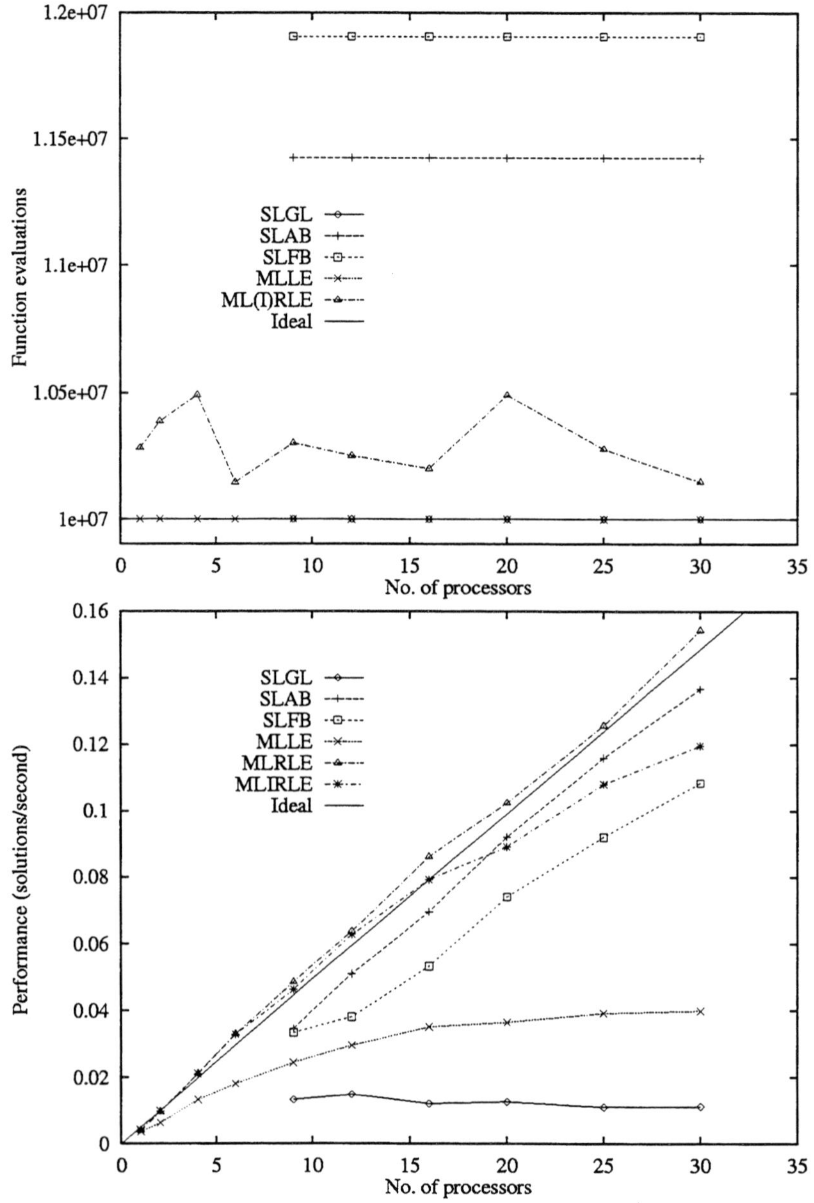

FIG. 4.2. *Problem 2a: No. of function evaluations and temporal performance on KSR-1.*

100,000 items. For this problem the differences in performance are not so marked, and SLAB, MLRLE and SLFB all achieve close to ideal performance on up to 30 processors, and SLAB requires only marginally more integrand evaluations than SLGL. MLIRLE, MLLE and SLGL have poorer parallel performances; the shorter list of subregions means that the performances of MLLE and SLGL are better than for Problem 2a.

The performance of the algorithms on the 8-dimensional version of the oscillatory problem, Problem 2c, is displayed in Fig. 4.4. In this case the final list of subregions contains

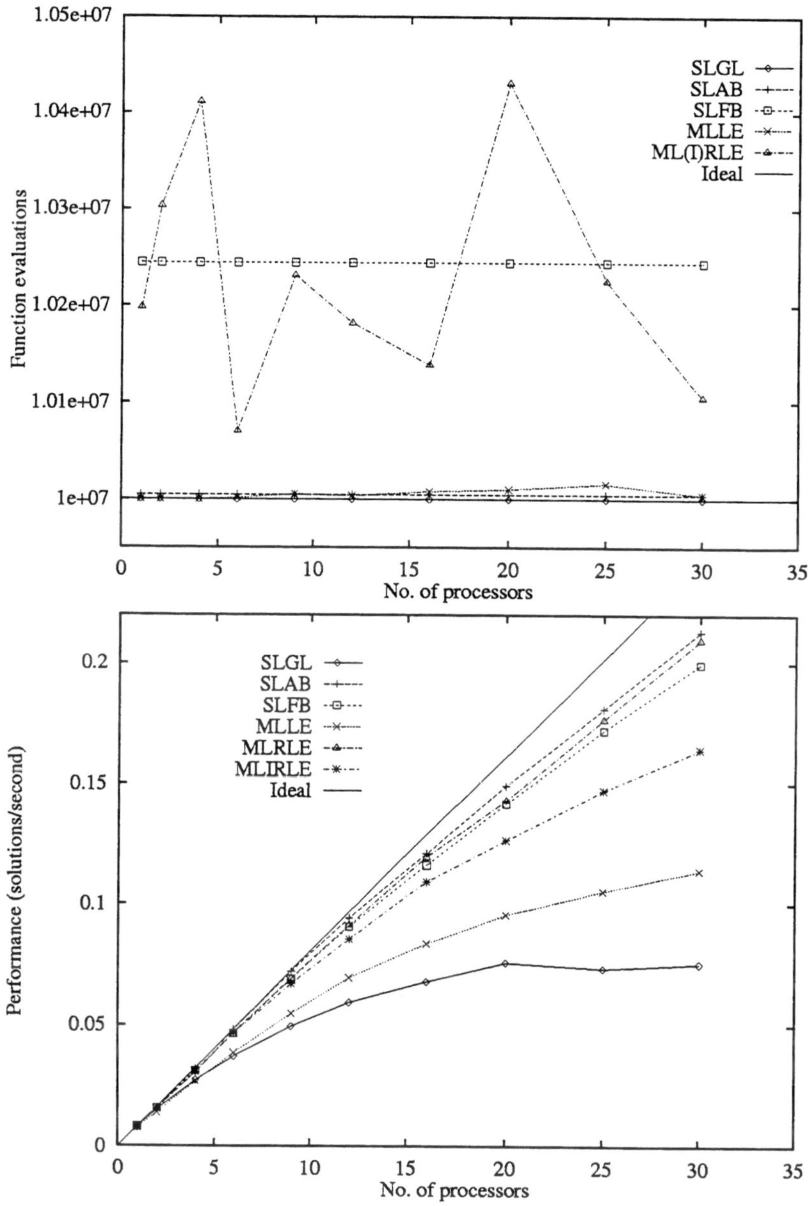

FIG. 4.3. *Problem 2b: No. of function evaluations and temporal performance on KSR-1.*

about 25,000 items, and the housekeeping associated with the list is considerably reduced compared with Problems 2a and 2b. All the algorithms display respectable speed-ups, with SLFB, SLAB and MLRLE displaying close to linear speed-ups. Compared with Problems 2a and 2b, there is much less difference between the best (SLFB) and the worst (MLLE) algorithms.

In Fig. 4.5 we display the performance of the algorithms on Problem 3, which is a 3-dimensional problem with a singularity at the origin. The final list of subregions is relatively

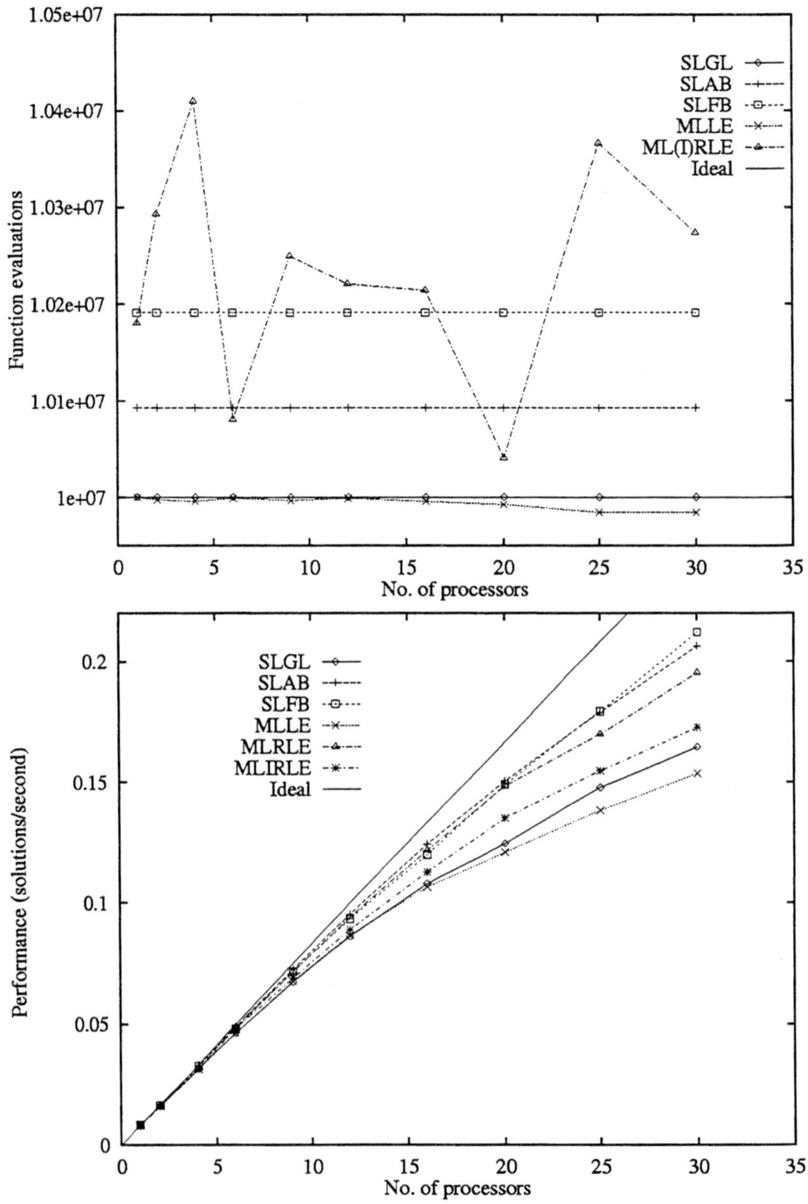

FIG. 4.4. *Problem 2c: No. of function evaluations and temporal performance on KSR-1.*

long, with about 300,000 items. MLRLE performs significantly better than the other algorithms with close to linear speed-ups for up to 30 processors. MLIRLE, SLFB and SLAB have similar performances with speed-ups of about 22 on 30 processors. MLLE and SLGL perform significantly more poorly, primarily because of the synchronisation and housekeeping costs associated with processing the long list of subregions. The number of integrand evaluations required by the algorithms is surprising. SLFB requires about 8% *fewer* evaluations than SLGL, and SLAB also requires fewer evaluations than SLGL. This is unexpected,

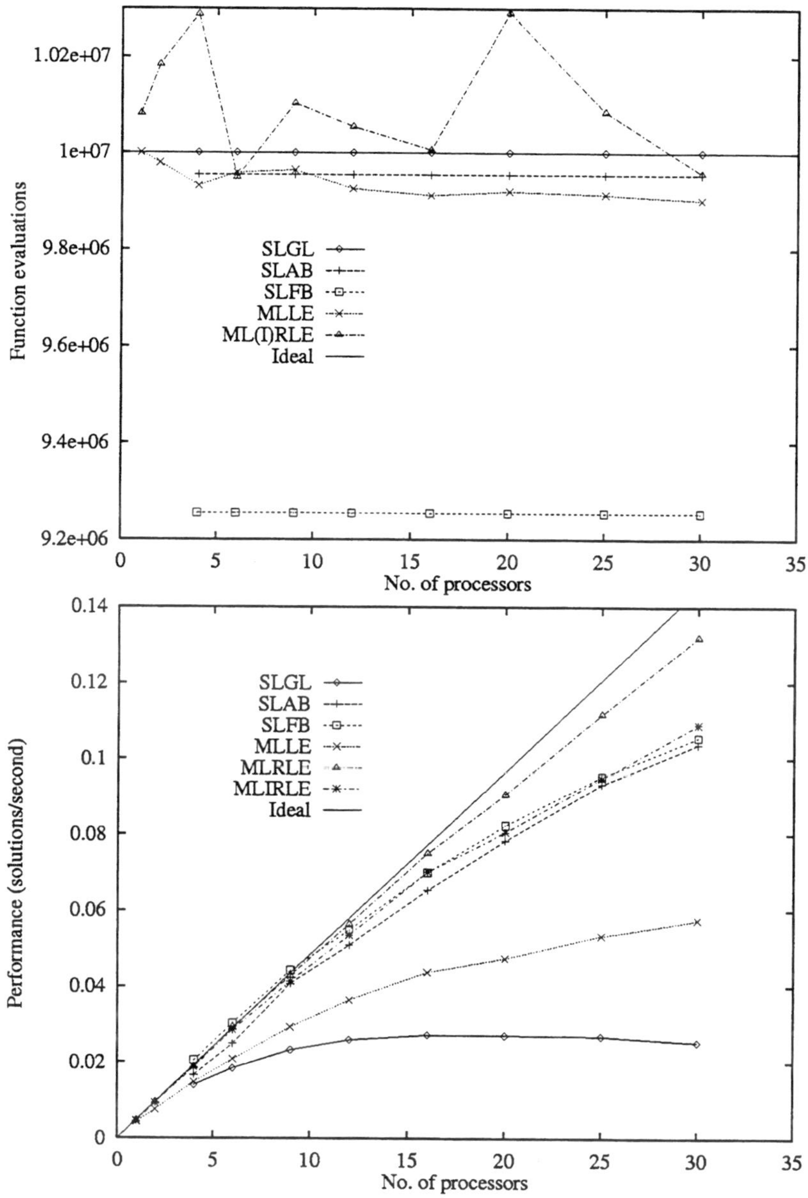

FIG. 4.5. *Problem 3: No. of function evaluations and temporal performance on KSR-1.*

and we believe that it is caused by poor error estimation for this problem. In general we have found that error estimation is much less reliable for multi-dimensional problems, compared with 1-dimensional problems, and this can lead to severe underestimation of the local error and unexpected behaviour of the adaptive algorithms.

5. Discussion and Conclusions. We have shown that efficient and scalable parallel algorithms for globally adaptive numerical integration can result from both the single list and multiple list approaches. The major advantage of the multiple list approach is that it can be readily implemented in either a message passing or a shared memory programming paradigm, whereas the single list approach is suitable only for shared memory. The multiple list approach makes better use of data locality, and thus has lower communication overheads than the single list approach. This is particularly important for problems where the list of subregions grows very large. On the other hand, obtaining good performance from the multiple list algorithm is strongly dependent on choosing a good value of γ. By comparison, the Adaptive Bins and Fixed Bins algorithms are relatively insensitive to the choice of b. Another advantage of the single list algorithms is that if we only use bisection to divide subregions, the course of the algorithm does not depend on the number of processors. Unlike the multiple list algorithms, the single list algorithms are not restricted to numbers of processors which can form a suitable toroidal grid.

Acknowledgements. The authors wish to thank the referees for suggesting a number of improvements to the original version of this paper.

REFERENCES

[1] J. Bernsten and T. O. Espelid, *A Parallel Global Adaptive Quadrature Algorithm for Hypercubes*, Parallel Computing, 8 (1988), pp. 313–323.

[2] J. M. Bull and T. L. Freeman, *Parallel Globally Adaptive Quadrature on the KSR-1*, Advances in Computational Mathematics, 2 (1994), pp. 357–373.

[3] J. M. Bull and T. L. Freeman, *Parallel Algorithms for Numerical Integration in One and Several Dimensions*, Applied Numerical Mathematics, 19 (1995), pp. 3–16.

[4] J. M. Bull, *Parallel Algorithms for Globally Adaptive Quadrature*, Ph.D. thesis, Department of Mathematics, University of Manchester, 1997.

[5] K. Burrage, *An Adaptive Numerical Integration Code for a Chain of Transputers*, Parallel Computing, 16 (1990), pp. 305–312.

[6] M. D'Apuzzo, M. Lapegna and A. Murli, *Scalability and Load Balancing in Adaptive Algorithms for Multidimensional Integration*,Parallel Computing, 23 (1997), pp. 1199–1210.

[7] E. de Doncker and J. Kapenga, *Parallel Systems and Adaptive Integration*, Contemporary Mathematics, 115 (1990), pp. 33–51.

[8] E. de Doncker and J. Kapenga, *Parallel Cubature on Loosely Coupled Systems*, in Numerical Integration, T. O. Espelid and A. Genz, eds., Kluwer Academic Publishers, Dordrecht, 1992, pp. 317–327.

[9] S. Frank, H. Burkhart and J. Rothnie, *The KSR1: Bridging the Gap Between Shared Memory and MPPs*, in Proceedings of Compcon '93, IEEE, 1993, pp. 285–294.

[10] A. Genz, *The Numerical Evaluation of Multiple Integrals on Parallel Computers*, in Numerical Integration. Recent Developments, Software and Applications, G. Fairweather and P. M. Keast, eds., NATO ASI Series **C203**, D. Reidel, Dordrecht, 1987, pp. 219–229.

[11] A. Genz, *Subregion Adaptive Algorithms for Multiple Integrals*, Contemporary Mathematics, 115 (1990), pp. 23–31.

[12] A. C. Genz and A. A. Malik, *Remarks on Algorithm 006: An Adaptive Algorithm for Numerical Integration over an N-dimensional Rectangular Region*, J. Comput. Appl. Math., 6 (1980), pp. 295-302.

[13] I. Gladwell, *Vectorisation of One Dimensional Quadrature Codes*, in Numerical Integration. Recent Developments, Software and Applications, G. Fairweather and P. M. Keast, eds., NATO ASI Series **C203**, D. Reidel, Dordrecht, 1987, pp. 230–238.

[14] I. Gladwell and M. A. Napierala, *Efficiency of Globally Adaptive Quadrature*, in The Quality of Numerical Software: Assessment and Enhancement, R. F. Boisvert, ed., Chapman and Hall, London, 1997, pp. 326–329.

[15] K.S.R., *KSR Fortran Programming*, Kendall Square Research, Waltham, Mass., 1991.

[16] M. Lapegna and A. D'Alessio, *A Scalable Parallel Algorithm for the Adaptive Multidimensional Quadrature*, in Proceedings of the Sixth SIAM Conference on Parallel Processing for Scientific Computation, R. F. Sinovec, D. E. Keyes, M. R. Leuze, L. R. Petzold and D. A. Reed, eds., SIAM, Philadelphia, 1993, pp. 933–936.

[17] V. A. MILLER AND G. J. DAVIS, *Adaptive Quadrature on a Message-Passing Multiprocessor*, Journal of Parallel and Distributed Computing, 14 (1992), pp. 417–425.

[18] M. A. NAPIERALA AND I. GLADWELL, *Reducing Ranking Effects in Parallel Global Adaptive Quadrature*, in Proceedings of Seventh SIAM Conference on Parallel Processing for Scientific Computation, D. H. Bailey, P. E. Bjørstad, J. R. Gilbert, M. D. Mascagni, R. Schreiber, H. D. Simon, V. J. Torczon and L. T. Watson, eds., SIAM, Philadelphia, 1995, pp. 647–651.

[19] N.A.G., *N.A.G. Fortran Library Manual, Mark 15*, N.A.G. Ltd., Oxford, 1991.

[20] R. PIESSENS, E. DE DONCKER, C. ÜBERHUBER AND D. KAHANER, *QUADPACK, A Subroutine Package for Automatic Integration*, Springer-Verlag, New York, 1983.

[21] J. RICE, *A metalgorithm for adaptive quadrature*, Journal of the ACM, 23 (1975), pp. 61–82.

[22] I. H. SLOAN AND S. JOE, *Lattice Methods for Multiple Integration*, Oxford, 1994.

GENERIC OPERATIONAL DECOMPOSITION FOR CONCURRENT SYSTEMS: SEMANTICS AND REFLECTION

ANNIE MARCOUX, CHRISTINE MAUREL, FRÉDÉRIC MIGEON & PATRICK SALLÉ*

Abstract. We present in this article reflection in concurrent languages, and in particular, in PlasmaII which is an implementation of the actor model defined by C.Hewitt and G.Agha. We propose to implement structural and behavioural reflection with an approach based on a fine-grained decomposition of actors management.In this reflective architecture, the actor life cycle is described as a system of cooperative elementary entities that can be easily changed. This approach provides the user with an expressive and concise description of reflective programs.

The paper describes this architecture and how it is used to fit various paradigms of concurrent systems such as the actor model of Hewitt and Agha. We also present several examples and emphasize the components specialization leading to black-board communication, ported-object system, or rendezvous synchronization. We also use the semantics of Agha's actors to formalize components cooperation and its ability to treat concrete examples. We compare our approach to others such as facets of CodA or Meta-Interpreters and Meta-Object of ABCL/R3.

Key words. Actor Languages, Operational Reflection, Concurrent Systems, Meta-Level Architecture, Generic Description, Actor Semantics.

1. Introduction. An application in distributed systems is described by a community of cooperative concurrent entities.Within this context, problems such as fault-tolerance, entities distribution or synchronization between entities are crucial. Management of these problems is often mixed with functional description and raises problems such as *inheritance anomaly* in distributed object-oriented languages. Solutions to this kind of problems deal with separation between application logical part and management part.

Reflection gives the possibility to any system (operating system, application) to reason and act upon itself dynamically. We obtain system self-representation by materializing some of its structural and computational features in order to consult or to modify them, while changes are checked dynamically at run-time. In practical use, reflection allows dissociation between the application description and its execution features. Without modifying the application, reflection enables to change, for example, communication protocols, evaluation modes, objects or resources distribution, and so on.

Our work concerns reflection in concurrent languages, and in particular, in actors languages. Our main goal is the extension of concurrent systems to reflection. However, as a first step, we work on individual reflection, i.e. reflection for each entity. Afterwards, group reflection will be introduced to describe the whole system management.

In object-based systems, various architectures (like in [1] and [2]) have been proposed which provide operational decomposition of objects. They are usually described as structural and operational components which cooperate with each other. However, these reflective architectures do not allow dynamic objects modifications. In these cases, reflection is used as abstraction of management mechanisms.

We propose, in §2, a modular and dynamic description of entity operational management ([3]) and present how to use genericity to describe different concurrent entities management. This description is obtained by cooperation of components, in which each of them describes a precise part of the entity management.

*Institut de Recherche en Informatique de Toulouse (IRIT), Universit Paul Sabatier, 118 Route de Narbonne, 31062 Toulouse Cedex, France, e-mail:{marcoux, maurel, migeon, salle}@irit.fr Tel: +33 (0) 561 556 765 Fax: +33 (0) 561 556 258

Thereafter, we describe the specialization of these components to fit particular paradigms. We emphasize the specialization for actor language PlasmaII ([4]) in §3 and state semantics of components in that particular case. We also show how to use the decomposition genericity to implement different concurrent entities management such as blackboard communication, Ported-Objects ([1]) and rendezvous synchronization in §4.

Section 5 contains a view of how to extend the decomposition to obtain reflective entities. We firstly present description and semantics of extensions; then we give a practical use of reflection with *regularity* property implementation.

Finally we conclude with related works and perspectives.

2. Generic operational decomposition.

2.1. Purposes. We propose to realize operational management of a concurrent entity so that we obtain a description that:

1. enables easy implementation of reflective entities.
2. is abstracted enough to suit many distributed systems.
3. is not too monolithic to minimize changes. If only a part of the description needs to be changed, we do not want to rewrite the unchanged portion.
4. is little enough to be practical.

We propose to built the operational management of every entity as the cooperation of operational components which can evolve dynamically. This allows to adapt decomposition granularity to every particular entity management and also to reflective modifications.

2.2. Operational decomposition of concurrent entities. A concurrent entity has capabilities to deal with its community - i.e. an interface which specifies communication and creation protocols - and computational capabilities. Therefore, we implement its management with six operational components that could be classified according to the concepts: Community Interface, Computation and Execution Cycle.

- Community Interface: *Reception* and *Emission* components describe the information exchange mechanisms while *Creation* component manages entity creation.
  - *Reception* : It considers information coming from the outside; it is the end of the information travel, which was under the control of the system communication manager. It administers the different entry points and organizes a possible waiting of information according to FIFO, LIFO or priority policies.
  - *Emission* : It sends information to the outside. This transfer may be, for example, synchronous or asynchronous, to a single entity or a group, and so on.
  - *Creation* : It runs dynamic creation according to physical resources allocated by the underlying operating layer. When entities are statically created, this component doesn't exist.
- Computation : For every piece of information, computation consists in determining entity reactions using *Selection* and *Execution* components.
  - *Selection* : It chooses the next information to compute among those waiting. This choice, for example, is depending on some pattern matching criteria, on preconditions or guards to satisfy, et cetera.
  - *Execution* : The chosen information is executed according to the entity functionality and resources provided by the system.
- Execution Cycle : Component *Cycle* coordinates communication and computation mechanisms. Using the physical parallelism allocated by the system, it manages

the concurrency. In sequential mode, *Cycle* administers control transfer from component to component.

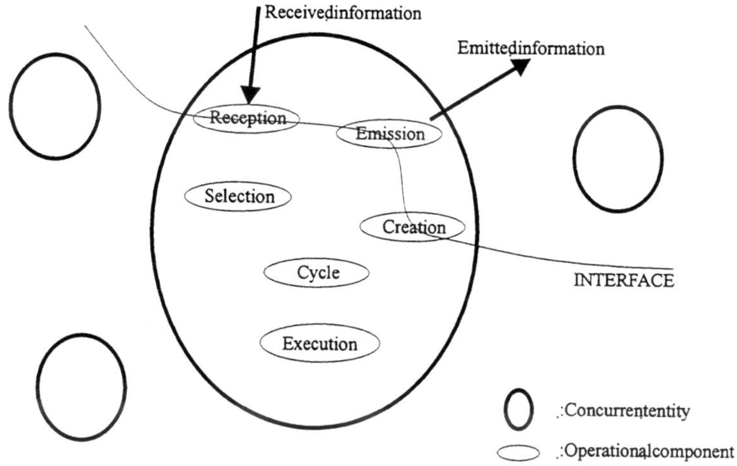

FIG. 2.1. *Generic operational decomposition of concurrent entity*

The above decomposition, illustrated in figure 2.1, deals with operational parts of a concurrent entity regardless of implementation choices and doesn't restrict therefore the systems that could be described (object-based systems, actors systems, prototype-based system, and so on).

3. Specialization and semantics for PlasmaII actors. To give semantics of a particular concurrent language with the generic decomposition seen above, it is necessary to specialize previous six components and to define data structures which were implicit until now and which are used to manage the entity functionality.

We see, in this section, how the decomposition is specialized for actor language PlasmaII.

3.1. PlasmaII actors.

3.1.1. The actor model. The actor model defined by C.Hewitt [5] and G.Agha [6] addresses the description of concurrent computations in which a problem is resolved by actors community, made of independent entities which communicate and cooperate for the resolution of a common goal. Each actor of this community works in an autonomous way in its own domain, communicating and exchanging information by message passing. Actors represent conceptual or physical objects which appear in the application. Messages correspond to information queries or answers to these requests.

Message passing is the only way for actors to exchange information; it is *point-to-point*, *unidirectional*, *safe* and *asynchronous*, which requires a queue or buffer. An actor is identified by its reference, which is a kind of mail address.

An actor is completely defined by a triplet made of its reference, its behavior and the set of messages received but not computed yet. The actor *behavior* is composed of *acquaintances* (known actors) and a *script* which describes its reactions to the received messages.

The *life cycle* of an actor is a loop which consists (1) in extracting the first waiting message from the buffer and (2) in computing it. During calculation, an actor can (1) dynamically create new actors, (2) send messages to some acquaintances, and (3) replace its current behavior by the one intended to perform the next message.

3.1.2. PlasmaII implementation. The language PlasmaII [4] is a realization of the actor model extended with built-in functions, communication protocols and data structures which increase expression power and efficiency (like, for example, communication protocol of synchronous messages, communication management with priority and data structure list).

The actor's script is a list of *receivers* (methods) made of a pattern and a list of actions. *Pattern matching*, second order semi-unification, is realized between a message and a *pattern* to select the receiver adapted to the message. The set of patterns describes the messages structure that the actor will accept. Pattern matching is also an operation that creates execution environment.

The language was implemented on the distributed virtual machine Smart [7] which insures the system portability on many architectures.

3.1.3. Operational decomposition of PlasmaII actors. It is necessary to specialize the operational components to adapt them to the description of PlasmaII actor management:

- Community Interface : *Reception* and *Emission* components are specialized to implement asynchronous point-to-point message passing. *Creation* becomes a component able to create PlasmaII actors.
  - *Reception* : It stores received messages in a Buffer-like data structure.
  - *Emission* : It forwards the message to the communication manager. The message is sent in an asynchronous way and delivered to a single actor.
  - *Creation* : In actors systems, creations are dynamic. They consist in the allocation of a computation power to make the actor autonomous.
- Computation: The computation steps are now (1) pattern matching selection, then (2) computation of the adaptated behavior.
  - *Selection* : The waiting messages management is specialised in a FIFO policy.
  - *Execution* : The chosen message is performed according to actor script. This computation is done in several steps. In the first one, a receiver is chosen by pattern matching. Then, this receiver is computed with respect to the syntax and the semantics of the language constructions. To describe these different steps, we have enriched this decomposition with the following components:
    * *Error* et *Complaint*: These are components which describe error management for computational errors and pattern matching errors.
    * *Script_Choice*: When the selected message is passed to *Script_Choice*, it returns the adapted computation, if there is one.
    * *Compute*: It's the part of the computation which consists in evaluating the actions produced by the message acceptation.
- *Cycle* : It describes the components cooperation to realize messages execution.

Moreover, the following structural components have been added:

- *Behavior* which stores *acquaintances* and *script*, and
- *Buffer* which queues all the messages received but not processed yet.

This default decomposition (cf. Fig. 3.1) is not fixed and could be reduced or extended in order to be adapted to some particular works. However, this fine-grained decomposition of actor operational mode brings good expressiveness for reflective operations (cf. §5.3).

3.2. Components semantics. According to the semantics of the actor model presented in [8], we give formal semantics for the decomposition of PlasmaII actors in terms of Agha's actors.

Initially, every component is an Agha's actor. Therefore, a PlasmaII actor is described

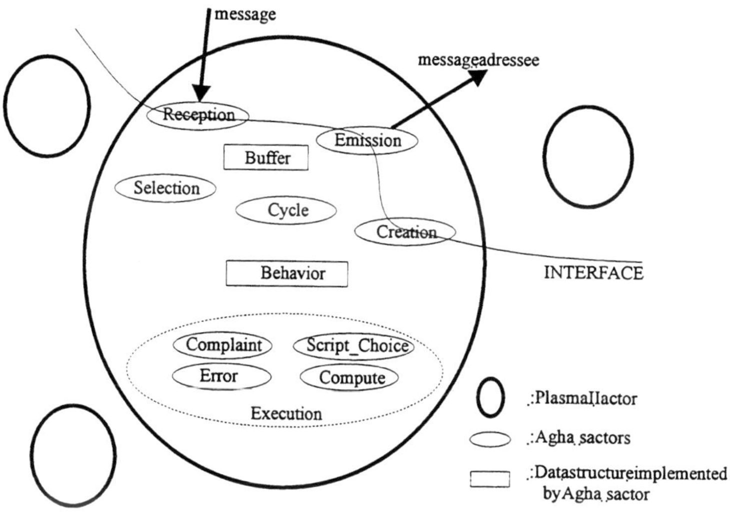

FIG. 3.1. *Operational decomposition of PlasmaII actors*

by a system of Agha's actors. We present here the different default behaviors of the actors involved in the decomposition.

We suppose that operational and structural components definitions are mutually recursive.

We will use two data structures, Buffer and Behavior, known by every component of a same PlasmaII actor, without showing the management problems due to concurrent accesses. These structures could have been managed by actors which would have serialized the operations. However, this management simplification doesn't change semantics presented here. Moreover, we consider that the function *Update()*, which updates the structures values, solves the accesses problems.

We use the syntax presented by Agha in [8].

3.2.1. Cooperation. *Cycle* component describes the cooperation between the principal components of the architecture (cf. Fig. 3.2).

When the message to be processed is received, *Cycle* delegates to component *Script_Choice* the choice of a computation adapted to the message, then it changes its behavior to become an actor that will accept the answer (1). *Script_Choice* calculates the execution environment and the actions list to be computed. When the answer received by *Cycle* is an error signal (2), *Cycle* tells component *Complaint* to manage it, asks *Selection* to give the next message, and changes its behavior to be able to accept a new message (3). If there isn't any error, *Cycle* asks *Compute* to evaluate the expression *expr* in the environment *env*, then it changes its behavior to become an actor waiting for the answer (4). If the evaluation produces a fatal error, component *Error* is told so (6); otherwise, *Cycle* asks for the next message (7).

Compute, like *eval* in functional languages, evaluates the PlasmaII syntatic expression *expr* in the environment *env*; it is not presented here.

If the expression *expr* is a behavior of a PlasmaII actor, its syntatic form is (A_METH $\langle pattern\rangle\langle body\_of\_method\rangle$) or ($CASES(A\_METH\langle pattern\rangle\langle body\_of\_method\rangle)^{+}$) that *Com-*

[1] $\langle ELT1, ELT2\rangle$ is a notation for the couple

```
Behav_Cycle =
 (λ mess.
  let {Behav_Computation =
    (λ ⟨env, expr⟩.¹
     if (env = fail)                                          (2)
       seq ( send (mess, Complaint),
             send ('Start, Selection),
             become (Behav_Cycle)),                           (3)
       let {Behav_Error =
               (λ result.
                  if (result = err)                           (5)
                     send (⟨env, expr⟩, Error),               (6)
                     seq ( send ('Start, Selection),
                            become (Behav_Cycle)))}           (7)
        seq ( send (⟨⟨env, expr⟩, self⟩, Compute),
               become (Behav_Error)) )                        (4)
    }
   seq (send (⟨⟨Behavior, mess⟩, self⟩, Script_Choice),      (1)
       become (Behav_Computation)) )
```

FIG. 3.2. *Semantics of component Cycle*

pute evaluates and gives as a result a closure which has the form $(BEHAVIOR\ \langle environment\_of\_definition\rangle\langle body\rangle)$ (cf. p.232).

3.2.2. The community interface. It is constituted of the three components : *Reception*, *Emission* and *Creation*.

```
Behav_Reception =
  (λ pol_recep λ mess. Update (Buffer, pol_recep (mess, Buffer)))

Behav_Emission =
  (λ ⟨addressee, mess⟩. send (mess, addressee))
```

FIG. 3.3. *Semantics of Reception and Emission components*

Reception component is defined by means of a reception policy (the default is FIFO) and the buffer of waiting messages ; after receiving a message, *Reception* stores it with respect to the reception policy and updates the buffer.

The sending mechanism in PlasmaII is the same as the one defined by Agha : with the reference of the adressee and a message, *Emission* sends the message to the specified actor.

As in Agha's model, creation consists in creating a new reference, where messages will be sent to, that is linked to a behavior. The reference (mail address) is then returned to creation client (1) and life cycle is started by sending a message to *Selection* component(2).

```
Behav_Create =
  (λ ⟨behav, client⟩.
    letactor {adr_Emission = Behav_Emission,
              adr_Reception = Behav_Reception (Reception_FIFO),
              ⋮
              adr_Cycle = Behav˙Cycle,
              adr_Buffer = Empty˙Buffer,
              adr_Behavior = behav,
         }
     seq (send (adr_Reception, client),                              (1)
          send ('Start, adr_Selection)))                             (2)
```

FIG. 3.4. *Semantics of component Creation*

Technically speaking, components know each other as they are defined in a *recursive let* (cf. Fig. 3.4).

3.2.3. Computation. Computation process is defined by means of *Selection* component and *Execution* component cooperation. *Execution* is itself composed of *Script_Choice* component, of *Error* and *Complaint* components, error managers, and of *Compute* component which is an interpreter for actions defined in the actor's behavior.

Selection is defined by means of a selection policy (the default is FIFO). It uses it to choose the next message to be computed and stores in the buffer the remaining messages (cf Fig. 3.5).

```
Behav_Selection =
  (λ selec_pol λ buff λ starter.
      let {⟨mess, buff⟩ = selec_pol (buff)} send (mess, Cycle))
```

FIG. 3.5. *Semantics of component Selection*

The two components *Error* and *Complaint*, presented in figure 3.6, uses a message constructor. When a wrong message is received, they display an explanation.

```
Behav_Complaint =
 (λ Construct λ mess. send(Construct (Behavior, mess), Output))

Behav_Error =
 (λ Construct λ ⟨env, actions_list⟩. send(Construct (env, actions_list), Output))
```

FIG. 3.6. *Semantics of Complaint and Error components*

As described in figure 3.7, a behavior and a message are sent to *Script_Choice* which begins different computations with respect to plasmaII actor script structure (1). In the default case, the client is *Cycle* component.

```
Behav_Script_Choice =
(λ ⟨⟨behav, mess⟩, client⟩.
 (case² behav                                                    (1)
  (= (BEHAVIOR :env_def (A_METH :pattern :body))³                (2)
     let {env_calc = match (pattern, mess)}                      (3)
      if (env_calc = fail)                                       (4)
       send (fail, client),                                      (5)
       send (⟨append_env (env_calc, env_def), body⟩, client))    (6)
  (= (BEHAVIOR :env_def (CASES (A_METH :pattern :body) :other_scripts))  (7)
     let {env_ calc = match (pattern, mess)}
      if (env_calc = fail)
       send (⟨⟨(BEHAVIOR env_def (CASES other_scripts)), mess⟩, client⟩,
                                                         self),  (8)
       send (⟨append_env (env_calc, env_def), body⟩, client))
  (= (BEHAVIOR :env_def (CASES))                                 (9)
     send (fail, client)) ))
```

FIG. 3.7. *Semantics of component Script_Choice*

If the behavior has a single receiver (2), *Script_Choice* calculates pattern-matching environment by means of function *match* (3). If the result is a failure (4), the error is reported (5), else pattern-matching environment and definition environment are appended and sent to the client with the list of actions to be executed (6).

If the behavior contains several receivers (7), the failure launches a recursive call with the receivers not tried yet (8). Case (9) is for trivial case of recursive call.

4. Specialization for other concurrent systems. This architecture, based on dissociation between communication and data computation is still appropriate for other concurrent systems. Moreover, run-time changes of components will provide reflection to these systems too.

Next, we present several examples of system descriptions. We emphasize the components specialization leading to blackboard communication, ported-object system, or rendezvous synchronization (see Fig. 4.1).

4.1. Blackboard communication. Blackboard communication is a particular communication mechanism used in multi-agent systems. It is based on information sharing between agents. The reading and writing operations are made in exclusive mode. We assume that each agent starts its work as soon as it is created.

The blackboard data structure is implemented by a specific entity of the underlying layer, named BB in the example of the figure 4.2, and known by the whole system. For each agent, the *relation* mechanism consists now in sending messages to this server for storing

[2] Multiple selection expression is (*case* ⟨*exp*⟩ ⟨*selector*⟩$^+$)

[3] cf. p.229

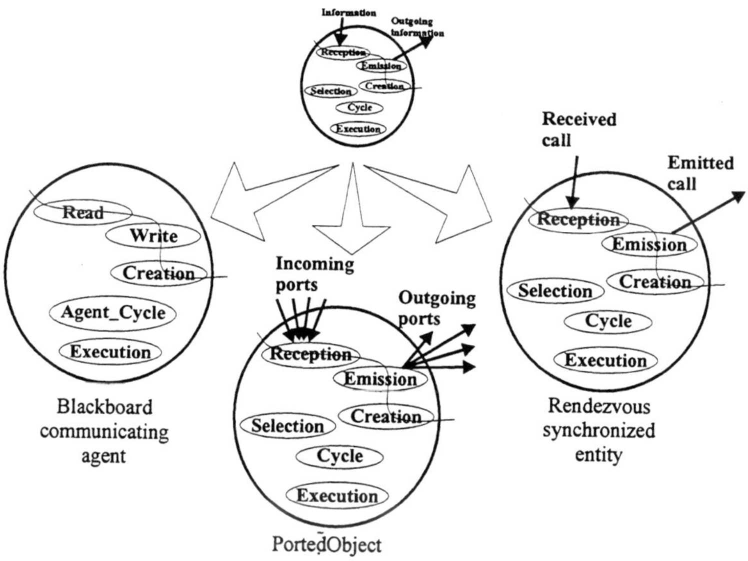

FIG. 4.1. *Multiple specialization for different concurrent systems*

Behav_Write =
(λ symbol. λ value.
send (['Update symbol value], BB))

Behav_Read =
(λ symbol.
send (['Get symbol], BB))

FIG. 4.2. *Semantics of Read and Write components*

and reading data. Therefore, *Emission* and *Reception* components are replaced by *Write* and *Read* ones.

Selection component disappears as no more waiting messages are stored, and *Cycle* component becomes an *Agent_Cycle* which expresses the behavior execution at creation-time.

4.2. Ported-objects system. We illustrate in this section the components specialization to meet specifications described in [1]. Ported-objects are objects with a set of incoming and outgoing ports over which data flow. When data in the appropriate quantity and form arrive at the input ports, the object carries out some computation. If the computation results in producing some data , they are written to output ports and thus sent to other objects.

In this example, *Emission*, *Reception* and *Selection* are specialized to deal with several communication media (cf. figure 4.3).

- *Emission* realizes broadcasting through a specific communication port. With underlying point-to-point communication, this is simulated by extended *Emission* so

```
Behav_Emission =
  (λ mess. λ PortId.
    ForEach obj in receivers( PortId )                           (1)
      do send (mess, obj))

Behav_Reception =
  (λ pol_recep λ Buffer. λ mess. λ PortId.
    Update (Buffer[PortId], pol_recep (mess, Buffer[PortId])))   (2)

; extraction as soon as a message is present in any queue
Behav_Selection =
  (λ selec_pol λ PortList. λ buff λ starter.
    ForEach id in PortList
      do let {⟨mess, buff[id]⟩ = selec_pol (buff[id])}
           send (mess, Cycle))
```

FIG. 4.3. *Specialization for Ported-object Computation*

that it can store all the objects connected to each channel. Then, semantics becomes "send message to each receiver of the channel" (1).

- *Reception* doesn't handle a single entry point any more, but controls as many entries as there are incoming ports connected to the object. Each channel is associated to a particular queue managed in FIFO style (2).
- *Selection* implements synchronisation between queues. For example, it can extract a message from a queue as soon as it arrives, whatever is the non-empty queue; or it can wait for all the queues to contain at least one message.

4.3. Rendezvous synchronized entity. Here, we specialize the operational decomposition to process rendezvous synchronization. This kind of communication is particularly used by Ada tasks. There are two possibilities of synchronization:

- If a calling task issues an entry call before corresponding accept statement is reached by the task owning the entry, the execution of the calling task is suspended.
- If a task reaches an accept statement prior to any call of that entry, the execution of the task is suspended until such a call occurs.

If several tasks call the same entry before a corresponding accept statement is reached, they are queued. During execution of accept statement by the called task, the calling one remains suspended.

We describe in figure 4.4 how *Compute* component interrupt itself to send or accept rendezvous calls.

On the one hand, when *Compute* is evaluating an accept statement (1), it asks *Selection* the next call waiting for the rendezvous *rdv.* Then, it changes its behavior to be able to compute accept statement body (3). Execution suspension is obtained with *Selection*, which will be the only one to send message to *Compute* at this time, replying only if a call has been reccived.

Once *Selection* has returned arguments values and caller's reference, *Compute* evaluates the body and returns to caller the result (4). Then, it changes its behavior to deal with the

```
Behav_Compute =
 (λ ⟨⟨env, expr⟩, client⟩.
  (case expr
    ⋮
   ; rendezvous accept statement
   (= (ACCEPT :rdv :body)                                              (1)
     let {accept_computation =
          (λ ⟨env_call, caller⟩.
            let {cont =
                 (λ val. send (send (val, caller), client))}
              seq (send (⟨⟨append(env_call, env), body⟩, cont⟩, Compute), (4)
                   become (Behav_Compute))) }                          (5)
      seq (send (⟨⟨Next_Call, rdv⟩, self⟩, Selection),                 (2)
           become (accept_computation)))                               (3)
    ⋮
   ; rendezvous call statement
   (= (CALL :task FOR :rdv)                                            (6)
     let {call_back_computation =
          (λ result.
            seq (send (result, client),
                 become (Behav_Compute))) }                            (9)
      seq (send (⟨⟨task, rdv⟩, self⟩, Emission),                       (7)
           become (call_back_computation)))                            (8)
    ⋮))
```

FIG. 4.4. *Semantics of Compute component for rendezvous synchronization*

rest of the execution (5).

On the other hand, when *Compute* is processing a call statement (6), it delegates to *Emission* the call sending (7). Thereafter, it changes its behavior and waits for the answer (8). Here again, execution is suspended as long as the called task, which will be the only one to send a message to *Compute* at this time, has not replied.

When the call result is received, *Compute* resumes computation.

5. Extension for reflection. In traditional systems, management policies such as fault-tolerance, synchronization or distribution policies are mixed with the application description, i.e. the program functionality. Reflection allows dissociation between the application description, that is left at base-level, and its management (execution features), placed at meta-level [9]. We obtain system self-representation by materializing some of its structural and computational features in order to consult or to modify them, while changes are checked dynamically at run-time. Therefore, complex operational management may be described regardless of the base-level application. It gives more reusability, modularity and readability of programs and operational managements. As it is presented in §5.3, it allows to implement particular communication policies such as regularity. We have also experimented reflection in placement policy which is described in [10].

5.1. Extension for PlasmaII paradigm. The decomposition presented above allows to precisely manage the operating cycle of a PlasmaII actor. However, this actor doesn't have the ability to modify its operational components.

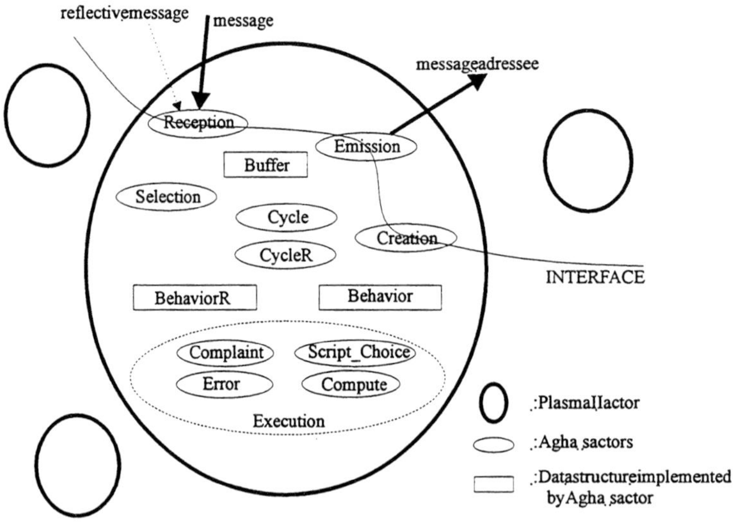

FIG. 5.1. *Operational decomposition for a reflective PlasmaII actor*

Every actor implementing a component can only be modified on its own decision (actor integrity). Therefore, actor-components have to be extended to be able to accept consultation and modification messages coming from the component responsible for reflective messages computation.

Consultation and modification operations are realized on a PlasmaII actor by sending particular messages called *reflective messages*. So, it is necessary to extend the operational decomposition of PlasmaII actors so that they can understand reflective messages. This extension (cf. Fig. 5.1) consists in adding:

- the component *CycleR* which describes components cooperation for reflective messages computation,
- and the structural component *BehaviorR* which describes computation for each reflective message.

5.2. Formal description of the extension. On the one hand, we present in this section, a formal description of component *CycleR*. On the other, we describe actor-components extension to deal with consultation and modification messages.

5.2.1. Formal description of a reflective actor's life cycle. *CycleR* differs from *Cycle* only in steps (1) and (2). First, a reflective computation is searched in *BehaviorR* component (1) as it was done for traditional computation with *Behavior* (cf. §3.2.1). If the message is not accepted, it is delegated to *Cycle* (2), considering it may be a traditional message.

```
Behav_Cycle_R =
 (λ mess.
  let {Behav_Computation =
   (λ ⟨env, actions_list⟩.
    if (env = fail)
      seq ( send (mess, Cycle),                                      (2)
            become (Behav_Cycle_R)),
      let {Behav_Error =
              (λ result.
                 if (result = err)
                   send (⟨env, actions_list⟩, Error),
                   seq ( send ('Start, Selection),
                         become (Behav_Cycle_R)))
      }
       seq ( send (⟨⟨env, actions_list⟩, self⟩, Compute),
             become (Behav_Error)) )
  }
  seq ( send (⟨⟨BehaviorR, mess⟩, self⟩, Script_Choice),              (1)
        become (Behav_Computation)) )
CycleR = Behav_Cycle_R
```

FIG. 5.2. *Semantics of component CycleR*

5.2.2. Formal description of actor-component extension. Let *old_script* be the script of an actor implementing an operational component. Figure 5.3 shows the extension which allows the actor to understand consultation and modification messages.

```
(λ mess.
  (case mess
    (= ⟨Consult, : client⟩  send(Behavior_of⁴ (self), client))
    (= ⟨Modif, : f⟩          Update(Behavior_of(self), f(Behavior_of(self))))
    (= :mess               old_script(mess)) ))
```

FIG. 5.3. *Actor-components extension*

5.3. Example: the regularity. The architecture described in this paper enables a very flexible and comfortable use of reflection. The operational components correspond to precise steps of actor messages computation; semantics and manipulation are therefore more intuitive.

We give now an example of *regular communication* to illustrate the power of the reflective language obtained. It's an example of management policy, short enough to be interesting to

[4]The function *Behavior_of* returns the actor's behavior whose reference have been passed to

be presented. Of course, more important implemetations have been realized such as actor placement, synchronous message passing or persistence.

The regularity property assures that between two actors S and R, if S sends R the message M1 followed by M2, then R will process M1 before M2. This property which isn't satisfied by the model is introduced by reflection. Here, we present a simple implementation.

As it is described by the specification, the property couples the message sending process of the sender S and the selection mechanism of R. Therefore we specialize the *Emission* component of S and the selection policy of R's *Selection* component.

In order to control the messages order, we define an ordering relation at sending-time, which is controlled at selection-time. Thus, regularity implementation concerns two actors (S and R) and two functions of ordering (*succ* which gives the ordering number for the next emitted message and *succ?* which verifies that the number of the selected message is the one expected). Finally, between two message sending or two receptions, the components must have stored the ordering numbers previously used.

Send_Reg =
  (λ succ λ order_num λ R λ ⟨addressee, mess⟩.
    if (addressee ≠ R)
      send (addressee, mess),
      let {order_num = succ (order_num)} send (⟨⟨REG_S, order_num⟩, mess⟩, R))

Mk_Emission =
  (λ addressee. Behav_Emission (Send_Reg (Label_Succ, 0, addressee)))

FIG. 5.4. *Emission component specialization for Regularity implementation*

For S message sending mechanism, when addressee is R, a regulation message is constructed by adding a numbered label.

For R selection policy described in figure 5.5, if the extracted message is a regulation message coming from S (1), with a good labelling number (2), then it is chosen to be the next one to be computed (3). If the label isn't the expected one, it is left in the buffer and another one is chosen (4). In case the extracted message is not coming from S (i.e. without any label), it is chosen as it is (5).

Next, changes are realized by reflective messages sending to the sender and adressee.

6. Related Work. A *reflective architecture* [11] is defined as the toolkit to explicitly handle reflective computation. In such an architecture, the meta-level is considered independently from the base-level.

Reflection was implemented with different architectures:

- *Individual reflection* associates a meta-entity to each entity in order to express its features, as in 3-LISP [12], BROWN [13] or 3-KRS [11].
- *Group reflection* provides relations between objects of a group to be represented by a community of meta-objects, as well in object-oriented languages like Smalltalk-80 [14] or MUSE [15] as in actor languages such as ACT/R [16], ABCL/R2 [17] or Reactalk [18].
- The *meta-object protocol (MOP)* [19] exploits the object-oriented programming advantages in order to define reusable meta-level objects. A meta-object associated

```
Selec_Pol_Regul =
  (λ succ? λ order_num λ S λ buff.
    let {⟨message, buff_rest⟩ = Head (buff)}
     if (message = ⟨⟨REG_S, : mess_num⟩, : mess⟩)                    (1)
       if (succ? (mess_num, order_num))                              (2)
         let {order_num=mess_num}
            ⟨mess, buff_rest⟩,                                       (3)
         let {⟨chosen_mess, new_buff⟩ =
                  Selec_Pol_Regul (succ?, order_num, S, buff_rest)}
           ⟨chosen_mess, Cons (message, new_buff)⟩,                  (4)
       ⟨message, buff_rest⟩)                                         (5)

Mk_Selection =
  (λ sender
    Behav_Selection (Label_Succ?, 0, sender, Buffer))


Regulation =
  (λ Sender λ Adressee.
    seq ( send ('(MODIF (λ c. Mk_Emission (Adressee))), Sender),
         send ('(MODIF (λ c. Mk_Selection (Sender))), Adressee) ))
```

FIG. 5.5. *Selection component specialization for Regularity implementation*

to a base-level object describes its management. The meta-object interface, called *meta-interface*, enables the application designer to adjust the object implementation to his particular needs without modifying the traditional interface (of the base-level object). A lot of languages and systems (Apertos [20], OPEN C++ [21], MPC++ [22], Iguana [23], etc.) integrate this notion which leads to the definition of *open implementations* [24].

- The *meta-component approach* is based on an operational decomposition of concurrent entities.

CodA and the decomposition in "facets".[1] Rather than describing a particular language, and trying to generalize its representation, Jeff McAffer builds an operational decomposition of object behavior, whichever the underlying system is. So, he gets seven "*facets*" (*send, accept, queue, receive, protocol, execution, state*) which describe the behavioral steps of an object in an abstract way. From a structural point of view, he makes this single hypothesis: each object has an associated set of slots in which it can store other objects; it can execute methods and send messages. These structural constraints seem sufficiently little restraining in order to enable the description of most objects systems. Each facet is implemented by an object called *meta-component* which, in turn, can be split in seven facets.

ABCL/R3: meta interpreters and meta-objects.[2] In order to create a simple and extensible language in which the user can define his own constructions, the ABCL/R3 designers associate every object to a meta-object constituted of four structural components (*class*, *state-vars*, *message-queue* and *evaluator*). Moreover, objects operational mode is punctuated of methods calls (*(message m)*, *(accept m)*, *(become env)* and *(process_next)*) that can be statically modified. The component *evaluator* is a *meta-interpreter*, object of the meta-level, which manages the execution of base-level methods and functions.

The meta-component approaches are modular and abstracted enough to fit concurrent systems management. However, these two architectures suffers from several drawbacks:

- Although CodA facets brings modularity because of the decomposition in operational components, we think this quality could be improved by adding a new component that deals with facets cooperation. As we see with our *Cycle* and *CycleR* components, without modifying the other ones, it is possible to describe particular object life cycle.
- We also find that metalevel architecture of ABCL/R3 could be describe with finer grains. Life cycle of entity is divided in four pieces. We think that operations such as communications (message sending) and object creation will be difficult to express with such an architecture. That's why we provide our metalevel architecture with ten fine-grained operational components that, moreover, may be changed dynamically to obtain useful granularity.
- At last, it seems that dynamic changes of CodA facets or ABCL/R3 metaobjects are not possible. Because these languages are compiled, metalevel program is preprocessed and merged to base-level part. From this point, changes are prohibited. This use of reflection allow the user to abstract management mechanisms from functional part of the application and also somewhat efficiency due to compiled code. Our point of view is that dynamic changes are to be preserved rather than efficiency. This reason explain why we use an interpreter and lazy creation of meta-components.

7. Conclusion and perspectives. Currently, our researches are planned along three axes:

- *Group reflection.* Such a functional decomposition of every actor allows to easily express all modifications on operational cycle by means of predefined reflective operators. However, it only concerns the structures and mechanisms of every actor. The actor represents a fine grain of activity. From a software point of view, it is often judicious to consider it within a group, for example, a group of actors with the same behavior (class based),a group of actors of a same application, etcetera. From hardware point of view also, all the actors of a same site represent a particular subgroup from the whole actors system.

  The notion of group reflection enables to define a set of entities having in common some structural or operational features. In a concurrent and distributed framework, this raises the problem of how to place this global knowledge in a distributed environment. Considering, for example, a broadcast mechanism, two solutions could be imagined. On the one hand, in a distributed and local manner, the message sending component could know the whole actors group list and send the same message to each one. But this solution requires the diffusion of updating messages in case of elimination or introduction of an entity in the group. On the other hand, an actor server, known by the entire group, could centralize the list. Each actor which wants to broadcast, asks this server. This adds therefore a message for every wanted diffusion, and puts foreground the localization problem of this server with regard to the localization of every member. We study an implementation of groups for concurrent languages and in particular for the language PlasmaII.

- *The reduction evaluation cost problems.* The present implementation in PlasmaII aimed to validate the reflective architecture. The translation of the reflective extensions proposed in virtual machine Smart's code will allow to reduce this overhead. Then, dynamic compilation and binding techniques, or partial evaluation will allow both efficiency and power of reflective expression [25].
- *Dynamic composition of reflective operations.* We have studied dynamic composition of reflective operations, that is to say, the possibility of adding or cancelling a reflective operation at run-time. For this purpose, we added to PlasmaII actors a structural component which stores the sequence of all reflective modifications done. We are working now on composition efficiency. When reflective operations are cancelled, our first approach consists in re-composing all the operations left in the sequence. This can be optimized if we can identify and preserve states of unchanged components.

REFERENCES

[1] JEFF MCAFFER, *Engineering the meta-level*, In Kiczales [26], pp. 39–61.

[2] H. MASUHARA, S. MATSUOKA, AND A. YONEZAWA, *Implementing parallel language constructs using a reflective object-oriented language*, In Kiczales [26], pp. 79–91.

[3] FRDRIC MIGEON AND PATRICK SALL, *Generic reflective description of concurrent systems*, In the 5th International Conference on Advanced Computing, K.M. Mehata & A.K. Somani R. Mittal, Ed. December 1997, pp. 155–161, Tata, Mc Graw Hill.

[4] A. MARCOUX, C. MAUREL, P. SALL, AND G. LAPALME, *Prsentation du langage PlasmaII*, Tech. Rep., L.S.I., Universit Paul Sabatier, Toulouse, France, 1990.

[5] CARL E. HEWITT, *Viewing controll structures as patterns of passing messages*, Journal of Artificial Intelligence, vol. 8, no. 3, pp. 323–364, 1977.

[6] GUL AGHA, *ACTORS : A model of Concurrent Computations in Distributed Systems*, The MIT Press, Cambridge, Mass., 1986.

[7] F. FRANCS, A. MARCOUX, C. MAUREL, P. SALL, AND M. SALOM, *An actor-based distributed virtual machine*, In 4th International Symposium on Computer and Information Sciences, A. Doga & E. Gelenbe, Ed., Cesme, Middle East Technical University, Turquie, 1989.

[8] GUL A. AGHA, IAN A. MASON, SCOTT F. SMITH, AND CAROLYN L. TALCOTT, *A foundation for actor computation*, Journal of Functional Programming, vol. 7, no. 1, pp. 1–72, Jan. 1997.

[9] J.-P. BRIOT AND R. GUERRAOUI, *Objets pour la programmation parallle et rpartie: intrts, volutions et tendances*, Technique et Science Informatiques, vol. 15, no. 6, 1996.

[10] J.-P. ARCANGELI, L. BRAY, AND P. SALL, *Le placement des acteurs : problmatique et mthodologie*, In JRPRC2 Deuximes Journes de Recherche sur le Placement Dynamique et la Rpartition de Charge. Laboratoire d'Informatique Fondamentale de Lille (LIFL), may 1998.

[11] PATTIE MAES, *Concepts and experiments in computational reflection*, In Proceedings of the Conference on Object-Oriented Programming Systems, Languages, and Applications (OOPSLA), Norman Meyrowitz, Ed., New York, NY, Dec. 1987, vol. 22, pp. 147–155, ACM Press.

[12] BRIAN C. SMITH, *Reflection and semantics in Lisp*, In Conference Record of the Eleventh Annual ACM Symposium on Principles of Programming Languages, Salt Lake City, Utah, Jan. 1984, pp. 23–35.

[13] DANIEL P. FRIEDMAN AND MITCHELL WAND, *Reification: Reflection without metaphysics*, In Conference Record of the 1984 ACM Symposium on Lisp and Functional Programming. ACM, Aug. 1984, pp. 348–355, ACM.

[14] A. GOLDBERG AND D. ROBSON, *Smalltalk80, the language and its implementation*, Addison-Wesley Publishing company, Reading, Massachussetts, 1993.

[15] T. MINOHARA AND M. TOKORO, *Multiple meta-objects support an object*, In ECOOP/OOPSLA'90 Workshop on Reflection and Metalevel Architectures in Object-Oriented Programming Proceed-

ings, Ottawa, Canada, October 1990.

[16] T. WATANABE AND A. YONEZAWA, *An actor-based metalevel architecture for group-wide reflection*, In Proceedings of REX School/Workshop on Foundations of Object-Oriented Languages, Noordwijkerhout, the Nederlands, May 1990.

[17] SATOSHI MATSUOKA, TAKUO WATANABE, AND AKINORI YONEZAWA, *Hybrid group reflective architecture for object-oriented concurrent reflective programming*, In Proceedings ECOOP'91, P. America, Ed., Geneva, Switzerland, July 15-19 1991, LNCS 512, pp. 231–250, Springer-Verlag.

[18] S. GIROUX, *Agents et systmes, une ncessaire unit*, Ph.D. thesis, Universit de Montral, C.P. 6128, succursale A, Montral, P.Q. H3C 3J7, Août 1993.

[19] G. KICZALES, J. DES RIVIRES, AND D. BOBROW, *The art of the metaobject protocol*, The MIT Press, Cambridge, Massachussetts 02142, 1991.

[20] Y. YOKOTE, *Kernel structuring for object-oriented operating systems: the Apertos approach*, Tech. Rep. SCSL-TR-93-014, Sony CSL, 1993.

[21] S. CHIBA, *Programmer's guide for version 2*, Tech. Rep. SPL-96-024, Xerox Parc, 1996.

[22] Y. ISHIKAWA & AL., *Design and implementation of metalevel architecture in C++ - MPC++ approach -*, In Kiczales [26], pp. 153–166.

[23] B. GOWING AND V. CAHILL, *Meta-object protocols for C++: the iguana approach*, In Kiczales [26], pp. 137–152.

[24] GREGOR KICZALES EDITOR, *Foil for the workshop on open implementation*, 1994.

[25] J. MALENFANT, M. JACQUES, AND F.-N. DEMERS, *A tutorial on behavioral reflection and its implementation*, In Kiczales [26], pp. 1–20.

[26] G. KICZALES, ED., *Proceedings of the Reflection'96 Conference*, San Francisco (California, USA), April 1996. ParcPlace-Difitalk, Object Technology International, Xerox Palo Alto Research Center.

A NEW FAST MESSAGE PASSING COMMUNICATION SYSTEM FOR MULTIPROCESSOR WORKSTATION CLUSTERS *

ZHENG WEIMIN, SHEN JUN, WANG JU†

Abstract. In this paper, a fast message passing communication architecture (FMP) is proposed in order to reduce the software overhead of communication, which has been a great impediment to the good performance of workstation clusters. A FMP system is implemented over the SUN Ultra2-Myrinet platform. Measurements show that this implementation has achieved a one-way latency of 11.2us for one-byte packets in network communication, and only 4.9us in local communication. Its bandwidth can reach as high as 338Mb/s for 8KB packets in network communication, and more than 770Mb/s in local message passing. These results tell us that FMP can really exploit the performance of supercomputers and high-speed networks.

Local communication is implemented through shared memory within a single host, while the methods to decrease overheads of network communication depend on user-level communication protocol, pipeline transmission, credit flow control and multithreading. Furthermore, the whole system provides the same interface for both network and local communication.

Key words. communication,message passing, overhead, performance, network of workstations, protocol

1. Introduction. Cluster of Multiprocessors, i.e., Multiprocessor workstations linked together by high-speed networks, could be the model of supercomputers in the future. The communication system in such a cluster plays a significant role in many aspects, such as the efficiency of parallel computing, the scope of application and the scalability of the system. Therefore, in addition to advanced computing workstations, a high-performance cluster also needs an efficient communication system with low latency and high bandwidth. Generally, a communication system can be divided into two parts: Network Communication (communication among different hosts using networks) and Local Messages (communication among different processes within a single host). Improvement of both of them will result in a well-developed communication system.

A common way to achieve high performance of network communication is to use high-speed local-area networks such as Fast Ethernet, ATM and Myrinet[3] for workstation clusters. The bandwidth of these networks can reach as high as hundreds of megabits or even gigabits per second, which is much better than conventional Ethernet. However, measurements show that the actual performance of those networks in practice is not so good as expected. For example, the TCP/IP peak bandwidth of Myrinet is only 42.6Mb/s and its round-trip latency of 1506us is even higher than a 10Mb/s Ethernet.

Ultra-fast workstations are used to improve the speed of computation. While the "side effect" of that is obvious: the hardware can offer a data transfer-rate as high as the data bus would permit. But existing message passing systems can only use a small part of it. In SUN's SPARC 20, for example, a conventional UNIX domain socket can only achieve a bandwidth of about 170Mb/s, which means that a large part of bandwidth SBUS offers has been wasted by the socket. ¿From those examples, we can see clearly that hardware is no longer the bottleneck of communication performance for high-speed communication system.

Communication latency is primarily composed of software overhead and transfer latency (time of flight). The term software overhead is used here to refer to the time spent by the processors at sending or receiving ends on handling messages. Although high-speed network

*This research is supported by the National High-Tech Program of China under Grant No. 863-306-ZD-02.

†Department of Computer Science and Technology, Tsinghua University, Beijing, 100084, China (zwm-dcs@tsinghua.edu.cn, shen@est4.cs.tsinghua.edu.cn, sswang@solaris.bjpu.edu.cn).

and ultra-fast data bus can reduce the latency of data transmission, it does not decrease the software overhead. So the software overhead became the bottleneck of the improvement in communication performance.

The communication protocol and the operating system are the main generators of software overhead. Firstly, the communication protocol overheads include buffer management, message copy, checksumming, flow-control handling and so on. For TCP/IP protocol, since it is designed for interconnection of networks, it provides many complex functions, such as congestion control, routing, time management, flow-control and buffer management. These functions make the TCP protocol able to provide a reliable, ordered byte-stream, but they also lead to heavy overheads. Secondly, involvement of the operating system in communication sometimes causes context switching (e.g., from kernel mode to user mode) and interrupts. Those operations cost so much CPU-time that the overhead introduced by it can no longer be neglected.

Since the new generation networks used to build workstation clusters can offer very low latencies (less than a few microseconds) and very high bandwidth (in the 100s of MB/s range), they are called System Area Networks(SANs)[5]. Examples of SANs include the Myricom Myrinet and the IBM Vulcan switches. SANs can not only provide good performance, but have great potential in keeping this high performance to the end-user applications as well. Since the communication links of SANs are pretty reliable and their structures are relatively simple, it is not necessary to use heavy-weight software protocols like TCP/IP on them, which could severely affect their performance as mentioned before. As the result, it seems of great significance to study how to reduce the software overhead in order to achieve low latency, high bandwidth and reliable communication. In this paper, a fast message-passing communication system (FMP) is proposed, and a system based on FMP is implemented over the UltraSparc-Myrinet platform. Measurements of FMP on SUN Ultra2 workstations show that this implementation achieves a one-way latency of 11.2us for one-byte packets in network communication, and only 4.46us in local message passing; while its bandwidth can reach as high as 338Mb/s for 8KB packets in network communication, and more than 770Mb/s in local message passing for 2KB packets. These results tell us that FMP can really exploit the performance of supercomputers and high-speed networks.

The rest of this paper is organized as follows: techniques for mutual exclusion are discussed in Section 2. Section 3 describes the network communication architecture. Section 4 describes the implementation of network communication of FMP on Myrinet and the techniques used to improve communication performance. Section 5 describes the local message part of FMP and its implementation on SUN Ultra 2. Section 6 describes the performance of our system and compares it with other related work. Section 7 presents our conclusions and directions for future work in this area.

2. Techniques for mutual exclusion. In a traditional UNIX networking architecture, the communication protocol is usually implemented in the kernel space. The path taken by messages through the kernel involves context switching and several data duplication, and crosses multiple levels of abstraction between the device drivers and user applications. The resulting overheads limit the peak communication bandwidth and cause high end-to-end message latencies. One of the most promising techniques to reduce these overheads is to move part of the protocol into user space. As for network communication, it means that messages can be sent directly from user processes to the network interfaces or received directly from the network interface to user processes without involvement of operating system and unnecessary copies. While in the local message part, it means that messages can be copied directly from one process to another. This approach can largely reduce the communication overhead.

Obviously, areas shared by all the processes are needed to meet those requirements. Then here comes another problem: how to prevent processes from interfering with each other when they are accessing these public areas concurrently? Two approaches are suggested here:

1. Let the operating system do it.
2. Use a software-locking algorithm.

In the first approach, P/V atomic operations are implemented using some of the interprocess communication mechanisms (IPC) in UNIX such as semaphores. The involvement of operating system brings us an easy way to perform perfect concurrency management. But it will take about 50us to perform a P-V operation, which is too long for the FMP system, whose latency of one-way transportation is always around 10us. Therefore, we turned to the software-locking algorithms. There are many different algorithms about mutual exclusion. We have tried two of them: Eisenberg & McGuire's locking algorithm and a simple CAS (compare-and-swap) method.

Eisenberg & McGuire's algorithm is surely a good one. It provides every competing process a fare chance to enter the critical area. No starvation will appear here in this method under all circumstances. But its overhead of 6us in the atomic lock-unlock pair is relatively high. This is a fatal drawback, and we have to give it up.

```
proc init_lock(var my_lock);
[     my_lock := False;      ]
proc lock(var my_lock);
[
      reg := True;
      repeat swap (my_lock, reg) until reg = false;
]
proc unlock(var my_lock);
[     my_lock := False;      ]
```

FIG. 2.1. *The CAS Locking Algorithm*

The CAS method is very simple. It takes advantage of the swap instruction on SPARC architecture. The algorithm is shown in Figure 2.1.

This algorithm works provided that "swap" is atomic and no more than one processor can access a memory word at the same time. Many kinds of architecture including the SPARC family support all of those. The overhead of this method is really very low, only about 0.5us for a lock-unlock pair. But it is not a "fare" method due to its "simple-mindness". Starvation might occur when some of the processes kept competing for the control of critical region. However, we can avoid this in the upper level applications. Please refer to Section 5.4 for further discussion about the role mutual exclusion plays in a communication system.

Table 2.1 presents one-way communication latencies in microsecond for the three mutual exclusion techniques. The latency without mutual exclusion operations is 12us for single process. The IPC mechanism is the worst with the cost of 50us because of the involvement of operating system. The CAS method is the fastest, but is not a perfect one because of its

TABLE 2.1
One-way latency for mutual exclusion

Mutual exclusion techniques	One-way latency (us)
Without mutual exclusion	12
Eisenberg & McGuire's algorithm	18
IPC atomic operation	62
CAS Locking Algorithm	12.5

simplicity. However, we choose this one for the FMP system due to its low cost and high efficiency.

3. Network Communication Architecture. NCFMP (Network Communication in FMP) is a lean communication layer. To reduce the communication software overhead as much as possible, two key techniques are used here in NCFMP: queue buffer management and credit flow control.

3.1. Queue Buffer Management. Buffer management plays an important role in a communication protocol. The implementation of many functions, such as messages sending, receiving, retransmission and flow controlling, is related to buffer management. In order to design a highly efficient communication protocol, queues are used to reduce overhead in NCFMP. As shown in Figure 3.1, There are two queues in the system: S_Queue is used for sending messages and R_Queue is for receiving messages. Both of them can be accessed by the host processor and network interface (NI). For each queue, a head pointer (head) identifies the next item to be dequeued, and a tail pointer (tail) identifies the next free entry. The queue is empty if head and tail are equal, and full if tail is one item less than head (modulo queue size). A processor sends a message by simply enqueueing it in S_Queue. That is, it first checks for overflow, then write the message to the next free queue location and increments tail. NI retrieves the message from S_Queue and sends it to networks actually by first checking for an empty queue, and then reading the queue entry pointed to by the head. The message remains in the queue until NI explicitly increments head. Receiving a message is similar to sending operation. NI gets messages from network and enqueue them in R_Queue, then the processor retrieves messages at the head of the queue. When multiple processes send or receive messages at the same time, a tag is used in each message to determine its destination and processes only receive their own messages identified by the tag. Mutual exclusion operations are also necessary to prevent modifying tail or head pointer concurrently.

Using head and tail pointers of the queues is a very simple way to manage reuse of memory. No handshaking between the processor and NI is required to access the head and tail pointers. Consequently, the synchronization overhead is avoided and messages can be sent or received like a pipeline. With this buffer management, the potential bandwidth of networks can be delivered greatly.

3.2. Credit Flow Control. An important feature of any communication protocol is flow control. Because all networks have limited buffer size, flow control is necessary to achieve reliable delivery, ensuring that a receiver has enough buffer space to store incoming messages. Traditional flow control schemes include sliding windows which combine flow control, error detection and correction for fault tolerance. The Sliding window scheme is too complex for SANs, because bit errors or lost packets rarely occur on SANs. Moreover, many SANs even provide a back-pressure flow control scheme in hardware to prevent buffer

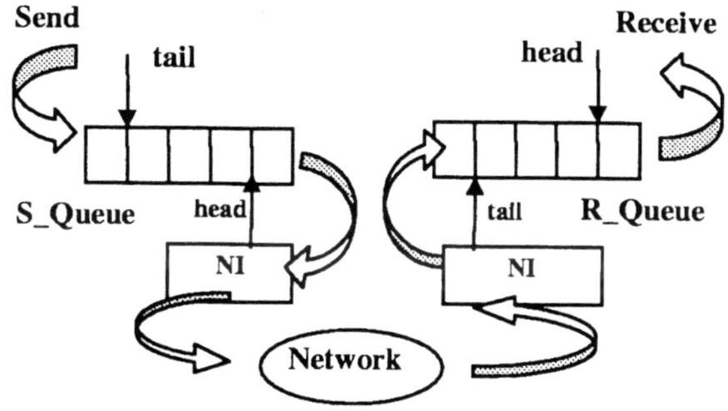

FIG. 3.1. *Queue Buffer Management*

overflow in the network interface. Therefore we designed a credit flow control to reduce the overhead incurred by the window scheme.

In the credit flow control scheme, a receiving queue is divided equally among all the nodes. Each node owns some sending credits to the receiving queue. The number of all credits stands for the size of the queue. When sending a message, a sending process first checks if it has a credit to its destination. If it does have, it can send the message and use up a credit. Otherwise it has to wait until a credit is returned from the receiver. At the beginning of communication, the sender can dispatch messages continually. When it uses up all of its credits, it will start polling for new credits. For message receiving, the receiver uses a counter to record the number of received messages. When the number is larger than the return-credit threshold, the receiver replenishes credits by replying a credit-acknowledgement message to the sender. Note that we can optimize replying a credit-acknowledgement message by piggybacking it on ordinary data packets.

The credit scheme is a simple flow control mechanism. It uses credits to avoid overflowing the receive queue during communication. However, the disadvantage of this approach is that the queue size scales with the number of processors and the depth of the network.

4. Implementation of Network Communication. The NCFMP communication architecture has been implemented on a cluster of Ultra 2 workstations connected by Myrinet network. The primary goal is to exploit the performance of Myrinet and provide a high-performance parallel computing environment on workstation clusters.

4.1. Hardware Architecture. The experimental platform appears in Figure 4.1. Each Ultra 2 contains two 200 MHz UltraSPARC processors with 512 KB of L2 cache per processor and a total of 512 MB of main memory. A Myricom M2F network interface card is on the SBus of each Ultra 2 workstation. Eight workstations are connected with an 8-port Myrinet switch.

Myrinet is a high-speed local-area network or system-area network for computer systems. The network link can deliver 1.28 Gb/s of bi-directional bandwidth. It also provides in-order network delivery with very low bit error rates (below 10^{-15}). On sending, the 8-bit CRC is computed by hardware and is appended to the packet. On a packet arrival, CRC hardware computes the CRC of the incoming packet and compares it with the received CRC. If they do not match, a CRC error is reported. Each Myrinet contains a 37.5 MHz 32-bit control processor called LANai (version 4.1) with 256 Kbytes of SRAM (Static Random Access Memory). The SRAM serves as the network buffer memory and also as the code and data memory of the LANai processor.

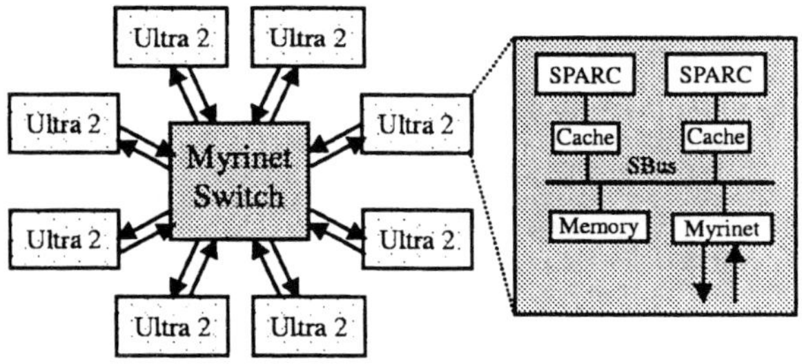

FIG. 4.1. *Hardware Architecture*

4.2. Software Architecture. As illustrated in Figure 4.2, NCFMP consists of two basic parts: the NCFMP protocol program on hosts and the Myrinet control program (MCP) on network interfaces. MCP is responsible for sending data to networks or receiving data from networks. The memory and registers on Myrinet interface are mapped into the user's address space by a UNIX system call – mmap(). Thus, the NCFMP protocol program can bypass the operation system and directly access the network without any extra data copy cost. This part completes the main functions of NCFMP such as buffer management, concurrency management and flow control. Compared with the traditional protocol TCP/IP, the architecture is quite simple.

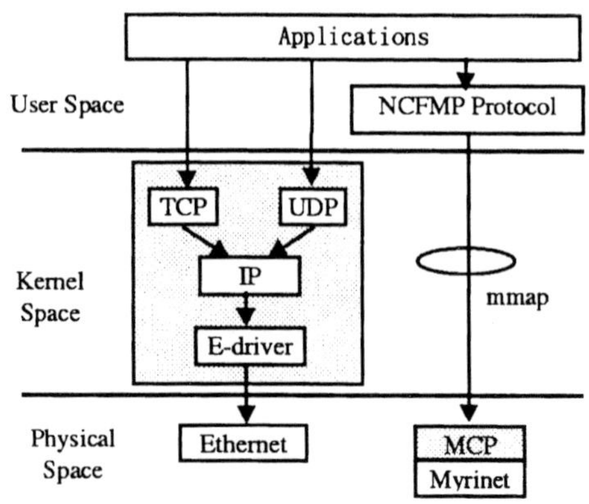

FIG. 4.2. *NCFMP Architecture*

4.3. Sending and Receiving Messages. In the existing systems, two ways are offered to move data between the processor and the network interface. First, the processor can perform directly load or store data to or from memory-mapped device registers. This way is called as programming I/O (PIO). PIO can start data transmission immediately, but it has very low bandwidth because it takes the processor much time to access the memory bus or the I/O bus in transmission and can only move data word by word. Second, the processor can initiate a DMA (Direct Memory Access) request either through a system call or through a user-level DMA request, which activates the DMA engine in the network interface. DMA is a way in which we can make full use of the bandwidth of I/O bus and do not consume any host CPU time during data transmission. However, the initialization time to start a

DMA operation is much more than that PIO needs, because the DMA operations could not be started until DMA pointers to the buffer on workstations become valid. DMA pointers have different requirements on different platforms and operating systems. For example, on SPARCstation20s running Solaris 2.4, they must be aligned on a 4-byte boundary, and must be in whatever space the OS requires them to be in. The memory must be locked down so that it cannot be paged or swapped. All data offset and length must be a multiple of 4-bytes. As there are so many restrictions on DMA operations, DMA have to spend a lot of time on align data to meet the above requests. Figure 4.3 shows the raw bandwidth of PIO and DMA for the Myrinet interface on Ultra 2 workstations. For small messages (their size is less than 128 bytes), its PIO bandwidth is better than the DMA performance. For large messages, the maximum bandwidth of DMA is up to 50 MB/s, but the PIO bandwidth is only 23 MB/s when the message size is 8192 bytes. This result reflects the different characteristics between PIO and DMA. According to the above analyses, we use different ways to transmit data in order to get the best performance. When handling small messages (less than 128 bytes), the initialization time to exchange the information between the board and the host becomes predominant over the transmission time itself, therefore PIO is adopted to decrease latency. On the other hand, when dealing with large messages (larger than 128 bytes), since the transmission time dominate the whole overheads, DMA is used to get better bandwidth performance than PIO.

In order to move data between the user space and the network interface through DMA operations, a buffer named as UBLOCK is allocated in the kernel of OS. Because the memory pages are pinned in the kernel and cannot be swapped out to disk, UBLOCK can meet the restrictions of DMA operations. As illustrated in Figure 4.4, the host processor sends short messages directly from the user space to the send queue in SRAM of Myrinet through PIO, or first copy large messages into send buffer in UBLOCK, then DMA them onto Myrinet interface. The process of receiving messages is similar to the sending process.

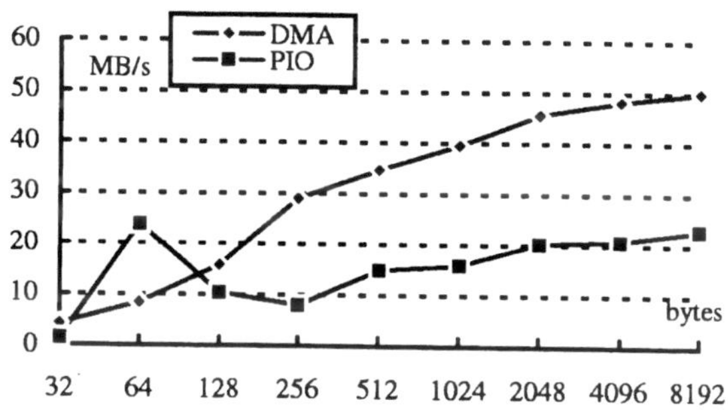

FIG. 4.3. *Raw Bandwidth of DMA and PIO*

4.4. Pipelined transmission. As we discussed earlier, the following procedures are needed to transfer data between main memory on each node.

1. Transferring the data by DMA from main memory to on-board SRAM.
2. Sending the data from on-board SRAM to the network.
3. Receiving the data from the network to on-board SRAM.
4. Transferring the data from on-board SRAM to main memory.

The sequential execution of DMA and message transmission cannot fully utilize the bandwidth of the DMA controller and the network interface. In this case, it is impossible to

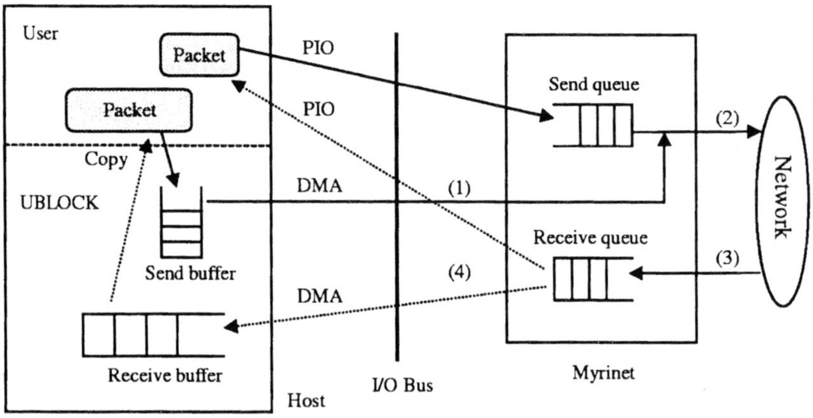

FIG. 4.4. *Sending and Receiving Messages*

achieve high throughput. Therefore we develop a technique called pipelined transmission to overlap the DMA transfers between the host and the network. We decompose a message into packets of equal size. On the sending side, the Myrinet initiates DMA of the outgoing message onto the network link as soon as it has received the first small packet. On the receiving side, the pipeline operation is performed in the same way. Figure 4.5 shows that pipeline transmission can reduce message transfer time compared to sequential delivery by hiding the latency of transfers on the host I/O bus. The performance of sequential and pipeline transmission is illustrated in Figure 4.6. The bandwidth of sequential delivery is 22.8 MB/s, while pipeline transmission achieves 42 MB/s for 8192-byte messages, increasing 84%. The latency of pipeline transmission is also much lower than that of sequential delivery.

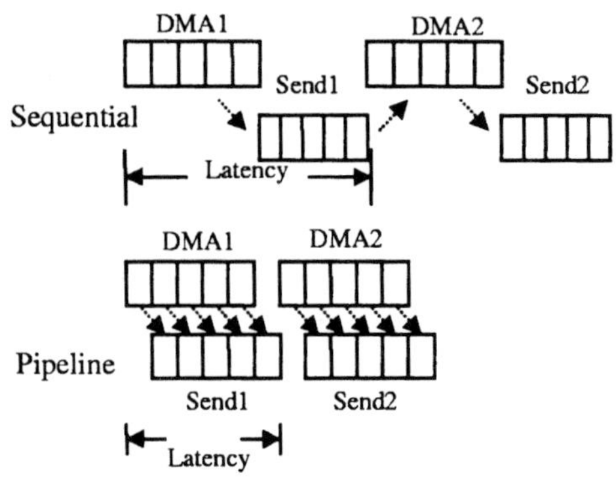

FIG. 4.5. *Pipeline Transmission*

4.5. Flow Control. Myrinet provides a back-pressure flow control scheme in hardware to control the speed of sending messages and prevent buffer overflow on the receiving side. When the sender transfers data faster than the receiver, the sender will block the sending operation until the receiver takes away the data in the receiving buffer or timeout happens

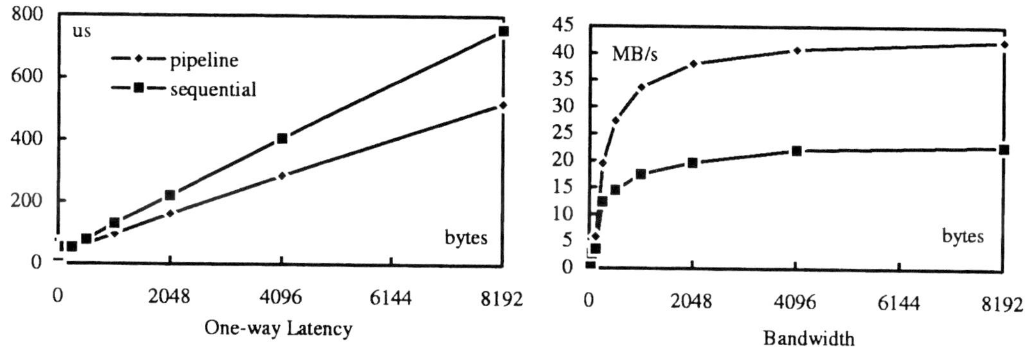

FIG. 4.6. *Performance of Sequential vs. Pipeline Transmission*

on the sending network interface. The timeout is used to prevent a communication deadlock in the network, but it causes the blocked part of the sender's messages to be dropped. As the hardware flow control may lose data when communication, the credit flow control is adopted in NCFMP to improve the communication reliability. Furthermore, in order to deal with the occurrence of bit errors, the flow control also detects the CRC of the coming message to make sure that it is correct. The receiver would ask the sender to re-transfer the message in case error occurs.

The overhead of the credit flow control is very small. Comparison between the communication layers with and without flow control indicates that the scheme incurs little additional latency. The communication layer achieves a round-trip latency of 20us without flow control and 24us with flow control, only increasing 4us.

4.6. Multithreading on Myrinet. Multithreading is a technique to hide communication latency and exploit the concurrency of programs. In NCFMP, this technique is used in MCP for the Myrinet LANai processor. The LANai processor is a dual-context machine. One context, which is called as user context, is interruptible. An interrupt during the execution of the user context causes

the processor to switch to the other, system context. The system context is not interruptible. It can be converted to the user context by executing a switch instruction. Therefore a sending thread and a receiving thread are designed respectively. The receiving thread runs in the system context and the LANai always works in the system context to detect if there is a message coming from the network. The sending thread works in the user context. Only when there is a message need to be sent from the user space does the processor switch to the user context to process the sending request. After the processing is finished, the processor returns to the system context. Although context switching causes somewhat overheads, the two threads can make full use of the bi-directional bandwidth of Myrinet networks. Measurements on the multithread model indicate that it achieves a round-trip latency of 22.4us and a peak bandwidth of 338 Mb/s, while the round-trip latency of the single thread model is 24us and its maximum bandwidth is 270 Mb/s.

5. Local Message Communication. LMFMP (Local Message in FMP) is another important issue. Since there are more than one CPU in a multiprocessor workstation such as SUN Ultra2, communication among processes within a single host is of the same importance as network communication.

5.1. Overview of Local Message Passing. Local message passing is a little different from network communication. Usually, the architecture of a Local Message Passing System is something like what depicted in Figure 5.1. There is a global message header queue in the system. A sender process inserts its message header into the queue, and a receiver process gets the message header it wants out of the queue. The body of the message is handled separately in a message buffer. The address of the message body is indicated in the message header. Because all of the involved processes share a block of physical memory, there are no actual transmission operations taken during communication. Therefore, some critical issues in network communication, such as flow-control, no longer exist in LMFMP. Here we are more concerned with how to organize the message queues and how to allocate or free a shared-memory block.

As shown in Figure 5.1, both the sender processes and the receiver processes will access the message header queue. So efforts should be taken to minimize the chance that these processes would compete for the critical region. In the next subsection, we will discuss how to construct message header queues to avoid competition. It is the most important issue in LMFMP, but is not all. We will also talk about how to allocate/free a shared memory block with fixed size or arbitrary size.

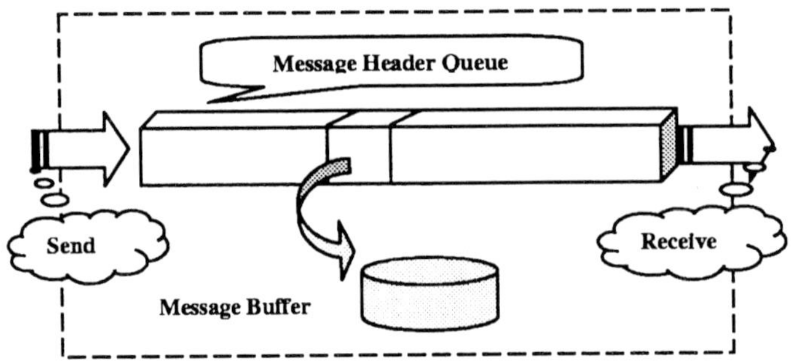

FIG. 5.1. *Architecture of Local Message Communication*

5.2. Structure of Message Header Queue. Consider the case of having only one global message header queue in the whole system, we will find that receivers have to probe in the whole message queue for messages sent to them. It means that a receiver process can remove a message header in any position of the queue, and also means that all of the receiver processes have to compete for the critical region, i.e., the message queue, with not only themselves but all the sender processes as well. It is too complicated for LMFMP. What we need is a simple and efficient one. So we build private incoming message queues for each of the processes in the system (Figure 5.2).

Every process in the system has a unique "channel number", and every channel has a private incoming message queue. Now, the sender processes just need to insert messages into the message queue of the receiver. While the receiver only need to check its private message queue to decide whether there are messages. This will save a lot of time spent in probing for a specific message in a large message queue for the entire system. Moreover, there will be no competition among receivers any more, and receivers can work independently now.

Our goal is to let all the processes work as independently as possible. Since it will be very expensive to avoid competition among all the senders, (N^2 message queues will be

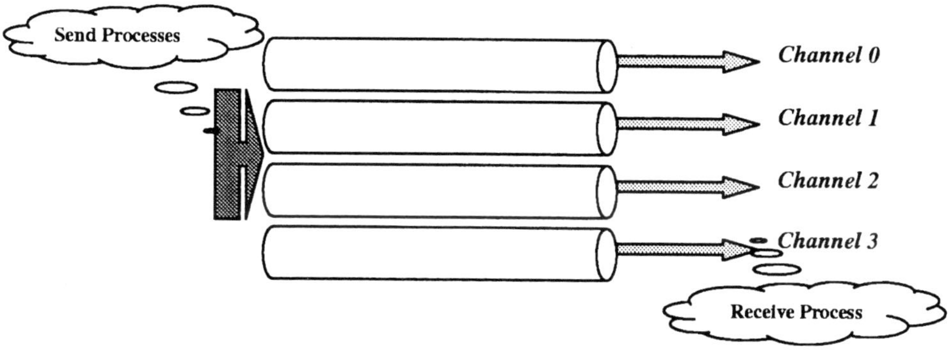

FIG. 5.2. *Message Header Queue for Multichannel System*

needed for N channels), we decide to think better of it and focus on how to avoid competition between senders and receivers.

If the receiver will receive all the messages sent to it, the message header queue will work as a FIFO, and competition could be avoided entirely. The data structure of the queue is depicted below in Figure 5.3.

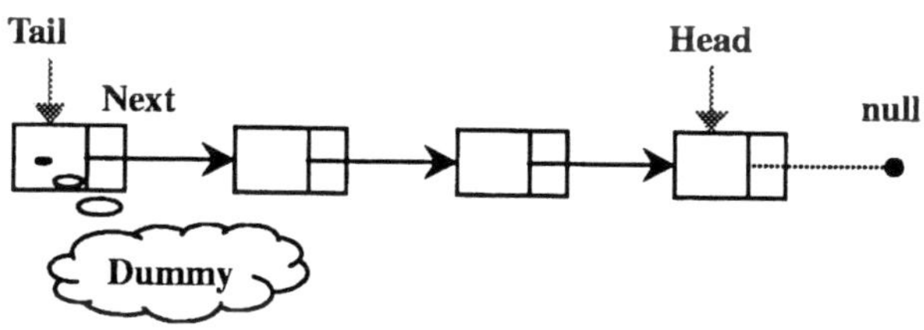

FIG. 5.3. *Data Structure of a Queue*

A dummy element is employed to avoid collision between "Tail" pointer and "Head" pointer of a valid queue. The queue is defined as empty when its "Tail" equals to its "Head". Therefore, the enqueue and dequeue operation could be defined as in Figure 5.4.

In the common case, where receivers will receive any message sent to it, the send operation is just an "enqueue", and the receive operation is a "dequeue". Obviously, there is no critical region between enqueue and dequeue operations. So there will be no competition between senders and receivers.

But in parallel systems FMP supports, such as PVM and MPI, receivers can choose to receive some specific messages. In this case, the message header queue will not work as a FIFO any more. Receivers can access any element in the queue. It means that it is possible that a sender and a receiver could access the same element at the same time. It happens only when the receiver wants to remove the element at the head of the queue as shown in Figure 5.5.

The receiver is trying to change Head to P1, while the sender is trying to change it to P2. If the sender and the receiver work one after another, the element Head is pointing to currently will be removed, and Head will then be changed to P2. Then the pseudo-code of send and receive is something like what is shown in Figure 5.6.

```
PROC enqueue (MSG_TYPE *Msg, QUEUE_TYPE *Queue);
[
      Msg->Next := NULL;
      Queue->Head->Next := Msg;
      Queue->Head := Msg;
]
PROC dequeue (MSG_TYPE *Msg, QUEUE_TYPE *Queue);
[
      If ( Queue->Tail = Queue->Head ) // the queue is empty
                  Return NO_MESSAGE;
      Else  Begin
            Msg := Queue->Tail->Next;
            Queue->Tail := Queue->Tail->Next;
      End
]
```

FIG. 5.4. *Enqueue and Dequeue*

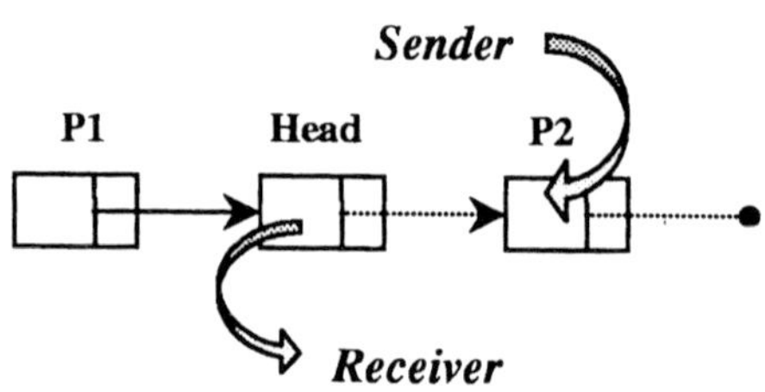

FIG. 5.5. *Competition between Senders and Receivers*

In the critical region, there is only one branch instruction for the receiver and two assign instructions for the sender. So the overhead of competition is slight for both of them. In most cases, receivers do not compete for the critical region at all. Therefore senders and receivers can almost work independently. That will greatly improve the performance of LMFMP as discussed in Section 5.4.

5.3. Memory Management. Since the size of a message header queue is always changing, memory blocks should be allocated or freed dynamically. Here we have to deal with two kinds of memory blocks: fixed size blocks and blocks with arbitrary size.

1. Management of fixed size blocks

Message headers have a fixed size, and ought to be allocated or freed quickly. As was discussed before in section 5.2, competition between allocaters and freers should be avoided to enhance the overall performance. We used a heap-like structure here. (Figure 5.7)

PseudoHeap is an array of fixed-size blocks. Items located above the position Pointer is pointing to have never been allocated before. Free-list works as a FIFO (see section 5.2), and it will collect freed memory blocks. When allocating a block, it first checks whether the free list is empty. A block will be allocated from the free-list if the list is not empty; otherwise a block will be allocated from the PseudoHeap. When freeing a block, the freer

```
PROC Receive( MSG_TYPE *Msg, QUEUE_TYPE *Queue);
[
      Msg points to the element to be removed;
      Temp points to the precursor of Msg;
      If (Msg = Queue->Head )
      Then Begin
            Lock( MUTEX );
            If ( Msg = Queue->Head )
            Then Queue->Head := Temp;
            Unlock( MUTEX );
      End;
      Temp->Next := Msg->Next;
]
PROC Send( MSG_TYPE *Msg, QUEUE_TYPE *Queue);
[
      Msg->Next := NULL;
      Lock( MUTEX );
      Queue->Head->Next := Msg;
      Queue->Head := Msg;
      Unlock(MUTEX);
]
```

FIG. 5.6. *PseudoCode of Send and Receive*

only needs to insert the freed block into the free-list.

In this way, the competition between allocaters and freers can be totally avoided, and the operations of allocating and freeing are very simple. Another merit of this PseudoHeap is its robustness. Trying to free a never allocated block can be easily detected.

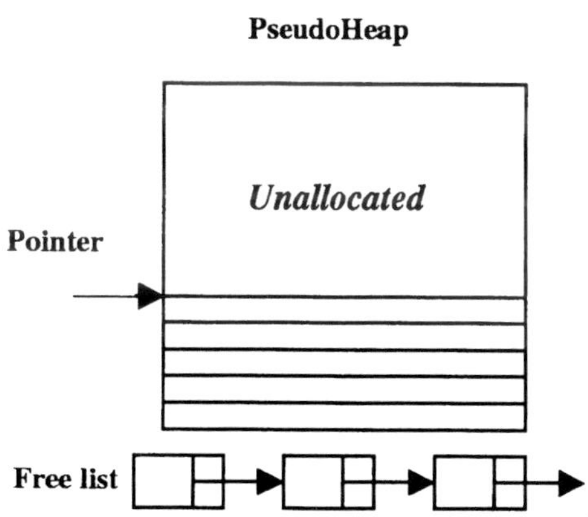

FIG. 5.7. *PseudoHeap*

2. Management of blocks with arbitrary size

The size of messages is arbitrary, so the method in section 5.3.1 could not be used to manipulate message bodies. We have to find another way out.

As shown in Figure 5.8, a link list is employed here to meet our needs. Every item in the list has the same size of 1KB for example. When allocating a block of 2.5KB, 3 items from the list will be allocated with the handle of the first one as the address of this block. This Null-terminated link list will be transparent to the user interface, when a new routine of memcpy() is defined.

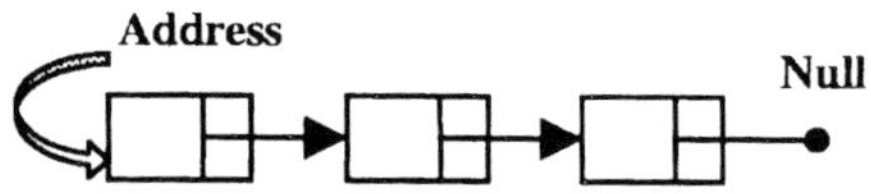

FIG. 5.8. *Block with arbitrary size*

5.4. Issues about Competition. In previous sub-sections, our goal is to avoid competition, because competition can greatly set back the performance of LMFMP. Testing results on Ultra 2 can prove it:

In a system without any effort to avoid competition, the latency of sending a 4-byte packet is very unstable. It ranges from 6us to more than 100us. In our optimized system, that latency is always around 4us on a light-burdened workstation.

The reason here has something to do with the operating system. For a competing process, it can not work until it has the control of both the critical region and CPU. There are chances that a process has CPU resource but has to wait for the critical region to be freed, while the process that has control of the critical region is waiting for its turn to get CPU. So competing processes keep waiting for each other to release resources, none of them could work until control of CPU is switched from one process to another. It means that the performance of LMFMP will be partly determined by the way OS switching its processes. This is the reason why in a crude system without effort to avoid competition, the performance of LMFMP is very unstable.

In our optimized system, competition rarely appears. Even though it happens, the process in the critical region has only a few operations to do, usually two or three instructions, so it can finish its tasks quickly and leave the critical region instantly. Moreover, in a multiprocessor system such as Ultra 2, the sender process and the receiver process can work almost collaterally, while in a crude system sender and receiver have to work serially. That is why the performance of our system is quite stable while a crude system is not.

6. Performance and Related Work. This section gives the performance of two parts of FMP, NCFMP and LMFMP, over the Ultra 2 workstation cluster. All measurements of network communication (NCFMP) have been made between two Ultra 2 workstations connected through a Myrinet switch.

The latency and bandwidth of LMFMP is shown in Figure 6.1. The one-way latency of a 1-byte packet is only 4.45us, while the bandwidth of a 2KB packet is more than 770Mbps. The performance of LMFMP is far more better than conventional UNIX domain sockets. The latency of a 1-byte packet is about 100us, while the bandwidth of a 2KB packet is less than 50Mbps.

Figure 6.2 illustrates the latency and bandwidth of NCFMP and Myrinet application programming interface (Myrinet-API). For small-size messages, the latency of NCFMP is much lower than Myrinet-API. NCFMP achieves a one-way latency of 11.2us when the message size is one byte. For large messages, NCFMP obtains the bandwidth of 338 Mb/s when the message size grows up to 8192 bytes, which reaches up 84.5the Myrinet-API bandwidth

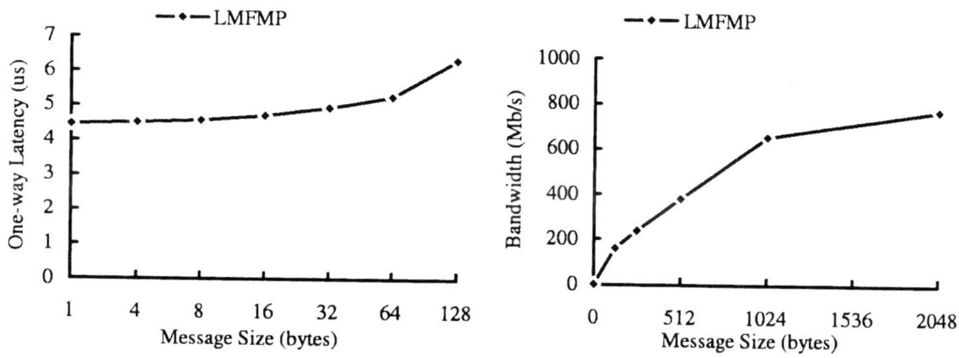

FIG. 6.1. *Latency and Bandwidth of LMFMP*

is 261 Mb/s. These experimental results demonstrate that NCFMP can significantly reduce the communication latency and get a high bandwidth. However, the maximum bandwidth of NCFMP is quite lower than the Myrinet link bandwidth of 1.28 Gb/s. The factor that greatly restricts the bandwidth performance of FMP is the performance of SBus. Tests on Ultra 2 workstations show that the highest DMA bandwidth of SBus is only 400 Mb/s, less than one third of the Myrinet link bandwidth. It is the low performance of the I/O bus that sets an upper bound for any user-level communication protocol. It means that the I/O bus has become the bottleneck limiting the performance of high-speed networks. If the I/O bus has higher performance, NCFMP will obtain a better performance.

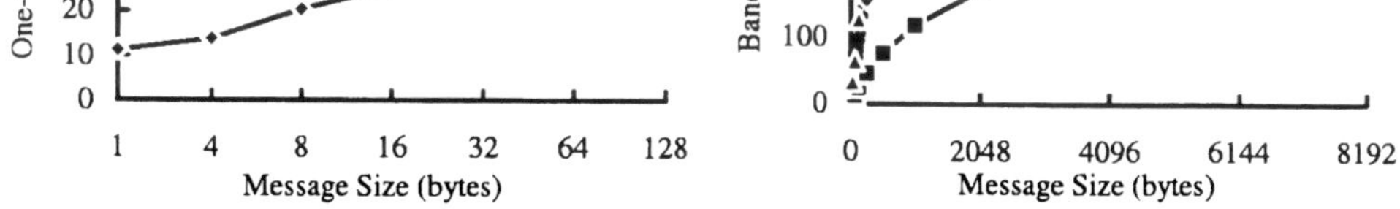

FIG. 6.2. *Latency and Bandwidth of NCFMP and Myrinet-API*

The Myrinet networks have been used by several different research projects to produce high performance message passing interfaces. These include Active Messages (AM-II) from the UC Berkeley[2][6], Fast Messages (FM1.0, FM2.1) from UIUC[7] and Virtual Memory-Mapped Communication (VMMC) from Princeton University[8]. The performance of these systems is shown in Table 6.1. The table illustrates that the performance of VMMC and FM2.1 are the best among the five systems. VMMC achieves a peak bandwidth of 864, and

TABLE 6.1
The Performance of Five Message Passing Systems

System	Network	Computer	One-way Latency(us)	Peak Bandwidth(Mb/s)
FMP Tsinghua	1.28Gb/s Myrinet (SBus)	Ultra 2	11.2	338
AM-II UC Berkeley	1.28Gb/s Myrinet (SBus)	Ultra 1	22.5	314
FM1.0 UIUC	640Mb/s Myrinet (SBus)	SPARC 20	14.5	140
FM2.1 UIUC	1.28Gb/s Myrinet (PCI)	Pentium Pro	11	616
VMMC Princeton	1.28Gb/s Myrinet (PCI)	Pentium 166	9.8	864

FM2.1 gets 616 Mb/s. One important facet contributing to their excellent performance is that both of them are built on PCI based Myrinet interfaces. The bandwidth of PCI DMA can be up to 1Gb/s, while Sbus DMA only reaches 400Mb/s. Therefore the performance of the I/O Bus has become another bottleneck which limits the performance of communication system.

7. Conclusions. This paper describes the architecture and implementation of Fast Message Passing communication (FMP) for a workstation cluster composed of Myrinet and Ultra 2. FMP can not only provide low latency and high bandwidth communication, but also guarantee the reliability of message delivery and supports multiple senders and receivers in a multi-user environment. We implemented FMP with several techniques to reduce the software overheads, and managed to develop a high performance PVM (Parallel Virtual Machine) parallel computing environment based on FMP. In the future, we will research on following issues:

1. To study the effects of I/O buses on network performance and implement FMP on PCI based platforms.
2. Implementation of ADI (Abstract Device Interface) for MPI (Message Passing Interface) on Myrinet-Ultra2 platform.
3. A new version of FMP in which NCFMP (network communication) and LMFMP (local message passing) will be integrated. Network communication and local communication will be transparent to users.

REFERENCES

[1] C.L. DONG, W.M. ZHENG, ET AL., *A scalable parallel workstation cluster system*, Proc. of APDC'97. pp. 307-313.

[2] T. VON EICKEN, D. E. CULLER, S. C. GOLDSTEIN, AND K. E. SCHAUSER, *Active messages: a mechanism for integrated communication and computation*, In Proc. of the 19th ISCA, May 1992, pp. 256-266.

[3] NANETTE J. BODEN, DANNY COHEN, ROBERT E. FELDERMAN, ALAN E. KULAWIK, CHARLES L. SEITZ, JAKOV N. SEIZOVIC, AND WEN-KING SU, *Myrinet: a gigabit-per-second local area network*, IEEE Micro, 15:1, February 1995, pp. 29-36.

[4] J. KAY AND J. PASQUALE, *The importance of non-data-touching overheads in TCP/IP*, In Proceedings of the 1993 SIGCOMM, pp. 259-260, San Francisco, CA, September 1993.

[5] GORDON BELL, *1995 Observations on Supercomputing Alternatives: Did the MPP Bandwagon Lead to Cul-de-Sac?*, Communications of the ACM, 39(3): 11-15, March 1996.

[6] STEVE RODRIGUES, TOM ANDERSON, DAVID CULLER, *High-Performance Local-Area Communication Using Fast Sockets*, USENIX '97 , 1997.

[7] MARIO LAURIA, AND ANDREW CHIEN, *MPI-FM: High Performance MPI on Workstation Clusters*, Journal of Parallel and Distributed Computing, Jan 1997.

[8] C. DUBNICKI, A. BILAS, K. LI, AND J. PHILBIN, *Design and Implementation of Virtual Memory-Mapped Communication on Myrinet*, In Proceedings of the 1997 International Parallel Processing Symposium, April 1997, pp. 388-396.

EFFICIENT DELAY COMPUTATION METHODS FOR REAL-TIME TRAFFIC IN AN ATM NETWORK*

JOSEPH KEE-YIN NG[†] AND SHIBIN SONG[‡]

Abstract. ATM is a connection-oriented technology. Before two hosts can communicate, a connection have to be established between them. Consider a real-time communication application running on top of an ATM network. In order to provide the real-time service, we require the connection to provide a performance guarantee. Such deterministic guarantee can only be possible if there exists an absolute worst case delay bound on all the ATM cells within the real-time connection. In this paper, we first present a framework for this worst case delay within an ATM switch. Later on, in estimating the real-time arrival traffic, we use the Deterministic Bounding Interval Dependent (D-BIND) traffic model [11] to characterize the burstiness and the temporal correlation structure of a real-time message stream. We then derive the worst case delay bound for an ATM switch with some typical output port schedulers. We find out that our proposed method is no harder than the other existing methods in finding such worst case delay in terms of computation complexity. Hence, we have an efficient and effective way to estimate the worst case delay for the connection admission control for an ATM network.

Key words. Real-Time ATM Networks, Worst Case Delay Analysis, Efficient Delay Computation, Distributed Computing.

1. Introduction. In recent years, the demand for real-time communication services in ATM networks has grown rapidly. Recalling that ATM is a connection-oriented technology. Before two hosts can communicate, a connection have to be established between them. For real-time communication services over an ATM network, we require the connection to provide a performance guarantee. Such guarantee should be deterministic and can only be possible if there exists an absolute worst case delay bound for all the ATM cells in this real-time connection. Many recent research focus on the Guarantees of Service (GoS) and in particular the delay guarantees [1, 4, 7, 10, 11, 12, 13, 17, 19, 20, 21, 22, 27, 28] for real-time communication. Such delay guarantees are crucial to the Connection Admission Control (CAC) of an ATM network. When a new connection that requires a certain quality of service (QoS) arrives, the CAC can only admit this connection if the network can guarantee the requested QoS of this connection without violating the guarantees committed to the currently active connections. In order to guarantee that the real-time requirements are met for each connection, we must derive the worst case delay experienced by the ATM cells in each of the connection within the ATM switch. Furthermore, the method to find out the worst case delay bound should be both efficient and effective. It has to be efficient because the CAC need to react fast in accepting a connection, and have to be effective because a tighter delay bound means admitting more connections into the network, hence, fully utilize the available bandwidth.

The deterministic delay bounds have been studied by many researchers [1, 2, 9, 11, 12, 14, 15, 17, 25, 26]. Similar to Cruz [7] who obtained the delay bounds by the arrival curve and service curve, we find the delay bound by utilizing the inverse function of the arrival and service functions during an ATM switch's busy period.

*The work reported in this paper was supported in part by the RGC Earmarked Research Grant under RGC/97-98/54, and by the FRG under FRG/96-97/II-103.

[†]Department of Computer Science, Hong Kong Baptist University, 224, Waterloo Road, Kowloon, Hong Kong. Email: jng@comp.hkbu.edu.hk .

[‡]Department of Mathematics, Zhong Shan University, Guang Zhou, 510275, China. Shibin Song is a visiting research scholar in the Department of Computer Science at Hong Kong Baptist University.

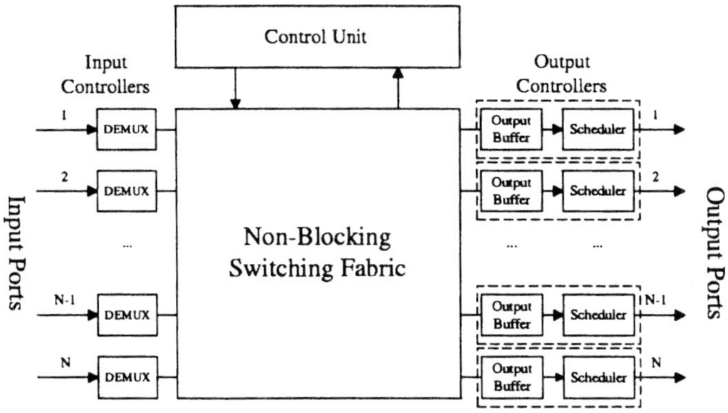

FIG. 1.1. *The ATM switch architecture.*

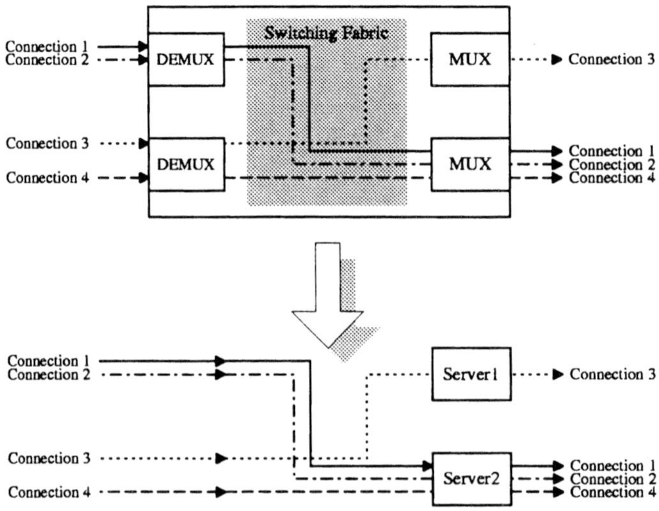

FIG. 1.2. *Connection-server graph.*

To be more specific, in this paper, we first present a framework for the worst case delay computation. Network elements, such as schedulers, regulators, and communication links are considered as servers. The streams of cell arrival traffic will be served by these servers. For the traffic descriptions, we use the arrival function concept similar to Cruz et al. [1, 5, 6, 7, 25] where the actual arrival function is bounded by a maximum arrival function (or arrival curve) [7]. The service provided by the server to serve the connection's cell is given by a service function. From our previous works on ATM delay analysis, the delay of a cell can be obtained by utilizing the inverse functions of the arrival function and service function during the busy period of an ATM switch[17, 19, 20]. Our method is proven to be simpler and more efficient than the previous methods [7, 11, 12].

The rest of the paper is organized as follows: Section 2 describes the real-time connections and the model for the ATM switch. Section 3 presents a general framework for our worst case delay. In section 4 and 5, we apply the results from Section 3 to a delay-based admission control. In estimating the real-time arrival traffic, we use the D-BIND traffic model [11] to characterize a real-time message stream's burstiness properties and temporal correlation structure. The D-BIND maximum arrival function is a piecewise linear function in which the slope of each segment is decreasing. In section 5, the computation delay formulae of the worst case delay for the D-BIND real-time traffic are given for some typical ATM output port schedulers.

Section 6 shows that the computation complexity for our delay formulae are $O(N + K)$ where N, K are the numbers of segments for the piecewise linear arrival, and service functions, respectively. In terms of computation complexity, our methods are proven to be no harder than the previous results [7, 11, 12].

Furthermore, although the accuracy of our methods rely on the number of segments of the arrival and service functions, we find out from our CAC experiment that a 5-segment traffic function is all that is necessary to provide a good estimate for the worst case cell delay. And these results are shown in Section 6. Lastly, we concluded the paper in Section 7.

2. Connections and ATM Model.

2.1. Connections. As mentioned before, ATM is a connection-oriented packet-switched technology. Before two hosts begin to communicate, a connection has to be set up between them. The term *connection* is then often referred as a stream of messages sent from a source host to destination host. In ATM networks, messages from individual connections are divided into fixed size packets called *cells*. We assume that time is normalized in terms of a cell transmission time as one time unit.

A hard real-time connection has a stringent deadline constraint on the delay of its cells. The admission control for a hard real-time connections is: when a new connection request arrives, the network must determine if all the cells within the connection can meet its deadline constraint and without violating the guarantees already provided to the currently active connections.

2.2. ATM Switch Model. As cells belonging to different connections traverse through the network, they may share network resources such as communication links and ATM switches. Referring to Figure 1.1, an ATM switch itself consists of input ports, switching fabric, and output ports. A cell that arrives at an input port of a switch is transported by the switching fabric to an output port where the cell is then transmitted along the physical link associated with the output port.

The scheduling policy at an output port controller of an ATM switch determines the order of the cells (from different connections) being transmitted. Typical scheduling policies utilized in the ATM switches are either FIFO or priority driven. However, there are other scheduling policies such as GPS(Generalized Processor Sharing) [21, 22], EDF(Early Deadline First), ... etc.

2.3. Connection-server Graph. To simplify the delay analysis, these network components are abstracted as servers. These servers supply transmitting cells service. An ATM network can be model as a connection-server graph in which the nodes are the servers.

The servers are classified into two categories: constant servers and variable servers [4, 23, 24]. A constant server offers a constant delay to each cell that traverse through it. A variable server, on the other hand, offers different delay to each cell. For example, physical links and switching fabric are constant servers. Since the function of an input port is to de-multiplex and achieved a constant time delay to each cell, so an input port is also a constant server. The output port, on the other hand, is a multiplexor and therefore, must be considered as a variable server and the delay suffered by a cell in this server should depend on the queue length in the buffer and the scheduling policy.

Note that the constant servers serving a connection only add a fixed amount of delay to its cells and do not change its traffic characteristics. Hence we can subtract the appropriate constant delays encountered by a connection from its deadline. We eliminate all the constant servers from further consideration and focus only on the variable servers. Thus, we can view a connection as being served by a sequence of variable servers only. Figure 1.2 shows how we can construct a connection-server graph from an ATM switch having 4 real-time connections passing through it.

In the next section, we give a general framework for the worst case delay of a connection's cells in a variable server.

3. A Framework for the Worst Case Delay. Consider a server system with some connections. Suppose in any time interval of length I, the maximum number of the cells from connection M_i that can arrive at the server is upper-bounded by the following constraint function $F_i(I)$, we can select $F_i(I)$ to be an increasing, right-continue and sub-additive function [3, 15].

Let $F_i(t, I)$ be the number of cells arrived from connection during time interval of $(t, t + I]$. Then, for any $t \geq 0$

$$F_i(t, I) \leq F_i(I) \tag{3.1}$$

Given this relation, $F_i(I)$ is called the *maximum arrival function* for connection M_i.

Now, we can specify the definition of an inverse function. Let $H(x)$ be a non-decreasing function. $H^{-1}(y)$, the inverse function of $H(x)$ is given as

$$H^{-1}(y) = \inf\{x | H(x) \geq y\} \tag{3.2}$$

DEFINITION 3.1. *A server is* sequential *if for every connection it serves, cells from the same connection are served in the order of their arrivals.*

A *busy period* of a connection in a server is the time interval during which any extra cell from the connection arrived at the server, the cell must be waiting for the service. Obviously, we are only interested in the busy period. We further state that an instant time t is the *starting point* of a busy period if at t^-, that is, at any time before t, the queue of the server is empty and starting at t, it is not. For the sake of simplicity, any time interval mentioned in the rest of this paper has its left boundary being a starting point of a busy period.

Cells of a connection are delayed at a server because the server does not serve the connection in the full rate. For the FIFO scheduler and the priority driven scheduler, this may happen due to the fact that the server is shared with other connections. For the sake of delay analysis, we need to quantify the service available to a connection from a server.

From $F_i(t, I)$, we can find the arrival time of the c-th cell in the busy period starting at time t. Denote t_c , T_c be the arrival time of the c-th cell when the arrival functions are $F_i(t, I)$and$F_i(I)$, respectively. Then

$$t_c = t + F_i^{-1}(t, c), T_c = t + F_i^{-1}(c), T_c \leq t_c, \tag{3.3}$$

where $F_i^{-1}(t, c), F_i^{-1}(c)$ are the inverse functions of $F_i(t, I)$ and $F_i(I)$ with respect to the variable I, respectively.

DEFINITION 3.2. *$S_i(t, I)$ is the service function for connection M_i during the time interval $[t, t + I)$ in a busy period starting at time t. That is, $S_i(t, I)$ specifies the number of*

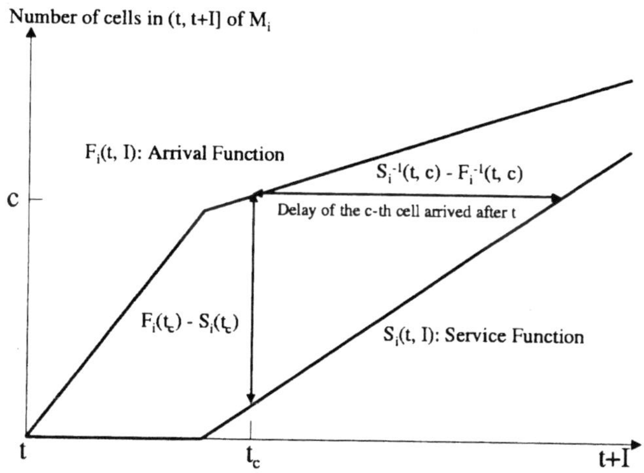

FIG. 3.1. *Traffic and service functions.*

cells from connection M_i that can be served (i.e., transmitted) by a server during the time interval between t and $t+I$.

From $S_i(t, I)$, we can find s_c, the departure time of the c-th cell in the busy period started at t.

$$s_c = t + S_i^{-1}(t, c) \tag{3.4}$$

If a server is lossless and sequential, from Equation (3.3) and (3.4), we can compute $d_i[t, c]$, the delay of the i-th cell in the busy period started at t, as follows:

$$d_i[t, c] = s_c - t_c = S_i^{-1}(t, c) - F_i^{-1}(t, c) \tag{3.5}$$

Then, in the busy period started at t, the maximum delay of M_i is given by

$$d_i[t] = \max_c (S_i^{-1}(t, c) - F_i^{-1}(t, c)) \tag{3.6}$$

And the maximum delay of connection M_i is

$$d_i = \max_{t,c} (S_i^{-1}(t, c) - F_i^{-1}(t, c)) \tag{3.7}$$

where t is the starting point of any busy period.

Figure 3.1 shows conceptually how we can compute the delay of the c-th cell for a connection M_i during the busy period starting at time t, by given the arrival function $F_i(t, I)$ and the service function $S_i(t, I)$.

Because it is very difficult to know the exact arrival and service functions, we must have some other estimates in order to compute the delay. In many occasions, an upper bound of the arrival function and a lower bound of the service function are known.

Let $F_i(I)$ be the maximum arrival function for connection M_i, and $C_i(I)$ be the lower bound of the service function for M_i. $C_i(I)$ is defined as

$$C_i(I) \leq S_i(t, I), \tag{3.8}$$

for any busy period starting at time t with a time interval of length I.

THEOREM 3.1. *Given $F_i(I)$ and $C_i(I)$, the upper bound of $F_i(t, I)$ and the lower bound of $S_i(t, I)$ respectively, the worst case delay bound for the cells from connection M_i is*

$$d_i \leq \max_{c \geq 0}\{C_i^{-1}(c) - F_i^{-1}(c)\} \tag{3.9}$$

where $F_i^{-1}(c)$ and $C_i^{-1}(c)$ are the inverse functions of $F_i(I)$ and $C_i(I)$, respectively. *Proof.* Since $F_i(t, I) \leq F_i(I)$ and $C_i(I) \leq S_i(t, I)$, we have

$$F_i^{-1}(c) \leq F_i^{-1}(t, c) \text{ and } C_i^{-1}(c) \leq S_i^{-1}(t, c) \tag{3.10}$$

Replacing $F_i^{-1}(t, c)$ and $S_i^{-1}(t, c)$ with $F_i^{-1}(c)$ and $C_i^{-1}(c)$ in (3.7) respectively, we have (3.9). Q.E.D.

Cruz et al. [1, 2, 6, 7] present a service curve method for the delay computation. The service curve of a connection is the lower bound of our service function. However, the delay bound in Theorem 3.1 could be overestimating sometimes. There are other methods to compute a more accurate worst case delay.

DEFINITION 3.3. *The input of a server is greedy if all the arrival functions are always maximum from the starting point of the busy period. That means*

$$F_j(t, I) = F_j(I),$$

for all j where t is the starting point of the busy period.

DEFINITION 3.4. *$S_i(I)$ is the service function for connection M_i when the input of the server is greedy starting at time zero, the beginning of a busy period.*

For FIFO scheduling server, Priority scheduling server, Leaky bucket server and GPS server [21, 22], ... etc, the worst case delay occurs when the input of the server is greedy. We have proven the same results for a regulated priority driven server and a regulated FIFO server in [17, 19, 20]. Because of this, the worst case delay computation by (3.7) can be simplified as stated in next Theorem.

THEOREM 3.2. *If the worst case delay for a connection M_i occurs when the input of the server is greedy, then the worst case delay is*

$$d_i = \max_{c}(S_i^{-1}(c) - F_i^{-1}(c)) \tag{3.11}$$

where $F_i^{-1}(c)$ and $S_i^{-1}(c)$ are the inverse functions of $F_i(I)$ and $S_i(I)$, respectively.

For the proof of the Theorem, please refer to the technical report [18].

4. D-BIND Traffic and Delay Analysis.

4.1. D-BIND Traffic. Among different types of real-time traffic, some have variable bit rate (VBR) characteristic, such as the transmission of MPEG videos. To provide a deterministic service, it needs a deterministic upper bound on the arrival traffic. The tightest time invariant deterministic bound on arrivals in an interval of length I is defined as

$$\epsilon(I) = \sup_{t \geq 0} F(t, I) \tag{4.1}$$

$\epsilon(I)$ is called the minimum envelope process [3]. The maximum arrival function, as a deterministic upper bound on the arrival traffic, must be an upper approximation to $\epsilon(I)$.

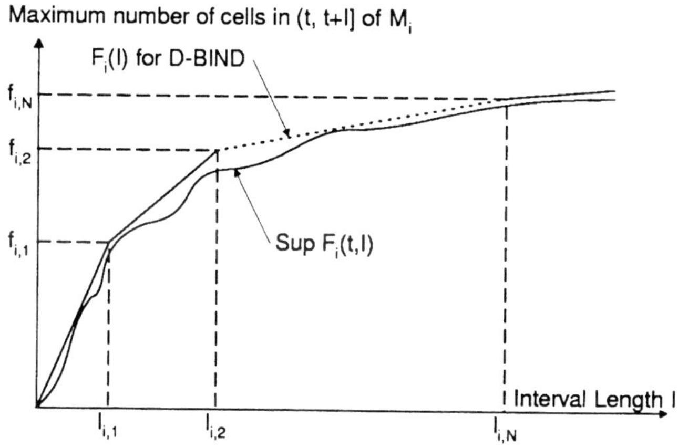

FIG. 4.1. *Traffic Functions.*

There are some traffic models such as the (σ, ρ) leaky bucket model [4], the $(X_{min}, X_{ave}, I, S_{max})$ model [8] and others [11, 15] that follows this approximation. Among all the models, the D-BIND model provides a good upper bound that can closely bound $\epsilon(I)$ for a wide variety of sources. On the other hand, since the D-BIND maximum arrival function is a piecewise linear function, its inverse function and the delay computation are easy to cope with.

The D-BIND traffic model of a connection M_i consists of N rate-interval pairs, $\{(\mu_{i,j}, I_{i,j}) | j = 1, 2, \ldots, N\}$ is shown in Figure 4.1, where $\{I_{i,j}\}$ is increasing and $\{\mu_{i,j}\}$is decreasing. The maximum number of cells at the input of a connection M_i in any interval of length I is

$$F_i(I) = \begin{cases} f_{i,j-1} + \mu_{i,j}(I - I_{i,j-1}) & I_{i,j-1} < I \leq I_{i,j} \\ f_{i,N} + \mu_{i,N}(I - I_{i,N}) & I > I_{i,N} \end{cases} \tag{4.2}$$

for $j = 1, 2, \ldots, N$, where $F_i(0) = 0, f_{i,j} = F_i(I_{i,j}), \{\mu_{i,j}\}$ is decreasing and $f_{i,0} = I_{i,0} = 0$.

4.2. Delay Computation. We consider service systems with infinite waiting buffer and lossless service. We can derive the worst case delay from Theorem 3.1 and 3.2 when the input traffic follows the D-BIND model and the lower bound of the available service function is piecewise linear. Consider the input of M_i is bounded by $F_i(I)$ as in (4.2). The lower bound of the available service function of M_i at the server is given as

$$C_i(I) = \begin{cases} c_{i,j-1} + \nu_{i,j}(I - T_{i,j-1}) & T_{i,j-1} < I \leq T_{i,j} \\ c_{i,K} + \nu_{i,K}(I - T_{i,K}) & I > T_{i,K} \end{cases} \tag{4.3}$$

for $j = 1, 2, \ldots, K$, where $C_i(0) = 0, c_{i,j} = C_i(T_{i,j}), \{\nu_{i,j}\}$ is increasing and $c_{i,0} = T_{i,0} = 0$.

From Theorem 3.1, we can derive the following Lemma:

LEMMA 4.1. *Let $F_i(I)$ and $C_i(I)$ as in (4.2) and (4.3), be two piecewise linear functions for the upper bound of M_i's input and the lower bound of M_i's service, respectively. If $\nu_{i,K} \geq \mu_{i,N}$, then the worst case delay of M_i satisfies*

$$d_i \leq \max_{c \in G}\{C_i^{-1}(c) - F_i^{-1}(c)\} \tag{4.4}$$

where $G = \{f_{i,1}, f_{i,2}, \ldots, f_{i,N}, c_{i,1}, c_{i,2}, \ldots, c_{i,K}\}$.

When the input of the server is greedy starting at the beginning of a busy period, the service function $S_i(I)$ is piecewise linear and can be expressed as:

$$S_i(I) = \begin{cases} s_{i,j-1} + \nu_{i,j}(I - T_{i,j-1}) & T_{i,j-1} < I \leq T_{i,j} \\ s_{i,K} + \nu_{i,K}(I - T_{i,K}) & I > T_{i,K} \end{cases} \tag{4.5}$$

for $j = 1, 2, \ldots, K$, where $S_i(0) = 0, s_{i,j} = S_i(T_{i,j}), \{\nu_{i,j}\}$ is increasing and $s_{i,0} = T_{i,0} = 0$.

Then, from Theorem 3.2, we can derive the following Lemma:

LEMMA 4.2. *If the worst case delay of M_i occurs when the input of the server is greedy starting at the beginning of a busy period, and that the maximum arrival function $F_i(I)$ and the service function $S_i(I)$ are piecewise linear with $\nu_{i,K} \geq \mu_{i,N}$, then the worst case delay of M_i satisfies the following equation*

$$d_i = \max_{c \in G}\{S_i^{-1}(c) - F_i^{-1}(c)\} \tag{4.6}$$

where $G = \{f_{i,1}, f_{i,2}, \ldots, f_{i,N}, s_{i,1}, s_{i,2}, \ldots, s_{i,K}\}$.

Now we can apply Lemma 4.1 and Lemma 4.2 to some typical output port servers and find out the worst case delay for the connections.

5. Delay Analysis for Typical Servers.

1. *FIFO Scheduler:* For M connections entering a FIFO server, the maximum arrival function of M_i is given as in (4.2). The worst case delay of M_i occurs when the input of the server is greedy starting at the beginning of a busy period. At this point, the total maximum arrival function is

$$F(I) = \sum_{j=1}^{M} F_j(I),$$

and the total service function is $S(I) = I$, therefore, the worst case delay is given as

$$d_i = \max_{c \in G}\{c - F^{-1}(c)\} \tag{5.1}$$

where $G = \{f_{i,1}, f_{i,2}, \ldots, f_{i,N}\}$.

2. *Static Priority Scheduler:* Now we analyze the worst case delay for a static priority scheduler. By assigning P priorities to a set of connections, $\mathcal{M}$, the connection set is partitioned into P disjoint subsets:

$$\mathcal{M} = \mathcal{M}^1 \cup \mathcal{M}^2 \cup \ldots \cup \mathcal{M}^P$$

where $\mathcal{M}^j$ contains the connections with the assigned priority $P(\mathcal{M}^j) = j$. Suppose $M_i \in \mathcal{M}^j$, because all cells within the connections of $\mathcal{M}^j$ are served by the FIFO scheduling policy, the maximum arrival function $F^j(I)$ is

$$F^j(I) = \sum_{P(M_k)=j} F_k(I) \tag{5.2}$$

Since $F_k(I)$ is piecewise linear, $F^j(I)$ is also piecewise linear. The lower bound of the available service function for $\mathcal{M}^j$ is

$$S^j(I) = \begin{cases} 0 & 0 \le I \le I^j \\ I - \sum_{P(M_k)<j} F_k(I) & I > I^j \end{cases} \tag{5.3}$$

where I^j satisfies $I^j = \sum_{P(M_k)<j} F_k(I^j)$.
Since $S^j(I)$ is also piecewise linear, so the worst case delay of $\mathcal{M}^j$ can be computed by (4.6).

3. *EDF Scheduler:* Consider an EDF scheduler has accepted M connections with maximum arrival functions $\{F_k(I)\}$. When a new connection with maximum arrival function$\{F_{new}(I)\}$ arrives, we can compute the delay that an EDF scheduler can guarantee. The service function the scheduler can provide for the new connection is lower bounded by:

$$S_{new}(I) = \begin{cases} 0 & 0 \le I \le I^* \\ I - \sum_{k=1}^{M} F_k(I - D_k) & I > I^* \end{cases} \tag{5.4}$$

where D_k is the deadline for connection k and $I^* = \sum_{1 \le k \le M} F_k(I^* - D_k)$. Using Lemma 4.1, the worst delay of the new connection can then be derived.

4. *GPS Scheduler:* For a GPS server with M connections, and M_i being assigned a parameter ϕ_i, the lower bound of M_i's service function (see [21]) is given as

$$C_i(I) = \frac{\phi_i}{\sum_{j=1}^{M} \phi_j} I \tag{5.5}$$

Given a piecewise linear maximum arrival function, $F_i(I)$, we can derive the worst case delay bound from Lemma 4.1.

6. Performance Evaluation. Since Knightly and Zhang are one of the few researchers that proposed methods to find the delay and actually presented delay formulae for the worst case bound. In this section, we therefore, compare our worst case delay bound formulae with the one proposed by Knightly and Zhang [11]. We then introduce the performance metric and evaluate the effectiveness of a connection admission control using our delay formulae. In this set of experiment, the ATM switch adopted a FIFO scheduling policy at its output ports.

6.1. Comparison of Delay Formulae. We compare the worst case delay bounds by our method and the method proposed by Knightly and Zhang [11].

For the FIFO scheduler: the delay formula by our method is:

$$d_i = \max_{c \in G}\{c - F^{-1}(c)\} \tag{6.1}$$

where $G = \{f_{i,1}, f_{i,2}, \ldots, f_{i,N}\}$, in which N is the number of segments for the arrival function.

On the other hand, by Knightly and Zhang's method, the delay is:

$$d_i = \max_{I \ge 0}\{F(I) - I\} \tag{6.2}$$

Given the function $F()$ and $F^{-1}()$, both algorithms are of the order of $O(N)$, hence, the computation complexity for the two formulae are the same for a FIFO output port scheduler in an ATM switch.

For a static priority scheduler as the output port controller: Assuming $M_i \in \mathcal{M}^j$ and $F^j(I)$ and $S^j(I)$ are given as in (5.2) and (5.3) respectively, the delay derived from our method is:

$$d_i = \max_{c \in G}\{S_i^{-1}(c) - F_i^{-1}(c)\} \tag{6.3}$$

where $G = \{f_{i,1}, f_{i,2}, \ldots, f_{i,N}, s_{i,1}, s_{i,2}, \ldots, s_{i,K}\}$, in which N, K are the number of segments for the arrival and service functions, respectively.

Given the $S_i^{-1}()$ and $F_i^{-1}()$, our method can compute the worst case delay in $O(N+K)$ since we only need to calculate every $c \in G$.

On the other hand, by Knightly and Zhang's methods, the delay is:

$$d_i = \max\{I \geq 0 | b_j(I) \geq I\} \tag{6.4}$$

where $b_j(I)$ is defined as

$$b_j(I) = \max_{t \geq 0}\{F^j(t) + \sum_{k=1}^{j-1} F^k(I+t) - t\} \tag{6.5}$$

For Knightly and Zhang's method, the computation depends on the complexity of $b_j(I)$ and it in turn depends on any $t \geq 0$ in (6.5). The delay computation in (6.5) is very difficult and almost impossible to analyses because the value of t is arbitrary.

In anyway, from the above, our method is no harder than Knightly and Zhang's method in terms of computation complexity for the FIFO server. Furthermore, since our method can apply to other kinds of typical servers as described in Section 5, our method is more general and thus, a better method in estimating the worst case delay bound for the real-time connections within an ATM switch.

6.2. Performance Metric. Since we are interested in computing the worst case delay bound for each connection and use it for Connection Admission Control, the performance metric we are interested in is the admission probability. By admission probability, we mean the probability that a hard real-time connection can be admitted to the ATM network. Recall that a hard real-time connection is admitted if and only if its worst case delay can meet its deadline constraint without violating the deadline constraints of connections that are currently active in the system. Obviously, the method to derive the worst case delay will make its impact on the admission probability. During the experiments, the admission probability P_{adm} is defined as follows:

$$P_{adm} = \frac{N_{accept}}{N_{accept} + N_{reject}}$$

where N_{accept} is the number of connection being accepted and N_{reject} is the number of connections being rejected.

6.3. Simulation Experiment. We have written a discrete event simulation program to simulate the ATM network. We use here a set of workload that models the transmission of different types of MPEG videos over an ATM switch. We ran our experiments with three

MPEG Parameters	MPEG-II Main Profile	MPEG-II Low Profile	MPEG-I
Data Rate	9 — 15 Mbps	2 — 4 Mbps	0.666 — 1.767 Mbps
Startup Latency (VBV_Buffer)	1,835,008 bit	475,136 bit	327,680 bit
Resolution	720 × 576	352 × 288	352 × 288
Frame Rate	30 fps	30 fps	30 fps

TABLE 6.1
MPEG files system parameters.

Simulation Parameters	MPEG-II Main Profile	MPEG-II Low Profile	MPEG-I
$\rho = \frac{DataRate}{155Mbps}$	0.058 - 0.0968	0.0129 - 0.0258	0.0042 - 0.0114
$\beta = \frac{VBV\_Buffer}{8Bit/Byte \times 48Byte/cell}$	4,779	1,238	854
$D = \frac{1/30sec \times 155 \times 1024 \times 1024bps}{8Bit/Byte \times 48Byte/cell}$	14,109	14,109	14,109
$I_{max} = \frac{\beta}{1-\rho_{max}}$	5,291	1,271	864

TABLE 6.2
Simulation parameters for the MPEG videos.

types of MPEG traffic: 1) MPEG-II Main Profile; 2) MPEG-II Low Profile; and 3) MPEG-I; Each of the corresponding system parameters are listed in Table 6.1 [16].

There are altogether five system parameters for our simulation: λ is defined as the mean of inter-arrival rate between the video connections; ξ is the mean of the life-time of each connection; ρ is the average connection workload, I_{max} is the maximum value of I as defined in Section 3 and $I_{max} = \frac{\beta}{1-\rho_{max}}$ for a FIFO server. Lastly, D is the relative deadline for a connection. The actual values being used in each of the simulation experiments are listed in Table 6.2. For each connection, ρ is chosen from an uniform distribution. The inter-arrival time and the lifetime of connections are chosen from an exponential distribution. Hence, we obtained our estimated switch utilization of the ATM switch as $U = \lambda \times \rho/\xi$.

For the priority assignment at the output port, we adopt the FIFO scheduling policy. For each run of our simulation experiments, we generate over 2,000 connections according to the predefined system parameters, and start the simulation with no connection in the ATM switch initially. To eliminating the warm-up effect, we let the system to run into a steady state before collecting the data. In particular, we let the system run through at least U/ρ number of connections before recording the data. For each connection arrival, the worst case delay bound for each connection are calculated. The system then decided whether to accept or reject the newly arrived connection.

6.4. Simulation Result. We ran the experiments with each of the three types of MPEG traffic and look into the admission probability at various utilization under different traffic functions. All three simulation runs produce very similar results and the results from the MPEG-II Main Profile, and the MPEG-II Low Profile are shown in Figure 6.1

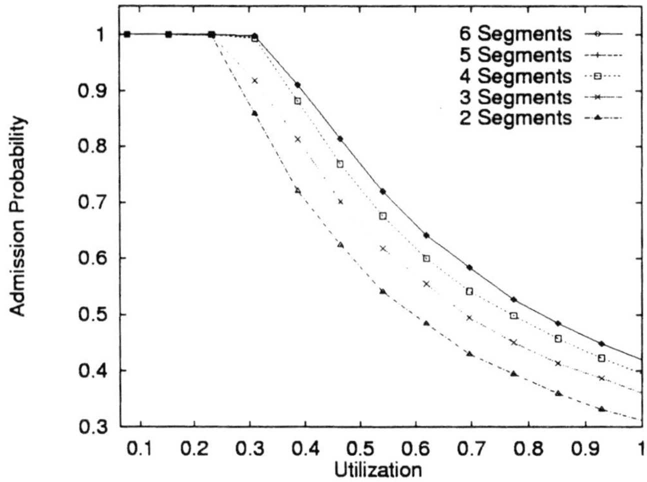

FIG. 6.1. *MPEG-II Main Profile.*

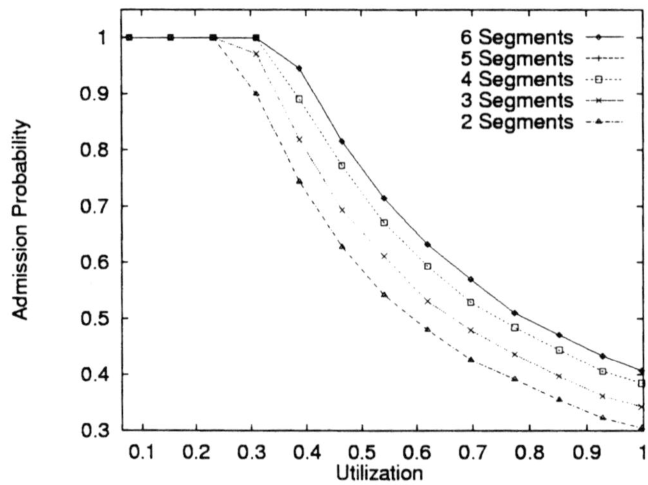

FIG. 6.2. *MPEG-II Low Profile.*

and 6.2, respectively. Because of the similarity of the results, we will mainly describe the observation for the MPEG-II Main Profile traffic from Figure 6.1. With a 2-segment traffic function, the admission probability starts to drop when the utilization reaches 0.25. As the switch utilization increases, the admission probability decreases. When the switch is fully utilized, the admission probability for this 2-segment traffic function is at 0.3. The overall performance can be improved if a multiple segment traffic function is used. It is because a multiple segment traffic function can better described the real-time MPEG traffic. However, as Figure 6.1 and 6.2 have shown that the improvement levels off and does not show any further improvement beyond a 5-segment traffic function. Notice that the performance curves by a 5-segment traffic function is the same as a 6-segment traffic function in Figure 6.1 and 6.2. For Figure 6.1, when a 5-segment traffic function is used, the switch will accept all the connection until the utilization is 0.3, then the admission probability starts to decrease and eventually when the switch is fully utilized, the admission probability is about 0.425 which is higher than the 0.3 when a 2-segment traffic function is used.

7. Conclusion. In this paper, we first present a framework for the worst case delay within an ATM switch. In estimating the real-time arrival traffic, we use the D-BIND traffic model [11] to characterize the burstiness and the temporal correlation structure of a real-time message stream. We then derive the worst case delay bound for an ATM switch with some typical output port schedulers. Later on, we evaluate the real-time connection admission control utilizing these worst case delay analysis, and we find out that our proposed method is no harder than the other existing methods in finding such worst case delay in terms of computation complexity. Furthermore, our experiments in connection admission control had shown that although the tightness of the delay bound depends on the number of segments in the traffic description functions, no significant improvement is observed beyond a 5-segment traffic function. Thus, our method is both efficient and effective for the connection admission control of an ATM network.

As for the future work, we would further investigate the effectiveness of our delay computation with different kinds of traffic other than the MPEG video traffic. Moreover, to investigate whether a 5-segment traffic function can always well describe the network traffic in general also remains to be one of our future work for this study.

Appendix A. The Proof of Lemma 4.1.

Lemma 4.1. Let $F_i(I)$ and $C_i(I)$ as in (4.2) and (4.3), be two piecewise linear functions for the upper bound of M_i's input and the lower bound of M_i's service, respectively. If $\nu_{i,K} \geq \mu_{i,N}$, then the worst case delay of M_i satisfies

$$d_i \leq \max_{c \in G}\{C_i^{-1}(c) - F_i^{-1}(c)\} \tag{A.1}$$

where $G = \{f_{i,1}, f_{i,2}, \ldots, f_{i,N}, c_{i,1}, c_{i,2}, \ldots, c_{i,K}\}$.

Proof. By Lemma 3.1, the delay bound can be given as

$$d_i \leq \max_{c \geq 0}\{C_i^{-1}(c) - F_i^{-1}(c)\} \tag{A.2}$$

Given two piecewise linear functions $F_i(I)$ and $C_i(I)$ as in (4.2) and (4.3), we can compute each of their inverse function:

$$F_i^{-1}(c) = \begin{cases} \frac{1}{\mu_{i,j}}(c - f_{i,j-1}) + I_{i,j-1} & f_{i,j-1} < c \leq f_{i,j} \\ \frac{1}{\mu_{i,N}}(c - f_{i,N}) + I_{i,N} & c > f_{i,N} \end{cases} \tag{A.3}$$

where $j = 1, 2, \ldots, N$.

$$C_i^{-1}(c) = \begin{cases} \frac{1}{\nu_{i,j}}(c - c_{i,j-1}) + T_{i,j-1} & c_{i,j-1} < c \leq c_{i,j} \\ \frac{1}{\nu_{i,K}}(c - c_{i,K}) + T_{i,K} & c > c_{i,K} \end{cases} \tag{A.4}$$

where $j = 1, 2, \ldots, K$.

Denote $D_i = \max_{c \geq 0}\{C_i^{-1}(c) - F_i^{-1}(c)\}$, we need to prove that $D_i$occurs at $c \in G$. Due to the fact that $C_i^{-1}(c) - F_i^{-1}(c)$ is piecewise linear, if $\nu_{i,K} \geq \mu_{i,N}$, $C_i^{-1}(c) - F_i^{-1}(c)$

must have a maximum. In each segment, the maximum should occur at the two end points. Hence, D_i will occur at $c \in G$ and we have,

$$d_i \leq \max_{c \in G}\{C_i^{-1}(c) - F_i^{-1}(c)\}.$$

Q.E.D.

REFERENCES

[1] R. Agrawal and R. Rajan, Performance bounds for guaranteed and adaptive service, *IBM Research Report*, May, 1996.

[2] J. Boudec, Application of network calculus to guaranteed service networks, Accepted for *IEEE Trans.Inform.Theory*, 1998.

[3] C. S. Chang, Stability queue length, and delay of deterministic and stochastic queueing networks, *IEEE Trans. Automat. Contr.*, vol. 39, no.5, pp. 913-931, May 1994.

[4] R. L. Cruz, A calculus for network delay, Part I & II, *IEEE Trans .Inform. Theory*, vol.37, no.1, pp.114-141, Jan. 1991.

[5] R. L. Cruz, Service burstiness and dynamic burstiness measures: A framework, *J. High Speed Networks*, vol. 1, no.2, pp.105-127, 1992.

[6] R. L. Cruz, and M. C. Chuah, Consequences of rate control in exhaustive service polling systems, in *Proc.27th Ann. Conf. Inform. Sci. Syst.*, Johns Hopkins University, Mar. 1993, pp.119-125.

[7] R. L. Cruz, Quality of service guarantees in virtual circuit switched networks, *IEEE. J. Select.Areas Commun.*, vol.13, no.6, pp.1048-1056.

[8] D. Ferrari and D. Verma, A scheme for real-time channel establishment in wide-area networks, *IEEE J. on Selected Areas in Comm.*, vol.8, no.3, pp.368-379, Apr. 1990

[9] V. Firoiu, J.Kurose and D.Towsley, Efficient admission control for EDF schedulers, *Proc. IEEE Infocom'97*, April 1997.

[10] L. Georgiadis, R. Guerin, V. Peris and K. N. Sivarajan, Efficient network QoS provisioning based on per node traffic shaping, *Proc. IEEE Infocom'96*, March 1996.

[11] E. Knightly, H. Zhang, Traffic characterization and switch utilization using deterministic bounding interval dependent traffic models, in *Proc.IEEE INFOCOM'95*, pp1137-1145.

[12] E. Knightly, H-BIND: a new approach to providing statistical performance guarantees to VBR traffic, in *Proceedings of IEEE INFOCOM'96*, 1996.

[13] J. Kurose, On computing per-session performance bounds in high-speed multi-hop computer networks, in *Proc. ACM Sigmetrics*, Perform.'92, 1992.

[14] C. Li, W. Zhao, and R. Bettati, Delay computation and priority assignment for ATM networks with static priority scheduling, *TAMU Tech. Report*, 1997.

[15] J. Liebeherr, D. Wrege, and D. Ferrari, Exact admission control in networks with bounded delay services, *IEEE/ACM Trans. Networking*, vol.4, no. 6, pp. 885-901, Dec. 1996.

[16] J. Mitchell, W. Pennebaker, C. Fogg, and D. LeGall, *MPEG Video Compression Standard*, Chapman & Hall, International Thompson Publishing, 1997.

[17] J. Ng, S. Song, and W. Zhao, Integrated Delay Analysis of Regulated ATM Switch, *Proceedings of the 18th IEEE Real-Time Systems Symposium (RTSS 97)*, pp. 285 — 296, December 1997.

[18] J. Ng, S. Song, and W. Zhao, Integrated Delay Analysis of Regulated ATM Switch for Real-Time Applications, *Technical Report (JNG05-97.ps)*, Department of Computing Studies, Hong Kong Baptist University, May 1997. Also available at http://www.comp.hkbu.edu.hk/~jng/Tech-Rpt/.

[19] J. Ng, S. Song, and W. Zhao, Integrated End-to-end Delay Analysis for Regulated ATM Networks, submitted to *Real-Time Systems*, 1998.

[20] J. Ng, S. Song, C. Li and W. Zhao, A New Method for Integrated End-to-end Delay Analysis in ATM Networks, submitted to *Journal of Communications and Networks* 1998.

[21] A. K. Parekh and R. G. Gallager, A generalized processor sharing approach to flow control in integrated services networks: the single node case, *IEEE/ACM Trans .Networking*, vol.1, no.3, pp. 344-357, June 1993.

[22] A. K. Parekh and R. G. Gallager, A generalized processor sharing approach to flow control in integrated services networks: the multiple node case, *IEEE/ACM Trans. Networking*, vol.2, no.2, pp. 137-150, Apr. 1994.

[23] A. Raha, S. Kamat, and W. Zhao, Guaranteeing end-to-end deadlines in ATM networks, In *Proc. 15th IEEE ICDCS*, June, 1995.

[24] A. Raha, S. Kamat, and W. Zhao, Admission control for hard real-time connections in ATM networks, in *Proceedings of IEEE INFOCOM'96*, pp. 111-119, Mar. 1996.

[25] H. Sariowan, L. Cruz and G. Polyzos, Scheduling for quality of service guarantees via service curves, *Proc. Of ICCCN'95*, Sept. 1995.

[26] D. Wrege, E. Knightly, H. Zhang and J. Liebeherr, Deterministic delay bounds for VBR video in packet-switching networks: fundamental limits and practical trade-offs, *IEEE/ACM Trans. Networking*, vol. 4, no. 3, June, 1996.

[27] D. E. Wrege and J. Liebeherr, A near-optimal packet scheduler for QoS networks, *Proc. IEEE INFOCOM'97*.

[28] D. Yates, J. Kurose, D. Towsley and M. G. Hluchyj, On per-session delay distributions and the call admission problem for real-time applications with QoS requirements, In *Proc. ACM SIGCOMM'93*, pp. 2-12, Sept. 1993.

Index

D

E

K

L

M

N

S

T